Praise for *American Moderns*

"Stansell's book is a triumph." —Eunice Lipton, *The Nation*

"A beautifully written evocation of bohemian Greenwich Village teeming with New Women and radical men dedicated to free speech, free love, free thought, and determined to emancipate American art, work, sex, and psyches from stifling Victorian constraints."
—Mike Wallace, coauthor of *Gotham: A History of New York City to 1898*, winner of the 1999 Pulitzer Prize in History

"A complex and exciting portrait of a crucial historical moment and the men and women who shaped it—and us."
—Katha Pollitt, author of *Reasonable Creatures: Essays on Women and Feminism*

"For most of the twentieth century, hard-core Greenwich Villagers looked back on the period from the eighteen-nineties to the nineteen-twenties as their golden age. Stansell shows why: she senses the time and place through its own eyes, ears, and fingertips." —*The New Yorker*

"A brilliant and beautifully written portrait of a generation of free-thinkers, reformers, talkers, artists, and dreamers. This is intellectual history at its finest." —Brian Morton, author of *Starting Out in the Evening*

"Stansell has ably captured the audacity of those who made New York the capital of modernity." —Robert Taylor, *The Boston Globe*

"In this original, searching look at turn-of-the-century bohemian New York, Christine Stansell explores the formative moment in American modernity—a time of vivid personalities, high ideals, and political, aesthetic, and sexual turmoil. A captivating story, wonderfully told."
—Jean Strouse, author of *Morgan: American Financier*

"Here they all are at last, Randolph Bourne, John Reed, Edna Mollay, Floyd Dell—the new Bohemians of Greenwich Village. But they were more than simple legends. *American Moderns* shows us for the first time how their lives and their hard-won beliefs—whether about the Wobblies or that New Woman—changed America forever. In this first-rate book, Chris Stansell tells us how they made our time what it is—and what it isn't."
—Nancy Milford, author of *Zelda Fitzgerald: A Biography*

ALSO BY CHRISTINE STANSELL

City of Women:
Sex and Class in New York, 1789–1860

Powers of Desire: The Politics of Sexuality
(coedited with Ann Snitow and Sharon Thompson)

AMERICAN MODERNS

AMERICAN
MODERNS

Bohemian New York and the
Creation of a New Century

CHRISTINE STANSELL

AN OWL BOOK
HENRY HOLT AND COMPANY   NEW YORK

Henry Holt and Company, LLC
Publishers since 1866
115 West 18th Street
New York, New York 10011

Henry Holt® is a registered trademark
of Henry Holt and Company, LLC.

Published in Canada by Fitzhenry & Whiteside Ltd.,
195 Allstate Parkway, Markham, Ontario L3R 4T8.

John Reed Papers quoted by permission of the
Houghton Library, Harvard University.

Library of Congress Cataloging-in-Publication Data
Stansell, Christine.
   American moderns : bohemian New York and the creation of a new century /
Christine Stansell.—1st ed.
      p.   cm.
Includes index and bibliographical references.
ISBN 0-8050-6735-3
   1. New York (N.Y.)—History—1898–1951.   2. New York (N.Y.)—Intellectual life—20th century.
3. New York (N.Y.)—Social life and customs—20th century.   4. Bohemianism—New York (State)—
New York—History—20th century.   5. Greenwich Village (New York, N.Y.)—Intellectual life—20th
century.   6. Greenwich Village (New York, N.Y.)—Social life and customs—20th century.   I. Title.
F128.5 .S79 2000   99–049928
974.7'104—dc21   CIP

Henry Holt books are available for special promotions and premiums.
For details contact: Director, Special Markets.

First published in hardcover in 2000 by Metropolitan Books

First Owl Books Edition 2001

Designed by Kate Nichols

Printed in the United States of America

1   3   5   7   9   10   8   6   4   2

For Sean Wilentz

Contents

Contents

V. FORMER PEOPLE

AMERICAN MODERNS

Prologue

In the first years of the twentieth century, many Americans felt they were living through an epochal change in human history. The tides of modernity, which had washed over Paris in the 1870s and subsequently over Vienna, Prague, Munich, Berlin, and London, had finally reached American shores. Everywhere the world had changed—so people claimed in 1910, or 1912, or 1913—faster, more entirely than it had ever changed before. "The world has changed less since the time of Jesus Christ than it has in the last thirty years," averred the French writer Charles Péguy in 1913. "On or about December 1910," Virginia Woolf famously insisted, "human character changed." In the United States, too, "something was in the air," claimed the Chicago editor Floyd Dell. "The atmosphere was electric with it." "The revolutionary pot seems to be boiling," exulted a radical trade unionist in 1912. "The day of transformation is at hand."

This book is about the men and women who ushered in that day of transformation in America, the people who embraced the "modern" and the "new"— big, blowsy words of the moment. The old world was finished, they believed—the world of Victorian America, with its stodgy bourgeois art, its sexual prudery and smothering patriarchal families, its crass moneymaking and deadly class exploitation. The new world, the germ of a truly modern America, would be created by those willing to repudiate the cumbersome past and experiment with form, not just in painting and literature, the touchstones of European modernism, but also in politics and love, friendship and sexual passion. This would be a modernism experienced as an artful, carefully crafted everyday life. One avid promoter, the journalist Hutchins Hapgood, cheerfully reported on how various were its manifestations: "Whether in literature, plastic art, the labor movement . . . we find an instinct to loosen up the old forms and traditions, to dynamite the baked and hardened earth so that fresh flowers can grow."

Nowhere did the instinct for the new flourish more extravagantly than in New York City, where a group of writers who collected in Greenwich Village between 1890 and 1920 transformed an unexceptional shabby neighborhood into a place glowing with a sense of the contemporary. The outlines of the Villagers' story are familiar: the reign of the "romantic rebels" has generated decades' worth of histories, memoirs, recollections, films, and biographies in which winsome young women throw morality to the winds (along with their Victorian corsets) in ardent love affairs, golden young men plot peaceful revolution, poets and playwrights conceive their creations in scintillating talk in late-night cafés. Everyone knows everyone else; politics are thrillingly efficacious and entertaining, not dull and dutiful. Small knots of intimates lead thousands in fiery demonstrations, captivate thousands more with their radical journals, impress sophisticated Manhattanites with their homegrown avant-garde theater. A tipsy crowd of revelers climbs to the top of the arch in Washington Square to declare Greenwich Village an independent nation. Everyone is always dancing wildly, discoursing eloquently, flirting, making friends or making love; rents are low, apartments charming, and restaurants cheap.

But these stories, endlessly recycled, fail to identify, let alone explain, the complexities of this startling and influential historical moment: the confusing sources of change, the shifting balance of old habits and emerging hopes, the unintended consequences of well-meant actions. There is something inevitable, even providential, about the history as it has been told, as if the explosion of the 1910s were simply meant to be. The penchant for mythmaking, in fact, began with the protagonists. They loved to picture themselves riding the zeitgeist of modernism, zipping straight to the future, high above the heads of ordinary mortals. Their insistent self-dramatization shaped subsequent accounts, enshrining them in legend but also cordoning them off from the rest of American history. Ironically, a generation of willful, ambitious arrivistes has become in historical memory a band of kindly, colorful dreamers. Their nervy inventiveness and presumption have faded into charming idealism, just as their preferred colors— jarring fauve yellows and purples—paled into pleasantly antique sepias and mauves in *Reds*, the Hollywood version of their story.

Yet it was the bohemians who made modernity local and concrete, tangible to a popular American audience. Their innovations reached would-be moderns elsewhere through their published stories, plays, essays, and reportage, through lecture tours (and even through a few silent films). They created the first full-bodied alternative to an established cultural elite, a milieu that brought outsiders and their energies into the very heart of the American intelligentsia. They developed an unrivaled vision of feminism—with its powers to recast men's and women's lives—as a critical ingredient of modern culture. With intuitions and perceptions nurtured by experiments in the arts, they achieved distinct forms of sociability—in conversation, friendship, and sexual love—which they thought could carry the hopes of the age into the future. They injected into the politics of the left a new cultural dimension, as well as psychological identifications between working-class and middle-class people, that lent tremendous flexibility and originality to the popular politics of the era.

The perspective was both local and cosmopolitan, narcissistic and grandiosely trained on the whole world. The bohemians were terrific self-dramatizers and self-aggrandizers, adept at creating themselves as a cast of fascinating characters: not only exuberant artists but plucky New Women, idealistic New Men, brilliant immigrant Jews, smoldering revolutionaries, and farsighted workers, all vaunting their renovations of artistic endeavor, politics, and sociability. They made Greenwich Village into a beacon of American possibility in the new age.

In this they were very much New Yorkers, inventors of a form of

Manhattan self-importance that is still with us today. They are in fact part of the bigger story of New York's ascendancy to ultimate American city in the first part of the twentieth century. New York had long been an interesting place but never one that exerted special appeal. As late as 1900, other cities held their own, rival capitals of thriving regional cultures. Boston may have begun to drift into the backwaters of gentility, but still it harbored its own bohemian set and sophisticated gay male circles. San Francisco supported a milieu of writers and painters attuned to the glorious light-washed landscape and to an aesthetic that over time would foster a distinctly West Coast secular mysticism. New Orleans was a showcase of musical experiment where Afro-American jazz artists created a glorious, uniquely American modernist form. And Chicago also had a strong claim to the spirit of the age: with its huge polyglot population, mammoth industrial base, and gorgeous skyscrapers, it was the newest city in the age of the new, the shock city of the early twentieth century as Manchester, England, had been the shock city of the nineteenth.

So when Herbert Croly, the editor of the *Architectural Record*, argued in 1903 that New York was the one American city where "something considerable may happen," he was expressing only a distant hope. Yet by the second decade of the century Croly's prediction had been fulfilled: all the other cities, even Chicago, had turned into provincial capitals, oriented toward New York as the arbiter of contemporary culture. Helped along by its self-conscious moderns and its phenomenally vigorous publishing and advertising industries, New York had become the source of images and texts that defined Croly's notion of "considerable" for the rest of America. New arrivals came to the city to live in ways they had already read about elsewhere, to reside in neighborhoods already settled by others whom they were prepared to imagine as kindred spirits. Business, habits of metropolitan display, an emerging culture of celebrity, and popular fiction all combined to make the city's bohemia a theater of contemporaneity to which spectators flocked in the hope of playing a part.

By 1915, even Europeans had overcome their snootiness to pronounce New York as that place to which all roads led. Fleeing the war, a coterie of avant-garde artists from Paris—Marcel Duchamp, Albert and Juliet Roche Gleizes, Francis Picabia, Jean Crotti—found themselves not at the ends of the earth but in the middle of a city that thrilled them and that was perhaps, Crotti believed, destined to be the artistic capital of the modern world. For the first time, New York actually appeared beautiful, an enchanted city promising magical transformation; the expatriates rendered its imploded glories from many

Albert Gleizes. Downtown. *Pencil on paper, 1916.* ©2000 ARTISTS RIGHTS SOCIETY (ARS), NEW YORK/ADAGP, PARIS

vantage points, their pencils lingering over the delicate detail etched within the cubist forms.

The English poet Mina Loy, who had been living in Florence, dreaded the tedium of American exile, but her first sight of the New York skyline as she sailed into the harbor—"an architecture conceived in a child's dream"—converted her. The "glittering clamor of myriad windows set like colored diamonds" beckoned with bounteous promise. True, the praise could be ambivalent, betraying unease about the character of modernity itself, the cruel pace, the glut, the hard edges. Another European cosmopolitan, Leon Trotsky, also in exile and biding his time in the city in late 1916, judged New York the apogee of the era. "More than any other city in the world," the European cosmopolitan charged, "it is the fullest expression of our modern age . . . a city of prose and fantasy, of capitalist automatism, its streets a triumph of cubism, its moral philosophy that of the dollar." Yet whether or not one welcomed the modern age, clearly New York had become its showcase. As long as tradition counted, London, Paris, and Rome had no peers. Once novelty set the cultural rules, New York in its grasping, temporary, fertile inventiveness became a world-class city, America's first.

In the bohemian geography of the imagination, Greenwich Village was proximate and permeable to the Jewish Lower East Side, twenty blocks to the south, crawling with its own bohemians and sizzling with its own ideas of modernity, and to the plebeian hurly-burly of Union Square to the north. Its reach extended uptown, too, to precincts of money and power, where certain old-style business-minded publishers as well as new cultural entrepreneurs welcomed the infusion of novel material and self-congratulation the moderns provided. Theirs was a community of dissidents who prided themselves on living a life apart—a modernist secession—even as they shrewdly identified and exploited certain openings in the establishment they denounced. The bohemians went farther afield, too, traveling evangelists of the new to help in the field. Writers and sympathizers dipped in and out of strikes, wars, and revolutions in America, Mexico, Europe, and finally Russia. Their education in modernity's capital had prepared them, confident tourists of the revolution, to go wherever the spirit of the new touched down.

The lyrical tone of the Villagers' celebrations of modern life echoed Walt Whitman's fifty years earlier, except that the basis was now different: the twentieth-century bohemians praised not Whitman's male fellowship of tender comrades but a colloquy of both sexes. Running through their creations—the salons, literary productions, sexual arrangements, theatrical ventures, and forays into politics—was an implicit belief in a new space for the sexes, where metaphorical sisters and brothers might carry on "life without a father," a phrase of Gertrude Stein's that could stand as an epitaph for a generation. Certainly never before, and probably not since, did a group of self-proclaimed innovators tie their ambitions so tightly to women, and not just a token handful but whole troops of women, waving the flag of sexual equality. There were other new characters in the mix, too: an infusion of immigrant Jews—not assimilated Germans but Eastern Europeans just off the boat—as well as a dash of others from humble class and ethnic origins, contributed to a milieu that made democracy a palpable experience rather than a civic catchword. These efforts to equalize and animate the relations of men and women seemed to spin threads of empathy between self and other social strangers. It was as if revitalized relations between the sexes could bring the classes, too, into amity and honest conversation, both political and social.

Modernity, we are taught, is about machines, speed, electricity, explosions, abstraction, the autonomy of language, the autonomy of paint, the death of God, and the divided self. All true, and yet this first full-blown generation of American moderns experienced the imperatives of the age as plainer, if no less complex: the pressures of democracy and the claims of women. As they mused upon and polemicized about their favorite subjects—free speech, free love, free expression—they shaped their writings, social lives, and love affairs to conform to the new story, in which questions of sexuality and sex roles merged with those of class equality. The "new temper of mind," cheered an enthusiastic Walter Lippmann, enriched "whatever it approached," tying innovations in theater, painting, and literature to emotions and politics. The adjective *new* seemed to put whatever phenomenon it blessed into an analogical, mutually sustaining relation with every other *new*, so that the New Woman somehow benefited from the new theater, and the new psychology fructified the new politics. Using this idea of sharp contemporaneity, the American moderns converted familiar issues of the nineteenth century—women's rights, labor versus capital—into arresting problems of the modern self and polity that audiences throughout the country could recognize.

The moderns were a raffish lot, assembled from many different places and circumstances in America and Europe. Some were revolutionary socialists, others moderate progressives; some were middle-class, native-born, and college-educated; others had come up the hard way, from the shtetlach of Russia and the hard-bitten factory towns in New England. They would be subject, much later, to drastically different fates; some would end up in bitter political exile while their old friends back home became well-heeled pundits of morals and manners. Their ranks included novelists, journalists and reporters, painters, political thinkers, revolutionary zealots, trade unionists, hangers-on, artists' models, secretaries, theater people, chess whizzes, poets, restaurateurs, feminists, and cultural impresarios. There were people who turned out to be eminent (although they weren't necessarily so at the time)—Alfred Stieglitz, Georgia O'Keeffe, John Sloan, Eugene O'Neill, Margaret Sanger, Isadora Duncan, John Reed, Emma Goldman, Walter Lippmann, Mabel Dodge, Randolph Bourne, Claude McKay, Max Eastman. There were others who played major roles then—the charismatic political leaders, the bon vivants who magnetized the parties, the writers du jour, and the dashing seducers—but have since devolved into minor characters. Taken together, all these figures were quite a crowd, and their collective effort to fashion modern possibilities—an effort at once cooperative and idealistic, conflicted and self-deluding—shapes our expectations of American culture to this day. One story of modernism often told begins with the exiled, solitary artist gazing out from his rented room onto the streets of the strange and unknowable city below. But another starts off with an eclectic assortment of people in a downtown café— women and men, patrician-born and barely educated, Yankees and Russian Jews—absorbedly talking, feeling their odd concourse to be in league with something new on the streets outside. This is the story I tell in this book.

I
—
BOHEMIA

PREVIOUS PAGE: *Jacob Epstein. "In These Cafés They Meet after the Theatre or an Evening Lecture." From* The Spirit of the Ghetto, *by Hutchins Hapgood.*

1

Bohemian Beginnings in the 1890s

In New York in the 1890s, there were certain places that suddenly vibrated with importance. These were not the fashionable resorts of the rich but shabby restaurants and grubby saloons, bare plastered rooms graced solely by massive, ornately carved bars. Those who poured in, late evenings, were mostly poor immigrants, but—and this was the novelty—a few gentlemen and ladies came too, drawn to a glittering life of the mind mysteriously manufactured from the dingy surroundings. Schwab's, and Maria's, and Mould's Café provided, oddly enough, cosmopolitan excitement difficult to come by in the swish and swirl of monied life. The seedy crowds harbored brilliant students of the latest European ideas and the garish light and deep shadows made a stage where all rules were suspended: workers might expound upon Nietzsche, ladies could go unchaperoned, and gentlemen could speculate about the coming revolution, as everyone drank steadily and ploughed through great heaps of spaghetti, or bratwurst, or brisket.

The conversation would have been loud, ostentatiously intellectual and self-involved, full of brilliant disquisitions and dashing contretemps. When the talk was loudest and beer and wine had loosened up the crowd, people might start to change places, opinionated workingmen squeezing in at the sophisticates' table to argue about the opera or some production of Shakespeare at the Yiddish theater, a curious gentleman pulling up a chair to pitch into some workers' dispute about anarchism. The women would have listened, laughed, and murmured to one another, but occasionally one of them might join in, too, and a few firebrands must have held their own at the center of the conversation. These saloons were unconventional but respectable, so the women, both working- and middle-class, were ladies, not tarts; there was no lovemaking or sexy dancing. But they did smoke cigarettes and they did flirt: even arguing with men in this late-night world could be read as a sinuous invitation.

To the sophisticates, such evenings temporarily suspended the dictates of well-heeled respectability. The shabby decor and cheap food were elements of a new connection to the city—and, by extension, to an America in the making. Unlike their well-to-do contemporaries who also might dip their toes into the world of the laboring classes, these people were not slummers and they were certainly not philanthropists; they came to revel and discover, not to aid and uplift. They took to seeing themselves as bohemians, priding themselves on a hedonistic familiarity with the city and its gaudy, besmudged riches. The distance between the life to which they had been raised and the one they were trying to make was wide, so it took rebellion and a little luck to bring themselves to the place where they could improvise.

The story of becoming bohemian is articulated in various coming-to-New-York accounts from the 1890s. Consider two instances: first, Hutchins Hapgood, that champion of cultural dynamite, a midwestern manufacturer's son who had gone to Harvard. He might have come to New York, as many of his classmates did, to take up a place as a leading man in business or the law. Instead he chose to become a reporter for the *Commercial Advertiser*, a tony paper that hoped to tap the talents of the best and the brightest. Quickly, his friends and his research led him to the vast stretch of tenements below Fourteenth Street. There the Harvard man found unexpected kinships with people remote from the circle he had been raised to inhabit: immigrant Jews, street hustlers, and demimondaines. In his autobiography he remembers his forays across the class line as a source of enjoyment: "other kinds of men and women than I had ever known, other social groups than I had ever touched upon before, made me each morning keenly expectant of the pleasures of the day before me." The radicals of the Lower East Side would soon count Hapgood an anarchist and he, for his part, came to consider himself a fellow traveler of the working class.

Headstrong and fanciful, Mary Heaton Vorse, another memoirist, was on the run from the mannerly, insular society of Amherst, Massachusetts. Eventually, she, like Hapgood, became a journalist and labor sympathizer. In the 1890s, however, she was a young artist and she went to New York to launch herself as a commercial illustrator, unchaperoned for the first time in her life. In the beginning, things did not go well. She had little luck finding work and she was often lonely and discouraged. Despite everything, though, she prospered mentally. She, too, gravitated to the downtown circuit. "I am part of the avant garde," she crowed after a string of late nights. "I have overstepped the bounds!" Out walking, bantering with music critics and newspaper sketch artists in the cafés, Vorse found her own pleasures, exchanges tinged with a diffuse sensuality and a newfound awareness of "impossible and forbidden things" that must have come from that silent traffic in erotic glances with which the New York streets bustled (and still do).

The bohemia into which Hapgood and Vorse stumbled, almost by happenstance, owed its inspiration to prototypes from Europe. Beginning with Pfaff's, a basement saloon of the 1850s that Walt Whitman had frequented, Americans borrowed episodically and haphazardly from the European tradition, but nothing vital or full-blown came of their adaptations. In the 1880s, in fact, bohemia in the United States was more likely to denote a gathering of ribald gentlemen (as in the upper-class Bohemian Grove of San Francisco) than a group of artists in revolt. But toward the turn of the century, some artists and journalists in downtown New York began to turn the European models to their own uses. "In New York, as in Paris, the café is the poor man's club," observed the arts critic James Huneker, a committed devotee. "It is also a rendevous for newspaper men, musicians, artists, Bohemians generally." They found the idea of bohemia well-suited to distancing themselves from the middle-class destinies laid out for them, and they also discovered its attractions to other metropolitans, working-class people with their own motives for rebellion. Improvising, fantasizing, dramatizing, they expanded and enriched bohemia so that by the end of the decade it was a coherent milieu with distinctly American protagonists: gentlemen at odds with their class, women at odds with their roles, and immigrants seeking conversations outside the ghetto. "It is the best stamping-ground for men of talent," Huneker went on to boast. "Ideas circulate. Brain tilts with brain. Eccentricity must show cause or be jostled." And if perhaps there was a little too much drinking, there was "the compensation of contiguity with interesting personalities." Greenwich Village was yet to come: this fin de siècle bohemia was makeshift, taking its cues largely from cheap fiction about an older, mid-nineteenth-century Paris than from the actual bohemia (of Verlaine and Jarry) flourishing there or from the bohemias of Vienna, Barcelona, Berlin, and London at the time. Nevertheless, the layers of fantasy accrued, and by the beginning of the century the seductions of downtown bohemia were known in many interesting corners of the city.

The turn to bohemia was one manifestation of gathering revulsion against a society that seemed locked in a stranglehold of bourgeois resolve. Many felt this, not just young dissidents. "So cheerful, and so full of swagger and self-satisfaction," the patrician Henry Adams described the country in 1900; Henry James wrote of a populace divided into the satisfied classes and the swindled. In politics, the misery created by a devastating depression in 1893–94 had not led to a successful challenge to the leaders of the two major parties, who were preoccupied with tariffs and monetary policy. The political drift was strongly conservative. State and federal troops crushed labor dissent, and the Populist threat was quelled in the election of 1896. African Americans in the South endured endemic violence and brutal segregation throughout a period now considered the nadir of post-Emancipation race relations, and Anglo-Saxonism—the belief that Americans of English descent were a "race" fitted by their inheritance to uplift the lesser peoples of the world—was the filter through which large numbers of educated people viewed the flood of immigrants into the country.

Indeed, the distance between the educated and the laboring classes was so great as to be more properly seen as a chasm. The great numbers of immigrants—Eastern European Jews, Slavs, Poles, southern Italians, and Irish (just clambering into the lower middle class)—still appeared to most of their social betters in the Victorian guise of "lowlife." Hostility to the immigrants strengthened antipathy to the cities, expressed in images of urban squalor and degradation. In New York, the gentry closed ranks and squared off against the masses in a campaign to seize back the government of the city from the corrupt immigrant-dominated Democratic machine. This was the urban variant of Henry Adams's "swagger," a determination to dig in one's heels and resist change, social heterogeneity, modernity itself.

But what was to some a social order to be maintained at any cost seemed an enormous political obstruction to others, particularly those who came of age in the North toward the end of the century. Children of the generation that had fought the Civil War, they were looking for their own generational project adequate to the idealism inherited from their parents. The enterprise of fashioning a new America, one that included workers and immigrants rather than simply policed or shot them (as had happened at the Haymarket massacre of 1886, a formative moment for many young liberals and radicals) seemed like just such a grand labor. This vision led many people to reform politics, to campaigns for municipal playgrounds, workers' housing, and publicly owned streetcars and utilities—the array of schemes for improvement known as progressivism.

This story of reform is familiar: the progressives were energetic, hardworking, and aggressively civic-minded people who bustled through Europe to study the impressive achievements in social policies there and, once at home, did the drudge work of policy change: sifting through piles of data and research, drumming up allies, lobbying intransigent politicians. But there was also a lesser-known, cultural dimension to politics. "The Social Gulf is always an affair of the imagination," one young reformer, Jane Addams, recognized, implying that an act of the imagination could close it. The progressives' brisk polit-

ical work could be transposed into a dreamier key: in order to understand those one would aid on the other side of the class divide, one
must first be able to imagine them. This was in part a problem of art,
of representation, of creating stories and images that eschewed
Victorian condescension and helped a middle-class public comprehend the lives of the millions separated from them by poverty, labor,
and upbringing.

Bohemia, a liminal zone in the city, was uniquely equipped to
launch idealistic young people across the boundary. Its associations
with revolt against bourgeois convention fit with the inclinations of
restless artists and writers to see the tawdriness of the cities, the jumble of languages and cultures, the mixing of the classes and the sexes
not as threat or problem but as opportunity—psychological, artistic,
and commercial. These developments were not exclusive to New
York; bohemias sprouted in other places as well, a few shoots at a time:
in Chicago, Boston, New Orleans, and San Francisco. But the urges
collecting in New York were acute. Self-styled sophisticates fanned
out across the poor neighborhoods to soak up "experience," construed
as familiarity with plebeian life. To them, the actors in the Yiddish and
Italian theaters, Eastern European revolutionaries, street hustlers, and
loud-mouthed market women were picturesque characters, not
squalid lowlifes.

Against the presumptions of a mood anxious about or downright
antagonistic to the city, these small groups of self-conscious urbanites
developed another narrative of an urban life brimming with transformative encounters. Their approach was not as radical a departure as
they liked to believe: others before them had challenged the discourse
of urban harshness and squalor. But in invoking a sphere that lay
beyond bourgeois propriety, they took the sensibility much farther,
past genteel amusement to a conviction that meetings with social
"others" might not simply entertain but foster more fully realized
selves. This view of the metropolis as the cradle of liberated personae
is now so familiar to us, so embedded in our literature and thought,
that it seems unremarkable. Who does not know that, in the city, closeted identities can come out from their hiding places? But in the 1890s
the idea broke with a long tradition that cast the city as threatening
and harsh, a place that shattered romantic illusions. The result was an

optics of pleasure that revolutionized the way cities appeared in the early twentieth century.

When they imagined bohemia, turn-of-the-century Americans called up an imagery of art, hedonism, and dissent from bourgeois life that originated in Paris in the 1830s. Bohemia was originally the name of a Central European kingdom (today a region of the Czech Republic) from whence the Gypsies supposedly came, and thus it conveyed a loose and vagabond nature that flourished outside society, an antibourgeois resolve. By midcentury the word had acquired a wider meaning, as an enclave of rebels and impoverished artists, following the popular success of Henri Murger's melodrama *La Vie de Bohème*, staged in Paris in 1849, and an edition of Murger's sketches of bohemian life published shortly thereafter.

In France, England, and the United States, bohemia proved to have enduring fascination. As a lived experience it was never quite separate from its celebration (and condemnation) in print and on stage: Puccini's opera *La Bohème* (1896) is a famous example from a string of now-forgotten plays, novels, and sketches throughout the nineteenth century. In the 1890s bohemia was on everyone's minds because of the English and American publication of the runaway best-seller *Trilby* (1894), a novel about a love triangle of English art students in Paris that updated the Murger prototype. These popular renditions of bohemia were pitched to respectable audiences charmed by themes of thwarted male genius, impoverished creativity, doomed love affairs, and perpetual bonhomie.

The notion of the bohemian reflected a nineteenth-century habit of mind already attuned to discovering and observing stock "types" in their particular metropolitan niches. Journalists' sketches and guidebooks highlighted different city spaces as stages that presented little dramas and set pieces featuring various urban specimens, easily identifiable from their appearance, clothes, and bearing. Writers in Paris, London, and New York all produced this kind of protoethnographic literature of the city (think of Dickens and Balzac), structured as a journey between the respectable, sunlit side of town and the vice-ridden, shadowy neighborhoods of laboring people. *New York by Gas-Light*

(1850), a typical guidebook, led readers around Manhattan to peer at "the courtesan," "the newsboy," and "the seamstress," all secreted in their respective habitats, "the fashionable assignation house," "the saloon," and "the tenement lodging." To people already interested in explorations of faraway lands, the metropolis itself became an adventure for brave gentlemen willing to risk danger in its nether regions.

For nineteenth-century audiences, bohemia readily fit into this mental landscape. It was peopled by its own "types," youthful libertines who despised bourgeois respectability and material success. The sociological reality, however, was more complex. Bohemia's self-designated types always existed in symbiotic relation to bourgeois culture rather than in opposition to it. While bohemias signaled dissent from the profiteering of the cultural marketplace, they also provided their affiliates—beginning with Murger, who dined out on "bohemia" the rest of his life—the means to parley that dissent into careers.

In turn, the widespread interest conferred a sense of importance on the participants. To be a part of bohemia was to elevate oneself and one's ambitions—to enhance one's identity—beyond the mundane lot of the illustrators, journalists, actors and actresses, art students, fiction writers, and playwrights who were its clientele. It was to enter an arresting plot. It was also to locate oneself advantageously in a market eager for cultural products bearing bohemia's imprint. Everywhere, bohemias, supposedly so out of the way and disdainful of success, guided their affiliates into commercial work and even celebrity. Nowhere was this paradox more marked than in the late-nineteenth-century United States, where cultural entrepreneurship was so vigorous. Bohemia in the 1890s supported pleasant youthful anomie—disgust at the power of Mrs. Grundy in the culture—but it also supplied young men and women materials to turn that alienation into professionally appealing innovation.

In the 1890s, the symbiosis was at work in that circle of talented young writers that included Hutchins Hapgood, reporters for the newly revamped *Commercial Advertiser*. The *Commercial* was a consciously literary alternative to both the staid reforming newspapers and the sensationalist yellow press. Overshadowed by the behemoth newspapers of the day, the *Commercial* nonetheless marks an important transition in liberal journalism from a moralistic reform perspective to human-interest writing. Edited by the famous muckraker Lincoln Steffens, it was a magnet for bright Ivy Leaguers looking to become serious writers. Steffens was a veteran of the city's dailies who had grown bored with the moral strictures of reforming journalism. A decade later, he would appear to Greenwich Village as a sententious stick-in-the-mud, but in the 1890s he was something of a bohemian himself, rambling around the city, consorting with immigrant Jews (to the horror of his anti-Semitic upper-class wife), and festooning his apartment with Near Eastern draperies and exotic curios.

Steffens disliked the working reporters he knew from the city's newsrooms, scantily educated hard-boiled men he viewed as time servers and ward heelers. He recruited his people through English professors in the Ivy League; he wanted open-minded writers who could train an appreciative, warm gaze on urban life, respectable vagabonds who would see "the beauty in the mean streets of the hard, beautiful city." The men he hired tended to be amiably at odds with their families' expectations, but they were decidedly at the well-bred end of the bohemian spectrum, no riffraff. The sole woman on the staff, Neith Boyce, was a little different; she came not from college but from her father's progressive journal in Boston, where she had worked as his assistant. Boyce, quiet, lovely, and self-contained, harbored strong literary ambitions and was determined to launch a career that would spirit her away from the destiny of marriage and motherhood. For all the writers, but especially for Boyce, the workaday office took on a lyrical gleam, so different did their kind of journalism seem from the hackwork of their colleagues at the big dailies.

Steffens set them all to write journalism conceived through the optics of pleasure, articles that would represent their city so "New Yorkers might see, not merely read of it, as it was: rich and poor, wicked and good, ugly but beautiful, growing, great." The *Commercial*'s metropolis was different from the New York of sunlight and shadows exemplified by Jacob Riis's lurid reporting in *How the Other Half Lives* (1890). Instead of exposing the horrors of remote regions, Steffens wanted to create common ground. In the *Commercial*, well-to-do readers could meet (at least in their minds) a gallery of city dwellers: Jewish garment workers on strike, conniving criminals, Irish police, wealthy philanderers. Unlike the big dailies, however, the *Commercial* regarded its subjects not so much as urban types—although the stereotypical elements lingered—but as delineated characters, endowed with histories replete with the details of human interest. Corrupt Tammany hacks were not merely the villains denounced by the Mugwumps but amusing, even faintly likeable characters.

Pitched at middle-class readers interested in expanding their knowledge of the city, the *Commercial* created a distinctive voice by softening and domesticating rather than playing up social differences. It could be seen as a pioneer of the I Love New York genre, parlaying Manhattan knowingness from the central conceit that "we"—the city-dwelling writers and readers—"knew it all": the city's "sorrows, joys, and underhanded ways." The Tammany pol, Steffens explained to his reporters, was a crook, but "he's a great crook," a New York crook, "and therefore a character for us and all other New Yorkers to know intimately and be proud of." The exposition aimed to elicit an intense civic sympathy: the goal of a murder story was to describe the criminal and the crime so sympathetically "that the reader will see himself in the other fellow's place."

Small incidents were deemed newsworthy, their significance drawn from a collection of minor, homey details. A toddler falls to her death from a tenement window in June 1899. The *Commercial* expertly proffers a few telling particulars—the child was perched on a chair by the window peering down at the street, her mother turned away to get her a glass of water—to frame the story as a tragedy recognizable by readers, any readers (how many, in this era before window guards, would have snatched a child back from an open window, heart in throat?). Yet the compilation of facts pointed to a different end than did the same ethnographic method in reform journalism: whereas social investigators intended to galvanize readers into political action, the *Commercial* aimed to create an intangible web of readerly empathy.

Steffens's literary urbanism was not initially distinguishable from the genre of the gentleman's ramble, the pleasant stroll around town taking in the sights, uptown to downtown, enjoying the sheer variety of urban life and encountering quaint plebeian characters (usually Irish, and dialect speakers) along the way. These expeditions were more or less formulaic and the encounters predictable: affable walks down Broadway or the Bowery, never venturing into the shadows farther east. The types were plucked from Victorian writing, although cleaned up a bit and rendered more comic, less menacing. Much later, the Village writer Randolph Bourne, burning with a new kind of radicalism, would remark appositely that the literary gentleman, for all their vaunted urbanity, had no idea "what a world of horizons and audacities they lived in." What distinguished the *Commercial* was the alacrity and interest with which its writers ventured away from these well-worn paths, heading instead toward the Lower East Side, then terra incognita for anyone except earnest social investigators.

It was the longing for bohemia that enabled these young people to catch a view of the horizons on the other side of the class divide. At this point, they made their outposts a couple of restaurants, but they treated the huge area of Manhattan south of Fourteenth Street as a circuit of potentially bohemian convocations and curiosities, known only to the cognoscenti. The *Commercial* writers, one particular circle, bumped against, sometimes joined forces with, and passed by other groups of writers, journalists, and art students also tinged with bohemian esprit. The floating milieu created its own ritualized ramble. Starting with the vaudeville shows and theater restaurants of Union Square, where Hapgood and Boyce might have shared a table with the arts critic James Huneker and his urbane friends (including Mary Heaton Vorse), pleasure seekers wound their way down to the Italian and French restaurants in what came to be known as Greenwich Village, and ended in the lively cafés of the Lower East Side. In the 1890s Eastern European immigrants were piling into the tenements and spilling out onto the streets; by 1905 New York was the most populous Jewish city in the world. To Jacob Riis, it was all dank horror; to James Huneker, it was "the fabulous East Side."

The Lower East Side surged with the energy of a population on the verge of enormous achievements, and it also introduced the WASP explorers to compatriots schooled by the European literature and social experience of *la vie de bohème*. Some Jews brought Europe's idea of bohemia with them from stopovers in Paris and London; others transported the closely related boulevardier sensibility from sojourns in Petersburg and Moscow. Konrad Bercovici, an immigrant from a well-to-do Romanian family expelled from the country during anti-Semitic violence in 1899–1900, picked up bohemian ways on the Left Bank in Paris. When he walked into the cafés on East Broadway, he felt right at home. Down on the Lower East Side, the air of bohemia settled over some of the scores of restaurants, cafés, and saloons where people gulped tea and swilled beer, smoked and argued relentlessly. The intelligentsia—cataloged by one artist as "students, journalists, scholars, advanced people, socialists, anarchists, free-thinkers, and even 'free lovers'"—staked out their spots along the avenues, quite separate from the cafés that men of religion frequented and fiercely defended from secularist incursions. In their own haunts, they carried on a ferociously productive intellectual and cultural life that encompassed Yiddish newspapers and theaters, literary societies, clubs, night classes, discussion groups, and obsessions with the writings of Gorky, Zola, Tolstoy, Gogol, Chernyshevsky, and Walt Whitman.

Politics and art mingled in discussions over endless glasses of tea. Socialist, anarchist, and Zionist controversies reverberated through the lecture halls, saloons, and tenements, the preoccupations of a "modern-minded European working class for whom Yiddish was its primary medium of expression." The grave and precise debate, both aesthetic and political, was remarkable even for the United States, where traditions of autodidactic learning were strong among workers. Feuds raged between the main political camps—say, Zionists versus socialists—but quarrels also flared up over the nature of realism or the quality of a production at a Yiddish theater. Bercovici remembered a concert review in a newspaper that provoked a falling-out so bitter and long-lasting that it finally drove one of the disputants to move uptown.

It was an amazing place for young men whose intellects had been formed in the Ivy League of the 1890s, where a fashion for upper-class ennui tinted with European decadence reigned. On the Lower East Side, they received another education entirely. Intellectually, some of the talk was almost certainly over their heads, turning upon fine points of revolutionary dogma, European literature, or Continental philosophy. Much of it was also linguistically incomprehensible, since conversations tended toward Yiddish, French, German, or Russian. But by its very nature, bohemia invited the adoption of a transnational identity, one that piqued people's interest in one another. Some emigrés like Bercovici, open to fellow spirits from wherever they came, liked to serve as guides to the WASPs; some of the Americans spoke German (learned on postgraduate sojourns in German universities), which enabled them to keep up with the Yiddish. The *Commercial* crowd also found a friend in their colleague Abraham Cahan, a writer for the Yiddish press whom Steffens had hired for the *Commercial;* Cahan squired them around the ghetto, introducing them to important people, translating, taking them to the Yiddish theater.

The plunge of these gentlemen from proper Protestant families into the Lower East Side involved a complex relation to the Jews and, more abstractly, to questions of social prejudice. In the American context, bohemia tended to filter out the most virulent strains of class and religious bigotry, although the turn of the century was a period of rising anti-Semitism, both in the United States and in Europe, directed especially against the newcomers from the East. In Europe, wherever large communities of immigrants collected—in London, Prague, Paris, Berlin—the refugees were subjected to violence, disdain, or contempt, and a language of biological racialism fell full force against the Jews, discharging images of Jewish disease and degeneration. In the United States, too, ideas of distinct racial biology and heredity and fears of the depleting influences of the "objectionable races" gained tremendous strength. Each immigrant group was deemed a particular race—Slavs, Italians, Jews, Finns—with its own place on the ladder of civilization: at the bottom, the most "primitive" race, the African Americans; at the top, the bearers of culture and physical vigor, the Anglo-Saxons. The Jews, deemed dark-skinned and atavistic, lurked near the bottom with the blacks.

Scholars disagree on how preponderant American anti-Semitism was within the wide-ranging racial hatreds of the time, but though on the increase, it undeniably took a milder form than in Europe. Anti-Semitism was a strong element within American racialism, but so was anti-Catholicism and general fear of the "foreign peril." There was certainly hostility to Jews in business and adamantine anti-Semitism among the rich, who barred successful assimilated German Jews from exclusive clubs; lower on the social scale, stereotypes of the hook-nosed usurer and his greasy family had considerable currency, especially among the Irish. But there were no officially sanctioned episodes of violence or bursts of hysteria directed solely at Jews, no political parties organized around anti-Semitism, no boycotts of Jewish businesses as there were in Europe.

The most intense hostility against Jews existed outside New York. Boston was the seat of the upper-class Anglo-Saxonist crusade, which began in 1894 with the Immigration Restriction League. This does not mean that New York was a sanctuary—far from it. Several versions of anti-Semitism existed there: Irish street attacks, verbal and physical, on "Christ-killers"; earnest progressive campaigns to Americanize Yiddish speakers; workers' hatred for Jewish sweatshop bosses. To the New York gentry, though, the Jews seemed not that much different from other detestable foreigners, and the reigning tone in public was one of chilly reserve rather than out-and-out enmity.

Interestingly, there was, at the same time, a trickle of philo-Semitism, especially in the late 1890s, when European anti-Semitism gained force with the Dreyfus case in France and an outbreak of blood-libel charges throughout central Europe. A genial revulsion against the prejudices of the Old World set in, with its corollary a pride in a society that could open its doors to the quaint, hapless Jews. In 1892 *Century* magazine, something of a house organ for the New York elite, published a long article on Lower East Side Jews explicating their customs, religious ceremonies, and reasons for emigrating, and lauding their familial devotion, piety, and love of learning. Throughout the decade, New York houses published the British Zionist Israel Zangwill's fictional portraits of the London ghetto and his Orientalist romances of Jews through the ages, and the big New York papers all ran sympathetic features about the Lower East Side.

It was this strain of philo-Semitic interest that brought the *Commercial* writers to the Lower East Side, set them apart from the garden-variety bigotry of their time, and made their work commercially intriguing. Their observations appealed to an inquisitive public who wanted to peek across the "Social Gulf" without actually straying into the territory themselves. Their articles interested immigrant readers, too, who were pleased to see themselves as newsworthy in the English-language press. The connection worked both ways, making the immigrants available to the writers and making the writing more accessible to the subjects; Cahan's name propelled the *Commercial* into circulation in the ghetto. For the journalists, encounters with the immigrants yielded the type of personal, freely associative feuilleton then fashionable on the Continent, further tightening the writers' association with European bohemia.

Hapgood parlayed his Lower East Side newspaper sketches into his first literary success, *The Spirit of the Ghetto* (1902), a collection that cast him in the role of translator of the new Americans to the old ones. He addressed an implicitly urbane audience, skittish about the new-comers but not repelled. His armchair tourist of the city might find the Jews "queer and repulsive" at first, he acknowledged, but through investigation, he avowed, one could discover their charms. Hapgood—like other writers for the *Commercial*—never altogether transcended the genre of the picturesque: his Jewish subjects, if impressive and learned, are also slightly silly, harmless dreamers. The religious scholars appear "medieval, submerged in old traditions and outworn forms," but the political intellectuals, too, for all their learn-ing, are eccentrics of overheated, grandiose hopes. For all Hapgood's declarations of newfound comradeship, the immigrants do not yet appear to be compeers so much as characters in a metropolitan the-ater. Still, the philo-Semitic perspective, for all its limitations, opened up that theater to a new idea of a possible America.

Bohemian sensibility did not prove so elastic when it came to African Americans. This was a matter partly of demographics, partly of the place Manhattan's blacks occupied in the city's cultural geogra-phy, and partly of assumptions and prejudices against African Americans that ran strong among even the most open-minded white New Yorkers. In their search for amusement and stimulation among the poor, the bohemian young might have gone to the Tenderloin, the area south of Times Square that was the center of Manhattan's small black community and of a thriving, racially mixed nightlife. Here, some sophisticates did roam: Stephen Crane, for example, on the prowl for a new novel of the streets when he was caught in a vice raid there in 1896. Certainly the Tenderloin was known to outsiders; it promised the kind of pleasures men about town had traditionally sought in the city's "shadows"—saloons and brothels interspersed with hotels, theaters, stores, and tenements. Nightlife catered to black people from the neighborhood, white tourists (mostly male), interracial lovers, black professional athletes and entertainers, and their admirers of both races. You could dance to amazing music there—ragtime, newly minted show tunes, early jazz—and meet strong personalities: the Tenderloin was the showcase for African American celebrities before the wholesale move to Harlem.

Yet the Tenderloin's sporting life—the offerings of drink, gambling, and interracial sex—was too closely associated with late-Victorian habits of bourgeois culture to magnetize the attention of people interested in bohemia. It was known too readily to certain kinds of gentlemen and show business people; its shop talk ran to theater bookings and the music business, not to social revolution and Chekhov—there was as yet no full-fledged black intelligentsia in Manhattan to preside over high-toned discussion. And with its honkytonk music and low-down dancing, and the predominance of entertainers, the Tenderloin would have evoked for intellectually minded people a popular culture that had no place in their lexicon. Doubtless they went there, like other urbane New Yorkers, but the neighborhood did not count for them in the way the Lower East Side did.

Indeed, there is no comparing the Tenderloin, or any other working-class neighborhood—Italian East Harlem, the Irish tenement districts around Union Square—to the tawdry grandeur of the Lower East Side, with its concentration of intellectual and artistic energy. Rolling with controversies and passions, the Lower East Side represented a democratized high culture within which the bohemians were very interested in placing themselves.

That this bohemian beginning included women was by no means foreordained. Bohemia in its original incarnation had been all male. Earlier bohemias were never completely off-limits to women, but the inner sanctums were closed. In Murger's Paris, women were cast as grisettes—lovelorn working-class women and artists' models (though, in truth, they were sometimes artists themselves) who played supporting roles in the artists' dramas of male friendship and creativity.

At Whitman's Pfaff's, a few demimondaines hovered around but the milieu was overwhelmingly male. By the end of the century, a token female artist or two was a motif of modernism in European avant-garde circles, a flag for the men's advanced views, and the association of sexual integration with the most radical art made female minorities tolerable in fledgling bohemias everywhere, including New York. Aspiring artists like Neith Boyce and Mary Heaton Vorse tagged along, turning themselves, if only haltingly, into counterparts of the masculine flaneur, broadening their urban provenance.

The largesse of movement necessary to bohemian sociability did not come easily. Vorse, Boyce, and their compatriots took advantage of cracks in the order of what was still a man's city, where respectable women required men's symbolic protection, especially at night and especially in places that were noisy, smoky, and frequented by other men. In earlier decades, only actresses and prostitutes habitually ventured out at night without escorts; a lady would never have gone to a working-class saloon. To do so, in the strict gender code of the day, was to risk all, to invite associations with the paradigmatic "woman of the streets." But now, the nineteenth-century rules were buckling. Ladies went to work by themselves every day. They rode streetcars alone and the more daring smoked in restaurants and shed their corsets. They congregated in groups at the bohemian hangouts, sometimes accompanied, sometimes part of the crowd. Like other great cities with bohemias, New York was a world of opportunity where a handful of women might move into places once altogether forbidden them. Their presence bothered some, but it did not generate explicit opposition.

Everywhere, but especially in the United States, the women who gravitated to bohemia came from a population of single women supporting themselves outside traditional family situations, sometimes through work in the arts. The phenomenon of artistic professionalism that in the antebellum years had been confined to women writers—dismissed by Nathaniel Hawthorne as "scribbling women"—spread in the late nineteenth century to painting, music, theater, even sculpting.

Artistic careers changed from being a nearly inconceivable option for respectable women to a possible livelihood. The influx of ordinary women elicited mixed reactions. "There are . . . more would-be *prime donne* in Chicago than anywhere else on earth," sneered an opera singer, a successful prima donna herself. But a longtime patron of women in the visual arts celebrated in 1897: "There are today thousands upon thousands of girl art students and women artists, where only a few years ago there was scarcely one."

The "girl art students" and "would-be *prime donne*" belonged to a subset of the urban type known as the New Woman. Dignified yet free in her comportment, she could be seen on the streets, walking alone, or on the omnibuses on her way to work, marked by a graceful, athletic bearing and the lack of a wedding ring. New Womanhood overlapped but was not synonymous with the women's movement, which in the 1890s was committed to a view of American women rooted in marriage and the family. The discussion among New Women focused rather on how women might live outside traditional domestic roles. Usually historians locate New Women in medicine, college teaching, social work, the law, or the ministry. But there were also New Woman illustrators (Mary Heaton Vorse), art students, sculptors (Clio Huneker, married to the critic), journalists (Neith Boyce), book and magazine editors, actresses, and dancers: ill-paid, often undistinguished in professional achievement, yet yearning nonetheless for distinction. To women drawn to the downtown restaurants, the setting hinted at help in realizing those ambitions.

As women lingered at the edges of these urbane circles, they added a sense of themselves as heroines in a new story to bohemia's increasing store of plots. Just as bohemian identity was intimately intertwined with its representation in print, so was being a New Woman: what one read shaped how one lived. One could learn about the New Woman from novels and magazine fiction and admire her elegant image— slim, shirtwaisted, fine-featured, hair piled high—in the proliferating illustrations that accompanied them. The New Woman inspired a stream of Anglo-American writing, beginning with Henry James's finely wrought stories of young American women abroad in the 1880s and continuing in the novels of Arnold Bennett, George Gissing, and George Egerton in England and of Edith Wharton, Kate Chopin,

Theodore Dreiser, and Willa Cather in the United States. In fiction, New Womanhood turned upon a desire for experience and an attraction to the city's aesthetic possibilities rather than upon the ardors of getting through medical school. Characters who would have registered in a Victorian valence as schemers, adulteresses, sad spinsters, or courtesans blossomed into morally ambiguous modern women: women who longed to live and to matter.

This fiction was a prism through which young women in the cities might imagine their own lives and the lives of the women around them, and it contributed to the theatrical air of those who helped create bohemia. Mary Heaton Vorse's feverish exaltation about her life in New York unmistakably vibrates with her fictional counterpart's romanticism—a romanticism that, for her generation, was trained on meaningful work rather than love. She considered herself part of "the army of women all over the country" who were "out to hurt their mother [sic]," who had to "in order to work. . . . More and more and more of us are coming all the time, and more of us will come until the sum of us will change the customs of the world," she rejoiced. Vorse's coming-to–New York story eschewed the paradigmatic nineteenth-century urban plot, which cast young women alone in the cities as friendless, forlorn, and sexually vulnerable. She saw herself not as a woman adrift but as a plucky heroine, joining in a great search for feminine self-realization.

Writing about the New Woman contributed a variety of figures beyond the Victorian dichotomy of the "true" woman and the woman of ill repute: the Bohemian Girl was one neologism, the Gibson Girl and the Bachelor Girl were others. These images were reiterated and recycled so continuously in light fiction and social commentary that they took on independent weight and plausibility, announcing a widened spectrum of respectable femininity. The loosening of imaginary boundaries lent women mental resources to enter bohemias in the 1890s as protagonists in their own right. Especially for painters and sculptors, fictional New Women helped them shuck off cloying associations with the Victorian "woman artist"—amateur, sentimental, genteel—to align themselves with rebellion, bohemian artists' stock in trade. The community of New Women also gave a material basis for ambitions, since commissions for illustrations, busts, and paintings of various sorts of New Women often went, in an early form of identity politics, to women artists. Neith Boyce, living alone in a rented room, had no success writing human-interest stories for the *Commercial* and ended up shunted to the copy desk. But she did hook magazine assignments for articles on the Bachelor Girl, with whom she allied herself. "When I speak of a person of individuality, pluck, and a sense of humor, I am speaking of myself," she wrote.

These images were not templates from which women stamped out a stereotypical common identity, but proliferating magazines, novels, and newspapers did disseminate characterizations and stories that helped form female identifications. The avidity with which women incorporated fiction into their lives at the turn of the century was widely acknowledged, although usually as a problem. Henry James unhappily mulled over the relation between the diffusion of stories and other female reading and a new kind of collective female life. There were many women readers, many of them unmarried, he worried, and "they live in a great measure by the immediate aid of the novel."

What was this "aid"? For young women, casting oneself as a character popularized, glamorized, or even maligned in print was a way to sharpen claims of a selfhood historically muted within the domestic sphere. Popular writing assimilated by eager audiences gave force and vocational direction to the single woman who needed to "convince the world that she is possible," as Neith Boyce put it in *Vogue*. When Mary Heaton Vorse rhapsodized that she was "an escaped bird, flying through the clear air of heaven" in New York City, she echoed the language of an augmented female self that had been clearly articulated in print.

The penumbra of literature around bohemia had long worked to enhance the mundane lives of its participants. But in the 1890s young women from the lower echelons of cultural production, too, pushed their way in to share the glow. The newcomers were vivified by the imagery of feminine independence that surrounded them, an unfolding narrative of a generation of women that gave them a place in bohemia and visibility in a metropolitan spectacle.

The loosening of women's roles did not go uncontested. Novelists who wrote about New Women were admiring but also ambivalent and sentenced their heroines to solitude, humiliation, or death: recall the clouded destinies that await the variously independent protagonists of Chopin's *The Awakening*, James's *The Portrait of a Lady*, Gissing's *The Odd Women*. It was all but impossible to imagine a happy ending that outstripped the marriage plot. In social discourse, only the hardiest, most intrepid defenders of female paid work rose to defend women's prerogative to remain single and virtually no one dared defend publicly the benefits of bohemia for women. Rather, writers often updated an old Victorian morality tale about unsuspecting girls seduced and abandoned in the big cities, admonishing young women that their foolish infatuation with art could lead to dead ends and disappointments and, worse, disqualify them forever from marriage.

The roots of the discomfort are not hard to find. The appearance of the New Woman challenged patriarchal relationships that were so familiar, so threaded into the fabric of people's expectations of themselves and others, that they seemed to many (and not only to men) to be the essential stuff of human fellowship, not arrangements that normalized men's power over women. The New Woman appeared in too many masculine places where she didn't belong—medical practices, newly coed universities, reform politics—upsetting the soothing hum of men's bonhomie, competing with them and discouraging them with her infernal drive to matter.

And the undermining of customary gender relations fed into worries about other social instabilities, contributing to what contemporaries saw as a general failure of nerve among young men. Indeed, the concern over what might make an American man who could rule the country ran through so many discussions in the 1890s that the era's historians speak of a masculinity crisis. This loss of confidence was manifested in alarm over the supposed epidemic of neurasthenia among overly intellectual young men, in a celebration of sports and martial vigor as antidotes to the plague of effeminacy, in a vogue for bodybuilding (and its companion religion, Muscular Christianity), and, most famously, in the cult of the "strenuous life" and of "roughing it" in wild, restorative places with "primitive" manly men—Indians, cowboys, native guides. Fear of the immigrants, the black masses, and the labor movement blended with dislike of the New Woman, promoting appeals to restore traditional hierarchies in family and class relations. A new kind of man seemed necessary, a tough, vigorous, decisive figure to match modern women's capabilities, recuperate the certainties of masculine direction, and subdue the threat of anarchic sexual modernism.

Bohemia, for all its optimism and masculine poise, was susceptible to the disquietude. Art itself was deemed to be a peculiarly feminine interest at the end of the century and artists as a group were considered vaguely compromised men. Insipid female taste supposedly dominated American culture, and in this mental frame, male artists ran the risk of emasculation, prevented by sentimental women from creating the virile work demanded by the times. In truth, there was little substance to the charge, but the "feminization of American culture," an idea born of reactions against the small gains New Women did make in public life, was a truism by the end of the century and nagged at the self-assurance of men who made art.

In a culture bifurcated between men of business and women of delicate tastes, artists worked at such a remove from the masculine world that they risked being seen as sissies, as "a little off, a little funny, a little soft!" So lamented the dean of American literature William Dean Howells (who was living in New York in the 1890s), and if Howells, a good fellow, a family man, and a member of the Century Club (where men of business did rub elbows with well-to-do men of the arts), could fret over the artist's potency, how much more vulnerable were the bohemians, disdaining as they did conventional masculine affairs? Historically, and as an urban type, the bohemian never quite emerged from the semipublic, semiprivate milieu of the café or the garret to enter the centers of business and power; his narcissism gave rise to dandyism, and dandyism could slide into foppery. Oscar Wilde's arrest and trial for homosexuality in 1895 only added to the taint of effete decadence.

Some artists seem to have little minded the suspicions; the association with European decadence ratified their sense of sophistication. But others tried to keep these associations at bay and enlist bohemia in the service of vigorous masculine endeavor. In painting, the circle of Philadelphia realists around Robert Henri—a group in the process of relocating to New York, where they became the Ashcan School— used a masculine idiom to distinguish themselves from the "tea-drinking" artists of the establishment. In journalism, the writers at the

Commercial made the same link between male vitality and realism: the exploration of real life promised to rejuvenate feminized American letters and build up the role of the male writer in the process. The encounter with the underworld and the laboring classes, in the 1850s the exclusive business of the dandy, now took on virile connotations. A man could rough it even on the Lower East Side. Lincoln Steffens mused that he found in the ghetto what others found out West: he meant adventure, perils, brawny comrades.

It seemed possible, then, that bohemia, despite the risk of effeminacy, might give rise to a New Man, a hero whose active, intelligent participation in the modern age could make him an adequate companion for the New Woman. With its modern aspirations, its loose, flexible sociability, and its egalitarian sensibility, bohemia seemed a place where a liberal solution might unfold to problems between the sexes, where a kind and gentle male authority might arise, benign and brotherly rather than authoritarian and patriarchal. The impulse underlies a group of fin-de-siècle novels about bohemia, all written in the wake of the best-seller *Trilby*. Set in Paris and New York, the stories are about troubled gender relations, with bohemia figured as a male refuge invaded by women hungry for life. The heroines, lit by the high ambitions of their generation, set out to prove themselves in the world, rejecting romantic love, determined to find new stories for themselves beyond marriage. Always they come to a bad end, always they are saved by the bohemian heroes.

These books are really about the provisional welcome fin-de-siècle bohemia offered women, about how marriage eventually snatches them out of the sphere of bohemian fantasy and reasserts its sensible authority over their experience. Gertrude Fosdick's *Out of Bohemia* (1894) is a seduced-and-abandoned tale, a warning pitched to credulous families too willing to send their daughters to art school. A young woman from the States is ruined by the scandal mongering about her in the Latin Quarter of Paris (a prime destination for American art students) because, although blameless, she is careless about her reputation. She seeks the protection of a brotherly friend, who instructs her in painting and finally marries her to save her from social ostracism. William Dean Howells made women's inflated delusions of creativity, their silly attempts to *matter*, the brunt of gentle comedy in *The Coast of Bohemia* (1899), in which the heroine discovers that the way to becoming a good painter lies not in specious independence but in marrying her chivalrous teacher. Robert Chambers's *Outsiders* (1899) is a Pygmalion tale of a bohemian writer who, newly arrived from Europe and despising the women artists he meets in New York—he calls the city the domain of the "cultured hermaphrodite"—recovers his moral bearings by rescuing the one woman he meets who yearns for something "higher," a working-class daughter who is in danger of losing her sexual virtue. He installs her—on platonic terms—in his downtown bohemian lair and there, with the help of his friends, teaches her about books and music and turns her into a grateful New Woman submissive to his teachings. A manhood strengthened by confronting the moral perils of the city triumphs as patron of female ambition and virtue.

The novels encourage a belief in a new kind of man who might trump rather than repress woman's ambitions. Their bohemias need not be exclusively male to be vital: a few grateful women can enjoy the men's company. The stories invite young men of sophistication to believe that enlightened solutions—a shared urbanity rather than separate spheres, mixed company at cheap restaurants rather than same-sex jollity at gentlemen's clubs—might reconcile men's customary dominance over women with a belief in women's right to a wider sphere of action. This self-conscious attentiveness to the needs and sensitivities of the New Woman would become, over the next two decades, a leitmotif of heterosexual relations in bohemia. In its own way, it would end up as a liberal version of swagger, reworking feminist ideals of a sexually egalitarian life into a different set of male imperatives.

The Lower East Side, too, had its New Women, identifiable by their dress (plain shirtwaists with ties and neither the head coverings of Orthodox women nor the cheap finery of conventional working "girls"), physiognomy (serious), and manner (grave). The Jewish New Women were garment workers, political zealots, and writers for the neighborhood newspapers, which hired them to gather local "women's news" and compose advice columns. They came to modern ideas through socialism, anarchism, and ideals of female independence that had been circulating through the Jewish intelligentsia, especially in Russia since the 1860s. By the turn of the century, all sorts of thinkers and proselytizers—Yiddishists and Zionists, too—inveighed against the backwardness of gender roles in the Jewish community, calling for education for girls and release from the heavy expectations of reproduction, deference, and service to family that yoked women to an archaic past.

Jacob Epstein. "A Russian Type." From The Spirit of the Ghetto, *by Hutchins Hapgood.*

As New Women did everywhere, these Jewish women provoked dark and pitying commentary from conservatives about the price modernity exacted from them. To their critics, they seemed depleted by their lack of the respect and admiration that traditional gender relations, in theory, conferred upon Orthodox women. "They sit in an atmosphere of tea-steam and cigarette smoke . . . pallid, tired, thin-lipped, flat-chested and angular. . . . The time of night means nothing until way into the small hours." But among the women themselves, a different understanding prevailed, one that came from Nikolai Chernyshevsky's fictional critique of traditional marriage and his defense of a proudly modernized womanhood in *What Is to Be Done?* (1863), a canonical novel of radical sensibility in Eastern Europe. For intellectual and artistic immigrant women, as well as for their American counterparts, fictional creations were tangled with social and psychological life.

Emma Goldman was one Chernyshevsky reader who took the dicta of New Womanhood very much to heart. Her path from an oppressive traditional home in Russia to New York bohemia provides a glimpse of the interactions of fiction, political ideas, and social mobility in the lives of dissenting immigrant women. Leaving Russia as a teenager, she first lived with her sister's family in Rochester, New York, where a marriage to a sexless, boring fellow immigrant (in order to get citizenship papers) reminded her of the protests against loveless marriage in *What Is to Be Done?* Respectable, cautious, working-class Jewish Rochester came to stand for all that Goldman despised in immigrant life. She hated the conservative expectations that hemmed in women, the constant angling for financial security, and the pie-in-the-sky dreams of success. The Haymarket deaths in 1886 and her own misery working in the factories pushed her vague radical sympathies into full-blown anarchist fulminations, rants that provoked and frightened her family and friends.

Along with other would-be New Women at the end of the century, both Jewish and Gentile, working- and middle-class, she sensed that she could find a more hospitable life in New York City. In Rochester, cramped and disappointed, she came to imagine New York as the place where she might break with duty-bound marriage and enervating work to create the kind of life she heard whispered about back in Petersburg, where she was a girl in the early 1880s: a life based on the harrowing, intense political commitments of the nihilists, the soulful, martyred young whose "revolutionary mystery" pervaded the air of her childhood. So New York it was: knowing just about no one, she set out for the city in the summer of 1889. Her autobiography contains one of the loveliest of coming-to–New York stories, her arrival the defining moment of her life, the point from which the self, now released, can gather itself and the plot can proceed. The two volumes begin with this lyrical evocation of a sweltering Sunday in the city: "I was twenty years old. All that had happened in my life until that time was now left behind me, cast off like a worn-out garment. A new world was before me, strange and terrifying. But I had youth, good health and a passionate ideal. Whatever the new held in store for me I was determined to meet unflinchingly."

And like other arrivals who told their tales of sudden transformation, Emma Goldman claimed she discovered what she was looking for in New York that very first day. She must have been so easily recognizable as a type that any passerby could direct her to her proper niche in the ecology of the Lower East Side. She found Sachs' café, where fellow spirits gathered; there she met other New Women, kind comrades who advised her where to find work, and an impressive young man named Alexander Berkman—another emigré, soon to be

Emma Goldman in the 1890s
INTERNATIONAL INSTITUTE
OF SOCIAL HISTORY

her lover and eventually her lifelong comrade. Berkman took her with him to finish off the evening at a meeting of leading anarchists, European luminaries whom she had admired from afar when she read the radical newspapers. She was renewed, exhilarated, *found:* the pinched self of the provinces slipped away. "The door upon the old had now closed for ever. The new was calling, and I eagerly stretched my hands towards it."

Goldman rose quickly in the tiny sectarian circles of American anarchism. The cafés were full of talk of the anarchist *attentat*—the idea of principled murder that had fired the nihilist assassins of the czar in 1881. In 1892, during a bitter, bloody strike of steelworkers at the Homestead mills outside Pittsburgh, Goldman and Berkman, now intimates and incensed by the high-handed response of the owner, Andrew Carnegie, sought to make good on the theory by planning the murder of the chairman of the board, Henry Clay Frick. Berkman acted as the assassin, but he botched the shooting. He went to prison for fourteen years; Goldman was implicated but never charged. In the wake of the *attentat*, Goldman broke with New York's anarchist leaders, who, to a man, repudiated Berkman. She began to find her own way in the political movements of the Lower East Side. By 1893, she was already something of a celebrity in the neighborhood for her oratory during hunger demonstrations that winter and the resulting prison sentence on Blackwell's Island (the first of several). When she was released, nearly three thousand people packed into a Bowery theater to celebrate.

Bohemia became a showcase for her newfound fame. She would have already seen how performers in the Yiddish theater, poets, musicians, and political notables used the café scene to show themselves off to gawkers and make themselves available to reporters and critics. Goldman extended the practice. She settled in at Justus Schwab's saloon, a meeting place for neighborhood radicals and uptown bohemians. She printed Schwab's address on her cards and correspondence and used the place to talk to reporters and receive admirers. She mixed with new friends there, consorting not only with leading French and German anarchists, socialists who had escaped Bismarck's Germany, and graying veterans of the Paris Commune, but with American-born artists and critics as well.

Goldman's story is unusual: not every rebellious Jewish daughter attracted a crowd. Elsewhere, and especially for women, cosmopolitan contacts were scattered and episodic, hampered by the language barrier, class prejudices, and anti-Semitism. Still, Goldman's experience in the 1890s shows the mutual and novel recognition of a common bohemian allegiance. There were, at this point, no sustained political undertakings, although wherever the immigrants were, there was sure to be serious talk. But these early meetings captured, on the one hand, the desire of an American-born generation for an experience beyond their class and, on the other, the ambitions of a proletarianized Jewish intelligentsia. Bohemia turned outsiders into insiders, even as it enticed insiders with all that could be learned and enjoyed on the outside.

Historians describe the crisis of the bourgeoisie in the late nineteenth century as stemming from a pervasive sense of how unknowable their society had become, detached from familiar moorings and Christian belief, and how immaterial their own influence seemed. "For many, individual identities seemed fragmented, diffuse, perhaps even unreal," observes the historian T. J. Jackson Lears. "A weightless culture of material comfort and spiritual blandness was breeding weightless persons who longed for intense experience to give some definition, some distinct outline and substance to their vaporous lives." For the bohemians, however, there was nothing ethereal about New York. Life pressed its particularities on every side. The city produced clutter, not vapors—palpable things of the world.

Against images of the metropolis as the chaotic site of a harsh and undisciplined modernity, the bohemians promoted notions of the city as infinitely knowable and nourishing. The politics of progressive reform also signaled the discovery of a generational project that reached across class lines and made the city its staging ground. But progressive reformers were still highly class bound, their projects imbued with a conviction of the rightness of middle-class hegemony and strong prejudices against immigrants and Jews. Among the writers and artists, imaginations roamed more widely. Their fondness for working-class characters, their sense of affinity with fellow wage earners and urban travelers, and their fascination with women of independent lives would, in the next decade, converge with politics to create what we know as Greenwich Village.

2

Journeys to Bohemia

Around 1910, the diffuse elements of turn-of-the-century bohemia collected at one stop on the old circuit, Greenwich Village. Suddenly, it seemed, New York's avant-garde emerged as a coherent community, visible and audible not just to its protagonists but to the whole city—and the country. To the participants, the change seemed to occur in the modern manner—that is, instantaneously, irrevocably, as a rupture that severed everything that came before from all that came after. They were a much larger group than the drifting bands of the 1890s, and their claims to importance—social and artistic—soared. Bohemia had always been self-aggrandizing but now it was millennial. "Life was ready to take a new form of some kind and many people felt a common urge to shape it," proposed one of the enthusiasts, the impresario Mabel Dodge. "The most that anyone knew was the old ways were about over and the new ways all to create. The city was teeming with potentialities."

The congregation was sizable and eclectic. People who had never conversed with one another, it was said, who had never sensed even an inkling of one another's existence, now found themselves in the same rooms, eating the same food, agreeing on some matters, arguing about others, putting on plays and pageants and political demonstrations, ruminating about their love affairs. "Everywhere . . . barriers went down and people reached each other who had never been in touch before," Dodge observed.

Yet it was the energies of history, not some alchemy of the times, that brought these people together and prompted them to make so much of the conjuncture. Some of the sources of bohemia were the same as those that had supplied the avant-garde in the 1890s. But by 1910, recruitment followed a more established pattern as apprentice bohemians across the country trod well-lit paths to Greenwich Village. If you came of age in the first decade of the century, there was available, for the first time, a road map to American bohemia.

Greenwich Village was an old neighborhood in lower Manhattan. In 1910, Greenwich Village meant the area demarcated by Washington Square and Fifth Avenue to the east, Tenth Street to the north, Houston Street to the south, and the Hudson River to the west. Its old brick row houses and winding streets, remnants of New York's original street plan, distinguished part of the district from the rest of downtown, nestled as it was within a regular grid of hulking buildings and tenements. Max Eastman, who in 1912 became editor of the Village's famous monthly the *Masses*, described a place of "low houses, transformed bakeries and livery stables, and streets that meandered around until they ran at times almost into themselves," the sedate facades concealing warrens of courtyards, tunnels, alleyways, and little back studios crowded into the interiors of the blocks.

The idea of the Village as an appealing arty neighborhood—indeed, the name "the Village" itself—came from middle-class people who moved in after 1900. Working-class residents of the tenements that dominated the less charming spots called the neighborhood "the Ward" or "the Lower West Side." Indeed, a social scientist who interviewed plebeian Villagers in a 1935 survey argued that bohemian Greenwich Village was what we would call a commercial fiction, "very largely manufactured and imposed from without," not least by the realtors and landlords who reaped profits from the newly discovered attractions of rundown houses. Eastman, who had certainly imbibed "the life that flowed there so brimmingly" since he arrived in 1908,

Minetta Street MUSEUM OF THE CITY OF NEW YORK

always refused to call his neighborhood "the Village" because the insider's knowingness of the term irritated him so.

In 1910, there were corners of affluence in the Village but mostly it was a neighborhood down on its luck; "To Let" signs filled the windows of prime storefronts. A few old wealthy families remained on Washington Square and lower Fifth Avenue, left behind in the late nineteenth century as fashionable New York moved uptown, but most residents were workers and modest professionals unable to afford the new apartment houses elsewhere. The irregular street geography lent itself to varied demographics, pockets of Italians, Irish, blacks, and artists. Once people thought of it as bohemia, however, certain aspects of the locale but not others registered as "Greenwich Village." Although labor questions would become prominent in the bohemians' concerns, for example, they did not see their own neighborhood, packed with working-class residents, as a community of labor but rather as one of leisured sociability. When a terrible fire at the Triangle

Shirtwaist Company, a manufacturing loft right off Washington Square, killed 146 women workers in 1911, the horror was understood as a tragedy not of the Village but of a working-class New York situated in some vague elsewhere. Villagers' memories might well summon up the winding streets where Italian urchins played, but never the sweatshops and tenements where the Italians lived and worked. There was virtually no recognition of the Irish, who were a considerable presence, or of the black laborers who remained after an Italian influx pushed the residents of "Little Africa" on Houston Street (dating from the 1830s) up into the Tenderloin.

Greenwich Village, as it came to be celebrated, did not refer to an actual neighborhood so much as to a fictive community. It was a selective vision of city life that installed some people in the foreground as protagonists and shunted others to the background or offstage altogether. The notion of the "Village" enhanced the mutual awareness of newcomers but not that of longtime residents; in situ, artists and journalists, New Men and New Women could recognize one another but seldom their working-class neighbors. The compactness of the district, the plethora of cafés and saloons, and the little stoops at street level encouraged easy sociability, and the twists and turns of the streets fostered a kind of purposeful sauntering. It was a much more probable niche for bohemia than the modest 1850s beer cellar Pfaff's had been, or even the restaurants of the Lower East Side. Low rents (at least early on) allowed artists and writers to live there: indeed, a come-hither real estate market beckoned to anyone who fancied a life transformation.

The newcomers saw themselves as bohemians. But they also viewed themselves as intellectuals. The word itself was new, one of several keywords generated by the political left ("feminist" was another); it denoted professionals who supported themselves through some vocation in arts and letters. Originating as a self-designation of the Dreyfusards in France in 1898, "intellectual" had oppositional connotations; the term nodded toward men (women were problematic) of modest social backgrounds, not the gentlemen of property and standing who had devoted themselves to culture since the nation's founding. Greenwich Village provided a rich environment for precisely these people, who, although they lacked education, money, and connections, were determined to make their mark on America's culture.

The neighborhood's sense of noble enterprise bred an intense collective intimacy born of fidelity to a grand mandate. Critics sneered at the adolescent self-absorption, the narcissism of a world apart, but Villagers paid no heed. Rhapsody was the timbre of their commentary on the world's future and their own role in making it. "Instead of a world once and for all fixed, with a morality finished and sealed, we have a world bursting with new ideas, new plans and new hopes," wrote Walter Lippmann in 1912, just out of Harvard and braced by the spirit of the place. "The world was never so young as it is today, so impatient of old and crusty things." In the minds of its residents, the neighborhood acquired immense powers. Hutchins Hapgood had been living in and around the Village since he began working at the *Commercial*, but now he sensed a change. The metropolitan spirit, in his mind, seemed to charge across the country to swoop up lonely rebels in its folds. "Whenever a group of individuals—the men animated by a dislike of regular business or professional life, inclined toward the freedom of art and literature, the women of the same type, bored by some small place in the Middle West . . . filled with restless ambition to lead their own lives—came together, there was the Village."

Hapgood was already a proselytizer for metropolitan modernity. What was new in this refinement of the coming-to-New-York story was his sense of a tight connection between provincial iconoclasm and a particular part of New York. The roads to bohemia were broader, more clearly posted than they had been in the 1890s, when he and Mary Heaton Vorse chanced into the avant-garde. After the turn of the century, the circuitry of desire was in place: people moved to Greenwich Village, ideas and images flowed back out to the provinces, luring even more people to Greenwich Village. The sense of personal emancipation was not invented in the 1910s, nor was it unique to New York, but it became one of Greenwich Village's staple exports, an invitation to a life that could be found only in one place. There, remembered one emigré, "I first loved, and I first wrote of things I saw . . . there I got my first perceptions of the life of my time." "The only place for me," recalled another.

Who exactly were these self-styled rebels? Where did they come from and what barriers had they surmounted on their way? Most of the principals grew up outside New York and first formed their ideas of Greenwich Village from afar, often in Hapgood's "Middle West," in small towns that, as he correctly understood, had some ineffable affinity to Greenwich Village both as place and state of mind.

By the early 1900s, middle-class versions of bohemia existed across the country. Artists' colonies burgeoned—in Woodstock, New York; Carmel, California; Taos, New Mexico; the Roycroft group in Aurora, New York—blending an arts and crafts ethos with a touch of decadence. In small towns and cities, groups of artistic clubwomen, gentlemen, and racy young marrieds assembled under the bohemian rubric. Rooted in the press and art markets of their regions, these people mostly stayed where they were, the Taos crowd in Taos, the Woodstock group in Woodstock. In some places, however, bohemia was edged with the allure of something bigger. "A richly blended politico-aesthetic ambience," a historian has written of radical middle-class English homes in the period, a phrase that captures a particular kind of reform-minded, faintly cosmopolitan American milieu as well. Circles of small-town aesthetes overlapped with reformers. Socialist Party membership, labor sympathies, and municipal progressivism created connections between the classes and made restless people candidates for moving on.

Not since the great antislavery battles of the 1850s had political thought so thoroughly prepared provincial intellectuals to participate in a drama that transcended their local circumstances. Small-town culture in the North at the turn of the century may seem, on the face of it, suffocating and bourgeois, promoting neo-Victorian conceptions of culture as a WASP birthright, blocking working-class participation. But in fact, in those places where socialism, populism, or syndicalism cohered into organizations, there were mental and institutional spaces where middle-class and working-class people met each other. Not only political action but shared devotion to beloved radical classics (Tolstoy, Edward Carpenter, William Morris, Shelley, Robert Owen, Kropotkin) forged links otherwise unavailable in the class structure. Enthusiasm for Walt Whitman could be a ticket for some uneducated worker to friendship with the town's literati.

Little is known about this high-minded provincial life; its history is buried in separate accounts of progressive reform, or socialism, or feminism. And the memoirists, the veterans of this upbringing, reinforced the portraits of stultifying communities, so eager were they to underplay the cultural resources that propelled them on their journeys and to exaggerate their own heroism in rebelling against the small-town philistines. But in fact a serious and varied culture sometimes thrived in modest places. Reformers, readers, socialists, atheists, vegetarians, and feminists often knew one another, were sometimes the same people, and moved in contiguous channels of a lively intellectual life. The alignment of art with the liberal/left fight for the "good time coming" elevated, in the hands of the participants, petty municipal battles and mundane local arguments to a level of sophistication and significance.

One town that has supplied enduring evidence of this history is Davenport, Iowa. Davenport enters the record because several of its most gifted residents ended up in literary New York: Floyd Dell (co-editor of the *Masses* and future pundit on marriage and love), George Cram (Jig) Cook (impresario of the Provincetown Players), Susan Glaspell (short fiction writer and eventually Pulitzer Prize–winning playwright). They wrote enough about their origins to create a composite portrait, shot through with allusions to provincial narrowness, to be sure, but also unwittingly evoking an open, generous atmosphere. So for now Davenport will have to stand in for all the small places, mute in the historical record, where overlapping groups of reformers created a minor-league farm system for big-time arts and letters.

A small, thriving city on the Mississippi River, Davenport, population 43,000 in 1910, was the banking, trading, and transportation center for a rich rural hinterland. It could be the kind of town Sinclair Lewis pilloried in *Main Street* (1920): self-satisfied, mean-spirited, and unbelievably boring. And in fact the massive town history of 1910 does swell with a midwestern burgher's smug boosterish pride. "A Good Place to Live," one chapter announces, supporting the claim with lists of Davenport's post office branches, banks, and businesses—the infrastructure of bricks and mortar that in the Midwest united civic pride and pleasant profit.

The little city, however, was cosmopolitan in its way. German Jewish refugees from the revolutions of 1848 had turned a straggling trading post into a prosperous market town. A steady stream of Germans continued into the 1890s. One of the state's largest Jewish populations, first German peddlers and then Eastern European immigrants, made the town their home, eventually creating a solid Jewish middle class. Davenport's position as a Mississippi River town, servicing steamboat traffic and becoming the state's first rail terminus for the line from Chicago, meant that it was also a transit point for people moving up and down the river and in and out of Chicago. Steamboats stopped at the levee, where their bands and calliopes entertained for a night: the great jazz trumpeter Bix Beiderbecke grew up there and first listened to syncopated dance tunes, ragtime, and early New Orleans jazz down by the river.

It was, oddly enough, what we would now call a city of diversity. The German forty-eighters bequeathed the town a tradition of reform politics, intellectual inquiry, tolerance, and love of high culture. Abolition had been strong in Davenport—Dred Scott lived there for some time prior to litigating for his freedom—and the fact that John Brown had provisioned his raiding parties in Davenport remained a point of local pride. There was a small African American community founded by freedpeople, part of the hopeful migration of Southern black people looking for more hospitable environs after the Civil War. The city supported many musical organizations—choruses, study groups, instrumental ensembles—two opera and two vaudeville houses, and at least two theaters, one of which was German-speaking. Respectable culture (leaving out hot music on the river) was intricate, highly articulated in a network of voluntary associations, some men's, some women's, and some mixed: a society for philosophical debate, reading groups (a Shakespeare club, a Dickens reading circle, a history study group), and an Academy of Sciences.

This life of the mind was at its core middle-class but at its edges heterogeneous. It was carried on by lawyers and doctors, the Reform rabbi, and New Women, of whom Susan Glaspell, a college graduate and journalist who was writing a novel, was the most advanced. But the love of music cut across social divisions, and the abundance of fraternal organizations (Elks, Moose, Masons), ethnic brotherhoods (like the Hibernians), and trade unions (nearly fifty) also provided a public life for working people that could lead to serious reading and informed discussion. At the center of working-class intellectual culture were two small and vigorous Socialist Party branches—one English-speaking, one German-speaking—permeated by the passions of the self-taught. Socialism was strong enough that in the election of 1912 Eugene Debs won 11 percent of the vote, making Davenport the Red City of Iowa.

A few people moved between the different groups. Jig Cook was a newly returned native son, a Harvard graduate who came from a leading Davenport family. He left a job teaching literature at Stanford to come home in 1903 and pursue what he envisioned as a Tolstoyan life of contemplation tilling the soil. He poured his considerable mental and physical energies into meticulous chicken farming schemes, all failures. Mollie Price Cook, his second wife, was a voluptuous middle-class vagabond whom love had stranded in the Iowa fields. The daughter of an anarchist physician in Chicago, Mollie Cook had been an actress, an artist's model, and an assistant at Emma Goldman's New York–based journal *Mother Earth* before she married Cook and came to the farm, shocking the locals by sporting men's overalls and walking around barefoot.

Floyd Dell was another beneficiary of Davenport's distinctive culture. Having moved there from Illinois in 1904 when he was seventeen, the sensitive, impoverished, bookish boy (the oldest child of a failed butcher, he was already the breadwinner of his family) became a favorite son of working-class and middle-class intellectuals alike. He endeared himself to older people with his eagerness to learn, his earnest requests for advice and reading. The postman and the street sweeper pressed copies of nihilist tracts and socialist and populist classics on him; literary ladies and the librarian lent him New Woman novels and volumes of poetry; the rabbi argued with him about the future of society. He lazed in the town square with workingmen on market day, drinking beer and speculating on the future of labor. Intellectually gifted but dirt poor, he was supremely qualified to take advantage of opportunities only just developing. To working-class socialists, his background made him a child of the people who needed to be prepared for a role in the historic mission of raising his downtrodden brethren; to middle-class aesthetes, he was a natural poet in need of rescue.

Until he fell in with the Davenport intelligentsia, Dell was slated for a life of manual labor. "My destiny was to be a factory hand. I had no illusions of being able to rise from the ranks," he wrote in his autobiography. He was perhaps not disingenuous when he claimed that at the time he had no idea that such connections might lead to something, since in the early years of the century, the movement of working people into professional intellectual work was only barely imaginable. Once he left high school, middle-class friends found him a job as a reporter for the local newspaper, a literary arena that, if cramped, was still close enough to urban journalism in the 1890s mode. He adopted a bohemian soft collar and tie and roamed down by the river.

If Dell had simply been a socialist ideologue, it's doubtful he would have ever gotten much beyond Iowa, despite his charm. But his skill in "manufacturing a Bohemia for myself," as he put it, led his mentors to see "big things" in him. The interplay between his poetry and his socialism made him more than a star reporter: it cast him as a candidate for literary work in the metropolis. Mollie Cook saw his free-love disquisitions (worked out in essays but also in a surreptitious attraction between them) as a way to launch him into the national orbit of the anarchist press. The librarian, who had friends in Chicago, believed he was ripe for success in city journalism. And Jig Cook saw him as a romantic genius of rural life destined for glory in the city. When they met, Cook was brooding over his wasted youth and the sad fortunes of his chicken farm. He leapt on Dell as an audience for his quasi-mystical philosophizing. The boy would be his alter ego, he imagined, passing on to "big things" while he remained behind on the farm, true to his Tolstoyan ideals. "He is slight, has a cough, and in passion the gift of expression is like Shelley," Cook boasted to a crony in Chicago. "*He has never seen Chicago . . .* think what Chicago will be to him!"

With the help of his backers, Dell moved to Chicago in 1908 and took a job as a reporter, quickly rising in the ranks of the *Evening Post* so that in 1911 he became editor of the *Post*'s *Friday Literary Review*, the leading organ of literary modernism in America at the time. His youth in Davenport had educated him well for a job in which literary matters were also political ones. Jig Cook, fed up with idealistic chicken farming and now separated from Mollie and their two children, joined him as his assistant; Susan Glaspell, Cook's new lover, came soon after. But Chicago could not satisfy them. Everyone moved on in a few years to Greenwich Village.

The Davenport group was following a traditional path. In the nineteenth century, gifted young people tended to move within regional spheres, settling into local capitals—Boston, Philadelphia, New Orleans, Chicago, San Francisco, Atlanta. New York had dominated publishing and the art market since the 1850s, but these cities still retained vigorous, if smaller, networks of literary presses, newspapers, and art galleries. After 1910, however, other cities found themselves, despite their best efforts, pulled into New York's gravity, serving as points of departure in a way that would have been inconceivable in the nineteenth century. Bohemia—and, more precisely, the allure of Greenwich Village—played a part in the change.

Chicago, the country's second-largest city, was a real contender for national influence in the years before New York locked up its monopoly. More than any other American city except its great rival, Chicago inspired romantic hopes. The city's location in the center of the country gave it an edge in attracting intellectual and artistic talent from the Midwest and West. Industrially and financially, the city rose as a testament to the titanic powers of modern capital, a miracle of skyscrapers and industries, a Babel of nationalities. By 1890 the population was over a million, a figure that would triple by 1930. "Cattle, hogs, sheep, iron ore, coke, lumber, farm produce went in; meat, machinery, paper, and commodity futures came out," a cultural historian writes of the gargantuan economy.

Supported from above by a culture-conscious business class, Chicago boasted in the early twentieth century a symphony that rivaled New York's, a major art collection, a university with a faculty comprised of distinguished graduates of eastern universities, and several crown jewels of American architecture set in the business district of the Loop. The newspapers featured a circle of nationally known humorists and dialect writers. Chicago's publishing houses and magazines were not as extensive as New York's but they loyally encouraged midwestern writers. Nourished from below by a huge immigrant population and black migrants from the South, the city's popular culture encompassed a busy ethnic press, a variegated musical life that included early blues and jazz, and many foreign-language theaters.

Visitors and residents agreed it was impossible to describe the city. Chicago was too colossal, too anonymous, too populous, too diverse to be rendered in image or text. Ceaselessly changing, it outran nineteenth-century conventions of urban description. While writers also puzzled over how to describe New York (a theme of unrepresentability expressed in Henry James's *American Scene* [1903], in which people rarely intrude and architecture, instead, bears the weight of James's reflections on the city), Manhattan was at least geographically compact and offered approaching visitors a spatially integrated skyline that came to function as a visual and literary symbol of the metropolitan totality. Chicago, on the other hand, lay sprawled over miles of prairie, so large and inchoate that it baffled its visual artists, who engaged in no sustained attempt to paint or draw the city on the order of the effort that preoccupied New York artists.

Literary renderings of Chicago are brushed with grimness: the heroine of Willa Cather's *Song of the Lark* (1915), for example, a New Woman alone in the city while she studies opera, is exalted but imperiled, too, by the onrushing crowds, "the ugly sprawling streets, the long lines of lights." But an alternative strain surfaces as well, a lyrical celebration of precisely these features of anomie. Margaret Anderson, a young woman with literary hopes who came to Chicago in 1908, wrote of the enveloping glow of the city's "enchanted ground" and the exhilaration of walking in a city that seemed never to end. Because the city's elite prided themselves on helping talented newcomers, emigrés (if they were white) made their way to the inside easily enough. The powers of Chicago publishing, art acquisition, and taste—what a later generation called the Big Money—never sat on high in remote majesty as they had for so long in New York but rather seemed to lounge genially about the mahogany and gilt lobbies of the great hotels on the Loop. Not until Richard Wright's memoir of his miseries as a black writer in 1930s Chicago, powerfully titled *American Hunger*, would the sequence of loving tributes to Chicago be significantly interrupted.

Floyd Dell arrived in Chicago from Davenport in 1908 and immediately began jotting down his "First Impressions" in the mode of the 1890s feuilletonists, that style New York bohemians had learned from Europe and the Iowa bohemian learned from New York. "First Impressions" re-creates for us the relative ease with which an ambitious newcomer could traverse the range of Chicago culture, even making some significant contacts in his first few days. Dell moved around from high life to popular culture, public spectacle to intimate camaraderie, from the set piece that initiated any newcomer ("Arrival in Chicago; dark—crowds—big buildings") to an intimate spot known only to bohemian cognoscenti, the Price house, an anarchists' boarding house and rendezvous run by Mollie Cook's father. He made the rounds of high culture ("Lincoln Park; the flowers . . . Grand Opera . . . recital of Debussy and Maeterlinck") but also visited the Olympic Music Hall. Like the bohemians of the 1890s, he was uninterested in African American neighborhoods; his walks would not feature the pleasures of ragtime, blues, or jazz. But he was drawn to immigrants, so he took in the great Russian actress Nazimova in *The Comet* and the hit of immigrant life, Zangwill's *Melting Pot*. He easily located reform and radical Chicago ("Meeting where I saw Jane Addams; her voice and eyes" and "Anniversary of death of Haymarket victims"). He made the rounds of literary Chicago as well: the newspapers, the editors, the bookstores, the cafés where authors conversationally strutted their stuff. He met his fiancée, Margery Currey—a Vassar graduate, teacher, and ardent woman suffragist—in cheap ethnic restaurants, new venues in the courting life of the urban young ("Meeting Margery; the vegetarian restaurant; the chop-suey place").

Urban pride gave rise to the Little Room, a salon held in the beautiful downtown Fine Arts Building, an office building renovated into studios for local artists, playwrights, and writers. A proclamation over the doorway assured entrants "All Passes—ART Alone Endures." An elegant glass-doored elevator conveyed guests to a floor paneled in dark lustrous wood and decorated with exquisite pre-Raphaelite murals; the luxurious ambience spoke of the Midwest's belief in a felicitous alliance of business and art. The tone was refined, with a delicate touch of polite bohemia. Men and women sipped tea amid the exotica of a well-appointed artist's studio—a Russian samovar, heavy Spanish furniture.

By the time Dell came to Chicago, however, the Little Room's monopoly on Chicago arts and letters was being challenged. Young artists and writers with no interest in taking tea were moving to Jackson Park, a South Chicago neighborhood of flimsy frame storefronts that had lined the main approach to the Columbian Exposition of 1893. Each house consisted of a single high-ceilinged space fronted by a plate-glass display window; plumbing and heating were rudimentary (as in New York artists' lofts in SoHo's early days). Privacy came from curtains hung as partitions. Intense sociability and tacky restaurants suggested a "real" bohemia. Painters, sculptors, photographers, and writers lived there, many of them associated with the avant-garde Little Theatre. People dropped in and out of the chilly houses, modeled for the artists, and carried on love affairs.

Dell married Margery Currey—who came from a leading family in suburban Evanston—and the two set themselves up nicely in a roomy middle-class apartment. But they soon abandoned propriety to rent separate adjoining studios in Jackson Park. It was a startling choice for newlyweds. "What the 'ell are you and Margery going to do with two studios?" wrote a poet friend. "It sounds great, but madder than hatters." Currey, a strong feminist who insisted that her husband share the housework, seems to have liked the separate-but-equal arrangement and Dell, a dedicated lover of women, seems to have enjoyed his own bedroom. Whatever the case, the marriage broke apart in Jackson Park, the two amicably parting ways after only a year. "I have stepped back into my Margery Currey skin," she informed the readers of the Vassar alumnae magazine with the aggressive cheerfulness of a woman intending to be New. "I find it really nicer to be a single lady."

In 1890s New York, women were so scarce in bohemia that they functioned not as a group but as plucky individuals and tokens of the men's open-mindedness. Now women began to discover possibilities for leadership. Currey made herself the local *salonnière*, a hostess but a director, too, of people, ideas, and experiments. She attracted established artists who were restless in the humid atmosphere of the Little Room, liberal people from the university, the Davenport group. "Why does all of sharp and new; / That our modern age can brew; / Culminate in you?" an old friend teased. Margaret Anderson, very much a New Woman herself, a dazzling renegade from a wealthy

B. J. O. Norfeldt. Floyd Dell.
Oil on fabric. NEWBERRY
LIBRARY, CHICAGO

midwestern family (and like Currey looking for a profession), was moved by the gatherings to start a literary magazine, the *Little Review*, that would publish avant-garde work that Little Room writers would not touch. A Chicago Renaissance seemed to be in the works.

It didn't happen, though. Chicago, once a destination of a lifetime, turned like other regional capitals into a way station to New York. So many of the protagonists moved to New York that the Jackson Park circle fell apart. Dell and the Davenport emigrés were the first to go, followed by Margaret Anderson with her journal. There had long been complaints about the numbers of writers and artists who, once they made it in Chicago, took off to further their fortunes in the East. But these had been a minor note in an assertive Chicago urbanism that could depend upon regular infusions from villages and towns. The Davenport/Jackson Park exodus, however, signaled the regularization of travel along a new route: small city to big city, big city to New York. A new geography of culture was emerging, a fixed relation of periphery to center. The move from the provinces to New York would be the defining cultural journey of the country for most of the century, challenged only by the emergence of Hollywood as another magnet.

Ironically, the bohemia that looked like it might strengthen Chicago's claims to eminence actually hastened its subordination. The lure was New York's culture industries—newspapers, book and magazine publishing, art production, and the theater, all expanding at a pace that Chicago or any other American city could not match. Although local bohemias initially gathered in regional talent, they ended up redirecting ambitions toward New York in an unprecedented way. Jackson Park molded a local avant-garde that imitated popular images of an urbane intelligentsia, but in doing so it turned away from its own culture and in the direction of New York—the point of origin of that bohemian imagery. The same process went on elsewhere. San Francisco's bohemia, for instance, also lost talent to Greenwich Village. But in Chicago, the American city with the richest and most fully developed culture of its own, the shift was poignant, originating in a place that took such care to be hospitable to the gifted young. When Jig Cook moved, he continued to publish in the *Friday Literary Review* he once edited, but now in the form of a weekly "New York Letter" touting the personalities, daring, and discoveries of downtown Manhattan. If people were not restless to begin with, an awareness of Greenwich Village as a distant beacon of modernity ensured they would become so.

While Bohemia offered sanctuary to people traditionally excluded from the centers of culture, it also opened up escape routes to those who had access to those centers but found them too constraining—students at elite colleges and universities. This connection is so common in our culture that it seems unexceptional, but in the early twentieth century it was novel. For most of the nineteenth century, journalism and painting, the staples of bohemian vocation, lay outside the career orientation of college graduates. But a change came in the 1890s. Nationwide, the student body grew dramatically and even elite institutions opened up, admitting a few favored sons and daughters of lower-middle-class and working-class families. Some well-to-do progressives began to offer college tuition to exceptional working-class youths. A liberalized curriculum (from an emphasis on moral philosophy and the classical world to social science and "modern"—that is, postancient—history and literature) catalyzed political and intellectual debate on major campuses, interrupting a long tradition of upper-class hijinks, school spirit, and obsessive athletics. Wherever there were knots of teachers who promoted some sort of contemporary thought—whether the budding sciences of economics and sociology, reading Ibsen, or socialism—students construed the material as ratification of their desire to immerse themselves in experiences that lay outside their upbringings. One sign of the excitement was the formation in 1905 of the Intercollegiate Socialist Society, a federation of campus organizations that quickly grew to twenty chapters.

At the women's colleges, too, there were clusters of liberal teachers and chapters of the Intercollegiate Socialist Society. But perhaps more important, the association of female education with New Womanhood made the more daring students automatic prospects for bohemia. Feminists Crystal Eastman, Inez Millholland, and Edna St. Vincent Millay went to Greenwich Village straight from Vassar; other female moderns who ended up in New York studied at state universities. Though largely for the well-to-do, women's education was in fact more widely available than is generally thought, because of scholarships (Millay, from a poor Maine family, had one) and because of the state colleges and universities.

The generational romance of female independence made college something like a love affair. Dorothy Day, a child of the Chicago tenements, found supporting herself as a scholarship student at the University of Illinois was even "more thrilling than the idea of an education." Day was to become, in middle age, a radical ascetic, founder of the Catholic Worker movement. But when she was young, it was not religion but the saga of New Womanhood that made her poverty intoxicating. At university, she was on her own for the first time and away from the domestic responsibilities she had always assumed as the oldest girl in a large family. Although she worked endlessly, drudging for faculty families between classes to make ends meet, she felt nonetheless released. "Really I led a very shiftless life, doing . . . exactly what I wanted to do," she reminisced. The pleasures of easygoing independence made it easier for her to defy her family and move on after graduation to become a journalist in the Village.

For educated women, college was the launching pad to extended tours of self-invention in which bohemian props were crucial. But improvised their lives remained, fashioned out of chance rather than continuity, loose ends rather than warp and woof. Even young women with good educations and some backing had little to go on besides other New Women's sympathy. There don't seem to have been the clusters of admiring onlookers, the kind of believers who encouraged Floyd Dell, to applaud the transformation of promising young women into bohemians. If anything, families and well-wishers tried to shepherd them away from such compromises with respectability. For men, though, the passage from college to bohemia was generally achieved more smoothly. The story of the Harvard Renaissance shows how the privileges of a male elite could glide beneficiaries from a Cambridge elect of insiders to a New York elite of outsiders.

Harvard had undergone the changes that had affected higher education as a whole. By 1900, the forward-looking administration of Charles Eliot had turned a New England college into the country's leading university. A curriculum stressing modern subjects signaled at Harvard and elsewhere the weakening of the narrow and repressive intellectual politics that dominated campuses in the 1890s. Nationwide, it was social science that flourished, but at Harvard it was literature, philosophy, and the arts. Under Eliot's leadership and inspired by the powerful example of Harvard's beloved William James, a distinguished group of professors made their teaching a platform for advocating a searching relationship to contemporary life, whether through modern literature, drama, or Fabian socialism.

At Harvard, a purposeful curiosity about contemporary ideas opposed a fashionable dilettantism entrenched among the conservative undergraduate majority. Intellectual open-mindedness learned in classes emboldened an intrepid minority to challenge the rigid caste system of the campus. Harvard was divided into two groups: the patricians, ensconced in elegant clubs on the "Gold Coast" of Mount

Auburn Street, and the plebs, stuck in the shabby dorms of Harvard Yard. "Some men came with allowances of $15,000 a year pocket money, with automobiles and servants, living in gorgeous suites in palatial apartment houses," remembered John Reed, class of 1910. "Others in the same class starved in attic bedrooms." Buoyed by the liberal spirit of their studies, a group of social rejects consigned to Harvard Yard began to act instead like sophisticated secessionists. They were led by Walter Lippmann, the brilliant son of a wealthy German Jewish family from New York who was barred from the clubs because of anti-Semitism. The Harvard Yard rebels formed a Socialist Club, which became the flagship chapter of the Intercollegiate Socialist Society.

The Socialist Club, in turn, spawned more groups as the opposition—it amounted to a social revolution on campus—spread. There was soon a lively international club where foreign students discussed world politics with interested Americans, a Men's League for Women's Suffrage, an anarchist cell, a new theater group and an orchestra that performed only plays and music written by students. Progressives lectured, Emma Goldman held forth, a paper published muckraking essays on the university's treatment of its cleaning women. In 1912, while one contingent from Harvard motored out to a bitter textile workers' strike in Lawrence, Massachusetts, to serve in the state militia and have "their fling at those people," the socialists organized a demonstration in Cambridge to support the strikers. William James's moving 1908 dictum that educated youth might serve their society once they understood that "real culture lives by sympathies and admirations, not by dislikes and disdains" echoed the conviction of dissidents on his own campus.

Increasingly, a university that had been a finishing school for the New England patriciate oriented its talented students to a larger world. One result was that the collective gaze shifted away from Boston—or, alternatively, political office in Washington—and fastened on the city of New York. So many of the Harvard rebels went to Greenwich Village that John Reed, writing in 1912, saw Washington Square as pretty much an annex of Harvard Yard. Reed's lodging house in Greenwich Village was packed with classmates, whose exploits he travestied in a long comic poem, "The Day in Bohemia," in the fashion of the *Harvard Lampoon*. He also wrote a long paean to their undergraduate years, "The Harvard Renaissance," casting the dawn in Cambridge as the harbinger of a new day in the Village. Swelling pride in his own first successes writing for the New York magazines merged with the delighted conviction, shared so widely in 1912, that the world was on the verge of something big. "What happened at Harvard, and what is happening there, is the same thing that is happening in all the nations of the world." As Harvard went, Reed was thinking in his modest Harvard way, so went Greenwich Village, and as the Village went, so went the world.

By the time of the "Harvard Renaissance" essay, Reed had trimmed his sails to the Village winds and tacked to the left. But in fact at Harvard he played both sides of the street. Good-tempered and school-spirited (traits that served him well in revolutionary Russia), Reed was a relentless joiner of campus organizations with an unquenchable hankering to belong to the right set. Unlike Lippmann, whose Jewishness excluded him from the Gold Coast from the start, Reed kept coming just close enough to believe he might ultimately get in. His own family was well-to-do—his father was a leading lawyer—in Portland, Oregon, but that was not enough for Mount Auburn Street. Initially, "the rich splendor of college life" eluded him. He devoted himself to a striver's valiant round of extracurriculars, managing the water-polo team and cheerleading for football.

But once he threw in his lot with the political left, he gravitated toward an alternative order of success. From Charles Copeland, a Harvard English professor who in the 1890s had sent his students to work for Steffens at the *Commercial*, Reed learned that an educated man could exercise his talents in journalism. Through the socialists, he came to sense the possibilities of a liberal milieu of peers dedicated to art and politics. "The manifestation of the modern spirit," he called their aspirations, "for lack of a better name." At graduation, still only dimly aware he had lived through a "Renaissance," he had as yet no idea how dissent might connect to literary ambition. He did know that he did not want to follow the conventional route of the Harvard graduate. "It all comes down to this," he asserted with the portentousness of the undergraduate philosophe. "Happiness and experience, or money and a rut." For happiness and experience, he decided to look not in Boston or back in Portland but in Greenwich Village.

As they settled in dilapidated rooming houses on Washington Square, Reed and his friends formed a band of self-congratulatory brothers, radicals *avant la lettre*. The ease with which they took center stage in the Village must have been aggravating. Even as rebels, heralds of the new dawn, they had the confidence and authority of the old school ties. As Harvard has always wielded authority in New York, a secret cell of Boston influence, so they tended to position themselves nicely. They would take risks, to be sure—Reed most of all—and their commitment to innovation and self-invention was serious. But while they broke with Harvard power and privilege, they nonetheless arrived in New York fully costumed and prepared to take the stage, so they thought, for their roles as leaders of the new age.

Not all bohemians in New York came from elsewhere; the city itself also supplied recruits to the Village. Their journey was a mental one, a matter of relocating one's sense of vocation to another set of city blocks. There were particular points at which New Yorkers negotiated to exchange one life for another. An artistic calling was clearly a possible entrée to bohemia, but progressive politics was another. Political conviction—feminist, socialist, trade unionist—had never before been tied tightly to bohemia (although in Paris, revolution wafted through in 1848 and again in 1871), but now it became a distinguishing feature of the Village esprit. In particular, progressive reformers who had worked in the settlement movement and found themselves chafing at its restrictions were drawn to the Village intelligentsia.

The settlement movement began in the United States in 1889 when Jane Addams set up Hull House, a neighborhood center modeled on Toynbee Hall in London's East End, in one of Chicago's most impoverished immigrant wards. Scores of other houses in northern cities soon appeared, inspired by the Chicago example. Educated young people, men and women, took up residence in the settlements to live and work among the poor. These settlements departed from the premises of Victorian charity by stressing the interdependence of the citizenry, a belief that supplanted an older condescension toward the needy and harnessed a new generation's drive to learn about the "other half" firsthand. By 1910 there were some four hundred settlements across the country; of those in New York, three were south of Fourteenth Street, the University, Greenwich, and Henry Street houses. Initially motivated by the Protestant Social Gospel and a faith in their own WASP rectitude, residents saw their mission as uplifting immigrants to middle-class standards. But especially in Chicago and New York, where socialist influence was strong, the belief that workers, with middle-class support, could advance their own particular causes began to overtake Christian charity and make some social workers strong advocates of labor, politically holding up the left wing of the progressive movement. Residents included Protestant philanthropists formed in a late Victorian mold, but also young people who longed for "vital contact" and transported those yearnings into bohemia. With their experience of involvement with working-class people, the residents would help press labor issues on the attention of the downtown moderns and make Greenwich Village something more than a hive of aesthetes and privileged men on the make.

"Vital contact," a phrase used by Harvard rebels in the 1910s, distills a sensibility of dissent formed from the general agreement that privileged youth—especially, but not exclusively, men—were enervated by overeducation and overrefinement and that they could revivify themselves through contact with supposedly simpler, hardier, more spirited people. The notion suggested a form of elite renewal that could foster amity and shared goals across class lines. Unlike the thirst for vibrancy and authenticity in the 1890s, however, the yearning for vital contact was less oriented toward pleasure and self-development and more toward liberal political ideals. Working people would provide their privileged friends with an animating experience of simple charm and human drama; in turn, the educated mentors would teach the working poor good citizenship and civic organization. There was condescension at the heart of the effort, to be sure, but nonetheless the desire to socialize democracy made encounters across class lines in liberal settlement houses more reciprocal than they had been in the 1890s.

Vital contact was bleached of religious impulses. Not the search for "God" but the search for "life," not indwelling "grace" but "experience" shaped its imperatives, thereby separating its adherents from Christian do-gooders. Not in the first decades of the century or thereafter would these moderns go to church, pray, or even debate the existence of God; agnosticism was in the urban air they breathed. Occasionally, much later, some Villager under a cloud of misfortune sought solace in religion, though seldom in Christianity but rather in theosophy, Oriental mysticism, Gurdjieff, peyote. In this as in much else they found fellow spirits among the Jewish radicals. Secularists by virtue of throwing in their lot with socialism and anarchism, the Jewish moderns turned their backs on religious observance as archaic. This meant, for one thing, that varieties of anti-Semitism that required a Christian subsoil did not take root among left-leaning settlement residents.

The excitement of vital contact helped cast downtown New York, especially the Lower East Side, as a free-spirited, convivial quarter rather than the fetid bog of tubercular paupers that conventional reformers saw. The cafés never closed, marveled one settlement house resident, contrasting them favorably with the gentlemen's clubs with which he was also familiar. "Their convivial atmosphere and the lack of restraint such as the order and decorum of a club require, give more breadth to thought, more vividness to the imagination, more brilliancy to the expression." In particular, the Eastern European Jews were noted by all who came into contact with them for their astonishing capacities for flamboyant talk and hyperbolic argument. To American-born observers (and listeners), the cacophony of Yiddish, Russian, and accented English seemed "a brittle jabber," as Irving Howe describes it, and the din has been attributed, in the history of *Yiddishkeit*, to the garrulous and contentious character of the Jews. But that explanation isn't quite sufficient. The Irish, too, were (and are) a notoriously loquacious people, yet explorers of the Irish "shadows" of New York in the mid–nineteenth century seldom noted poor people talking, except for snatches of comic dialect or murderous screams. But because settlement workers were often political and intellectual people themselves, they were aware of the salience of what was being said in the immigrant cafés, the intellectual life that ran through them.

Their own preoccupations made them responsive to the talk of bookish shopkeepers, reflective women, penniless professionals, and proletarian intellectuals who studied Marx and Prince Kropotkin as
assiduously as their fathers had studied the Talmud in the shtetlach of
Eastern Europe.

Social workers, prompted by the example of 1890s journalists,
might become writers of human interest, turning fragments of speech
overheard on the street and sad stories learned from the poverty-
stricken clientele into feuilletonist ephemera and short fiction. "Few
have had material like that immense new field of life . . . in those early
years when the great pot seethed and boiled," recounted a Princeton
man who served his literary apprenticeship this way. True, even the
most sympathetic of settlement residents worked with assumptions
about the superiority of their "civilization" to the societies from which
their clientele had come, a stance that preserved a hierarchical relationship between them and those they would serve. Nonetheless, the
belief in the organic, reciprocal character of social bonds—"doing
good *with* people instead of *for* them," as an enthusiast encapsulated
the idea—promoted a more egalitarian strain of liberalism than the
Americanizing movements of uplift with which they are sometimes
now conflated.

To some degree, the boundary was open in the other direction as
well. Settlements led to relationships between native-born Gentiles
and immigrant Jews that in the nineteenth century would have been
unthinkable, alliances so unusual that they took on, de facto, a
bohemian defiance of WASP prohibitions. The marriage of Rose
Pastor, Jewish ex-cigar worker, and the New York patrician Graham
Phelps Stokes, a Yale-educated resident of the University Settlement,
was so extraordinary it became a newspaper sensation, with extensive
coverage of the tale of "the Cinderella of the tenements." The Stokes
family was huffy (at best) and kept Rose Pastor at arm's length.
Nonetheless, a few other couples—settlement house gentlemen and
immigrant women—braved upper-class anti-Semitism, including
Anna Strunsky, a Stanford graduate who was the child of Jewish shopkeepers, and the wealthy Socialist Party leader William English
Walling, so that by 1910 the Stokeses were living in Connecticut in a
wealthy little colony of mixed political marriages.

But these were anomalous matches. More significant were institutional arrangements that encouraged reciprocal interchange between settlement workers and immigrants. Sometimes these were only set pieces of self-conscious democracy, public debates in the settlement houses in which contending speakers—anarchists and socialists, labor activists and capitalist ideologues—presented their views and settlement residents acted as referees. In its more powerful manifestations, however, the ethos of cross-class exchange engendered by the settlements inspired political coalitions between socialists, trade unionists, and middle-class sympathizers. In the 1890s, such alliances had been rare, although there were exceptions—William Dean Howells lent his support to labor struggles and the Hull House staff organized relief for workers in the bitter Pullman strike outside Chicago in 1894. Ten years after Pullman, though, when the Women's Trade Union League was founded in New York in 1903, ideas about cross-class collaboration were so strong that middle-class "allies" and their working-class compatriots devised a governing board structure where workers were guaranteed a standing majority.

Altogether, this generation was more inclined to treat the newcomers as compatriots of substance rather than as picturesque dreamers. Bemusement at Eastern European quaintness never disappeared, but it did partially give way to greater respect. The shift made the plebeian Europeans more than stock types in the background of bohemia. It transformed them into necessary protagonists in a modern intelligentsia.

The turning point in the immigrants' status in the eyes of their intellectual compeers can be dated to the first Russian revolution, 1905–07. The struggle for constitutional democracy in Russia shook the Lower East Side and forced settlement house workers to regard these neighborhood radicals, who were knowledgeable and involved with the events, with new seriousness. Russian revolutionary politics were already a fertile ground for shared concerns. Since the late nineteenth century, Russia, seen as a country of arresting tragedy and deplorable autocracy, had inspired tremendous interest in the United States. Liberal Americans devoured the works of Kropotkin, Tolstoy, Gogol, and Turgenev and George Kennan's sensational

Century articles on the Siberian prison camps. And in 1903 news of the terrible Kishinev pogrom reenergized a "Free Russia" movement. When refugees from Kishinev docked in the harbor, their saber wounds still festering, there were people from the Henry Street Settlement there to meet them and publicize their plight.

Among the immigrants themselves, the connections to the revolution in Russia were amazingly close. "The radical East Side lived in a delirium," remembered Emma Goldman of 1905, "spending almost all of its time at monster meetings and discussing these matters in cafés." The Socialist Revolutionaries (SRs), one leading party of the revolution, sent organizers to New York, followed shortly by Catherine Breshkovskaya, whose years of suffering in Siberia made her a folk hero among Russian immigrants and a martyr to Kennan's American readers. The New York settlements arranged for Breshkovskaya to speak to wealthy liberals around the country. The American public, conveniently hazy about the socialism of the SRs, eagerly embraced the revolutionaries as rebels against autocracy and anti-Semitic terror.

The revolution and Breshkovskaya's successful tour hastened a recognition that the ideas of the Lower East Side were something more than abstract fulminations or romantic idealism. And the engagement with Russia, shared with the immigrants, pushed some settlement workers out of the more staid realms of reform into a bohemia open to different sorts of radicalism. The short history of the A Club, a cooperative boardinghouse set up in the Village by former settlement residents, shows how, in the heated political atmosphere of New York in 1905–06, settlement living could lead to political behavior that the older generation of reformers could not tolerate. The A Club was formed in those years by male cronies from the University Settlement and a half dozen women who were probably Women's Trade Union League activists ("A" was a cipher, later to be filled in by hostile newspaper coverage). Married couples shared the house with single people: occupants included Mary Heaton and her new husband (Albert Vorse, Harvard graduate, adventure writer, and former settlement worker himself), William English Walling and Anna Strunsky, Anna's sister Rose, and Rose's suitor, another middle-class settlement writer.

Cooperative housekeeping was in vogue, touted by feminists as the key to women's emancipation from domestic drudgery, and this aspect would have appealed to the Vorses, who had children by this time. They had been in Europe for two years, and Mary Heaton Vorse, excited by her contacts with the labor movement abroad, was elated to find so many like-minded people in one place: "Everybody a Liberal, if not a Radical—and all for Labor and the Arts." Located near Washington Square in a neighborhood of small hotels where Hapgood, Boyce, and other journalists had lived in the 1890s, the place was ideally situated for visitors to drop by. It became one of the first institutions of the Village, an informal salon where visiting radical celebrities—the labor agitator Mother Jones, for instance—mingled with notables and artists who were out for a stroll.

Involvements with the Lower East Side that had begun in the settlements led the A Club group to the Russian cause. Some traveled to Russia to help and actually to fight. The house on Washington Square functioned as an American press bureau; refugees arrived from Russia, Vorse remembered, "with ours as the only American address." When Maxim Gorky, visiting New York with his "paramour" to raise money for the revolution, ran into a press scandal engineered by the Russian embassy (Gorky could not legally marry his second wife because Russian law did not allow the dissolution of a first marriage), the A Club offered the couple shelter after every hotel in New York refused to take them in. It was then that the young residents' willingness to risk sexual scandal earned them the epithet "Anarchist Club" from the press. Interestingly, sympathetic as progressives in New York were to Gorky, everyone else flinched. Sexual heterodoxy was beginning to mark a divide between downtown radicalism and reform.

The political and social breaches of the wall in the early years of the century would, in time, lead to the crossover of immigrant Jews into the American intelligentsia in the 1930s, when the offspring of the first wave of immigrants became famous as writers, critics, and editors. But it was in the 1910s that a particular American chemistry had first gone to work, as if a dash of the "other," whether the Jew or the New Woman, was necessary to distill the modern from the cultural solvent.

The early crossover into bohemia was possible for other outsiders, too—a few Italian immigrants, sons and daughters of the Irish tenements, American-born workers like Floyd Dell—but not for blacks. The northern African American press celebrated the "New Negro" as a figure set into mutually beneficial analogy with all the other "new"s. But the New Negro would not appear on the bohemian spectrum until the Harlem Renaissance of the 1920s, and then only episodically.

This was partly a matter of a racism so deep it went unmentioned. Would a black person even have been served in a Village restaurant in 1910? Probably not. But the demographics of the city at the time made for few black candidates for bohemia. The African American intelligentsia in Manhattan was tiny; blacks were less than 2 percent of the population in the years before the Great Migration from the South turned Harlem into the capital of the African American world. W. E. B. DuBois did indeed spend some years in downtown New York—he came from Atlanta to edit the *Crisis* for the National Association for the Advancement of Colored People (NAACP) in 1910 and worked with William English Walling and Anna Strunsky, along with a group of black New York reformers. The office was on lower Fifth Avenue, in the heart of Greenwich Village. But by and large, his connection to the Village was tentative and to the Lower East Side nonexistent.

DuBois would in any case have been an unlikely candidate for Greenwich Village; he was a man too intensely conscious of his dignity—and vulnerability—to rub against the raffishness of bohemia. James Weldon Johnson, a less straitlaced figure, was a songwriter and diplomat who hung out in the Tenderloin, and here the association is more plausible. Johnson's wife, Grace Nail Johnson, belonged to Heterodoxy, a feminist club in the Village. A subscriber to the *Masses*, the flagship paper of modern radicalism published from Greenwich Village, Johnson was sufficiently aware of bohemia to draw the Tenderloin into analogy: the black neighborhood was a magnet for "colored Bohemians," he wrote in 1912.

The peripatetic writer Hubert Harrison, leader of a circle of West Indian radicals in Harlem, would also have been a likely conscript, since he was an outsider both proud of his marginal status and hungry for new connections. Born to a family of modest means in Saint Croix,

Harrison received his primary schooling there; then, like many other West Indian men, he extended his education by shipping around the world. In New York, he took menial jobs and went to night school. He threw himself into journalism and work for the Socialist Party and through these avenues came into contact with the Greenwich Village scene. By all accounts a brilliant speaker, Harrison worked with IWW leaders in a big strike of Paterson, New Jersey, silk workers in 1913, a cause célèbre in downtown New York. There he made acquaintances that led him to write for the *Masses*. As a Socialist Party member, an IWW supporter, and a *Masses* writer, Harrison would have been one of the few African Americans to know the principals and places of bohemia. But he apparently never found a compelling or sustained welcome there; or, conversely, perhaps he himself never found the Village compelling. By 1916 he had mostly abandoned his downtown left-wing involvements for a "Race First" politics—although still inflected with socialism—in Harlem.

For anyone black who sought admission, bohemia offered scant hospitality. In the 1940s, Richard Wright encountered bare bigotry from neighbors when he moved into a town house on a now-chic street in Greenwich Village. In the 1950s, even as Beat circles included a few black artists and interracial marriages, James Baldwin was assaulted in a Village tavern where hip writers mingled with workingmen. These grim facts, however, should not obscure bohemia's innovation. The early moderns had embraced a few Jewish artists and thinkers as the sponsors of a Lower East Side conceived as a fecund, politically animated community. The immigrants by their very presence gave a plebeian, ethnic, and at times racialized coloration to New York intellectual life quite different from the Anglophilia and Francophilia that had tinged the old elites. While this immigrant, largely Jewish crossover was distinct and in many ways unparalleled in the ensuing years, it did set into place a mechanism for incorporating other cultural outsiders, one that opened the way for the 1920s fascination with black intellectuals and artists. This is looking ahead, though. For the moment, it suffices to keep track of the charged relationships between modernist culture, commerce, and ethnic and racial others, relationships that determined who was included in "trans-national America," the concourse toward which downtown radicals would yearn.

The changes in manners and morals that Greenwich Village came to typify began in disparate places. Elite universities, provincial reform circles, other cities, and immigrant communities propelled people and ideas along widening pathways of accelerated mobility. But how such different people came together does not explain what they accomplished once they got there, how they transmuted earlier engagements with literature and reform into new metropolitan forms. It was the sensibility of modernism that now encouraged them to see themselves as a group residing on the near side of history. If they were not painters or writers at the cutting edge, they nonetheless might be inventors in other ways. The very substance of their community, flashing with unusual relationships, seemed a medium from which might be crafted forms like those the painters created on their canvases— forms that would shatter moribund, prettified conventions to inaugurate a more profound experience of human relations in talking, in writing, in sexual expression.

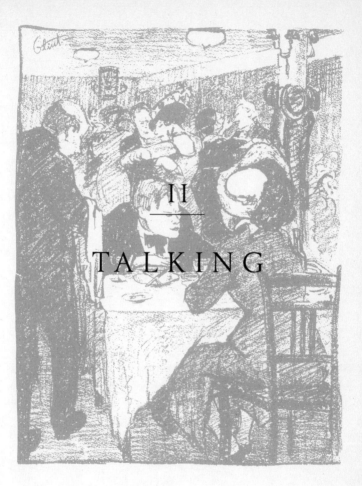

II

TALKING

PREVIOUS PAGE: *H. J. Glintenkamp. "He: 'Did you know that I am an Anarchist and a Free-Lover?' She: 'Oh, Indeed!—I thought you were a Boy Scout.'"* Masses, *December 1915* TAMIMENT INSTITUTE LIBRARY, NEW YORK UNIVERSITY

3

Intellectuals, Conversational Politics, and Free Speech

mbition took men and women to New York, and ambition
shaped their lives once they were there. But theirs was an
ambition broadly conceived. The desire was not so much to
be famous or rich—although those interests, in time, would figure—
but rather to *matter*, a determination to distinguish themselves in the
life of the country and in the epoch just beginning. But how, exactly,
to matter? Political engagement was part of the story; it was culture,
however, a distinctly metropolitan network of affinities and institutions, that provided the moderns the means to set themselves apart
from others and skirmish their way toward importance.

Speech—not just oratory and debate but focused conversation—
became one medium of distinction. Downtown New York turned talk
into a conspicuous secessionist style, setting the bohemians off as a
movement within intellectual life much as modern artists had set
themselves off in the world of painting. Radical talk expressed "a sense
of universal revolt and regeneration," in Max Eastman's description,
announcing "the just-before-dawn of a new day in American art and
literature and living-of-life as well as in politics." Bohemians had long
prized the rambling talk of the cafés. Now they picked up the pace and
transformed the agreeable palaver of men about town into a modish

assortment of subjects and arguments pieced together by men and women. Free speech was self-conscious, flashy, daring, ostentatiously honest and sexual. Shot through with a bohemian fondness for self-dramatizing, it flitted from poetry to birth control to the situation of the garment workers. It was "free-thought talk," Eastman added, not just socialism.

The talk was artful, with formal principles at work. The urbane, politically aware conversation was notable not for its discursive unity but for its juxtapositions: it was a pastiche of speech, a bricolage, a collage. Lack of cohesion was the fundamental principle, random items and topics from the vast range of American life assembled with tonic excitement. It was an aesthetic exercise in daily life, a quotidian American corollary to a European high-modernist aesthetics of language: think of Joyce's fascination with how words bobbed about in a modern city, unloosed from fixed referents. Broadly speaking, the astonishing linguistic play of *Ulysses* and the urbane stream of consciousness of Greenwich Village talk were fostered by similar urban forces: a booming print culture, the spread of advertising, and the compression of polylingual populations, all touching off an explosion of language.

The talk was more than just an avant-garde manner; it resonated with political changes in the United States. Intellectuals and artists developed a view of themselves as a select group uniquely equipped to speak to and for the poor and voiceless. When talk was free in the modern manner, new connections might emerge, both between Greenwich Village and the rest of the country and within the Village itself. Replete with the moral riches of empathy with the workers, free speech became a defining ethos of the radical milieu, an agent of cohesion for an intelligentsia in formation. Talk connoted a cultural triumph that was also political, modern sensibility and the social revolution fused. The rebellious talkers were buoyed by a cheerful conviction that language, unimpeded by convention or law, could create democratic communities with constituencies otherwise divided— men from women, the poor from the privileged, the untutored from the educated.

In the early century, opportunistic and idealistic outsiders alike could sense a vacuum in power in Manhattan. The WASP elites who ran the city's cultural institutions and overlapped with Republican political leadership were no longer able to inure themselves to the democratizing pressures of the day. Problems against which they had girded themselves in the 1890s had, by 1910, become urgent and acute. What was the nature of an aesthetic and intellectual life adequate to the great transformations of twentieth-century life: the influx of immigrants, the changes in women's roles, the growth of the cities? What might be the basis for a truly national culture, one that drew diverse people into proximity with one another? What was the character of American democracy in a time when economic power was concentrated to an unprecedented degree in the hands of the few? The rear-guard responses that had still seemed possible in the 1890s—the use of armed force to quell labor uprisings, the gentry's seizure of urban power from the immigrant-dominated political machines, the attempt to impose an anglicized neo-Victorian culture on the masses—seemed exhausted. At the same time, the possibilities for leadership, lying fallow in the hands of the city's reigning elites, seemed so enticing—what Herbert Croly had meant when he ventured that something considerable might happen in New York.

Who, then, was better equipped to talk to and for America—a fading patriciate of old men holed up in their gentlemen's clubs or a group of people, arrivistes of many sorts, gathered out of the crevices and far places of the country?

P rotecting free speech is now seen as a long-standing feature of American democratic politics, but before the 1890s the fight to protect the circulation of speech from government interference was sporadic at best. Agitation for the right to open public debate was in fact largely a turn-of-the-century phenomenon. Settlement house forums where radicals and settlement workers debated labor issues depended upon the principle, but their staged controversies were only a faint liberal echo behind closed doors of the tumult raging in streets and squares. The struggle for free speech turned into a concerted battle when towns and cities frequented by radical proselytizers passed laws to limit or ban open-air speechifying. With their denunciations of parasitic capitalists and their incitements to workers to join unions, Socialist

Party stump orators and, beginning in 1908, IWW militants in the Far West tested police, provoked reprisals, and landed in jail. But police intimidation and jail sentences sometimes galvanized not only socialists and union members but middle-class people and sympathizers from settlement houses. In 1902, there were already enough lawyers committed to taking on these cases to form a Free Speech League, which went on to push test cases up through appeals courts, their success aided by a new judicial propensity for constitutional review.

For the Wobblies and the Socialists, free-speech fights were a practical necessity but also an organizing tactic. Both groups depended upon open-air speaking to pull in recruits, since many of the working people to whom they preached could not read English or were illiterate in any language. One side effect of the free-speech battles was to catalyze coalitions of liberals and radicals. The networks surrounding the litigants made the cases flash points for agitation against the "plutocracy," especially among those middle-class and wealthy progressives who had no strong empathy for the rights of labor but were attracted to more abstract ideas of democratic politics. Across the country, when radicals went to jail for fulminating against capitalist injustice, they gained support from local doctors, editors, and progressive thinkers. Writers, theater people, and sex radicals also became involved, because an 1873 federal law—one of the famed "Comstock laws," after vice crusader Anthony Comstock—interdicted "obscene" material from being published, mailed, or performed. The Comstock law was used to suppress birth control literature and sex information, but from 1910 on, agents also went after novels, reproductions of nudes, and eventually avant-garde literature (Margaret Anderson's *Little Review*, for example, would be hounded mercilessly for serializing *Ulysses*).

Free-speech politics thus linked artists, writers, and professionals of a progressive bent to working-class militants. From liberal lecture halls to union rallies to soapboxes in New York's Union Square and Chicago's Bughouse Square, free speech left a trail of the fluid liberal/radical coalitions characteristic of this moment. While for Socialists and Wobblies free speech was a pitched battle against the plutocracy, for the many who lingered at socialism's margins, it was a cultural crusade, a means to affiliate with workers' grievances, to be sure, but more so a matter of cultural consumption, of the right to hear and entertain expressions of all sorts in the marketplace of ideas.

The effect was to detach free speech from class struggle and float it as a term signifying any form of expression that set itself against established authority. The Socialists in Davenport, Iowa, for example—the hardy band who helped Floyd Dell—waged their own free-speech fight in 1910 against the local library board. Dominated by Catholics, the board had vetoed the acquisition of a book of liberal theology. Denunciations pro and con rang forth from street corners; the controversy was the determining issue of the mayoral campaign. With fiery conviction, the Iowa free-speech forces saw their battle as one with the bloody Homestead Steel strike of 1892, the link being that Andrew Carnegie, who owned Homestead Steel, was also the philanthropist who donated the money for the Davenport library. The connection would seem to demand some irony, but Jig Cook drew a strict analogy between the two fights. "In view of the economic tyranny on which the Carnegie Public Library is based," he declaimed, "it is not surprising that another form of tyranny should make its appearance in the administration of it."

Such cross-class identifications could be politically vivifying, but they could also be strained, the lachrymose empathy liberals in the drawing rooms drummed up for hard-pressed people on the street corners. The Irish poet Eavan Boland, reflecting upon similar exchanges between Irish working-class radicals and well-off sympathizers before 1920, calls them "broken-hearted transactions"— broken-hearted because they metabolized the urgent needs of people under duress into a sentimental representation of those needs. The experience of censorship and police harassment aroused the sympathies of affluent liberals, but the ramifications of the free-speech fights were starkly different for working-class activists, who courted brutal treatment (and sometimes death) from vigilantes and the police. In Spokane, locale of the first IWW free-speech fight, a batch of Wobblies would be thrown into an eight-by-six sweatbox, its walls stained with the blood of previous prisoners, to swelter for a day until they were removed to icy cells without beds or blankets. In San Diego in 1912, when Emma Goldman and Ben Reitman, her lover and manager, arrived to help a hard-pressed free-speech campaign, a mob at the train station howled for Goldman ("We will strip her naked; we will tear out her guts"), and vigilantes abducted Reitman, drove him out to the desert, tortured him, and left him for dead. IWW free-speech fighters left the jails with scars, missing teeth, and broken bones, some of them with constitutions permanently weakened and impaired.

For affluent sympathizers, on the other hand, repression came in the form of police breaking up a lecture so that they were denied an evening's edification. For them—a group Floyd Dell described as "polite old-fashioned believers in the gradual improvement of mankind by going to lectures"—free-speech politics declared a desire to participate in an unhindered circulation of intellectual commerce, a view that, no matter how radical the substance, was commensurate with laissez-faire liberalism. Goldman excelled at creating coalitions around free speech but was always cynical about the strength of democratic solidarity on which free-speech liberals prided themselves. In 1909, the police, enforcing a recent New York law that criminalized anyone defending anarchist views, shut down a lecture Goldman was giving in the city on Ibsen and roughly dispersed the affluent crowd, which included plenty of "Americans"—as opposed to immigrants—and one Alden Freeman, an heir to the Standard Oil fortune. Freeman was irate. He plunged into a fight already boiling with IWW challenges in the West and poured money into the lawyers' Free Speech League. Goldman was happy to use Freeman's money but skeptical of his motives. The police had done far worse to her working-class audiences, she noted, but there had been no public outcry. "This time, however, the affront was offered to 'real' Americans, among them even the son of a millionaire. . . . Such a thing could not be tolerated."

Ultimately, these tensions would lead to a break between radical and liberal versions of free-speech politics, a break that produced the particular aesthetic of talk that characterized the moderns. The story of Greenwich Village's first institution for free speech and the conflicts within it shows the rupture. Founded in 1912, the Liberal Club briefly brought together older progressives and younger bohemians for debate and lectures. But the radical uses to which the bohemians turned the club unnerved the older people. A rift developed over talking—what to talk about, who could speak—separating the advocates of mankind's steady improvement from the champions of thoroughgoing revolt.

An earlier incarnation of the Liberal Club had been organized by a well-to-do Social Gospel minister, Percy Stickney Grant, who around 1910 began a weekly forum on social issues at his Episcopalian church near Washington Square. Grant brought in Socialists, Wobblies, and labor leaders to discuss with his wealthy parishioners, in a carefully moderated setting, the burning issues of the day. The church discussions were tremendously successful and Grant was moved to join with Lincoln Steffens and a few other progressives to found a permanent association nearby. They invited a mix of Village residents—old and young, Protestants and nonbelievers, socialists and feminists, bohemians and the respectable, men and women—to exchange ideas on social topics. But while the founders championed open discussion, they recoiled at the pressure to open up membership. When Hutchins Hapgood, a new member, proposed his friend Emma Goldman, and Walter Lippmann their fellow Harvard graduate W. E. B. DuBois, the founding clique went into a dither—so much so that the names apparently never even made it to a vote.

The breaking point, however, turned out not to be the issue of social integration but the spirited ways of one woman. When free speech courted sexuality, an unbridgeable gap appeared, separating progressive reformers from a new kind of radical. Henrietta Rodman was a feminist schoolteacher, tough and highly political, known around the Village for her eccentric appearance. Like many of her friends, she had her hair bobbed, but she also sported sandals and—reportedly—a straight shift that resembled a meal sack (presaging Gertrude Stein by several years). In 1912, she was leading a campaign against New York City's requirement that women—not men—report to their employers any change in their marital status. Seeking to force the issue, Rodman publicly refused to notify the Board of Education of her recent marriage. The fight hit the newspapers, which were ever alert to controversies involving New Women. Rodman and her supporters cast the matter as a free-speech issue because Rodman's transgression was to speak the truth—announcing to all the world that she was married—rather than to kowtow to antique discriminatory laws by keeping the marriage a discreet secret, as married female teachers typically chose to do. "She couldn't even do so conventional a thing as get married, without creating a terrific sensation and getting headlines," commented Floyd Dell, who barely coated his hostility with a veneer of fond condescension. The *New York Times* reported that Rodman was living in a free-love ménage and the scandal seeped into the Liberal Club, where she was a highly visible member. A Columbia professor whose wife also belonged even blamed Rodman for his divorce, charging that she and her friends had so lowered the moral tone at the Liberal Club that his marriage was irreparably damaged.

The scandal recalls Gorky and the A Club affair several years earlier, the same generational and political division falling between those who were willing to shrug off, even to court, conservative slurs and those who were aghast at any hint of sexual impropriety. A willingness to tolerate looseness in what women said and how they presented themselves in saying it separated the moderns from the progressives. For the latter, talk between men and women was proper if it was high-minded: behavior in mixed company, especially women's, was strictly regulated. The problems brewing at the Liberal Club also hearken back to a ruckus in the Fabian Society in London among a similar group of reformers three years earlier, when the affair of H. G. Wells with another member, a young woman, shook the group to its core. Any suggestion of sexual irregularity, even if it was simply rhetorical, brought such mixed groups dangerously close to the laxity of free-love bohemia, an intolerable situation for the older people, however sympathetic they might be to women's rights. In New York, dismayed progressives bolted the scene.

The third incarnation of the Liberal Club, now controlled by the champions of open membership and feminism, set up in a brownstone on narrow, decrepit Macdougal Street, south of Washington Square, in the heart of Greenwich Village. The new club blossomed with heterosexual conviviality and emancipated talk. "A Meeting Place for Those Interested in New Ideas," the letterhead advised—the casualness of "meeting place" as opposed to "club" advertising a come-hither sociability. The decor stressed this club's difference from other clubs: bare floors, wooden tables, cubist and fauve art on the walls. Bright colors were the fashion for furniture, fiery "futurist" oranges and acid yellows rather than the somber wooden surfaces and florid wallpaper of Victorian decor. The circulation between the clubrooms, Polly Holladay's restaurant downstairs, and the Boni brothers' bookstore next door undermined any interest in exclusivity that might have lingered. Weekly dances (not mannerly waltzes but the turkey trot and the shimmy, imported from "low," working-class dance halls), unceasing ragtime on the player piano, masquerade balls, and amateur theatricals further erased the boundaries between those who belonged and those who didn't, so that the Liberal Club hosted a free-floating clientele. A cast of drifters—"girls who had run away from their parents, women whose husbands had left them, Jewish anarchists, professional beggars of the intellectual order, visiting celebrities, Russian revolutionaries," as one poet described the crowd, surrounded the core of leftish intellectuals, writers, and theater people, the stalwarts dubbed by the curmudgeon H. L. Mencken "all the tin pot revolutionaries and

Polly Holladay's restaurant MUSEUM OF THE CITY OF NEW YORK

sophomoric advanced thinkers in New York." People began to gather in the late afternoon and stayed on, talking, dancing, and drifting downstairs to eat at Polly Holladay's plain board tables.

And drinking. It is not overstating the case to say that Greenwich Village initiated a long infatuation of American writers and artists with alcohol, a love affair that began to subside only in the 1970s, if then. The generation of the 1920s—Hemingway, Fitzgerald, Dorothy Parker—is better known for its booziness, but as it turns out, they were following in the footsteps of their bohemian predecessors. Blowsy paeans to alcohol billowed up from the moment. "An elemental thing like the sea: a universal mother," Floyd Dell crooned about liquor. Everyone drank hard, ventured Mabel Dodge, who doesn't seem to have drunk much herself. "But it was a very superior kind of excess that stimulated the kindliness of hearts and brought out all the pleasure," she averred. "The idea that anybody would drink too much was unthought of," Dell recalled of his Jackson Park friends. Drinking was virtually a social duty.

Part of the allure was that men and women could drink together. It was as if in this bracing modern space, hard drinking shed its connotations of sodden gentlemen's maunderings or, alternatively, masculine barroom bonhomie to become an elixir of modernity. "The women worked quite regularly, even when they, too, drank," Mabel Dodge observed brightly, meaning, probably, that the women still cleaned up and put the children to bed. There are only scraps of evidence to go on about the New Women and drinking, but it's intriguing to piece something together. Most certainly, hard drinking was a token of emancipation, like sex before marriage and talking about sex; it was understood as a constructive act of affiliation. Morphine addiction is what the women appear to have viewed as the feminine debasement to be avoided. But whiskey—so vigorous and proletarian!—and wine—so sophisticated and Continental!—must have seemed potions of transcendence into a genderless life or, even more loftily, a domain of profound community, in touch with the mysteries, to put it in the neo-pagan terms that Jig Cook was wont to use.

The Liberal Club's conviviality was at once cozily domestic and racy, as men and women glowing with emancipated fervor and lubricated with liquor discussed subjects formerly taboo. "The most energetically wicked freeloving den in Greenwich Village," a proud member called the place. Love affairs materialized among the crowd, and spouses cast off traditional roles to dance and debate as comrades, friends, and colleagues. There were different circles of interest, all which incorporated men and women, amateurs and professionals. The extensive cast of characters makes it worth listing a few. There were the poets, a set that included Dadaist Alfred Kreymborg and Edna St. Vincent Millay. The club's theatricals attracted a devoted, hardworking group, among them Floyd Dell, who found a role as drama impresario when he arrived from Chicago, the set designer Robert Edmond Jones (one of the Harvard men), Princeton dropout Eugene O'Neill, Ida Rauh, a suffragist and lawyer, and Stella Cominsky, Emma Goldman's niece. The writers were the largest contingent. A number were already established: Theodore Dreiser, Sinclair Lewis, Upton Sinclair, Steffens, Hapgood, Sherwood Anderson, and John Reed; others were still struggling their way out of the newspapers and the leftist press: Neith Boyce, Louise Bryant, Anna Strunsky Walling, Jig Cook, and Max Eastman. Around these cliques circulated an eclectic set of professionals: a psychoanalyst, a civil engineer, publishers, liberal lawyers, bookseller Albert Boni, and teacher/troublemaker Henrietta Rodman.

The concourse reminds one of the self-consciously shocking and intimate talk of Bloomsbury, spinning transgressions across the ocean at the same moment. Both groups were "conversational communities," bound together by emotional and sexual ties but also by devotion to vivacious, bold, and honest talk. Both despised the mannered conversation of the patrician drawing room and arty salon as well as the barren commonplaces of the middle-class parlor.

A reader might bridle at the comparison. Do we have to hear more about Bloomsbury? True, Bloomsbury was too elite and tiny to make the parallel between its "conversational community" and the Village exact. "Civil society" might be an alternative model to describe the American milieu: a sphere of civic fellowship and reasoned disputation that nourished democratic politics, its theorists believe, beginning with the habitués of eighteenth-century coffeehouses. But "civil society" is too abstract and dry to capture the robustness of these early-twentieth-century talkers, who implicitly defined themselves in contradistinction to cultivated discussants. For one thing, coffeehouse talk, rooted in the consultations and disputations of a male citizenry, was historically inhospitable to women. The traditions of coffeehouse talk would have fed, for example, the intense late-night bull sessions at Columbia or at Harvard—"hours of glorious fighting, keen arguing and splendid, if impractical visions," as John Reed described them. But glorious fighting and keen arguing were not the modus operandi of bohemian conversants. For another, the talk of civil society was structured by logic and ratiocination. It kept personal life and intimate relations at bay and put men into relations with one another as informed discussants. So "conversational community" better evokes the freewheeling, frequently erotic and knowing talk, although in Manhattan, far more than in Bloomsbury, that community opened out to a heterogeneous range of speakers, interlocutors, and topics.

The particularity of the new American talk lay in its randomness. A broad variety of weekly lecture topics took the Liberal Club well beyond interest in the gradual improvement of mankind. Members began to think of themselves as an intelligentsia with the ability to give coherence to a collection of subjects that others would find unrelated—or stupid. A friend who came with Henrietta Rodman found that "one could listen to the keeper of a house of ill fame, looking like a primary school teacher, speak one evening, and a pacifist clergyman, looking like a professional boxer, address an audience on the following one." A talk on the tango followed a lecture on the IWW. Horace Traubel, Whitman's disciple and chronicler, spoke on the poet; Vachel Lindsay, a tramp poet from the Midwest, chanted his verse; Emma Goldman gave some of her spicier talks, like "Is Man a Varietist or Monogamist?" on humanity's need for free love, and "The Intermediate Sex," on homosexuality; Carl Jung lectured, too. There were discussions of the slit skirt, nudism, and the music of Richard Strauss.

Such offerings—topics plucked from the potpourri of the city and positioned in an evening's talk—made a speech collage, something of a verbal equivalent to the experiments in painting and affixing that Braque and Picasso were conducting in Paris in 1913–14. Indeed, the collagist juxtaposition, heterogeneous elements assembled without connectives, can be seen as a governing principle of this wave of modernism, asserting itself in stream-of-consciousness narrative, unconventional typography, and jarring instrumentation as well as painting. There were no contemporaneous American artists of collage, but there were Imagist poets who depended upon juxtaposition for effect, and the Postimpressionist works shown at the Armory Show in 1913 would have familiarized New Yorkers with modernist ideas about the disruption of stable referents and narrative logic.

One close American analogue to collage, however, was the much humbler one of vaudeville. The association may seem frivolous, but there was indeed an odd connection. Vaudeville (or its European counterparts, the music hall and the café concert) was in fact a love of the avant-garde: the London Decadents, for example, prized vaudeville for its wordplay, the expanded linguistic diction of its patter. American vaudeville producers, for their part, saw some sensationalist potential in the downtown moderns. Oscar Hammerstein, vaudeville kingpin, offered Emma Goldman a thousand dollars a week—a princely sum in 1913—to go onstage. Vaudeville in the early twentieth century specialized not only in acts—acrobats, singers, comedians, musicians— but in "characters" who did nothing more than act like themselves: Eva Tanguay, for example, who performed her "cyclonic" personality by gyrating wildly while yelling a song about herself, was a star of freakish feminine vivacity. A parade of characters like Tanguay softened up audiences for more staid—but still curious—modern figures like Inez Millholland, a beautiful Village suffragist who appeared in one of Hammerstein's theaters on "Suffragette's Day" in 1912.

A free-speech evening, like a vaudeville evening, made entertainment out of a series of non sequiturs. The association can be seen more strongly in Chicago, where bohemian free speech also took root and where it actually merged with popular amusement. The Dill Pickle Club was founded some time in the early teens by an entrepreneurial IWW member, a former miner who turned out to be a master showman. Located in an upstairs room off Bughouse (now Washington) Square, where free-speech radicals and self-declared "nutcases" held forth, the Dill Pickle brought oratory indoors and turned it into stand-up acts. The tone was light, with heckling expected. As at the Liberal Club, members staged one-act plays, poetry evenings, and edifying lectures; performers included Eugene

Debs, IWW leader Bill Haywood, liberal lawyer Clarence Darrow, Emma Goldman, Irish radicals. But other speakers, like "a Spanish spiritualist who shaved her head and dyed it green," were meant solely to amuse. "A brilliant Negro whose first name was Claude would entrance us with his pyrotechnics in mathematics and logic," recalled a regular. A British crackpot, Malfew Seclew, whose real name no one ever knew, lectured—with charts—on his scheme of human progress, which ran from simpoleon to hopeoleon to demoleon to superman. "It was part of the fun to import odd characters, squeeze all the free entertainment possible out of them, and then make way for a new idol," a habitué explained.

The random, wacky quality of free-speech discourse and its replication of vaudeville variety appealed to one veteran hoofer out in Hollywood, Charlie Chaplin. Max Eastman met Chaplin when he ended up in Los Angeles after a cross-country speaking tour. The two, great womanizers both and at the time involved with the same woman (Florence Deshon, a brilliant New York stage actress), became fast friends. There was no equivalent to the Liberal Club in Hollywood, but already there were enough leftists and ex-leftists there to concoct free-speech entertainments. Chaplin and Eastman invented a game based on a grab bag of left-wing topics. Contestants drew slips on which were written characters and subjects; then they "had to make a speech *on* the subject and *in* the character, in hastily fashioned costume. Chaplin as the 'Toothless Old Veteran' discoursed on 'The Benefits of Birth Control' and as Carrie Nation, a famous anti-saloon crusader, on 'Some Doubts on the Origin of Species.'"

Eastman and Chaplin spoofed the ersatz profundity of free speech, its pretensions to social relevance and gravity. Moving to the Village from Chicago, Susan Glaspell couldn't help but notice the "lot of twaddle that goes on among our kind of folks." Randolph Bourne, who returned from Europe in 1914, also found bohemian talk off-putting. When he eased into the scene in the Village, he was hoping for conversation comparable to what he had overheard in intellectual circles in London and Paris. But exchanges at the Liberal Club seemed to him pretentious and predictable: "most of the people look as if life had knocked them around a bit, and they were trying to forget it; it took so much of their energy to be radical that they had no time left for the life of irony." Indeed irony, with its rigorous distinctions, was just what this sociable radicalism lacked. Free-speech conversation depended rather on habits of conflation, culture collapsed into politics, ideas collapsed into performance.

Yet for all its self-delusions, free speech constituted a political act, and those who listened and argued were also participating in a process of radicalism. To the audience, the collage of speech seemed to promise freewheeling action, as if by breaking intellectual rules, the jumps from one topic to another in themselves made a revolution. Listening affiliated the audience with a new kind of political engagement, not the structured party work of the Socialists or the unions but a more episodic and diffuse involvement. Free speech linked speakers and listeners by analogizing the unhindered discussion of ideas with the active defense of those ideas. Listening and discussing supported, it seemed, both the ethic of free speech and the stance under discussion, much as walking a picket line supported a strike. Both were forms of direct action in the IWW mold, action undertaken "directly by, for, and of the workers themselves"—participatory democracy without the mediation of leaders. The dynamic was at work when Margaret Sanger came to the Liberal Club to speak to an enthusiastic crowd right after she was released from prison in 1916, having been held for disseminating birth control information, and when Theodore Dreiser lectured on free speech in the midst of his court battle against the suppression of one of his novels. Sanger's and Dreiser's audiences included people who had taken part in their battles, those who might write in their defense, and plain sympathizers. But whatever the degree of involvement, the battle around free speech heightened the importance of listening, imparting meaning and unity to the audience as if their presence amounted to political organization in itself.

Thus, for people who moved back and forth between politics on the one hand and literary and professional work on the other, free-speech ideas lent grand significance—so they believed—to their own modest struggles. Far from the western towns where militants were sweltering (and freezing) in jail, intellectuals became grander in their own eyes because of the penumbra of working-class heroism that surrounded them. Henrietta Rodman's fight with the school board (and the graybeards of the Liberal Club) was one foray into free-speech action. For Hutchins Hapgood, the place to take a stand was the commuter bus to Westchester County.

Hapgood had moved up to a house on the Hudson River with Boyce and their children, who numbered four by this time. Theirs was a town controlled and governed by a manufacturer who was the sole employer. When a vicious strike resulted in the deaths of several workers, Hapgood wrote a series of exposés for his New York newspaper. The company retaliated by ordering him banned from the bus line, which it owned. Determined to fight for his right to speak the truth freely, Hapgood one day elbowed his way on board, sat down, and refused to move. The police hauled him off to jail.

Free speech joined the battles of a schoolteacher and a disgruntled suburban bohemian to the ventures of Emma Goldman and Bill Haywood into the teeth of vigilante bands. It was an identification of enormous power. To what extent it was realistic we shall see.

In this mélange, the various talkers testified by their very presence to the potent properties of the new. Immigrants, emigrés from the working class, IWW militants arguing with Harvard men and Vassar women about whether or not monogamy was an innate human capacity—these collections of conversants seemed to enthusiasts to enact on an interior stage a drama of American democracy that was also taking place out-of-doors. Conversational community assumed utopian connotations as a third space of intellectual mingling: it lay beyond the divisions of the Victorian gender system and the segregation of those who worked with their hands from those who worked with their brains.

In this third space women were absolutely central. If the new century was to be a time when customary social differences might be blurred or even undone, then the line between men and women would need to be erased immediately. The Victorian sexual ideology with which the participants had grown up assigned men to the world and women to the home. These separate spheres, to the moderns, had only bred "lies and ignorances and reticences," as one Village feminist put it, a social ethic of evasion and hypocrisy that supported other harmful divisions. But now, all had changed: men's and women's "swiftly developing ability to tell each other the truth about themselves and each other . . . is one of the most hopeful signs of these parlous times." The mingling of men and women in conversation came to seem the very essence, the condition of modernity.

This does not mean, however, that women in this supposedly emancipated milieu could always speak freely. There is much zestful testimony from women to the general freedoms of the moment, but one wonders how they actually fared. Although there were women speakers, women members, women performers at the Liberal Club, it seems unlikely that the intellectuals' interest in sexual equality and the simple assertion of newness easily overcame habits of conversational deference to men—the habit of being good listeners rather than big talkers—that had been drilled into women, no matter how New, for generations. There is little to go on here, except for a remark or two. In Margery Currey's Jackson Park salon, Margaret Anderson (a discerning analyst of the new heterosexuality) dryly remarked, Currey made herself a personage by pushing Floyd Dell forward and creating little platforms upon which he could step up to declaim. "He would never have spoken to anyone if she hadn't relieved him of all social responsibility and presented him as an impersonal being whose only function in life was to talk." In all probability, free speech was not as free from gender rules as its proponents might imply.

Hidden psychological constraints may have been a reason why some women were interested in practicing free speech away from men. Heterodoxy, a monthly discussion club for women only, was founded on free-speech principles in 1912, the same year as the Liberal Club, and met downstairs at Polly's Restaurant. Inez Haynes Irwin, a San Francisco journalist newly come to town, described it as "the easiest of clubs . . . no duties or obligations. There was no press. Everything that was said was off the record." The women talked "about everything . . . all opinions." The membership was wide-ranging although, as in other Village institutions, there were almost no blacks (Grace Nail Johnson, an NAACP activist married to James Weldon Johnson, was the exception) and only a smattering of Jewish women from immigrant families. Otherwise these were more or less the usual suspects from downtown crowds, overlapping with the constituency of the Liberal Club, the worlds of the magazine and newspaper writers, and liberal politics, everyone leaning toward women's suffragism and the left.

Heterodoxy's single-sex separatism was more epicurean than ideological. Members took great pleasure in the gatherings. Recollections of the prewar Village are always effusive, but the memoirs of Heterodoxy are even more fulsome. The tone is distilled in Mabel Dodge's memory of "fine, daring, rather joyous and independent women . . . women who did things and did them openly." The club's willingness to put social differences in the service of a broad humanitarian/political effort made the absence of men seem accidental, not required. At this point, the militant wing of the women's rights movement looked upon men as benign supporters rather than as the adversaries they would become much later in the century; and although men never came to the club's gatherings, they were invited to share the platform at the group's first public effort, a pair of mass meetings where Greenwich Village men joined Heterodoxy members to speak on "what feminism means to me." Women remained in control of the proceedings, but the event was insistently heterosocial and "human," with sexual difference held up to be transcended, not idealized. "We're sick of being specialized to sex," Heterodoxy's founder, Marie Jenney Howe, maintained. "We intend simply to be ourselves, not just our little female selves, but our whole, big, human selves."

Heterodoxy would have been the public manifestation of a submerged, informal network of women's talk. At least some of its members carried on a smaller discussion group in Patchin Place, a tiny, gloomy court tucked away off a main shopping street. The buildings lacked utilities, with metered gas flares for light and heat, pumps for running water, and outhouses, but the life there was shared and the furniture emblazoned in fauve colors. The apartments were something of a haven for the newest of New Women. Sometime in 1915, a supper group began meeting to discuss politics, women's rights, and culture. Only two men were asked to join: Randolph Bourne and his friend Carl Zigrosser, who was involved with Florence King, another regular. Everyone smoked cigarettes and the women had mostly bobbed their hair.

The topics at Patchin Place bounded from one thing to another in the modern manner. The madam of a brothel visited and denounced women who practiced free love as scabs on honest women's labor (prostitution must have been especially interesting to the group since at the massive courthouse opposite Patchin Place, arrested prostitutes were a nightly spectacle, yelling orders and imprecations from the cell windows to friends and pimps gathered below). A Finnish women's rights leader came for a discussion of Finnish epic literature. Carl Jung, who was lecturing in America and had already spoken at the Liberal Club, ended up at Patchin Place. Zigrosser remembered that "the atmosphere had been rather stiff and formal until Jung broke the ice by addressing a pet dog who was misbehaving with his leg: Come, come, be reasonable; I'm not a female."

The reactions of the two male participants indicate how unusual—how contrary to custom—women's free speech could seem. Bourne and Zigrosser studiously respected the single-sex character of Patchin; their being there on sufferance led them both to treat the group gingerly. Zigrosser, a modest man, believed that he "learned something of the fine art of conversation. I began to see that if one were present in a group, one should make some effort to participate." Although a great talker himself from his Columbia days, he found a special suppleness and camaraderie in the women's talk that was new to him: "One could air serious as well as amusing opinions, provided they were treated lightly and deftly. Wit and repartee and pungent point of view added zest to the conversation, and conversation was the flickering flame that held the group together." But Bourne had more intractable problems to work out. He was badly crippled—born with a twisted spine and a malformed ear and so short and hunched that he reminded people, one friend remarked, of the Frog Prince. He carried the burden of an unimpaired erotic capacity coupled with the diminished sexual opportunity that his handicap then entailed. His was a more complicated experience than Zigrosser's, his faith in the importance of friendship and conversational community darkened by a great need for intimacy with women that the Patchin regulars failed to reciprocate.

Despite his discomfort, his responses to the Patchin group are instructive about the unacknowledged obstacles to free speech between men and women. Bourne's short New York life (he died in the influenza epidemic of 1918) and the brilliant writing he did there were inextricable from a tangle of friendships and love affairs with feminists who were his primary orientation toward the modernity in human relations he prized. Bourne, we will see, would take the idea of conversational fellowship farther than anyone else, reworking it into a beatific vision of a milieu that he called, movingly and memorably, the "beloved community." "Thinking cannot be done without talking," he believed. He had come some way from the all-male world of left-wing Columbia, which had rescued him in 1909 from a pinched suburban New Jersey upbringing. He first learned about the sustaining powers of friendship at Columbia through the bonds he wove with friends there in hours and hours of talk. When he moved downtown after his year in Europe, he learned to translate that masculine sociability into a conversation that included women. But sophisticated free-speech palaver did not appeal. He preferred talk that would rummage around in rumination; that was, for him, the basis for being a radical intellectual.

Bourne was not altogether happy at Patchin Place, despite what others found to be intimate and searching conversation. The ostensible reason was that he found the conversants, as he had those at the Liberal Club, too stagy and given to posing. But the fact that they were women seems to have also provoked an animus unusual for him. "Fair and serious and life-denying woman," he characterized the typical participant, "who in the name of a career and her pride and the sacred independence of woman destroys not only you but herself." The opinions aired at Patchin Place, he complained, unfairly stereotyped him and diminished appreciation for his participation; discrimination was in the air, "the philosophy that you are not a man but Man, and therefore, in spite of your sympathy, personal quality, and contribution, really only a lustful Being who wants you to cook for him." Whether or not he was right about the women isn't so important to discern as the bitterness of his criticism. It was perhaps difficult for even this most determinedly modern of men to give up a habit of conversational superiority. He seems to have been more comfortable talking to women who listened intelligently than listening to women who talked intelligently. His habits of speech having been formed in an exclusively masculine milieu, he could not quite give up his sense of masculine prerogative. He liked talking in a group of women and listening to them, but then again, he didn't. In his writings on feminists, as well—precise, fond, cutting—he oscillated between wistful admiration, even bedazzlement, and resentment at giving up center stage.

Were free-speech salons and their effervescent talk simply an expression of youthful ebullience, a youth rebellion? Randolph Bourne thought so, and chroniclers have followed him in attributing the new forms of expression to a cleavage between the generations. "It is the glory of the present age that in it one can be young," Bourne crowed in one of his first published essays in 1912. "Our times give no check to the radical tendencies of youth."

Bourne was the first to write about the conviction of youthful revolution that was in the Manhattan air, but in doing so he summoned up a generational identification gathering force in colleges and universities elsewhere. Youth, its champions proclaimed, were the spokespersons for modernity, embodying prescience that eluded the elders. By our own time, the concept of youth has become so ingrained in ideas of modernity that it is easy to take such celebrations at face value, as sociological description. In reality, however, bohemian circles in the 1910s were as mixed by generation as they were by sex and social origins, with middle-aged people like the Hapgoods and Emma Goldman freely speaking with fresh-faced college graduates.

The ideology of youth as bearers of historical change is interesting. What explains its new appeal in the 1910s—as well as its subsequent application to Americans' understanding of the demography of modernity (and postmodernity)? Bourne and his peers placed their faith in a vision of a generational cohort coming together right at the edge of history. "It is only the young who are actually contemporaneous," he proposed. "They interpret what they see freshly and without prejudice; their vision is always the truest, and their interpretation always the justest." Youth overlapped with radicalism, generating the new in myriad forms: the idea would eventually become a cultural truism. But at the time, the idea that youth were innately equipped to lead the culture was just making headway against the received wisdom that authority properly resided with the elders.

Youth in the 1910s was not the developmental category or consumer marketing niche it would later become but rather a signifier of political import. Bohemia was clearly implicated, but it was only one element in a thick historical mixture. By 1912, generational consciousness of various sorts was bubbling across Europe—among the iconoclastic elite in Bloomsbury, among French conservatives, in transnational movements of pan-Germanism and Zionism in Central Europe. Villagers, whether young or middle-aged, used the conviction of their own youthfulness to affiliate their affairs with European sensibility. Socialist and anarchist internationalism encouraged these identifications across national boundaries. But the idea of young/old as the axis of political struggle—like another opposition gaining force, man/woman—also undercut the centrality of the class struggle to revolution and allowed an emerging intelligentsia to grant itself a greater imaginative role. When the world was divided into generations before it was divided into classes, writers and artists could see themselves as participants—not just bystanders—in a world-historic struggle.

The sense of compatriotism with European youth movements, however, came from not knowing much about them. The Village brand of youth—cosmopolitan, left-wing, feminist—could be found in England, Russia, and scattered Jewish circles on the Continent, but elsewhere "youth" might mean radically right: successive waves of *die Jungen* in Austria and Germany who pitted themselves against their liberal fathers, flirting with or embracing nationalist, anti-Semitic politics; *les jeunes gens d'aujourd'hui* in France, whose conservative ideas were tinted with anti-Semitism and blood-and-soil nationalism.

In Europe, Bourne brushed against the patriotic side of youth movements. Traveling in the summer of 1914 on a continent lurching toward war, he encountered *die Jungen* in Germany in July: on the day Austria declared war, he saw young men marching through the street into the night bellowing patriotic songs. "It made me very blue," he confessed to a friend back home. Yet mostly, like any other tourist of the revolution, he saw what he wanted to see. He was looking for a way to confer on intellectuals a more concrete political task than simply floating along with the zeitgeist and he believed he found it in European youth movements. In Paris, he made friends with Maurice

Barrès, a preeminent conservative man of letters whose anti-Semitism and Catholic language of youth's obligation to navigate the nation through the "spiritual currents of the day" Bourne utterly failed to comprehend. He took with him back to the States only a sense of left-wing generational promise: the relationships that Parisian youth were striking up with the "folk" might be replicated by New Yorkers with their own people.

Bourne was unusual in his knowledge of the European scene, but he was not alone. Other principals of the Village had lived in Europe and, of course, the immigrants were familiar with European as well as Russian politics, often having sojourned in the capitals before they came to the United States. News of various youthful insurgencies abroad accompanied reports of labor unrest in the United States in the pages of the *Masses* and the other little magazines; *Seven Arts* published an article on "Young America" in a series that highlighted Young Germany, Italy, Ireland, Turkey, China, India, and Japan as well. The image of youth across the globe primed to overthrow the rule of the fathers lent a stirring cosmopolitanism to domestic events and turned foreign politics into something familiar, no matter if the specifics were really quite vague.

The coming of World War I might be supposed to have dampened such enthusiasm, but in fact it worked youth into the mournful epic of the lost generation, brothers driven to slaughter by the callous fathers. Thenceforth in America, freedom would become the political soul-mate of youth; the international brotherhood—with a seasoning of sisters—would promise a shortcut to revolution untainted by the hypocrisy and failed accommodations of the fathers. To speak freely would be an act that testified to the largesse and frankness of people who, whatever their actual ages, saw themselves as a groundbreaking generation, activated by the vivacity of youth.

Under the banner of youth, free-speech causes and conversation enlisted recruits in unusual places. In 1911, a coalition of social-ists and anarchists opened the Ferrer Center on St. Mark's Place, a street that tied the upper reaches of the Lower East Side to the east-ern edge of Greenwich Village. The core of the center—named after the Spanish freethinker and revolutionary Francisco Ferrer—was the Modern School, a libertarian school for children, but the place attracted young adults in their twenties and thirties, too—mostly Jews, along with a few Italians and a sprinkling of vagrant Greeks, Scots, and English radicals. On St. Mark's Place and later far uptown in East Harlem (an Italian and Jewish neighborhood where the center moved the next year), the Ferrer Center offered evening lectures, experimental theater, political organizing committees, a tea and lunch room, painting and music appreciation classes, and discussions of sex hygiene.

The center's ties to the anarchist movement were close—Emma Goldman's friends helped run the school and many of the students were anarchists. But the anarchism that leavened free speech was not the orthodoxy of the older movement but a cluster of political ideas—political intuitions, perhaps—about the broader possibilities of individual expression. The offerings were a pastiche of class politics, modernist culture, and fin-de-siècle aestheticism: lectures on birth control, a one-act play by a Ferrer dramatist in which the characters remained immobile for its entirety, scent concerts emanating different perfumes, jaunts to Isadora Duncan performances, and reports on IWW strikes. Robert Henri and George Bellows taught painting in the realist manner for twenty cents a class. "Free expression of opinions and interchange of ideas is the working method," held an anarchist printer who was a founder. "To hold robust opinions without being dogmatic is a good war cry."

The Ferrer Center was similar to enterprises in Europe that aimed to use workers' political allegiances as incentives not just to political mobilization but to intellectual enlightenment; the original was the Escuela Moderna in Barcelona (founded by Francisco Ferrer), an anarchist school in London's East End, and the anarchist Université Populaire in the Faubourg Saint-Antoine in Paris. Immigrants might easily have passed through one or another of these on their trek to the United States: they were magnets for bookish poor people, like the "motley collection of the Parisian proletariat, Russian girl-students, Poles, Swedes, Arabs, Hungarians" whom Randolph Bourne saw reading in a neighborhood library in the evenings when he lived in Paris. These institutions were variously inspired by republicanism, socialism, and anarchism; their political thrust and (in France and Spain) anti-clericalism distinguished them from bourgeois philanthropic efforts.

For all its radical ideology, the New York Ferrer Center was not entirely dissimilar to the settlement houses. Educated American-born people ran affairs for an impoverished constituency. What did make the Ferrer Center unusual, though, was the prominence of foreign-born intellectuals. These were people who, because of their poverty and lack of English, were still operating in the doctrinaire venues of the left-wing newspapers, socialist branches, and anarchist cells. The Modern School, by institutionalizing an immigrant free-speech enter-prise, opened up a set of connections to the Liberal Club, its down-town analogue, and thus to the Village milieu. Benzion Liber, a Romanian Jewish socialist and physician, began his rise to prominence as a writer on what we would now call holistic health. The painters Abraham Walkowitz and Man Ray (born Emmanuel Radnitsky) had come to the Modern School from the Lower East Side and Brooklyn to study painting; through Robert Henri, they fell in with Alfred Stieglitz, who swooped them up into his Photo-Secession group downtown. A ragtag bunch of ne'er-do-wells, including Eugene O'Neill (fascinated at the time by the anarchists), perambulated between both locales, hitting up people for loans, hitting on women for sex, and spouting revolution. The writer Konrad Bercovici was in this coterie, thereby completing his transformation from Lower East Side cicerone to universal bohemian, "a kind of amateur Nietzsche . . . mustachioed and braggadocious, scorning morals, for-getting debts" (as one long-suffering comrade put it). Bercovici latched on to contacts in the Village and published his first book, a col-lection of short stories about the Lower East Side, with the already distinguished publisher Alfred A. Knopf in 1917, heralded by an introduction from John Reed—quite a feat for a penniless Romanian who arrived in the United States not speaking English. Other Ferrer members hooked up with Village political causes.

The circulation around and across class lines should not be over-stated. Mostly it was the American-educated idealists who came uptown to hold forth and the immigrants who went downtown to lis-ten. At Polly's Restaurant or the Liberal Club, the role of Ferrer rep-resentatives was to add foreign spice to the mix. "Romany Marie," a

Ferrer Center Fourth of July picnic, New Jersey, 1914 COURTESY PAUL AVRICH

Moldavian Jewish garment worker and Ferrer regular, capitalized on this market by turning herself into a Gypsy and moving to the Village to start a terrifically successful "exotic" tearoom. Hippolyte Havel, a ubiquitous figure, was treated as comic relief. A Czech anarchist, Havel was an excitable, intemperate man who knocked around between New York and Chicago editing fire-breathing newspapers and working as a cook. Although educated, cosmopolitan, and politically serious (he served five years in prison in Austria for fighting Germanization laws barring the Czech language in the schools), to his Village friends he was a parody of an explosive anarchist. Hapgood, who employed him to cook from time to time, thought that he acted the Dostoyevskian God-drunk fool to the point of absurdity.

Still, for all the posturing, free speech created real exchange. For the downtown radicals, contacts with the center augmented political opportunity. IWW men traveling back and forth between the Village and the center brought downtown bohemians into important citywide demonstrations against unemployment in the winter of 1913–14.

Margaret Sanger, who lived uptown in the early teens and sent her son to the Modern School, launched herself as a political person from the Ferrer Center. She staged her birth control protests with help from both communities and, even after she moved down to Greenwich Village, continued to draw on the working-class militancy of East Harlem along with the financial and media support she received from her downtown allies.

Plebeian as it was, the center also had ties to the artistic avant-garde. Man Ray, who was too high-spirited to stay long with the autocratic Stieglitz, left 291 and, with another Henri student from Ferrer, started a colony in Ridgefield, New Jersey. On the high cliffs over the Hudson River, they created an artists' version of the summer campsites anarchists and socialists sometimes staked out for retreats. Their belief that fauve painting could be the basis for an aesthetic allied with anarchism attracted poets and politicos, as well as more painters. Alfred Kreymborg, who had dipped into the center, moved to Ridgefield and promptly launched *Others*, an extraordinary review of contemporary poetry. The spot became a mecca for unknown and little-known poets whom Kreymborg, whose taste was exquisite, published early on: William Carlos Williams lived close by and liked to drop in; a very young Marianne Moore came for picnics and

Ridgefield Gazook, *March 1915*

poets' shoptalk. Then in 1915, Marcel Duchamp, who had fled Paris and the war, moved in. The miscellaneity of Ferrer sensibility must have appealed to Duchamp's antic nature. Man Ray and Duchamp began a lifelong friendship and collaboration and Ray announced to the world the advent of New York Dada in the premier issue of the marvelously titled *Ridgefield Gazook*.

So the playful gambits of New York Dada owed something to the random associations of immigrant free speech. Historians are used to describing working-class intellectual life as the product of labor or socialist pedagogy: windy lectures, heavy debates, education in the ideological fundamentals. At bohemian offshoots, though, plebeian talk spun out beyond those customary limits.

For those who stayed closer to home, there were Mabel Dodge's evenings in Greenwich Village. In 1912, Dodge, an heiress from Buffalo, returned to New York after years abroad in Italy. Casting about for an outlet for her considerable energies, she hit upon the idea of holding a weekly salon. The logic of her class position should have led her to set herself up as a hostess in the grand manner uptown, near Central Park, perhaps, to conduct a gathering in the European mode. But Dodge saw more interesting options and moved instead into a sumptuous apartment near Washington Square.

Dodge proved to be an extraordinary organizer of conversational community, changing herself from a rich woman of limited talents, an epigone of Continental fashions, to a New York celebrity who melded real political commitments with a love for fame. She drew an analogy between art and American conversation and in her proudest moments presented herself as an artist of talk, crafting an aesthetics of random metropolitan encounters in a way that echoed her friend Gertrude Stein's random linguistic encounters. She learned to mix politics with culture, men with women, artists with workers. "The essence of it all was communication," she proposed. Talk in the free-speech mode assumed quasi-mystical connotations: she saw herself acting as a vessel through which creative communications could flow.

Dodge had searched a long time for a way to distinguish herself. Endowed with ample generosity and a gift for friendship, she nonetheless lacked the education, discipline, or altruism to prepare her for a formed vocation on the order that other ambitious women chose—say, medicine, the law, or even journalism. She was married for a time to a wealthy architect, Edwin Dodge, with whom she had lived in Florence since 1905 as a mainstay of the exile colony. In Italy she had turned herself into a *salonnière*, a sexually ambiguous femme fatale. At her villa she entertained local aesthetes, artists, and visiting luminaries from the Paris circle of Gertrude and Leo Stein, including the Stein siblings themselves. But by 1913, when she sailed for home, she was tired of the exile's life, of living in a "lovely frame," as she put it, for which "the picture never

Mabel Dodge in Florence YALE COLLECTION OF AMERICAN LITERATURE, BEINECKE RARE BOOK AND MANUSCRIPT LIBRARY

was painted"; tacitly she was admitting how inadequate to her energies were both the role of *salonnière* and that of wife. In New York, she set to work shedding her marriage and moving herself into another frame.

Dodge's friendship with the Steins, who were still in Paris, proved fruitful in Greenwich Village. The brother and sister—he educated at Harvard, she at Radcliffe—were a link between the Continental avant-garde and the downtown intelligentsia. Through the Steins, Dodge met Hutchins Hapgood (who had known them in Europe); she and he became fast friends. The Stein connection allowed her to inveigle her way into the group of artists and collectors who were organizing the Armory Show of modern art, which opened that winter.

Images of violent revolution and of the dawning of an age swirled around the show. John Sloan compared it to a charge of dynamite, a metaphor that resonated in 1913 with suspicions of the Wobblies and industrial sabotage; the crusty art collector John Quinn, no left-winger but a devotee of modernist work, excitedly declared it "epoch making." The show featured some thirteen hundred works of art, from Ingres drawings to Marcel Duchamp's *Nude Descending a Staircase* (which was the succès de scandale). Scattered among realist portraits, genre scenes, and landscapes was a substantial representation of the French Impressionists, Postimpressionists, and Cubists, a remarkable sample of the advanced line of development in European painting since the 1870s.

New York had seen modern art before in Stieglitz's gallery, but the circuslike atmosphere (the show was mounted on partitions in a huge central space that looked like a circus tent) and saturation publicity turned this demonstration of the new into a blockbuster. The art-loving public was accustomed to American painting that took its cues from the rearguard academies of Europe. Now the exhibit subjected Americans to a shock treatment that transported them to the plane of the avant-garde present. "The implicit assumption," observes Harold Rosenberg, "was that America either had caught up with the European past or was ready to join with contemporaries overseas in cutting that past loose." Some seventy thousand visitors saw the exhibit, goaded by thousands of postcards sent out in advance, posters pasted all over the city, and, perhaps most of all, denunciations in the press. The *New York Times*, taking its responsibilities to pronounce upon innovation very seriously (as usual), declared the show could "disrupt, degrade, if not destroy, not only art but literature and society too." A Chicago paper a bit more lightheartedly urged prospective viewers to do drugs ("smoke two pipefuls of 'hop' and sniff cocaine") to prepare themselves for the pictures.

The show proved to be the making of Mabel Dodge. Sensing the possibility of stirring things up, Dodge published in pamphlet form a piece Gertrude Stein had written when she visited Dodge in Florence, "Portrait of Mabel Dodge at the Villa Curonia." With narcissistic abandon she distributed the pamphlet at the Armory Show, under no particular auspices except some vague association with modernism.

The irrelevance of the "Portrait" to the paintings perfectly suited the organizing committee's interest in playing up juxtapositions in the modern manner. The committee's head, Arthur Davies, quickly printed up cards for visitors quoting Dodge's rhapsodic tribute to the show.

The circulation of the "Portrait" and the attendant publicity announced the ascendancy to metropolitan celebrity of the theretofore unknown Dodge (and also introduced Stein to an American audience). Dodge's picture was roughed in: she had become a public figure whom she herself could render, with satisfaction, in quotation marks: "I suddenly found myself in a whirlpool of new, unfamiliar life and if Gertrude Stein was born at the Armory show, so was 'Mabel Dodge.' I had rapidly become a mythological figure right in my own lifetime." Later in life, she preened herself on her celebrity makeover, her facility at soaking up others' projections of the new. "The faculty I had for not saying much and yet for being there gave people's imaginations a chance to fabricate their own Mabel Dodge."

At this point, Dodge had the money and connections to become a patron of the fine arts, as collectors Walter and Louise Arensberg would soon do when they moved to New York from Boston. But her talents did not really run to connoisseurship and besides, the collector's role, while powerful, was too sedate to suit her. The Armory Show demonstrated the flash and dazzle immanent in the moment—more interesting to her than the art itself—and so she trained her sights on a new venue altogether, Greenwich Village bohemia.

With the help of Hapgood and a new friend, fanciful Carl Van Vechten, a music and drama critic for the newspapers, Dodge created a setting at once evocative of the upper-class salon and the free-speech assemblage. The clientele was an intellectual and artistic jumble (in Dodge's view), a mix blended through the guests' ventures "in an unaccustomed freedom a kind of speech called Free." Differences, arguments, open antagonisms were allowed, even encouraged.

Who was invited? Dodge in her memoirs proudly produced a collage of types. Socialists, trade unionists, anarchists, suffragists, poets, lawyers, murderers, psychoanalysts, IWWs, birth controlists, newspapermen, "Modern-Artists, Club women, Woman's-place-is-in-the-home Women," met and "exchanged a variousness in vocabulary called, in euphemistic optimism, Opinions." There was a coterie of educated bohemians, advertised by one invitation as "a number of people (most of whom you know)," the regular cast of conversational community. And there were also·outsiders, the guests ushered in by her intention to entertain irrespective of class distinctions: seedy visitors from East Harlem and the Lower East Side, battered Wobblies from far afield. Her preferred plebs were people given to performing themselves as revolutionary characters so, like Oscar Hammerstein, Dodge was drawn to the theatrical Emma Goldman; IWW leader Big Bill Haywood, burly, one-eyed, and truly big, spouting incendiary rhetoric and trailing the scent of dynamite, was also a favored guest. A more modest, mild-mannered, and cerebral IWW organizer, however, met chilly disinterest.

As at the Liberal Club, conversation was a hash of the labor question, the arts, feminism, and sexual radicalism. But the ornate setting, so different from the shabby Liberal Club, focused attention on the elegant and beneficent hostess. The apartment was swathed in silks and brocades and furnished with graceful lounges on which Dodge draped herself. She provided such a lavish meal at the end of each "conversation," as she called her evenings, that after a few months serious habitués vowed to purge the freeloaders who came only for the food and drink.

Speech was free, but it was also governed by unspoken rules. Dodge would never have used the term "uplifting" for her conversations—it was loaded with Victorian moralism—but nonetheless she wanted the speech she modeled to work for the good. Born and bred a lady, she was open to democratic energies yet at the same time wary of the taint of low morality. Men and women could mix freely but not without observing a code of polite demeanor that forbade any hint of vulgarity. Just as heavy drinking needed to be elevated in her mind to noble stimulation, so the presence of social outsiders like the Wobblies was necessarily sanitized by the gravity of the concerns—the "Opinions"—that brought them there. She was happy to entertain the cream of the Lower East Side, skimmed off from the masses of immigrant poor, but her hospitality did not extend to black New Yorkers, whose Opinions never seemed to have mattered. Perhaps DuBois, James Weldon Johnson or Hubert Harrison came once or twice, but when Carl Van

Interior of Dodge apartment YALE COLLECTION OF AMERICAN LITERATURE,
BEINECKE RARE BOOK AND MANUSCRIPT LIBRARY

Vechten, an aficionado of African American music, brought a pair of
black performers—probably blues performers from the Tenderloin—
to sing and dance, Dodge quailed at the straight-on dose of African
American popular culture unredeemed by the idealism of politics. The
combination of black people and "low" culture seemed to impinge on
her very sense of herself, calling up racial stereotypes of predatory sexuality. "An appalling Negress danced. . . . The man strummed a banjo
and sang an embarrassing song while she cavorted and they both leered
and rolled their suggestive eyes and made me feel first hot and then
cold, for I never had been so near this kind of thing before." The performance conjured sex itself, its heat and shivers, pleasures and perils.
In free speech, women—respectable ladies—could converse freely,
even about sex, but only when the topic was safely distanced from allusions to the body and authorized by what they saw as higher concerns—feminism, birth control, free love. Explicit erotic talk—or
play—had no place in Dodge's experiment with communication.

Still, compared with the tone the Arensbergs would set—formal
dress, classical music spiked with lots of alcohol, arch double-
entendres in French—that of Dodge's evenings was positively abandoned. Guests came dressed as they liked. The Wobblies—Haywood,
Carlo Tresca, and some of the hoi polloi (but not *too* many)—sat
cross-legged on the floor, "with uncut hair, unshaven faces, leaning
against valuable draperies," Margaret Sanger remembered. Dodge's
aim was not to enact the rituals of the aristocratic salon but to put
epicureanism at the disposal of an assortment of people. The hostess,
marked by her distinct demeanor and dress, then became a sort of
artist herself, one who could, with her prescience and generosity,
shape the motley crowd into a coherent whole. Dodge believed that
she worked as an artist to release the creative properties of conversation: "I wanted to try and loosen up thought by means of speech, to
get at the truth at the bottom of people." The enterprise would be
socially regenerative, overcoming outmoded divisions: "I saw quite
soon, in my New York life, it was only the separations between different kinds of people that enabled them to have power over each
other."

Consider the distance of the Dodge salon from the Boston reform
soiree of the 1880s whose puritanism Henry James mocked in *The
Bostonians* (1886). In a "long, bald room," the guests of the elderly
reformer Miss Birdseye range themselves in rows and along the walls;
awkwardness, taciturnity, and the earnest omission of amenities are,
for James, the distinguishing characteristics: "the occasion was not
crudely festive; there was a want of convivial movement, and, among
most of the visitors, even of mutual recognition." This was the reigning imagery of radical sociability—lifted slightly by the equally high-
minded but somewhat more festive socialist picnic—that Dodge
inherited and, with the aid of bohemian esprit, wealth, and strategies
of self-enhancement, went about refurbishing.

Having discovered at the Armory Show the properties of the New
York media, which could change the ordinary rich woman Mabel
Dodge into the fascinating celebrity "Mabel Dodge," she sensed the
commercial alchemy that free speech might effect. The unusual guests
attracted the New York papers, who sent reporters to the evenings.
The Armory Show had been an evanescent setting for "Mabel

Dodge," but the salon ensured that she found her niche as a striking exemplar of New Womanhood. Now she took on a democratic role, mediating between her gallery of metropolitan types and the reading public. The publicity made her a target for fan letters and hate mail. Correspondents angled for her go-ahead to show up at the evenings themselves, writers and creators of schemes to save the world beseeched her help in publishing their work, and haters of Jews, the IWW, and the New Woman castigated her:

"Women that smoke are similar to the street-walking class, they are vulgar and immoral."

"Let the Jews alone Rabbi Wise and Sheif the banker will look after them."

"The *Scum* of the Lower East side a Pretended Lady as you make out to be taking a lot of Dirt In your house. . . . Dirty Lazy I.W. W.'s who are looking for food and a place to sleep and sit on the Benches all day."

Dodge was unquestionably a self-promoter: a little frivolous and a little empty-headed, her story edges into hucksterism. Here's what Leo Stein wrote about her after the Armory Show:

> Mabel Dodge
> Hodge podge
> What is up,
> What is down,
> What is frown,
> What is passion,
> What is pose,
> What is guessing . . .

Hodge podge, yes. And shrewdness about what was up and what was down. Dodge's inflated sense of herself was acute but not, we have seen, idiosyncratic. Inordinate self-regard was a by-product of the time and place. It led people to do things that were both brave and silly: think of Hutchins Hapgood facing down the police on the commuter bus. Hers was a vanity and an egotism made newly attractive by her culture—and her particular place within it.

The time has been called, justly, "a new era of self-amplification." The newspapers led the culture in the great turn toward our contemporary fixation on celebrity and visibility. The new prominence of scandal and sensation-mongering, the coalescence of ideas of fame (people deemed interesting not for their achievements but for being known by others), the beginnings of a star system on the vaudeville circuit—these developments were the precursors of gargantuan mechanisms of cultural hype as we know them today. Dodge was especially skilled at tapping into the nascent system of visibility and representation, but she was not the only one of her set doing so. The theatrical dispositions that were always part of bohemia made the Villagers apt subjects for commercial culture.

But to leave it at that, as some do, neglects the moderns' undeniable substance and achievement—Dodge's, too. There *was* passion along with the pose. Dodge believed the milieu she created would foster political and aesthetic creativity among a new metropolitan elite, insiders and outsiders comingling. She long insisted, for instance, that Bill Haywood forswore his enmity toward the ruling class when he spoke face-to-face with rich people at her house. She prized the night when the editor of a mass circulation magazine confronted an angry pack of artists who despised the insipid art his journal published. The evenings were her attempt at a third space, where her own artistry could resolve clashes, breaks, and disconnections. The guests at her salon, she was persuaded, "were all unconsciously freed by a feeling that it was under my protection because there I was, strong and calm and understanding."

Not everyone accepted Dodge's version of things. Walter Lippmann, with his more orderly disposition, was sufficiently under the spell of his college socialism and a progressive penchant for efficiency to want the salon to run on some clearly stated principles. "You've got enough endowment to run all of Greenwich Village half a century, and experience enough to supply a regiment," he teased her, but intellectually she was a mess. "Your categories aren't any good. They remind me of a Fourth Avenue antique shop. . . . You have a chance to do something really inventive here. Do try to make something of it instead of letting it run wild. Weed it out and *order* it." Others couldn't suppress their antipathy. To his wife, Margaret, who loved the salon, Bill Sanger denounced the "Parlor Discussion, Parlor Artists, Parlor Socialists, Parlor Revolutionists, Parlor Anarchists." Mary Heaton Vorse, an established writer by 1913 and, next to Emma Goldman, the Village's reigning New Woman, could not bear Dodge's pretensions. To her Dodge was just "a rich woman amusing herself in meeting celebrities of different kinds."

Compared to Vorse, a self-supporting woman with a history of serious political engagements, Dodge does indeed look like someone who was dabbling in ideas the way other wealthy ladies dabbled in art. But placed against the common trajectory of women of her class into society charities and hostessing, she looks more singular. Politically, she leaned far to the left, serving on the advisory board of the *Masses* and guest editing an issue in 1914. During the Paterson, New Jersey, strike of silk workers in 1913, she spent a good part of her days there, driving picketers from place to place in her automobile. She attended meetings to organize legal and financial support for those arrested in New York in the unemployment demonstrations of 1913–14 and sat through their trials. She also helped organize a citizen's group to press labor's point of view onto the Commission on Industrial Relations, a presidential commission that, in the wake of the violence and turmoil in a number of big strikes, was appointed to clarify the causes of unrest. Of President Wilson's nine appointees, three were of either progressive or radical disposition, and Dodge's New York–based committee sought to strengthen their hand by organizing testimony and documentation they could use. Here was another motley Village crew: W. E. B. DuBois worked with her (the first topic they presented to the commission was union discrimination against blacks), along with Bill Haywood, Walter Lippmann, and future Washington insider George Creel.

There were, to be sure, other wealthy people who helped the radicals—the "radical rich" they were called—like Alden Freeman, Goldman's friend in the free-speech movement. Their motivations could run from principled conviction to a vague interest in art and ideas to a desire to create sycophants and dependents. But few did more than write bank drafts, and many demanded quite a price in deference in return. Alva (Mrs. O. H. P.) Belmont, for example, a devoted suffragist and funder of the cause, was a famously imperious woman who, according to Max Eastman, "liked to conceive of herself in the role of noble-born patron to people whom some talent had raised, not up to her height to be sure, but above the common level." Others were tight-fisted: a Ferrer School member recalled a wealthy patron of the anarchists as a man who "like other wealthy people . . . was forever proud of buying bargains in the 5 and 10 cent store" and refused the smallest loans to down-and-out comrades. Dodge, in contrast, was generous to a fault and politically committed. True, she was not as involved as a few heiresses who toiled day to day for the Women's Trade Union League and the suffrage movement. Nonetheless, she was unusual among the radical rich for her willingness to involve herself in the mundane workings of radical politics.

Yet it would also be wrong to romanticize Dodge as an intellectual engagée. Her case speaks to the lability of free speech as a cultural signifier with the power to draw its adherents into an imaginatively charged realm. She took pleasure in hobnobbing with such "Dangerous Characters" as she believed Emma Goldman to be, perhaps because she herself wanted to be the most dangerous woman in New York. "Emma and her bunch" brought her close to the swashbuckling risk taking of the IWW free-speech fights. "I felt I was playing with dynamite and thought I liked it dangerous, yet I was scared sometimes," she admitted.

Dodge's self-dramatization marked how far free-speech politics could be stretched. Her political psychology distilled all the confusions and possibilities of the moment; that was the source of her appeal. Her fantasies of the power of her own broad-mindedness could range so widely precisely because the intelligentsia was intent on collapsing the boundaries between politics and culture. John Reed, Dodge's lover in the early days of the salon, noted the confusion when Dodge, uninvited, followed him to Mexico, where he had gone on assignment to cover Pancho Villa's army in the Mexican Revolution. "I think she expects to find General Villa a sort of male Gertrude Stein," he wrote acerbically to a friend, "or at least a Mexican Stieglitz." On the basis of associations that now seem far-fetched,

"Mabel Dodge," modern heroine born of Gertrude Stein and the New York papers, implicated herself conversationally with revolution.

Throughout 1912 and 1913, members of the downtown intelligentsia experimented with roles as supporters of the labor movement, utilizing their closeness to the media and evolving methods of publicity. They abandoned tried-and-true methods of drumming up support—street speeches, handing out flyers—and adopted more arresting tactics. During the galvanizing strike of textile workers in Lawrence, Massachusetts, in 1912—the strike for which the Harvard socialists rallied in Cambridge—a committee headed by Margaret Sanger and Dolly Sloan, a feisty socialist married to the painter, arranged for the children of strikers to be cared for in New York by sympathetic families and orchestrated their arrival by train, many of them pale and gaunt from hunger, before a crowd of reporters and photographers. In 1913, a group from the Dodge evenings, organized by Dodge and John Reed, staged a colossal enactment of the Paterson

Paterson strike pageant, Madison Square Garden TAMIMENT INSTITUTE LIBRARY, NEW YORK UNIVERSITY

silk workers' strike in Madison Square Garden right as the strike was going on in New Jersey.

Lawrence ended in victory for the workers, Paterson in defeat. But both were extremely gratifying for the writers and artists who were involved. Their collaborations with fellow intellectuals and the excitement of touching the lives of working people, deemed the bearers of revolutionary purpose, made this kind of politics very different from the slow, methodical efforts of progressives, devoted to changing laws and policies. After these political theatricals, the downtown radicals were ready for something closer to home. The sojourns in Manhattan of top IWW organizers recuperating from the two strikes intensified the sense of connection between their own conversational community and working-class struggles elsewhere. The winter of 1913–14 was unusually bitter—"the snow never stopped falling," according to Vorse—and a downturn in the economy pushed unemployment high. In New York, as many as 325,000 people were out of work. A Labor Defense Committee of liberals and radicals came together to address the plight of the jobless. In the midst of their first meeting in early March, a cause startlingly materialized, as Vorse told the story later. Vorse, whose first husband had died several years earlier, had just married a labor journalist, Joe O'Brien, and the two were living with her children and their new baby in a row house on Sheridan Square. The committee was meeting there, Vorse recalled, when a latecomer burst in to announce, "We have your first case for you. Frank Tannenbaum and a crowd of two hundred men have just been arrested down at St. Alphonsus."

Tannenbaum was from the Ferrer Center. At age twenty-two, he certainly embodied the spirit of emancipatory youth. Having emigrated as a boy from Austria, he had gone on to become a star scholarship student at Columbia and would eventually become a pioneering historian of Latin America. In him were represented the ardor, political courage, and intellectual drive of the best of an immigrant generation. "Vivid," Emma Goldman pronounced him. In the demonstrations that winter, he presented himself, no doubt for tactical reasons, as a grassroots organizer, a simple man of the people who had been thrust into leadership by a spontaneous protest from below. In truth, he had probably learned about organizing from participating in

Frank Tannenbaum addresses a crowd of the unemployed, 1914 CORBIS-BETTMANN

a hotel waiters' strike in New York in 1912 and been backed from the beginning—perhaps even chosen—by IWW leaders.

In any case, he was fearless. For ten days or so he led a crowd of six hundred unemployed men—bums, respectable people would have called them—around lower Manhattan in a kind of proto–street theater. Each night the men gathered at some church and demanded food and a night's shelter. The church "raids" succeeded with a few acquiescent clergy, but when ministers refused the men—most did—the confrontation worked to expose the harshness of the church toward the suffering of the poor. On the last night, a call on a Catholic church provoked the priest to summon the police. A bloody melee resulted in 190 arrests, including Tannenbaum's.

The Labor Defense Committee jumped into the fray, immediately providing those detained with the services of Emma Goldman's lawyer, who was also a Liberal Club member. The committee set up headquarters in the Vorse-O'Brien house. Vorse carried on her domestic affairs, including nursing a new baby, amid a whirlwind of histrionically agitated Wobblies, reporters, and sympathizers. The defense committee brought in other downtown writers and liberals. Rife with bohemian disorder and importance, the movement "drew people to it as an arc light draws moths," according to Vorse. "Some came for vicarious excitement, some to help."

The committee organized roving demonstrations in support of the arrested, and these turned lower Manhattan into a stage for labor confrontations rivaling the derring-do of IWW demonstrations in the West. The police were very rough with the protestors and confrontations spiraled. Mass protests against police brutality drew more brutality. The pitch rose after Tannenbaum was sentenced to a year on Blackwell's Island. Crowds in Union Square and Astor Place called for relief for the jobless and decried the injustices of capitalism. To one leader, the times "were unequalled in this country since the stirring days of 1886"—that is, the Chicago labor demonstrations that culminated in the Haymarket massacre. The cadences rang with outrage customarily reserved for the treatment of strikers and free speechifiers in the field. "I was sick at heart last night," avowed Lincoln Steffens after one big Union Square rally. "I've seen such things for twenty years now, but I can't get used to it. It lifts my stomach every time I see a policeman take his night stick in both his hands and bring it down with all his might on a human being's skull."

Downtown writers and personages publicized the events in magazines and newspapers. Jig Cook, for one, sent the news on to Chicago in one of his weekly "New York Letters" for the *Evening Post's Friday Literary Review*. With their connections to the media and other reform movements, the bohemians mediated between the demonstrators and local literary and political luminaries. They drew in progressive city officials, settlement people, and eventually the socialists. With such respectable people on board, they saw their task as controlling the Ferrer School anarchists, who were doing much of the support work with the unemployed men: the Village organizers accepted their help but at the same time held them at arm's length from reporters. For Vorse, "that winter was a sort of welding process." Her still-young marriage, her life as a mother, her New York friendships, and her writing became continuous with a political effort fought with and for ordinary people. "In Lawrence we had, after all, been only spectators. . . . Now suddenly we were on the inside, part of the movement, with responsibility for these men."

"Anyone who has ever been involved with solidarity work will recognize the atmosphere . . . the late-night meetings, the heady resolutions, the infectious excitement of exotic politics." So a biographer of Lord Byron describes a very different group of sympathizers in a very different time, the London support committee who in 1823 raised money and agitated in the newspapers for the Greek Revolution. But the precedent can be extended to this much later New York experiment in the politics of empathy. So, too, can the suggestion that solidarity work inevitably hinges upon the self-valorization of the practitioners. In the early nineteenth century, it provided a chance to demonstrate fealty to ethical principle; in the early twentieth, it became a complex enactment of a neo-Romantic life, risk-taking, adventurous, open to multitudinous human connections.

Two weeks into the demonstrations, news of a terrible climax to a miners' strike in Ludlow, Colorado, reached the city. Since the previous summer, workers employed by a company owned by John D. Rockefeller, Jr., had been on strike demanding that the company abide by Colorado laws on working hours, safety, and cash payment of wages. The IWW had stepped in to lead. Rockefeller ordered the mostly immigrant workers evicted from company housing and they moved to a tent colony nearby, a forlorn, isolated place where they lived through the savage mountain winter in what became a ferocious conflict. In late winter, at the behest of Rockefeller, National Guardsmen attacked the tent colony with rifles and machine guns and then set fire to the tents. Twenty-two workers, including women and children, died from suffocation, gunshot wounds, and beatings.

The New Yorkers, who prized analogy, made the connection: the National Guard was to the Colorado miners what the New York police were to the local unemployed. Furious calls for vengeance— Italian anarchists spoke of a vendetta—joined denunciations of the winter's misery in both Manhattan and the Rockies. Ferrer School sympathizers, accompanied by novelist Upton Sinclair, took downtown street theater tactics up to the fashionable East Side, where they stood in vigil outside the doors of the Rockefellers' mansion. Sinclair then led a parade of silent mourners, dressed in black or sporting black armbands, past Rockefeller's Standard Oil offices. One militant managed to get into the building and threaten Rockefeller's life before police arrived. The pastor of the Church of Social Revolution invaded Rockefeller's Baptist church and challenged the minister to debate the cause of the Ludlow atrocities. When the Rockefellers retreated to their estate near Tarrytown, the radicals followed. Under the aegis of free speech the group tried to hold public meetings in the village square. For several weeks they tussled with police in the quiet river village, waging their free-speech battle there with the determination of seasoned Wobblies.

Soon enough, relations between downtown and uptown turned touchy. Few Liberal Club people joined the anti-Rockefeller actions. Emma Goldman was skilled at mediating between the two groups, but Goldman was out of town on her annual lecture tour for much of the spring. Alexander Berkman, the most genial of men and (it turns out) an unrepentant terrorist, was in charge of her journal, *Mother Earth*, in her absence. Berkman had never given up his belief in the moral justice of the *attentat* that had motivated his attack on Henry Clay Frick, and in his fourteen years in prison, he had never forgiven himself for bungling the attempt. In 1914, the deaths at Ludlow and the broken skulls in Manhattan merged for Berkman into a single injustice that demanded a dramatic reenactment of 1892. While some in the movement tried to find jobs for the roving Wobblies who had come to town to help and others gathered together great loads of books—among them, the complete works of Gibbon—to keep Frank Tannenbaum occupied in jail, Berkman secretly plotted an *attentat* on the Rockefeller estate at Pocantico Hills and conspirators from the Ferrer Center assembled a bomb in a tenement apartment on upper Lexington Avenue near the center. On a June morning, the bomb went off accidentally in the crowded immigrant neighborhood, killing three of the conspirators and a young female boarder.

The downtown moderns could encompass free speech, modern art, free love, and even militant class politics; they could cozy up to the newspapers and entertain thoughts of vaudeville. But they could not tolerate sectarian conspiracies of an older sort. Although Mabel Dodge took vicarious pleasure "playing with dynamite" in conversation, actual dynamite was not what she or others of the downtown intelligentsia had in mind. The radical rich scattered. Alden Freeman, who lived on Rockefeller's Standard Oil money himself, had financially backed the school wing of Ferrer; after the Lexington Avenue explosion he cut all his ties.

Goldman, who understood both the pliability and the limits of the American scene, was incensed. Even years later, when she wrote her memoirs, the outrage returned: "Comrades, idealists, manufacturing a bomb in a congested tenement-house! I was aghast at such irresponsibility." Berkman, in high ideological style, took the disaster as an occasion to turn the dead into martyred heroes, with a big demonstration at Union Square capped by another massive observance at the *Mother Earth* offices. This was all fine, as far as Goldman was concerned, a worthy tribute, but there was more to come. In her absence Berkman devoted an entire issue of *Mother Earth* to the calamity, reprinting in full violent harangues from the Union Square rally. *Mother Earth* was Goldman's living connection to a new audience—Ibsen lovers, small-town playwrights, free-speech doctors, liberal lawyers—in short, to a dissident fraction of the middle class. These readers, she knew, did not like bombs. She was appalled: "I had always tried to keep our magazine free from such language, and now the whole number was filled with prattle about force and dynamite."

"Prattle about force and dynamite" from conspirators was too much for downtown Manhattan. The unemployment demonstrations were the culmination of a series of local experiments with cross-class politics. The intrusion of sectarian violence made such efforts far less appealing. When the downtown radicals again took up the cause of "the people," it was with the largely female "masses" in the birth control movement of 1915–16, a very different crowd from the hotheaded male Wobblies. Cross-class politics would be revived in the 1920s and 1930s, but within the disciplined party structure of the Communists and the strictly supervised "solidarity" of the Popular Front. Bohemians and workers would not mix again until the 1960s.

The events of 1914 demonstrate both the strengths and limitations of Greenwich Village sensibility, so vividly expressed in the juxtapositions of free speech. Flush with a conviction of their historic role in the changing of the guard, a small group decided to talk the country into the future. Free speech was their medium.

Historians have already noted the enthusiasm for "intense personal intercourse" among the early moderns. But leaving the matter at "personal intercourse" reduces the community to merely an affective or a therapeutic milieu. It fails to address the complex relation between inward preoccupations and outward concerns. The moderns were peculiarly attuned to both registers, keyed to the pitch by faith in the new and animated by an instinctively canny sense of cultural commerce. With the hubbub around free speech, they pushed themselves out of their urban niche into the limelight that the New York media cast so brilliantly. In the early years of the century, this didn't require personal confession (as it arguably does now) but rather an aptness for placing themselves on the stage of history.

Talk—racy, jumpy—mediated between the bohemians' metropolis and the workers' world, between culture and politics. It may be tempting now to sneer. Our beliefs in the possibilities of such forms of sympathy and identification have, in the intervening near century, become greatly attenuated. Yet it is undeniable that free speech, with all its half-cocked identifications, could be politically efficacious. The easing of class boundaries did allow a few working-class intellectuals to infiltrate and shape the character of the new intelligentsia. Speech forms produced social relationships that at times turned into real political collusions and collaborations. A politicized sociability cohered into institutions and conversational communities and opened up channels for people and ideas. The mass demonstrations that swept Manhattan in 1914 translated a sympathy for working people into day-to-day action. And exchanges between writers, lawyers, and poor people all laid out the terms for a powerful twentieth-century coalition politics of the left, even if that politics has now all but disappeared.

There was, to be sure, something broken-hearted—to return to Eavan Boland's phrase—about the soirées where well-heeled editors queried poor Wobblies about hunger in the ranks. Since there was commercial profit to be made from such meetings—and bohemia launched other careers besides Mabel Dodge's—the democratic professions of solidarity may seem all the more empty and self-serving. Certainly the imperviousness of the milieu to racial questions and black intellectuals gives one pause and seems to call for yet another critique of middle-class intellectuals content to bruit about a warm liberal sympathy for the oppressed but do little more.

But such condemnation would overlook the specifics of the moment. Viewed against the backdrop of similar milieus in Europe, the democratic propensities are impressive. Nowhere in Europe did anti-Semitism have so little play. Nowhere in Europe, except perhaps in Bloomsbury—itself an exclusive elite—were women admitted on such relatively comfortable terms nor did they succeed, as they did in Manhattan, in making feminist ideas central to radical doctrine. If the cross-class political alliances that formed, locally and nationally, never cohered into the political blocs that socialist and labor parties made up in Europe, they nonetheless opened up the possibilities for a radical democracy of the imagination, institutions with commitment to publicizing that democracy, and a changed manner of negotiating social differences in cultural and intellectual life. That manner depended upon the fantastical, aggravating juxtapositions of an early-twentieth-century city. One of the great, extravagantly wrought emblems of the era was Emma Goldman, a figure who emerged from strong imaginative requirements of the moment. It is to her successes and failures that we turn.

4

Emma Goldman and the Modern Public

More than any other downtown modern, Emma Goldman took New York's free speech on the road. If Mabel Dodge made herself the doyenne of free speech in New York, Goldman turned herself into its emblem across the country. When this daughter of the Lower East Side stopped off to lecture in Saint Louis or Cleveland, it's doubtful that more than a few of her listeners would have thought of Hester Street or Second Avenue, but many probably thought they glimpsed the "Bohemian Greenwich Village" against which a midwestern minister inveighed in 1916. Goldman pressed the juxtapositions of free speech into precepts of radical doctrine, vague but rhetorically potent analogies, such as Marriage is to Love as Capitalism is to Labor, or fulsome associations between the plays of Ibsen and Strindberg and a revolution of the oppressed. Her celebrity status and compelling oratorical presence made these links plausible and persuasive, and indeed it is in no small measure due to Goldman that for the rest of the century memoirists and historians would see some natural coherence in ideas that she, through extraordinary force, made cohere. Politically, she utilized that assortment of unlike elements that characterized early modernism. Artists in Denver and feminists in Portland came to see some meaningful correspondence between their own difficulties and the battles of copper miners; IWW zealots came to see free-love practice as a blow against capital; hardened politicos were drawn to art and high culture as sources of vitality. The origins of these ideas were multiple, but Goldman played a critical role in their confluence.

Goldman's story is in itself a model of the modernist principle of merging disparate phenomena: she embodied both celebrity and politics, spectacle and radicalism, universality and self-aggrandizement. In the early decades of the century, she transformed herself from the small-time political agitator she had been in the 1890s—one among many zealots on the Lower East Side—into a national figure, at once vilified and adored. Familiar to both working- and middle-class audiences, she learned to work the borders between the two, in part by encouraging free-speech coalitions between liberals and radicals. Her skill at blending diverse audiences made her not just notorious but something more, an object of fascination, the quintessential anti-Victorian, the woman who broke all the rules and offered instruction to those who would do the same, if only vicariously. More a prima donna than an organizer, Goldman manifested her devotion to radical causes through her speaking tours—a major form of popular entertainment in an age when the movies had yet to take hold—which mixed support for labor militancy, especially in the service of IWW causes, with cultural politics. In her public persona, she represented the eclecticism of the metropolitan intelligentsia: an English-speaking Russian Jew who could switch to Yiddish when she chose, an exuberant bohemian, a daring New Woman, a cosmopolitan lover of literature.

Goldman's dazzle as a speaker came, in part, from her relentless fascination with herself, a narcissistic preoccupation she could effectively project to her listeners. But it also derived from her gifts in evoking the charisma of the metropolitan center. Hers was the sophistication of urban free speech. She championed modern dance and modern drama, free love, homosexuality, and martyrs of the labor movement. Her militant anticapitalism, roughly aligned with the IWW's syndicalism, was the vessel that freighted the cultural politics that at the time were her most dependable stock-in-trade. She owed much of her success to incredible energy and theatricality; a great performer, she made herself available to many different readings among members of her audiences. But she owed some of it to a dash of good luck, too, the fortuity of being in the neighborhood just when downtown Manhattan was seeking conversations with immigrants that went beyond strike tactics and sweatshop legislation.

The rise of an immigrant Jewish woman to national prominence was without precedent. After 1900, the Lower East Side bohemia in which Goldman first made her name opened out into other self-conscious enclaves of the city, although not the New York literary and intellectual establishment—entrance there for immigrant Jews would come only much later, and for immigrant women only provisionally. Rather, in the 1910s Goldman entered that third space outside the ghetto, Greenwich Village, which put her in a sustained relationship with nonimmigrant, Gentile intellectuals. There, the foreign anarchist—especially so American a foreigner as Goldman—became a piece in the modern collage.

Goldman's ascendancy to prominence was not without reversals. Recall that in the 1890s she was known and honored on the Lower East Side as an instigator of hunger demonstrations and a soapbox orator. By 1897, she had achieved enough recognition from the faithful to embark on a cross-country lecture tour—the first such tour undertaken by an anarchist. But the assassination of President McKinley in 1901 shattered her modest reputation. The assassin, Leon Czolgosz, was a self-declared anarchist and something of a Goldman fan, and the police tried to implicate her in the murder. Freed for lack of evidence, she found herself nonetheless a pariah everywhere in the country, New York included. The assassination unleashed a wave of nativist, antiradical paranoia and resulted in a draconian federal Anti-Anarchist Law in 1903.

To her enemies, Goldman's name became a byword for the foreign menace. Middle-class labor sympathizers and progressives with whom she had developed friendly relations were appalled by her association with murder; even old comrades distanced themselves from her tenderhearted sympathy for "the boy" Czolgosz. Lower East Side landlords, accustomed to renting apartments to radicals of every stripe, found Goldman too hot to handle. Isolated from her comrades and bearing "that terrible name," she could not rent a room in New York, lecture, or earn a living. In 1902, at thirty-two years old, she was a virtual exile from downtown politics, living alone under an assumed name (Miss E. G. Smith) and operating a facial and massage parlor for women in the shopping district around Madison Square.

In the long run, however, the McKinley assassination and the ensuing anti-anarchist campaign liberated her from the restrictions of the anarchist movement, freed her from the tremendous guilt she bore toward Berkman, and propelled her away from the immigrants toward a new public and the issue of free speech. In the next ten years she re-created herself. The older generation of leaders, mostly male, dictatorial, and sectarian in style, was dying off, leaving a vacuum in which Goldman could expand and experiment. In the absence of comradely authority, she worked to broaden the basis of support for anarchist ideas. She became a free agent just at the moment middle-class reformers were turning with interest to selected immigrant thinkers. The effect of the 1903 law, coupled with new state measures—all prohibiting anarchist speech and penalizing offenders with deportation—contributed to growing free-speech sentiment among progressives. Goldman, still operating under her assumed name, joined up with the Free Speech League. Her participation in the group of middle-class reformers would have been unthinkable for a Lower East Side radical in the 1890s.

The Russian Revolution of 1905 also helped her win a wider audience. Still acting as Miss Smith—although her true identity was widely known—Goldman worked as publicist and interpreter for Catherine Breshkovskaya, the Socialist Revolutionary leader who visited New York that year, and thus reentered liberal venues that had shut down to her after the McKinley assassination. When the Orlenev theater troupe, a company associated with the SRs, came to New York at the peak of Breshkovskaya's visit, Goldman became their manager. In her first of many acts of translation between immigrant and mainstream cultures, she turned the sensation the company created on the Lower East Side into a Manhattan tour de force. She pulled in wealthy German Jewish backers, and her old bohemian friend James Huneker, by then an influential voice in the arts, touted the troupe and its leading actress, the then-unknown Alla Nazimova (later a Broadway and then Hollywood star) as a smashing exemplar of Europe's avant-garde. In 1906, Goldman took the company to Boston and Chicago. There Miss E. G. Smith mingled with Barrymores, Roosevelts, Harvard professors, and well-placed Friends of Russian Freedom and periodically revealed herself to be the dangerous Emma Goldman, to the delight of her hosts. Her alliances with reformers and theater people provided glimpses of an audience, still only faintly visible, of writers, artists, and liberal professionals.

The first step in reconceptualizing her role as an American—as opposed to a Russian—radical was to become a writer in English, something that few immigrants (Abraham Cahan was the exception) and no immigrant Jewish woman had yet done. Immigrant writing thrived in the early twentieth century but within a balkanized culture of letters so divvied up by audience and language that Henry James spoke of a literary scene as "subdivided as a chessboard, with each little square confessing only to its own *kind* of accessibility." Irish American writers, insofar as they were known outside the ethnic press, were, until Eugene O'Neill, confined to dialect writing and journalism; Italian American writing outside the foreign-language press was negligible. Even Abraham Cahan remained on the Lower East Side editing the Yiddish *Daily Forward* and was known from his *Commercial* pieces solely as a chronicler of ghetto life.

Goldman envisioned a different place for herself within literary culture, an American place secured by the full authority of her intellect, not her ethnicity—or race, as Jewishness was then conceived. Nor was she content with the slice of audience dedicated to left-wing polemics and pedagogy. She did not want a journal like the Lower East Side political sheets—Cahan's *Forward*, for example, or the anarchist *Freie Arbeiter Stimme*. Rather, she conceived of a little magazine of arts and letters "that would combine my social ideas with the young strivings in the various art forms in America." With the help of an Orlenev troupe benefit and the backing of newfound literary friends, she gathered enough money to begin. The title she chose, *Mother Earth*, spoke to both an embracing revolution of the soul and her monumental fantasies of herself.

As she gained prominence, Goldman's life came to revolve around two poles of activity. She spent half the year in New York, editing the journal and living in an intense cooperative housekeeping arrangement—similar to the A Club but more intertwined—that bound together a *Mother Earth* "family" of friends, lovers, ex-lovers, would-be lovers, and relatives. For the other six months she crisscrossed the country, lecturing two to three times a week on a wide variety of topics, most of them current in downtown Manhattan. She kept up a grueling schedule of lecture engagements, one town after another—thousands of miles of railway travel, scores of cheap hotel rooms and honorary dinners.

In the process she loosened her ties with hard-core immigrant anarchists and deepened her involvement with bohemia. She never lost her moorings in immigrant life—her inner circle, except for her lovers, remained Jewish—but she distanced herself from the Lower East Side emotionally and geographically, moving first to an apartment shared with her *Mother Earth* comrades on Thirteenth Street and then up to East Harlem. She acknowledged the help the old comrades had given her in her early years, but she took pride in her subsequent detachment. Once they had made her work possible, she allowed, but their scope was too constricted. "They had never been able to reach a large American public. Some of them had been too centered in their own language-group activities to trouble about interesting the native element. The results during those years were scant and unsatisfactory."

She did sometimes lecture in Yiddish, a habit that signaled fidelity to her original audience, but her English-language lectures in the city moved steadily into the mainstream geographically and culturally, from the Liberal Club up to a theater in Times Square, the heart of show business, where in 1914 she gave a series of talks on modern drama. Once the Breshkovskaya/Orlenev association ended, she minimized her Russian past. It was not Russian writers she discussed in her lectures, although she was a great reader of Russian novels, but the modern dramatists Ibsen, Shaw, Strindberg, stressing always a Western European cosmopolitanism. Only during the great fight for birth control in New York in 1916 did she turn again with sustained interest to the Lower East Side. And then it was not to rekindle her contacts with neighborhood activists but to use the neighborhood as a staging ground for mass actions led by Greenwich Village feminists. In short, she styled herself a secular Jew who was in touch with her immigrant past but at home, intellectually and socially, in a heterogeneous milieu. One might even say she anticipated the persona Alfred Kazin would much later claim, mischievously, truculently, ironically—the "New York Jew."

The crossover achieved by Goldman was perhaps the most dramatic example of the move undertaken by more ordinary immigrants—the Ferrer intellectuals, for instance. In liberal sectors of the culture, Russians and Central Europeans shed the attributes of the picturesque and exotic ghetto dweller to assume instead a revolutionary modern cosmopolitanism. Benefiting from but at the same time modifying the older philo-Semitic fascination, they could be assimilated into leftish American preoccupations yet retain ethnic roots, appear sophisticated yet still plebeian, with touches of the manners and accents of the ghetto—quite different, in short, from their polite German Jewish counterparts. In left-wing politics, Jews became the reigning intellectuals, and in bohemia, too, they far outnumbered other immigrant groups. In Greenwich Village, one could count the notable Italian Americans on one hand (Carlo Tresca, Arturo Giovannitti), and there were only a few people of Irish descent, Eugene O'Neill being the most famous, followed by Elizabeth Gurley Flynn and John Butler Yeats (the poet's father).

The process within the intelligentsia was not identical to that at work in other parts of the culture but there were parallels. Slightly later, in the 1920s and 1930s, immigrant Jews would become influential in New York's entertainment industry, using their own experience as outsiders to broker the movement of other groups into cultural circulation, inserting ethnic expression into the national currency. An intricate network within the Lower East Side recruited talent for vaudeville, popular music, the stage, and the nascent film industry, taking both personnel and material from diverse locales. Historian William R. Taylor describes the transpositions Jewish songwriters wrought: a classic case is a Tin Pan Alley hit of the 1930s, "Bei Mir Bist Du Schoen," a Yiddish street song first arranged for black singers in Harlem, then translated into English for Jewish musicians in the Catskills, and finally rearranged for recording by the then-unknown

Greek American Andrews Sisters. The play of separateness and inclusion is complex among this generation of innovators, but across the board they proved skilled at negotiating the demands of an American culture that looked to them, by virtue of their own superior cosmopolitanism, to domesticate what seemed the irreducible foreignness of everyone else.

The world they moved in was not free of anti-Semitism but its overt expression was more muted than it had been at the turn of the century. American prejudice against the Jews at this moment continued to lack the obsessiveness of European anti-Semitism; racial hatred, insofar as it was diverted from antipathy toward African Americans, blurred into a general suspicion of "them," the dangerous swarthy immigrants of all casts. No doubt anti-Semitism still secreted itself in cracks and crannies. A bohemian lawyer on the West Coast, for instance, a radical who defended the IWW and the anarchists, liked to throw his friendship with Emma Goldman in the face of his shocked provincial family and publicly preened himself on transcending prejudice. Yet on a visit to New York, he wrote in his diary of his disgust at the Jews he saw on the beach at Coney Island, employing European images of a somatically enfeebled race: "scarcely one physically fit to be father or mother—undersized flabby fleshed and knock-kneed . . . flatchested humpbacked." Helen Marot, a Village feminist active in labor issues, stunned her Jewish coworkers in the Women's Trade Union League in 1911 when she announced that the organization should focus on "American girls," not on Lower East Side garment workers. Too emotional, Marot thought the intrepid Jewish women, too ideological and too much for the "Americans" to swallow. Other devotees of the new would have expressed their uneasiness by projecting anti-Semitic stereotypes onto the immigrant masses rather than onto their Jewish comrades and contemporaries—a time-honored American strategy of token acceptance.

But whatever the hidden workings of prejudice in bohemia, the result was nonetheless hospitality. The rejection of explicit anti-Semitism was part and parcel of the cultural revolt. It set these moderns off from analogous European circles where anti-Semitism penetrated the very marrow of modernity: think of the pejorative meaning of "the Jew" for T. S. Eliot, for example, or more notoriously for Ezra Pound. In the conversational community, the Jew (still with a Yiddish accent) took his or her place alongside the New Woman as a figure signifying modernity—beginning in the teens and continuing on, despite waves of anti-Semitism, up to the present day, when a dash of Yiddish is still welcome in the fashionable New York society of the mind.

Goldman was a pioneer of the process. In New York, as she moved between immigrant radicals and native-born reformers, she learned about the advantages of loose rather than literal translation of political allegiances. She acquired a knack for fusing disparate urban types into her public persona: thus the Jewish insurrectionary was not eradicated but humanized by her other roles as New Woman, bohemian, lover of high culture. The urban type, a literary figure inherited from the nineteenth century, was changing in the 1910s from a creature of surfaces—physiognomy, dress, gesture—to a character of psychological depth. Eugene O'Neill was the master of this shift as he redesigned the Irish American from a stock type of literature and the stage to an anguished hero of modern psychodrama. Goldman, with her intimations of a passionate private life, a tragic past, and untold riches of the soul, was a useful character for this new sort of reading. O'Neill, the Ferrerite and connoisseur of anarchism, had experimented with Goldman-like characters since his first college playwriting experiments. She later turned up as a pseudonymous character in *The Iceman Cometh*, a transposition that indicates how available she seemed for an imagery of psychological depth that stood quite independent of her politics.

Goldman's lecture tours took her translations to a national audience. She was an indefatigable trouper and she played scores of places, big and small: Saint Louis, Cleveland, Portland, San Francisco, Chicago, Minneapolis, Sioux City, New Haven, Denver, Seattle, Kansas City. Her subjects were anticapitalism (discussed in the abstract, almost metaphysical manner of anarchism), sex, and literature. She held forth on "The Failure of Christianity," Nietzsche, "Man: Monogamist or Varietist?" and "Sex: The Great Element for Creative Work." Like other enactments of free speech, the lectures were associative and free-flowing. Her emphasis on individuals and their creative capacities drew on nineteenth-century Romanticism, but it also played into the current fascination with the determining powers of personality——as opposed to the Victorian moral construct of character.

Obviously, Goldman was not palatable to everyone. On the road, the "Priestess of Reds," as her enemies called her, was target for conservatives of a reactionary and sometimes dangerous sort, viciously nativist and antilabor. In New York, nativism never gained a real foothold until war politics took over, but in the Pacific West where she often traveled, anti-immigrant feeling, which had waxed and waned since the 1880s, gathered considerable force in the early 1900s. There, decades of anti-Chinese activity produced a violent Anglo-Saxonism, now fueled by the menace of the foreign-born radicals who dominated the IWW union drives and engineered free-speech fights in the region. Halls where Goldman was scheduled to speak were closed at the last minute; police and thugs bullied and threatened her and her listeners. At times police turned her lectures into "veritable battle encampments."

But her notoriety also functioned as celebrity and pulled in the curious. The exciting meetings were those where devoted anarchists rubbed elbows with the uninitiated—doctors, lawyers, judges, newspaper editors, teachers, literary ladies, and stenographers sitting beside the radical riffraff. In her highest-flying years, from roughly 1908 until 1916, conservative opprobrium was so extreme that even the act of going to hear Goldman became something of a political statement. Like the self-important activity at the Liberal Club, the business of crossing the line—both political and ethnic/racial—to attend an Emma Goldman lecture and listen open-mindedly became a declaration of support for free speech and its eclectic social lineage. Thus Harvard socialist Samuel Eliot, grandson of a Harvard president, stirred up a Boston scandal by addressing Goldman as "Comrade" when he chaired her lecture in the Ladies' Room of the Harvard Union. And the aggressively conservative president of Columbia, Nicholas Murray Butler, forced the resignation of one of his young faculty members, Bayard Boyesen, the son of a distinguished Columbia professor and a socialite mother, because Boyesen was seen consorting with Goldman's New York associates in public (Boyesen took refuge in the Ferrer School, where he became head administrator in 1911).

The most famous case in which sympathetic listening to a Goldman lecture turned into a free-speech issue involved one William Buwalda, a soldier for fifteen years and veteran of the Spanish-American War. While stationed in San Francisco in 1908, Buwalda attended a Goldman evening and afterwards approached the platform to shake her hand. Observed by plainclothesmen staked out in the hall, Buwalda was arrested, court-martialed, and sentenced to five years at hard labor on Alcatraz. His case was so outrageous that free-speech liberals were able to mobilize the broadest grounds for sympathy: Theodore Roosevelt, serving out the last year of his presidency, pardoned him after ten months. Not surprisingly, Buwalda was profoundly transformed. After his release he became a pacifist and in protest returned the medal he had been awarded for his courage in the Philippines. Buwalda was an exception, however: far more of Goldman's listeners shivered with transgression at the lecture and then returned to their regular lives.

The causes Goldman championed on her tours were multifarious. She agitated against international injustices, although her choice of issues was idiosyncratic. The execution of a Japanese anarchist for conspiracy to assassinate the emperor drew her fire; so did the suppression of the Easter Rebellion in Dublin in 1916. Events in Russia usually held her attention, but events on the Continent seldom did unless an anarchist was directly involved, as in the police murder of Francisco Ferrer in Barcelona in 1909. She was interested in the Mexican Revolution, but not so much because of any particular knowledge of the Mexican situation as because of the turn to anarchism of the Magon brothers, liberal intellectuals jailed in 1911 for leading an ill-fated IWW-inspired antigovernment attack in the Baja peninsula. She seldom addressed the Jewish issues of the day, like Zionism, the blood libel cases in Europe, the Dreyfus case, or the Yiddish revival. When she did, it was to denounce Orthodox Judaism or to minimize the political importance of anti-Semitism: the pogroms, she argued in 1906, were really an outbreak of anti-anarchist violence against Jewish radicals. Hers was the complex relationship to

Judaism that characterized other left-wingers of her generation. In Europe, intensifying prejudice pushed some Jewish intellectuals in the first two decades of the century to search for meaningful identifications, but the logic of the U.S. situation led Goldman, and others like her, into what seemed a safe harbor of universalist allegiances—Jews as "the race of transcendental idealism," as Hippolyte Havel describes them in an introduction to a collection of her essays.

With American politics, she was more systematic. She raised money and heightened public support for the left wing of the labor movement, including the Wobblies. Hers were the reigning causes, with a few quirks. Like most socialists and anarchists of the day, she ignored the travails of African America: she never spoke a word about lynching, and the disenfranchisement of black people under Jim Crow laws was an issue too bound up with what she viewed as an illegitimate electoral system to pique her interest. But she could venture outside the staple protests of labor struggles. She took up, for example, the comparatively obscure cause of fourteen Mexican American Wobblies traveling through Texas to Mexico in 1914 to join the revolution, who were indicted for the murders of several Texas Rangers during a melée. She publicized all the big strikes of the period—the miners at Ludlow, the silk workers at Paterson, the textile workers at Lawrence, the hops pickers in Wheatland, California. She worked for jailed and convicted militants, speaking widely, for instance, in defense of the McNamara brothers, accused of bombing the offices of the fiercely antilabor *Los Angeles Times* in 1910. She and Berkman, who was released from prison in 1906, led a campaign to commute labor militant Tom Mooney's death sentence for a bombing at a preparedness parade in San Francisco in 1916. In this regard, she was no different from other showstopping speakers on the left-wing circuit, Socialist Party leader Eugene Debs, for example, or the firebrand Mother Jones.

Her lectures and her audiences, however, expanded beyond the provenance of these political speakers. It is interesting to place this aspect of her career against that of a female contemporary from a very different context in Europe, the Marxian socialist and Polish Jew Rosa Luxemburg. The two, although drastically different in politics and intellect, were similar in the power and charisma they exercised as token women in their respective milieus. But while Luxemburg gained

distinction by speaking and writing entirely within the socialist movement, Goldman crossed over to popular, non-party-aligned audiences.
She spoke to thousands, in 1910 alone giving 120 lectures to some ten
thousand people. The settings were labor halls, Elks' halls, YMCAs,
socialist clubs, public libraries, theaters (in 1916 she spoke in posh
Carnegie Hall), trade union halls, and literary societies, not to mention the Ladies' Room of the Harvard Union.

Her stage presence, by all accounts mesmerizing, blended several
oratorical styles. She was fluent within the heavily masculine tradition of
the appeal to reason, practiced magnificently by Debs. Like Debs, she
depended upon control, deliberate argument, and cool sarcasm rather
than the tub-thumping denunciations and exhortations of many anarchist and socialist speakers. But within this controlled discourse there
was also the excitement of a woman exercising male rhetorical power, a
combination in which some of the best women's suffrage orators also
excelled. Masterful, listeners marveled: spellbinding. In appearance she
was New Womanish, spectacled and severe, dressed in a simple shirtwaist, tie, and skirt, her hair pulled back in a bun. As she aged and grew
plump, she took on a motherly aura to some: "rather like a severe but
warm-hearted school teacher," Mabel Dodge described her slyly.

Her genius lay in the polyvalence of her presentation, the availability of her ideas to many uses. Conversation in downtown New
York had taught her to maneuver between the organizational imperatives of the left, the cultural imperatives of anti-Victorianism, and a
transformative psychology of the self, without collapsing one into the
other. Goldman's personification of the metropolitan center and its
modernity, what Margaret Anderson described as "something cosmic
in the air, a feeling of worlds in the making," was so powerful that
meeting her could in itself be a spur to leaving where you were and
going where you longed to be. She addressed herself implicitly to all
the people on the edge of leaving one thing—a marriage, a job, an
identity, a town—for something else. In her own anarchist way she
spoke to the virtues of social mobility; she stationed herself as the ora-
cle pointing in the direction of untested possibilities. Emma Goldman,
it was said, could change your life.

Margaret Anderson was one beneficiary. Meeting Goldman, she
became a merry fellow traveler of the left, linking the *Little Review* to

Emma Goldman speaks on birth control at a rally in Union Square, 1916
CORBIS-BETTMANN

free speech and to the cause of the IWW and continually publicizing Goldman's books and lectures. Others also cited their encounters with Goldman as a turning point. Henry Miller, the future novelist, was on the lam from a middle-class upbringing and working as a ranch hand in southern California when Goldman came to San Diego to support the big free-speech fight there. He didn't even hear her speak, only saw her hustled out of town, but he claimed it was "the most important encounter of my life. She opened up the whole world of European culture for me and gave a new impetus to my life, as well as direction." Almeda Sperry, a working-class New Woman, thought she had found in Goldman someone who could help her make a life as a lesbian. Christine Ell, a prostitute in Denver, followed her back to New York and became a cook for Greenwich Village restaurants, a bit player in the Provincetown Theater, and a principal in free-love intrigues.

At the upper end of her constituency, among the provincial literati, Goldman spoke to a middle-class hope that the high culture repre-

sented by the late-nineteenth-century writers she extolled could enno-
ble both the well-born and the lowly. In an odd way, her emphasis on
the potential of radical beliefs to enrich one's experience as a consumer
of art—as a reader or a theatergoer—conjoined with a still-powerful
Victorian faith in the unifying and uplifting effects of culture. A parallel can be drawn to Mabel Dodge: as cultural avatars, both presided
over a jumble of topics and both kept potentially vulgar and low elements at a safe distance. Emma Goldman never allowed any manifestation of popular culture—the movies, popular dance, popular
music—to besmirch her message about the uplifting power of great
art. Her sense of herself as a cultural innovator rested not on the
avant-garde character of the works she championed but rather on her
ability to bring the high-born and lowly together in mutual appreciation. Thus she took pride that her lectures on modern drama inspired
(at least to her own, not unbiased eyes) the same response from workers as from educated lecture-goers: Colorado miners who heard her
speak on Shaw down in the pit at lunch hour glowed with understanding, she modestly believed, just as did the well-dressed listeners
in a fancy Denver ballroom the next day.

Because she directed herself implicitly to the neophyte, her lectures could wear thin for those who had already arrived. Even
Margaret Anderson, whose sympathies for Goldman were bountiful,
had too much of her over the years and eventually fell out with her
over her moralistic compulsion to champion art only on political—
that is, improving—grounds. Sara Bard Field, a sharp suffragist from
Portland, was aided by Goldman's exhortations on free love to leave
her marriage, but over time she wearied of the didacticism. "More and
more I am coming to feel that she is a woman for those in the first
primer of radicalism . . . those who have not acquired the a, b, c's."
Goldman's famous drama lectures, which consisted of a plot summary
glossed by a political moral, reminded Field of her Sunday school
teachers' presentations of Bible lessons. "I think Ibsen would groan in
spirit and Hauptmann hold up his hands in horror."

Also like Mabel Dodge, Goldman proved adept at techniques of
publicity and self-amplification; she was pivotal in the transfor-

mation of ideas and politics into spectacle and celebrity and in using the space where the left and entertainment converged. Her success owed much to Ben Reitman, a Chicago physician who became her lover and manager in 1908. Reitman himself was a master of publicity and the art of turning an urban type into first a character and then a celebrity, at least (in his own case) a minor celebrity. The child of a Jewish peddler who abandoned his family, Reitman grew up at the bottom of the Chicago working class, running errands for prostitutes and, as one of the few Jewish boys in his neighborhood, fending off anti-Semitic street violence. At the age of twelve he took to riding the rails, a life of adventure that beckoned to boys of the underclass.

A chance encounter in the Horatio Alger mode with a wealthy Chicago doctor who recognized his intelligence brought a scholarship to medical school and propelled Reitman from rags to riches, at least modest riches. But unlike the fictional heroes of rags-to-riches tales, Reitman clung to his class origins. In the Chicago milieu of philanthropists, settlement workers, and working-class radicals that became his home base, there were advantages to be gained by preserving rather than extirpating his roots in urban lowlife. The varieties of the lumpen proletariat that had for half a century attracted literary fascination were now becoming the objects of academic study in the nascent science of urban sociology. At the University of Chicago, a center for the discipline, the tramp was of particular interest, in part because Chicago, as the major rail terminus for the country, was the capital of migrant labor. A "drainage basin" of vagrant and criminal types, the *New York Times* deemed Chicago. Thousands of hoboes, set adrift from jobs, homes, and farms by successive economic downturns, passed through Chicago on their way to and from itinerant jobs in the fields and mines of the West and Midwest.

Reitman, as born exemplar and enthusiast of the hobo type, was thus well positioned to take advantage of liberal dispensations. He had long since abandoned Judaism to become a model Christian and Sunday school teacher, which further increased his appeal to do-gooders. With the backing of an eccentric heir to a railroad fortune who was devoted to helping tramps, Reitman established a Hobo College in Chicago to provide medical care, social services, and education to itinerant workers. Adapting a style that mixed the bohemian dandy and the Wild West—elegant black tails, cowboy hat, flowing tie, and cane, a costume with authentic touches of the habits of the "unwashed" (Goldman would complain that his long, curly hair was dirty and that he never washed his hands)—Reitman cut a memorable figure around reform-era Chicago. To the press he rattled off exotic ethnographic catalogs of hobo life—enumeration of the different species of hoboes, elucidation of the argot, identification of specimens (Gin Ricky Jack, Hot Tamale Kelly, One Tooth Scully, and so on).

Reitman met Emma Goldman in 1908, when anti-anarchist sentiment bubbling in Chicago since the Haymarket affair of 1886 again came to a boil. Shortly before she was to arrive on a speaking tour, a follower of Reitman's and a disciple of Goldman's was killed in the course of trying to murder the chief of police. Goldman was drummed out of all the halls she had rented. Reitman offered her the one he used for his hobo meetings and enlisted a squad of tramps to clean it up. There was an immediate sexual pull between the two, although chance attractions and affairs were a novelty for neither. What was unusual was, on the one hand, Goldman's quick discovery that Reitman, dirty hair and all, was the love of her life and, on the other, Reitman's instant willingness to tie his fortunes to her own. Never one to ponder the niceties of political doctrine—Reitman was an affable, apolitical person on the lookout for the main chance rather than a governing philosophy—he became an instant convert to anarchism and offered to become Goldman's pitchman on the lecture circuit. The hoboes, too much in need of respectable support to sully themselves with hotheads and bomb throwers, were horrified at Reitman's alliance with the "anarchist queen." But for Reitman, a man always on the make, the national limelight around Emma Goldman was more attractive than the local Chicago stage of vaudeville sociology. He and his "blue-eyed Mommy"—his favorite endearment—hit the road together.

The shape of their passion will concern us later. But for the moment, what is interesting is the repertoire of publicity methods Reitman unveiled for Goldman's use. Typically, reformers and radicals on tour still relied on hand leafleting and street bills to announce their presence; their forums were almost always labor halls, public squares, and street corners. Reitman, in contrast, looked for respectable venues and supplemented handbills and flyers with newspaper coverage, which he solicited directly. For him, publicity was the important thing, not whether the papers would treat Goldman and her ideas sympathetically. Inside the halls, he drew on the rituals of vaudeville—and even the circus—to relax the audience. The cadences of the tout and pitch familiarized for the timid the forbidding atmosphere of the anarchist meeting and eased the strain of the serious lecture, as Reitman came out before the speaker and warmed up the hall with exhortations to "take a chance" on anarchist pamphlets and "invest a nickel" before the "big show" began.

Goldman depended on his showmanship at the same time as she condescended to it. One of her principal means of understanding their relationship was the opposition she set up between her refined temperament, so attractive to one of Reitman's lowly background, and his vulgar plebeian character, sexually alluring while personally loathsome (in the index to Goldman's memoirs, Reitman's name is followed by the subheading, "repellent characteristics"). Goldman in her judgment was only echoing the nearly universal dislike of Reitman, a man whom Margaret Anderson described as not too difficult to like if you could drop all your ideas about how a human being should look and act. Long after the love affair ended, Goldman sniffed at his love of publicity and "show," which she contrasted to her finer sensibilities: "he could not understand my deep-seated repulsion to the habitual imposition of newspaper men. He could not comprehend that one who had been so long before the public could still shrink from the vulgarity of being made a public show." But however she might retrospectively hold herself superior to him in this as in all other things, Goldman needed him. On her own, she was too much of a devotee of high culture ever to be fully capable of utilizing the rhythms and forms of American commercial culture. Reitman, in doing precisely that, helped her reach a different audience.

There is a parallel between Goldman and Isadora Duncan, another great self-created modern woman of these years. Duncan's problem in staging herself was analogous to Goldman's—how to create herself as priestess of a lofty endeavor and at the same time attract popular audiences. Duncan held on to the frame of Hellenism—the Greek togas, the mythological trappings—just as Goldman held on to the frame of great literature and utopian politics. Yet Duncan's success lay in transforming the opera house dance concert—an offshoot of vaudeville, with novelty acts and gimmicky, exotically costumed step dances—into an art that spoke to the modern soul's yearning for beauty and freedom. Like Goldman, Duncan believed her mission was "to bring taste and understanding to the working class" and, like Goldman, she succeeded in creating extraordinarily mixed audiences for her theater of the new: middle-class art lovers, yes, but self-styled bohemians and immigrant girls, too, who eventually went to the settlement houses to learn "aesthetic" and "natural" dance.

Six years or so of touring with Reitman actually did bring Goldman her offer from the vaudeville stage. Oscar Hammerstein, the great show-business magnate, had probably heard her lecture right in Times Square when she spoke about modern drama. He invited her to appear in a variety evening in one of his Broadway theaters. At first Goldman agreed, drawn by the huge salary. But while she could function as a star on the lecture circuit with the master of ceremonies Reitman, to find herself in the very heart of popular entertainment—sandwiched between a trained-dog act and a high-kicking dancer—was too much. The lover of Nietzsche and Ibsen fled American popular culture no less than she did the *Yiddishkeit* of the ghetto. In the end, she was revolted by vaudeville's "pitiful efforts to amuse the public": the cheap jokes of the comics, the "cracked voice" of the singer, the "flabby body" of the dancer, and the "coarse hilarity" of the crowd. "I could not stand up in such an atmosphere to plead my ideas, not for all the money in the world."

The vaudeville stage was a volatile point of ethnic and racial crossovers, but popular culture was not a place where moderns at the time wanted to dwell. A handful of New York artists in the 1910s were drawn to the vaudeville theater, Coney Island, even African American blues clubs, entranced by the potpourri of types and the visual splendor. But generally this generation of bohemians, except for the Dadaists in Ridgefield, banked on renewing rather than undercutting the sources of high culture. For all her appeals to the soul of the "people," Goldman's strategies of assimilation—as a political, a Jew, and a woman who spoke on sexual matters and lived with men outside of marriage—depended on her placing herself within a realm of tastes that were high-minded at the same time they were revolutionary and translating them into a workable cross-class American idiom. A sympathetic view of popular culture—and of the polyglot American energies it embodied—was unthinkable, even antithetical to that position. It invited the taint of the cheap and the immoral.

I t is hard, once we leave aside the particular issues that Goldman took up on her travels, to generalize about the political opening on which she capitalized so brilliantly. In her Russian youth her political understanding was forged within a rigid notion of the people's will to reach a kind of metaphysical freedom and she never entirely lost that deterministic, dogmatic language. Nonetheless, early-twentieth-century America pressed on her a suppleness she was not born to. How did a Jewish daughter of the Russian nihilists become an American symbol of modern freedom?

Certainly her experiences on the Continent in the late 1890s and the first decade of the twentieth century predisposed her to see how anarchist ideas could engage various sorts of dissenters outside the tried-and-true ranks of the proletariat. At its core, anarchism was violent, sectarian, and unyielding, but as it spread outside tight knots of true believers into the European art world it became more flexible. Compared with socialist doctrine, the anarchist theory of society rested on large generalities rather than a precise taxonomy of social class, and much more than socialism, anarchism prized notions of individual self-expression and freedom. Especially in France and the Netherlands, where Goldman traveled to several international anarchist congresses, but also in Spain, Germany, and Austria (she lived in Vienna in 1895–96 while she trained as a midwife), anarchism tinged the avant-garde—in Barcelona, Picasso's circle of painters and their fellow *modernista* writers and dramatists; in Paris, the theatrical group of Alfred Jarry, the poets around Guillaume Apollinaire, and some of the neo-Impressionist painters. In Prague, anarchist discussion affected Franz Kafka, a habitué of the young men's cafés, and inspired Jaroslav Hasek to run a comic campaign in 1912 as sole candidate of his own Political Party of Modest Progress.

Thus, anarchist sensibility occupied a wide spectrum in Europe, ranging from revolutionary conspiracies at one end to the symbolist movement and Kafka at the other. In between there was room for all sorts of bohemian defectors: followers of Nietzsche, antimilitarists, despisers of bourgeois society (including its own children), sympathizers of the working poor. In Europe no less than in the United States, there were sects and theorists, acrimonious debates over fine points of doctrine, and divisions. Goldman charted her way among these feuding parties. She could hold her own in disputation, but her facility for ideological jousting was less important to her American crossover than her European training in adapting anarchist ideas to cultural discussions.

In America, Goldman benefited from the *absence* of a clearly articulated theory of social change; this may account for the vagueness one senses now in the essays and lectures she left behind. There were unacknowledged tensions, the tethers to violent revolution tugging as she turned onto an American, Emersonian path of self-development, but the paradoxes gave a hovering energy to her incitement to live fully in defiance of the authoritarian structures—legal, social, economic—which cramp and limit the self. Such injunctions vibrate with the psychological preoccupations of the moment—a vision of the bounty of fully released personalities—but also with an older, Protestant evangelical tradition that likewise challenged the authorities who stood between the self and cosmic creation. Tapping these sources allowed Goldman to fire the soul for a secular age. She evoked her role as evangelizer and exhorter when she argued back to comrades contemptuous of her bourgeois audiences that it was "spiritual hunger and unrest," not just economic oppression, that drove people to rebel.

At the same time she framed the search for fulfillment in social terms, as dependent on a common effort that would bring together the needy and the privileged. She thus spoke to onlookers at the margins of political action. The closely reasoned expositions of Second International socialists had their own attractions: the lure of a theory backed by empirical reasoning and laws of history was considerable in an age fascinated with the promise of science. But for many, the science of socialism was simply "too cumbersome . . . autocratic and dogmatic." So complained a middle-class defector from Yale who found his bearings as a novelist at the Ferrer School. Anarchism, in contrast, brought him into "a big, wide world." It was a world of the imagination more than of concrete social movements and political debates: "art, music, craftsmanship, creative imagination of literature." "I could never listen to the socialists," Margaret Anderson flatly admitted. "Anarchism, like all great things, is an announcement. . . . Socialism is an explanation and falls, consequently, into the realm of secondary things."

Also, the Marxist theory of class struggle spelled out perhaps too clearly the doom of the property-owning classes and certainly left little room for artists and intellectuals other than those directly serving labor struggles and the envisioned workers' state—organizers, policy makers, ideologues, poster makers, composers of political allegory. The category of class, on the other hand, was never critical to an anarchism rooted in the Russian theory of a huge "people" to be awakened from their slumber. Anarchist ideas could blur into the general emancipationist ethos, compatible with ideas of change that came from the youth movement and feminism. In fact, Goldman was sometimes willing to let go of class struggle altogether. Anarchism, she proclaimed in defiance of the teachings of her predecessors, "builds not on classes but on men and women," on deracinated individuals whom some sort of rebellion had cut loose from their origins. In her mind, her audiences were composed of people in different stages of losing their class affiliations, by virtue of artistic endeavor, political sympathies, or sexual rebellion. She was not naive about the power of class in America—no immigrant could be. Nonetheless, she was willing to talk with rebellious plutocrats, work with them, and take their money: she was willing, in other words, to be open-minded in this as in other matters.

Over the years, the comrades grumbled. A printer in the inner circle of *Mother Earth* criticized Goldman for turning anarchism into "a movement for individual self-expression rather than collective revolution." In Europe, he maintained, anarchists fought capitalism; in America, they fought the Comstock laws. "Instead of participating in the trade unions, organizing the unemployed or indulging in soap-box oratory, we rent comfortable halls and charge ten cents admission." Goldman's friend Voltairine de Cleyre, her only female rival in the movement, griped about the "respectable audiences, respectable neighborhoods, respectable people." But if she was too respectable, Emma Goldman was also not respectable enough, since on matters of sexual politics, anarchists often were more conservative than the middle-class audiences Goldman courted. Her interest in free love—always conceived as heterosexual—fell within the anarchist canon of properly political subjects, but her championship of birth control was unusual and her addresses on homosexuality were decidedly improper, so that staid comrades squirmed at her talk of "unnatural" subjects.

Alexander Berkman, in particular, though utterly enmeshed with Goldman, excoriated her innovations. Goldman indignantly attributed his criticism to his difficulties in adapting to life after prison and in making the transition between "his dream world of 1892 and my reality." Tensions eased as Berkman fell in love with a younger woman, an anarchist militant, and still more as he made a place for himself as editor of *Mother Earth* when Goldman was out of town. Finally, after the crisis in 1914 over the Lexington Avenue bombing, he accomplished a significant, if in the end temporary, separation from Goldman by moving with his lover to San Francisco to start his own paper, the fire-breathing *Blast*. Still, the strains between the orthodox revolutionary and the exponent of free love and Ibsen never disappeared. Psychological undercurrents moved between opposing gender poles of imputed and suspected difference, the hard-headed man of the gun squaring off against the soft-headed woman of culture. Berkman carped at Goldman's dependence on "chance" audiences, rather than congregations of the faithful, to build a movement; Goldman raged at his unending dogmatics, what she had denounced in the 1914 debacle as his prattle about force and dynamite.

Berkman, an adherent of strict doctrine to the end, believed there was an impregnable wall between the working class and the propertied class. Goldman's genius was to sense the ways in which progressive coalitions, feminism, and cultural democratization were opening up passages. The bourgeoisie that orthodox radicals imagined as a massive social bloc was in fact unstable at the edges, susceptible to secessions and defections. The "respectable people" whom Goldman touched included rabbis and public librarians like those Floyd Dell knew in Davenport, the radical rich, settlement house idealists, municipal reformers, polished college graduates—as well as working-class intellectuals hungry to make their marks not in the trade unions but in literature and the arts. Goldman gave something to all these people. She provided in her person and her polemics a basis for an anti-Victorian cultural authority that promised, in the hopeful years of the new century, a basis for a democratized cultural elite.

As fluid as her politics were, however, it is important to see that Emma Goldman was not endlessly adaptable. There were outposts of liberal sensibility in which a radical immigrant Jew, even in 1916—her high-water mark—was not welcome. Back in Manhattan, some doors remained closed. She did not drop in on the Arensbergs' uptown salon; she never appeared in the pages of *Seven Arts*, organ of high cultural radicalism. And although Walter Lippmann's Socialist Club had hosted her at Harvard back when Lippmann was an undergraduate, she never seems to have been invited to the elegant New York townhouse that housed the *New Republic*, where he was an editor from 1914 on. Rather, her Manhattan engagements were mostly along the north-south axis of downtown radicalism, from the Lower East Side through St. Mark's Place and up to Union Square, with a broad swath of territory through Greenwich Village to the west.

Interestingly, in these quarters the interpretations of Goldman were fairly narrow. What the Village intellectuals wanted from her was not so much free-love advocacy or reading lists of European novels as a shortcut to working-class militancy and a representation of intellectual seriousness aligned with revolutionary force. While the New York anarchists criticized her drift toward respectability, the Village intelligentsia—including Eugene O'Neill—fixed on her old association from the 1890s with revolutionary violence. Where the comrades saw wishy-washiness, the intellectuals saw dynamite. Max Eastman's EG, sketched in his 1948 memoir, was a nineteenth-century bomb-throwing anarchist: "a square little solid block of blue-eyed belligerent energy. . . . Her whole life wisdom consisted of comparing reality with an absolute ideal, and breaking her neck, and if need be all necks, in some obviously desperate leap for the ideal." Hutchins Hapgood, a good friend, respected, "the vigor and passion of her personality" but also saw her as an ideologue, espousing concepts he disdained as "too simple," "too orthodox," "a faithful expression of the traditional revolution of the working-class."

But it was Mabel Dodge, a wicked observer of other powerful women, who dissected Goldman's Village persona most precisely. Goldman and her friends always elicited from her, she remembered, "a mixture of wonder, horror, and admiration" and a longing for a closeness that she, Dodge, could never attain. The problem, she felt, lay in the insistent dramaturgy of revolution that the circle enacted, the hushed, scarcely veiled "Plans" that set them aside from other guests at her evenings. "I felt they had Plans. I knew they had. I knew they continually plotted and planned and discussed times and places. Their obvious activity seemed to be publishing the anarchist magazine *Mother Earth*, but beneath this there was a great busy humming complex of Planning; and many times they referred to the day when blood would flow in the streets of New York."

Dodge was an inveterate self-dramatizer and so was Goldman. It's impossible to judge whose theatricality was most salient in this account of feminine rivalry played out in political posturing. What we can see is how interested Dodge was in putting herself for just a moment into imaginative proximity with blood in the streets, an act she could accomplish simply by inviting Goldman to one of her evenings. "I wanted these people to think well of me," she recalled. "They were the kind that *counted*. They had *authority*." Goldman's "authority" over the rich woman, her power to render meaning—to make something count—is strong testimony to the ambivalent invitation that, in the early century, open-minded Manhattan issued to brilliant outsiders. Straining toward an awareness of social and intellectual heterogeneity as the basis for a modern cosmopolitanism, the guardians of an alternative cultural order extended a welcome at once democratic, voyeuristic, and self-serving to the New Woman and the New York Jew.

III
———

WRITING

5

Art and Life: Modernity and Literary Sensibilities

New York in the 1910s was a writer's city, literature the paramount art form. Downtown, books and magazines were the chief forms of entertainment and obsession, not painting or music, and bohemian conversation sooner or later settled on what the talkers were reading that week. And what they were writing: the bohemians' own forum of letters was "free expression," their term for a new literature that claimed an aesthetic expansiveness at once political and emotional. Free expression was a corollary of free speech, another vehicle for bringing people together, imaginatively, across divides and distances. "The artist does not run counter to his age; rather, he refines the propensities of his age, formulating their aesthetic equivalent": so the critic Kenneth Burke, who came to Greenwich Village in 1915, summarized the nebulous urges of this generation. If writers could turn into the equivalents of revolutionaries, then readers might become revolutionary sympathizers and politicoes could line up with artists. Writing was another point of crossover.

Literary culture in the United States in the early years of the century produced no counterpart to Woolf, Joyce, or Kafka, but it did create the basis for what developed, over the long run, as a distinctly American modern culture of letters—an assemblage of writers, publishers, and readers quite different from what had come before. The consortium sustained itself on both the materials of political dissent and the opportunities of an expanding literary market. Within lower Manhattan, sympathetic publishers, newly mindful of political dissent, and writers giving expression to the full spectrum of modern aspirations came together, their collaborations growing out of the polyglot urban life around them. Publishers and writers spied the outlines of a book- and magazine-buying public, for whom modern sophistication, left-wing affiliations, and metropolitan seductions were interlaced. In this literary culture, politics and art, commerce and idealism all played a part.

The idea that literature could be a transformative force in society had long antecedents, most recently in nineteenth-century Romanticism. In the United States in the 1910s, it gained momentum with a call to arms that echoed earlier campaigns for literary realism waged by Howells and Twain. On many fronts, though, the campaign to represent the "real" in American life had already been won by the older generation—Frank Norris, Stephen Crane, the regionalist writers, Howells and Twain themselves. So while the moderns were not simply reenactors of bygone battles—there were serious skirmishes to be fought, especially over writing about sex, as conservatives retired from the field—they did face a problem in turning themselves into youthful standard-bearers. What exactly was the new literature they championed? Always creatures of self-amplification, they sought their own way by inflating literature's importance, folding realism into the catchword of "free expression" and making free expression a habit—even an imperative—of a fully realized modern life. Art, creativity, and politics circled around and blended with one another, catalyzing writing that purported to evoke—and in the process, to bring into being—a democracy of plot and character. Characters who had once been relegated to the background moved up to the literary foreground. Plebeian social types became modern heroes and heroines, promoted by writers who themselves were crossing over from journalism to fiction, from obscure left-wing journals to big magazines, from small towns to big cities, and from ethnic enclaves to the metropolitan center.

Politics and art were associated in a loose sense that has by now been lost to us. The presumptions of the 1910s were perhaps better expressed by earlier generations of moderns—the French Impressionist painters, for instance—than by the explicitly political artists who came after the Russian Revolution (the writers of the Popular Front, for instance). Just as the first painters of modern life sought to escape the rigid structures and dictates of a highly regulated Parisian art establishment, American writers of the early twentieth century believed in the benefits of an unrestricted market for cultural goods (in their case, a market free of censorship), the opening of the literary profession to outsiders, the creation of a new public, the diversification of subjects. These impulses drew ethical strength more from the anarchists than from the aesthetically timid socialists; notions of ideological, instructive art that promoted left-wing party agendas would come only later, from the Bolsheviks, who through the Communist parties in the West would put an indelible stamp on politicized aesthetics, especially on the realist tradition. In the 1910s, attempts to knit together art and politics into a fabric of imagined democracy were not theoretically rigorous, but they were ebullient and flexible, resembling not so much a formal marriage as an easy-going bohemian free love union, colored by credulous good nature.

In Europe, literary modernism was characterized from its earliest moments by a readiness to turn on its own certainties, a willingness to grasp a world pregnant with its own contraries; its voice was self-mocking as well as self-aware. The Americans moved in a different direction—not toward modernism's exiled posture but toward Whitmanian affirmation. This was not a generation born, as was said of Emerson's generation, with knives in their brains. With them there is confidence, discovery, self-delight, not fine distinctions, irony, and refusal. These writers liked expansiveness and embrace, not doubt and mockery; crossing over lines, not drawing them. Their hopes for American culture—more precisely, about literary culture—were boundless.

Most downtown New Yorkers were invested in seeing themselves as artists. Their chroniclers have called them intellectuals, and so have I, but they were much more likely to see themselves as artists-writers than as intellectuals, reformers, journalists, or revolutionaries. Somehow there seemed more to being an artist. To claim artistic identity was to put oneself in high relief in the culture, to inherit the plots of a raft of bohemian novels. There were exceptions. Randolph Bourne, for one, wanted to get away from the posing that "art" entailed to strengthen the alternative identity of the political intellectual. To most of his peers, however, it was the "artist" who contained the essence of modernity. Artists and would-be artists in downtown New York were typically writers: everyone was writing novels or poetry or plays, and if they were writing nonfiction, it was supposed to be crafted nonfiction. But people with artistic inclinations also battened on to downtown Manhattan's communal theaters (the Paterson Pageant, the Provincetown Playhouse), turned the Armory Show and exhibitions of modern painting at Stieglitz's Gallery 291 into symbols of radical esprit, and made the writing of free verse a virtual entrance requirement for bohemia.

In their determination to merge art and politics, the bohemians laid the groundwork for a liberal metropolitan elite committed as much to matters of cultural taste and innovation as to social reform. An attraction to modern, "revolutionary," and "political" art, jumbled together, would henceforth run through American culture, leading enlightened audiences and artists to advertise their solidarities with the "people" and to see themselves, by virtue of the books they read, the art they admired, or the plays they attended, as subverting the status quo. At the time, though, the affinity between the politics of the left and artistic engagement was novel. In Europe, there was a tradition of alignment between sympathetic artists and revolutionary or labor movements dating back to the French Revolution. One thinks of David, the revolution's artist, of Courbet and his allegiance to the Revolution of 1848, and of the Impressionists, who were partisans of the Third Republic; in England, of the revolutionary-minded William Blake in the late eighteenth century and, a hundred years later, of the socialist William Morris. But in the United States, the labor and socialist movements, while occasionally drawing the sympathies of individual writers, never claimed their work.

This changed in the early twentieth century. Free speech and free expression encouraged the maxim that life was art and vice versa. The equation had been around since the 1890s but now the bohemians began to speak of art as work and of workers as artists, thereby giving it a political twist. The image of the worker as artist, which had been central to the English Arts and Crafts movement, migrated abroad via the anarchists (explaining why Picasso, for one, paraded around Paris for a time in workers' overalls rather than the usual bohemian garb). But in America, the identification of work with art entered not only artists' circles but also the left wing of the labor movement. Emma Goldman, as we have seen, preached the virtues of art appreciation to the rank and file, but some in the proletarian vanguard considered themselves not aspiring appreciators but the artists in need of appreciation. The last words of Joe Hill, IWW free-speech troubadour convicted of murder in Utah and executed in 1915, rang with the identification: "I have lived like an artist, and I shall die like an artist"—a declaration that made him a hero for Margaret Anderson's *Little Review*. Recovering in Greenwich Village from his labors in the field, Bill Haywood not only dined at Mabel Dodge's but also visited Robert Henri's studio and scribbled poetry in Washington Square. Haywood's prominence in bohemia led the *Dial* to gibe that he was popular in the Village much like a sports hero was on a college campus.

In part the association of art and life came from anarchist beliefs in a self whose creative powers were unleashed by revolutionary ferment—a theme that Goldman worked continuously in New York and on the road. "I have never known a people more rabid about art than the anarchists," averred Margaret Anderson. "Anything and everything is art for them—that is, anything containing an element of revolt." But the anarchist view of the creative imagination was also compatible with the hopes of bohemian amateurs, the conviction that hidden artistic powers lay buried within them, waiting to be tapped. Writing was the medium of choice because it offered access to commercial channels that, in America, modern painting did not. The result was an outpouring of politically tinged confessions, short stories, novels, plays, and poetry, all originating as products of daily collective life.

A tremendous expansion of print in the early century—a publishing boom in newspapers, magazines, and books—encouraged the transformation of amateurs into professionals and scribblings into published work. This affected both male and female writers as well as immigrant newcomers to the Anglophone press. Literary activity among radicals was both a cause and a consequence of growth in publishing, as advertisers and investors moved into what had been, in the nineteenth century, family firms and changed them into big operations, hungry for copy and writers.

The left press enjoyed its own boom. On the eve of the First World War, there were more than three hundred socialist publications in the country, some with circulations of over a hundred thousand (and the figure does not include the papers and journals of the women's movement, the anarchist journals, the progressive papers, and the nonsocialist labor papers). The need of these small publications for copy, in fact, can be seen as a latter-day equivalent of the vigorous Victorian religious press, whose demand for pious sentimental writing sprang many aspiring writers into print in the nineteenth century.

Eager for articles to fill up their narrow columns of dense exposition, the leftist periodicals welcomed unknown writers as long as they were conversant with the discourse that prevailed in their respective pages. Louise Bryant, for example, married to a dentist in Portland, Oregon, was a would-be bohemian who longed to be some kind of an artist, any kind; her first break came when she placed some pieces with Alexander Berkman's magazine, the *Blast*. Eugene O'Neill (who in 1914 was lurking around the Ferrer School signing his letters "Yours for the Revolution") first published in *Revolt*, an anarchist paper that his drinking buddy Hippolyte Havel started, and sent his hearty revolutionary doggerel off to a variety of little magazines and socialist rags ("What cause could be more asinine / Than yours, ye slaves of bloody toil? / . . . bleed and groan—for Guggenheim! / And give your lives for Standard Oil!"). The trajectory from journalist to writer, a rarity before the *Commercial Advertiser* in the 1890s, was common by the 1910s. "Everyone on the city desk was writing a play or a book," remembered Dorothy Day, who after graduating from college worked first on the Chicago dailies and then, in New York, on the socialist *Call* and the *Masses*. "All of us were going to write novels," Floyd Dell similarly recalled.

The combined effects of expanding commercial opportunity and a literary turn among journalists blurred lines of sexual difference that had once been inviolable. Although in the nineteenth century journalists from humble backgrounds—Whitman, Twain, and Howells come to mind—did achieve distinction, this avenue had mostly been closed to women; Victorian journalism confined them to poetry, essays, and domestic fiction. But after 1910, reporting was more open to women than it had been in the 1890s, when Neith Boyce was the sole woman on her paper and Nelly Bly was so unusual as to make news in herself. "Girl poets" of the feminist and labor lefts swarmed around Chicago and New York newspapers, Dell reported. Women's push into journalism strengthened an alliance with bohemian urbanity that, by the late teens, was so strong that reporter Djuna Barnes could swagger around as a more-or-less open lesbian-about-town in her job as a roving New York journalist, writing hermetic, involuted essays on Village life.

Immigrant Jews also benefited. Later, New York intellectuals who came of age in the thirties would speak grandly of the journey from the ghettos to the heights of liberal Manhattan as one of the longest journeys in the world. But actually, by the time they made it to Columbia and/or the *New Republic*, the route had been pretty well established by enterprising if less-memorialized travelers of the previous generation: writers Rose Strunsky, Anna Strunsky Walling, and Konrad Bercovici, magazine editor Sonya Levin, book editor Saxe Commins (Emma Goldman's nephew), and so forth. For immigrants, the way from outside to inside often came through socialist and anarchist networks connected to the downtown intellectual scene. There they received tips on the ardors of the trek from margins to center, the price of the ticket, the promised payoff, and the know-how to handle their baggage once they arrived.

Official prewar American culture might seem to have been a bastion of official Anglo-Saxon values, with its refined defenders hunkered down for a last stand against modern imperatives—this is in fact the view historians have habitually taken. In fact the situation was more ambiguous, with a stream of realist reportage and polemics flowing from liberal and left quarters into the big magazines and newspapers. Reform sympathies and a widespread fascination with "real life" meant that styles learned in writing social commentary for the small journals could be transposed with some ease into a mainstream press characterized by intense competition for sensational material. The thirst of the magazines and "yellow" newspapers for human interest stories gave journalists writing about workers an entrée into a print culture supposedly hamstrung by the ruling class. Even family magazine like *Harper's* and *Everybody's* published muckraking articles and human interest pieces sympathetic to labor, and radicals graced by some sort of respectability wrote for them. Louise Bryant's career is a good example of literary mobility launched from the left. In 1916, she left her dentist husband and Portland to live with John Reed in New York. In the Village, she began placing her work in the *Masses* and utilized her lover's connections with the magazines to win an assignment in France as a war reporter; with Reed, she made her name on the spot during the Russian Revolution; and by the early 1920s, she was a top writer on the Hearst syndicate.

In book publishing, too, alternatives took shape to the old New York WASP family firms that had long ago, in Walt Whitman's day, ousted their Boston rivals and then settled in for a comfortable half century of shaping American writing. The established publishers—Frank Doubleday, Charles Scribner, Henry Holt, among others—operated with tastes that had changed little since the 1870s. While not impervious to the realists' pressures to open up American writing, they understood, correctly, that their accustomed mixture of romantic fiction, historical romance, westerns, and uplifting stories of contemporary life was a winning one. They sponsored such 1910s best-sellers as the novels of Eleanor Stratton-Porter (*Laddie*, *Pollyanna*, and other Stratton-Porter books brought Doubleday a million dollars a year). The choices were obdurately American, with the addition of approved writers from England, still seen as the standard-bearer of excellence; the rest of Europe—not to mention Russia—was literary terra incognita. "Before 1914," Alfred A. Knopf reminisced, "few American publishers ever visited the Continent in search of books; when one left London it was to go on holiday."

The established publishers are often remembered as their downtown critics saw them—aging, smug, priggish, stodgy—a characterization that, not incidentally, helped cast the newcomers as glorious innovators. Publishing was a chummy gentleman's club, "a closed universe," run by the "high and mighty," remembered Max Schuster, who would go on to cofound Simon and Schuster. In fact, the best of these men had played, in their heyday, a liberal role. By the lights of their youths in the 1880s, they were democrats, upholders of the absolute value of high culture—its nobility, its moral purity—but also believers in a socially conscious creed summed up in the writings of Matthew Arnold, convinced that through the mass market they commanded they could bring the riches of culture to people outside the elite. They wanted not to create an aristocracy of taste but to win over a majority to what they saw as the highest of cultural standards.

By the 1910s, however, what was once cultural liberalism had been pushed far to the right. The old-guard publishers favored writing that they thought would move readers—all sorts of readers—to the kind of lofty sentiment and purpose looking at an Old Master or thrilling to an aria might inspire. Realism could go only so far: an article of faith was the necessity—both commercial and moral—of protecting the "family" audience from disturbing representations, a dictum that forbade any but muffled references to sex, so that Dreiser's publisher, Frank Doubleday, buried *Sister Carrie* (after his wife, a "family" reader, sampled the book and was horrified) even though the heroine's erotic liaisons are never described, only alluded to. Even genial skepticism about the existence of God or the divinity of Jesus was forbidden. And Anglo-Saxonist fears that a polyglot American population would bastardize the language turned publishers into protectors of standard English, resistant to infusions of slang, vulgarity, or "foreign" words. The biases extended to their choice of authors: editors depended on a pool of WASP talent, often writers connected personally to them through shared family or college backgrounds. While some publishers (Henry Holt, for example) dabbled in modern tastes—Holt published a few left-leaning books in the teens—they were skittish, quick to bolt at any sign of trouble. To the generation just coming into its own downtown, their extreme caution, coupled with their homogeneous social backgrounds and ignorance of European literature, made the older men appear complicit with provincial puritanism and Comstockery.

Still, the camps were not always as divided as the moderns liked to believe. The moderns, too, saw art as uplifting and educative—although in revolutionary, not bourgeois values. They, too, sniffed at any hint of popular culture. And they, too, even as they refused to become the monitors of the language their predecessors were, stuck to standard English in their writing, resorting to patronizing, heavy-handed dialect when representing colloquial or accented speech. But although the linguistic experimentation that would be the touchstone of 1920s modernism eluded them, they nonetheless laid the groundwork for a new configuration of literary production. They turned away from the tyranny of the family audience, orienting themselves toward subject matter that had been excluded: the aspirations of the working poor, the sexual desires of women. Once that had been accomplished and a new public staked out, there could be a reshuffling of market strategies, authorship, and writing itself.

In the shining "now" as opposed to the discredited "then," the idea went, dissident writers could represent American subjects, narratives, and experiences the establishment discounted or denied. The critic James Oppenheim expressed the common view: "all of us had lived through the cigar store Indian period, wooden and dead, when nice people went in for 'social work,' when Howells was dean of American letters, and when stiff white collars held your chin up." Now, there was the "shock of joy . . . when simultaneously, rockets of poetry went up and burst in the sky over the heads of an amazed people." Established publishers, not quite aware that roles in a pageant of generational struggle were being assigned, were before they quite knew it cast as pettifogging shopkeepers (reigning over cigar stores) or, worse, soldiers in the allegorical drama of Reaction versus Revolution, standing at the barricades uptown vainly attempting to forestall the moment when "the literary sansculottes would swarm over."

A group of independent publishers, mostly well-off German Jews, emerged to take on work that the older firms left up for grabs. Small operations at first, presses run by the young Alfred Knopf, Mitchell Kennerley, Horace Liveright, B. W. Huebsch, and bookseller Albert Boni published young writers from downtown and reprinted contemporary work from Europe. They mixed innocuous moneymakers—romantic fiction and spiritualist communications from beyond the grave—with stunning literature. Knopf went in heavily for the Russians and the French, introducing translations of Gogol, Kropotkin, and Maupassant. Ben Huebsch offered Hauptmann, Chekhov, Strindberg, and Gorky, as well as H. G. Wells and James Joyce's *Portrait of the Artist as a Young Man*; Kennerley brought D. H. Lawrence's *Sons and Lovers* to the States. The Modern Library, a fabulously successful offshoot of Boni and Liveright, published in its first years Oscar Wilde, Nietzsche, Dostoyevsky, and Maeterlinck; and Boni and Liveright under its own imprint brought out in 1918 an English translation of Trotsky's *The Bolsheviki and World Peace*. But the new publishers were also drawn to homegrown talent, writers they might well meet at the Liberal Club or a Village café, whose literary oddities or youth or radicalism made them risky for the established publishers. Alfred Kreymborg, Walter Lippmann, Konrad Bercovici, Van Wyck Brooks, Max Eastman, Dreiser, John Reed, Eugene O'Neill, and Edna St. Vincent Millay all published in the teens under the new imprints.

The fervor of the cultural moment, emanating at once from a market expansion and a political upheaval, meant that writers with negligible experience and education and no connections in the traditional sense could with some reason hope to place their work in national circulation. Of course, not everyone who tried the left-wing route succeeded. A hapless charity worker whom Rose Pastor Stokes had befriended tried to peddle her socialist stories of the poor through Stokes and failed. "I feel so *pained* & *hurt* to think that the stories over which I worked so hard, have been left to rot at the *New Republic*," she lamented. "I'm on the verge of going under from sheer exhaustion—Do let me know if they were thrown away." But the point still holds. That a self-taught immigrant writer should have tried, with the help of a wealthy socialist (who had her own literary hopes), to place her tales of poverty in an influential journal is evidence of unusually fluid influences.

Although the literature of the new was commercially viable, it still faced opposition. The new writing did well; it fed the bottom line. But its political nature brought it into conflict with the government over censorship law, and here there were problems. In the early twentieth century, censorship still meant Anthony Comstock, who in a quasi-official capacity zealously enforced until his death in 1915 the obscenity statutes named after him. The Comstock laws were initially directed at medical pamphlets that included birth control information, pornography, and papers advocating free love, but they were broad enough to be used over the years to ban from circulation and sale all kinds of papers, books, and journals. Even as the Victorian moral system that had initially supported Comstockery atrophied, the continuing zealotry of Comstock himself created a climate in which prudence ruled publishing.

Comstock had come to New York from rural Connecticut after the Civil War to work as a clerk. In 1872, backed by the Young Men's Christian Association, he began his crusade against the "obscene" publications that abounded in New York's streets and bookshops—pornography, pamphlets of contraceptive advice, spicy novels, and scandal sheets. Over the years, his animus against sexualized speech had, unquestionably, a chilling effect. Especially in book publishing, Comstock's ideas of obscenity conjoined with the tastes of the old guard of editors. Dreiser, to cite a famous example, had perennial trouble with the publishers over his "disgusting details" of illicit liaisons and abortions, details that now seem quite mild, and any mention of prostitution or out-of-wedlock pregnancy was bound to create a stir.

In retrospect, the gradual lifting of censorship appears as a slow but inevitable progression toward an enlightened age. Yet the opposition to censorship that came together in the teens was not preordained. It resulted from the connections between a small number of innovative publishers, left-wing writers already exposed to free-speech tactics and poses, and a liberal public that believed itself entitled to unfettered consumption of cultural goods. For the writers, the censors were simply another version of the police who shut down soapbox speakers elsewhere, and censorship fights provided more political opportunities to translate wishful identifications with working-class militants into credible action. Battles over the censorship of fiction and journalism were a means by which they could, in the free-speech manner, convert their professional situation into a political one. When they fought for free speech in print, they too became (at least in their own minds) revolutionaries.

In 1913, Comstock raided the offices of Mitchell Kennerley, one of the new publishers, and confiscated copies of *Hagar Revelly*, a novel about a fallen woman that was a tepid version of *Sister Carrie*. In the past, publishers had always folded immediately when Comstock threatened them, but Kennerley fought back and, represented by John Quinn, the lawyer who had enthusiastically backed the Armory Show, won an acquittal. When Comstock died, John Sumner, a Christian stockbroker, stepped in to lead the Society for the Suppression of Vice, which Comstock had founded. Sumner broadened the attack on the new literature, going after a novel published by Knopf and several "smart set" journals, Margaret Sanger's birth control pamphlet, and sex manuals sold in the bookshop of the *Masses*. The Comstock laws had traditionally borne down on small booksellers and publishers in New York's demimonde. But now the targets included legitimate publishers with resources to stand behind the work.

Censorship was a legal battle that was a contest for cultural authority as well, a battle over who was to determine the content of literature: fusty unlettered zealots who rarely read themselves—"ignorant postal clerks, clergymen of archaic convictions, and lower court judges of the tobacco-chewing, common saloon type," as a *Little Review* writer described the censors—or an "advanced" public of serious readers and eager intellectual consumers. Consequently, the fight for literature became a free-speech cause, marshaling strength from a connection that had been unavailable to the birth control advocates and small pornography publishers who were Comstock's earlier victims. Now that high culture was at stake, liberals and radicals joined to defend free commerce in ideas. The *Masses* editors, whom Sumner took to threatening, were delighted to find themselves free-speech heroes. They turned their case into a send-up of repressive authority, vowing to parade en masse to Sumner's office every month to read aloud the contents of each issue so that he might give his permission to go to press.

Kennerley's triumph laid the groundwork for further legal opposition. When Dreiser's *The Genius* went to court on obscenity charges in 1917, several years of experience in free-speech battles paid off in an organized defense, with Dreiser backed by the Free Speech League, the Liberal Club, and a coalition of liberal and radical New York writers. Although Dreiser's lawsuit came to nothing on a legal technicality and anticensorship politics virtually shut down during the war, the new alliance of writers, lawyers, and publishers would reemerge and play a critical role in the 1920s, when obscenity law met sustained—and successful—challenges from the defenders of books.

The importance the moderns accorded to battling print censorship speaks to how much this was a politics constructed from books, magazines, and the talk that surrounded them. In America, to affirm the modern was still primarily a literary act, secondarily a visual one: neither New York nor Chicago was a city of painters in the way that Paris was. "Words, words, mountains of words," Kenneth Burke marveled in his first days in the Village. The formative context for the bohemians was reading and writing: people were bound together partly by reading the same periodicals and each other's works. It was reading, most of all, that gave the bohemians their sense of themselves as artists and their convictions about what exactly was modern.

The early Villagers spent their youths reading for pleasure and instruction. Other mass entertainments were around at the turn of the century: popular theater (melodrama, Shakespeare, and blackface minstrelsy) and vaudeville traveled through the country, reaching even rural hamlets. And the cities were packed with amusements—dance halls with ragtime pianos, nickelodeons, and movie theaters for silent films, operas, and classical music performances. Nevertheless, this was a world where imaginative pleasure and curiosity came not so much from the eyes—as it comes now—as from the ears and the reading mind. The most common and dependable entertainment to while away the hours, for all classes and both sexes—the analogue to flipping on the TV today—was reading.

How these people lived in books! Memoir writers of radical sensibilities habitually included long lists of the books they had read in their nineteenth-century childhoods as not just primary influences but capsules of recollections, the titles unleashing riffs of sensations and vignettes. People who were adults in the teens had, as children, read great swaths of Shakespeare, Walter Scott, and Dickens. Dreamy youths had dipped into Goethe, Shelley, and Keats. Everyone had a dose of Walt Whitman. The men had read adventure stories, especially Kipling and, later, Jack London. And male and female alike, they all had devoured dime novels, the equivalent of pulp fiction, thrilling stories of Diamond Dick and Nick Carter. Theirs was the English literary upbringing common for their American generation—except for Twain and Frank Norris, few American novelists appear on the lists, not even Henry James. There was occasionally Emerson, but no Hawthorne or Melville (Melville's works were read as boys' books until the 1920s). The immigrants, of course, had read the Russians—Turgenev, Dostoyevsky, Tolstoy—and a number of them, too, had discovered the delights of Dickens. Both native-born and immigrant readers had often worked their ways through the canon of the late-nineteenth-century European literary left: H. G. Wells, George Bernard Shaw, William Morris, Ibsen and Strindberg, Maeterlinck. They cut their political teeth on the theorist-oracles in which the late nineteenth century abounded: Nietzsche, Kropotkin and Bakunin (for the anarchists), a smattering of Karl Marx, Theodor Herzl (for the Jews), the American utopian Edward Bellamy.

These lists show that serious American readers who came of age just as modernist prose was exploding in Europe formed their notions of new literature not from stylistic and narrative innovation but from a realist tradition that dwelt on contraband subject matter. Even accounting for the time lag between the United States and Europe, the most searching experiments in form went mostly unheeded. American moderns had little interest in the Decadents' explorations of the sensuous, fugitive nature of language; Conrad's experiments in unloosing narrative from nineteenth-century conventions remained foreign. Rather, the American writers saw their task as telling the truth of modern life, an act that, in their minds, amounted to revolutionary realism. A renovated realism presented itself as a solvent of bourgeois society, stripping away florid excesses of moralistic language and sentimental effusions to reveal the truth of social relations and individual souls. This social iconoclasm was one factor that precluded, or at least forestalled, the sense of exhaustion with the realist tradition that affected writers in Europe.

But a realism taken from the fin-de-siècle and given new life was not the only ingredient. This generation of readers and writers fused realism with psychological depth, imbuing sociological types and characters with emotional and spiritual drama. Grafted onto realism's inherent fascination with visible surfaces was a fixation on the evanescent soul, a mysticism that seems odd for an age that prided itself on its secularism. The French philosopher Henri Bergson is one source for the moony reflections on the spirit that wind through the pontification and poetry of the century's first two decades; his ideas on evolution as a series of stunning jumps effected by a mystical power of élan vital enjoyed enormous popularity. But there were also literary sources for the endowment of urban types with anguished souls.

In part Americans learned about the soul—especially the female soul—as a repository of modern yearnings from New Woman novels: Thomas Hardy's *Jude the Obscure*, George Gissing's *The Odd Women*, Olive Schreiner's *Story of an African Farm*. But the stronger models of inner exploration were Russian and Irish; indeed, it is to these two literatures we need look for multicultural influences on American letters at the beginning of the century. Both traditions provided languages of spiritual life that, because they were untainted by American Protestantism, could be admitted, watered-down, into freethinking circles. Through Jewish immigrant fiction writers (Abraham Cahan, later Anzia Yezerskia and Henry Roth), the tormented Russian soul entered the youthful immigrant hero or heroine struggling to reconcile the legacy of Judaism with the need to escape the clutches of smothering family and neighborhood. The Irish Renaissance, which roused considerable interest in America through the successful 1911 tour of Dublin's Abbey Theater and through support for the 1916 Easter Rebellion, also transfigured stock ethnic characters—Irish drunks and old crones—into psychologically complex, yearning heroes and heroines. The Abbey playwright J. M. Synge—with his deep pessimism and dark lyrical dialogue—had great influence on the Provincetown Players, especially on Eugene O'Neill, himself of Irish descent, whose movement from socialist doggerel to breakthrough dramas of family neuroses within the ethnic context was inspired by Synge's explorations of the Irish soul.

The amalgam of depth with realist typology can be sensed in

Alexander Berkman's *Prison Memoirs of an Anarchist*, published in 1912 by Goldman's Mother Earth Publishing Company. *Prison Memoirs* chronicles the fourteen years Berkman spent in jail in Pittsburgh for the attempted murder of Frick. Mixing genres, *Prison Memoirs* begins as an allegory of revolutionary martyrdom in the Russian manner, the narrative of a mind in extremis as the underpinnings of politics and morality Berkman learned on the "outside" fail him and he must construct a mental universe that can comprehend the surreality of prison. Berkman's book hearkens back to Dostoyevsky's *Notes from the Underground* but it also anticipates the postwar literature of altered consciousness—Beat accounts of criminal and drug subcultures, for instance. As Berkman educates himself in the anguished realities of prison life, his relationship with Goldman (the unnamed "Girl" in the text) fades and he moves toward close colloquy—relations that are suggestively eroticized—with his fellow prisoners. Yet depth remains tied to sociological observation: the story of a soul in torment is surrounded and enlivened by a human interest exposition of the hard-bitten types he meets, accomplished with a remarkable feel (for a nonnative speaker) for working-class American speech.

The reception of Berkman's book marked how much had changed in literary politics. For all the sympathy shown the men convicted and hanged for inciting violence at the labor demonstration in Chicago's Haymarket Square in 1886, the self-published memoir of one of the widows did not circulate outside socialist and anarchist ranks. Berkman's *Prison Memoirs*, written in an English inflected with tragic Russian accents, layered with anarchist elocution and American slang, and peppered with grievances against a self-centered New Woman, crossed over from a sectarian audience to address the liberal mainstream. It spoke to a modern reader situated outside the anarchist set, the empathetic "you" addressed by a critic for the *Little Review*, who stressed the book's universal appeal: "Berkman becomes so near, so dear, that it pains to think of him. You are with him throughout his vicissitudes; you share his anguish, loneliness, suicidal moods; your spirit and your body undergo the same inhuman tortures." For the reviewer, *Prison Memoirs* permitted politics to drain into psychology. It was a story for all "seeking, striving, courageous souls" who declared themselves in revolt—against capitalism and Carnegie Steel, yes, but also against the common plight of living an "empty grey life in this normal land." The ideological and didactic elements of the memoir disappeared in such a reading, subsumed by the soul yearning for freedom from convention.

Berkman was unusual in his choice of genre. Memoir writing was not yet the conduit for the emancipated soul it became at the end of the twentieth century. Poetry, rather, was the favored means of expression. It is safe to say that in the 1910s, the vogue for writing free verse— poetry that was unrhymed and unmetered—became what landscape painting had been for young people, especially young women, in the 1890s, a way to define oneself as an artist and to distinguish oneself from a family background seen as philistine or soulless. The position of free verse—itself a baggy term—within high literary modernism was complex: it was related to (but not identical with) Imagism, hearkened back to French Symbolist poetry, and aroused both the enthusiasm and the condemnation of serious poets like Amy Lowell, Ezra Pound, H.D. (Hilda Doolittle), Richard Aldington, and William Butler Yeats. But setting aside the formal issues, consider the tremendous middlebrow enthusiasm free verse elicited, an enthusiasm remarkable for what was, its champions believed, an avant-garde form, publicized by the insurgent little magazines. "The new poetry *is* revolutionary," attested a mainstream magazine. "It is the expression of a democracy of feeling rebelling against an aristocracy of form"—a fervor that horrified Pound, self-appointed high priest, who wanted to protect the art from loathsome populist incursions.

The release of verse from the "straight-jacket" of rhyme and meter did indeed encourage untutored readers to turn themselves into writers and free speechifiers to become free versifiers—Bill Haywood scribbled poetry in Washington Square and edited an anthology, Wobbly doggerel loped off into unrhymed lines; Margaret Anderson held a vers libre contest for all comers in the *Little Review*, judged by William Carlos Williams. Tugged and stretched by its audience, vers libre proved a pliable form. The new publishers turned out volumes of free verse: long Whitmanian lines adorned with profuse description, ornate sentiment, and thick soulfulness, or clipped lines of elliptical allusiveness, revelations of the inner life.

The "free" of free verse hailed the emancipationist ethos. The *New*

York Times linked free verse poets to political anarchism—not an entirely silly charge, since the Ridgefield colony, bohemian outpost and center of free verse, was indeed a hotbed of anarchism (although it was anarchism tending toward Dada rather than bombs). The openness of free verse circles to women made the new poetry seem the handmaiden of free love and woman's suffrage. In Albert Kreymborg's little magazine *Others*, published from Ridgefield, women made up anywhere from a third to half of the contributors. Entire issues were given over to Mina Loy and Djuna Barnes, and the apprentice poets Marianne Moore and Louise Bogan published there. Free verse was "free footed verse," a reporter for the *Tribune* found when she visited Ridgefield, modern women—freewomen—gamboling about in print like Isadora Duncan dancing. And as in Isadora's dances, erotic connotations abounded. Amy Lowell, who had a vaudevillian's love of publicity but was, after all, still a Lowell from Boston, was sufficiently worried about the association to try to copyright the term to keep it pure. For the *Times*, the revolt against syntax was a revolt against "decency." For the new poetry's followers, it was thrilling. "It is easy to forget," critic Helen Vendler notes of Mina Loy's vers libre, "how bold a one-word line was, and how 'obscene' it was for a woman to write nakedly about the hours of childbirth."

The convergence of realism, poetry, and a language of inner life created a new caste of literary aristocrats of modern subjectivity. "They burn with hot fire," Max Eastman wrote of the Russian Jews in a novel by Anna Strunsky Walling. "Their being is self-justified. They live and are sources of life." He, the pallid reviewer, could only marvel: "I used to wonder if they ever sleep, for I could not imagine them sleeping. As for me, I loaf, and smoulder, and dodge life, and tinker with trivialities." They were types delineated in the ethnographic manner of the nineteenth century—clothes, physiognomy, habitations—but also in the psychological manner of the twentieth—alive with pain and longing. The feminist, the prostitute, the revolutionary worker, the "rebel girl" worker, the poor Jew, O'Neill's tormented Irish drunks—these figures became available not just for readers' curiosity and sympathy but also for their identifications, as they coped with their own dramas of sexual, familial, and class emancipation.

P erhaps the most successful purveyor of art and life was the *Masses*. Published from offices in Greenwich Village on busy Greenwich Avenue, near the Sixth Avenue elevated railway, the *Masses* turned free speech into print for an audience beyond Manhattan. The monthly journal fused left-wing socialism with an image of downtown New York's conversational community. Between 1912 and 1917, when the federal government succeeded in shutting it down, the magazine became the country's premier venue for mixing labor and sex radicalism, always spiked with modern graphics and literature. Its pluralism was the eclecticism of free-speech association; its collage of political commentary and polemic, poetry, fiction, and labor journalism was the hodgepodge of a night at the Liberal Club or Mabel Dodge's; its implicit reader was an Emma Goldman listener, mentally poised in some small place for flight to some place bigger.

The *Masses* was the first Manhattan journal to base itself on the talk of the democratic salon, on editors luring into type conversations spun out extemporaneously the week before, as historian Thomas Bender has characterized the New York journalistic dynamic. Attracting contributions from nearly every up-and-coming writer of the day and some established ones, as well as cartoons and sketches from the leading New York realist artists, the *Masses* can be seen as New York's bid to capture literary sophistication from Chicago, where it lodged in the modern reviews: before the *Masses*, the important journals—the *Friday Literary Review* and *Poetry*—were west of the Mississippi.

The *Masses* began publishing in 1911, edited by a Dutch immigrant socialist, Piet Vlag, and backed by a wealthy Socialist Party businessman. Originally, the journal was nothing more than a formulaic contribution to the socialist press. Its pages sagged with chunky type; icons of brandished fists and allegorical illustrations of heroic workers and evil bosses embellished long dry expositions of socialist doctrine and the virtues of workers' cooperatives. With a circulation limited to Socialist Party circles, a scant ability to attract advertising, and a tedious emphasis on the cooperative commonwealth, the journal failed to sustain itself; the businessman withdrew his backing and Piet Vlag moved to Florida. But a few contributors—artists and writers—were interested in keeping the *Masses* going, this time as a different kind of publication. They formed an editorial board and decided to continue to publish as a cooperative, without any financial backing (to keep on publishing without money—"something nobody but artists would think of doing," quipped cartoonist Art Young, a moving force in the change). They invited—or commanded, as the story goes—Max Eastman to become the editor, issuing their funny ultimatum on a piece of torn-off drawing paper: "You are elected editor of *The Masses*. No pay."

Having come to the Village in 1907, Eastman was already an established figure, known in liberal circles as a mesmerizing orator (for the Men's League for Woman Suffrage, which he organized in 1909) and a writer in the leading monthlies. The journal had little to recommend it to a promising young man, but Eastman needed steady work and the board convinced him to put out one issue with an appeal for funds: if enough money came in, he could draw a salary. The venture succeeded; Eastman stayed on and within a few months he revamped the magazine, introducing sophisticated elements of graphic design (a layout that in the 1920s, Eastman claimed, inspired the design of the *New Yorker*), giving over the centerfold to drawings and cartoons, expanding the pool of writers, and greatly widening the scope of political discussion. Although cooperative ownership never succeeded in making the *Masses* run in the black, Eastman was such a charming solicitor of money from the radical rich that he published steadily for five years.

It was Eastman's gift to sense the existence of a national readership for free-speech sociability and an audience for the play of eclectic metropolitan minds. Circulation increased from ten thousand to, in the best months, upward of forty thousand issues. In his hands, the journal played up the vitality of free-speech bohemia; its Village and Ferrer School contributors wrote, as they boasted to their readers, unrestrained by either the limits of the magazines or the dogmas of the left. From the beginning, Eastman remembered, the journal enhanced his sense of himself and his surroundings. "The whole scene and situation lent itself to my effort and my then very great need to romanticize New York life and romanticize the revolution."

The original *Masses* preached a socialist creed nourished by republican traditions, a nineteenth-century faith in cooperation, reason, independence, and moral virtue, alloyed with Marxist ideas newly cur-

*Max Eastman addresses a
protest meeting in Union
Square during the Lawrence
strike*
COURTESY YVETTE
SZEKELY EASTMAN

rent in the United States. That brand of socialism, symbolized by the charismatic, morally compelling leader Eugene Debs, held together a variety of dispositions, from people committed to electoral politics and moral respectability to radicals, including the free speech radicals, who prized confrontations with the state. In 1912, however, while Debs, the Socialist Party candidate, was conducting a stirring campaign for the presidency, antagonisms broke out within the ranks, phrased in fact as a free-speech fight. Right-wing socialists sought to disassociate the party from the radical IWW by amending the constitution to prohibit any member from advocating violence or sabotage. Industrial sabotage for the Wobblies, if mostly an empty threat, was nonetheless their rhetorical stock-in-trade and they would not be reined in. Bill Haywood and his supporters walked out of the convention and split the SP, reducing the membership rolls by almost half, just as its electoral strength crested.

Eastman, like the rest of the radical intelligentsia in New York and Chicago, sided with the IWW. But the *Masses'* choice of him as editor indicates the board had more in mind for the paper than turning it into a platform for socialist dissidents. Eastman had inherited a radicalism in an American grain. Both his parents were ministers—his mother's ordination was rare for a woman—and Eastman and his sister, Crystal, were raised in an idealistic upstate New York milieu of liberal Protestantism, summer chautauquas, women's rights, vegetarianism, and literary discussion. Blessed with golden good looks and a quick mind, Eastman had nonetheless come out of his starry years at Williams College something of a neurasthenic, suffering from a bad back and bouts of lassitude (despite immense and abiding sexual energies). It was not socialism but feminism that galvanized him. Despite strong (if always unacknowledged) ambivalence toward the women's rights tradition exemplified by his mother and sister, Eastman's involvement with the Men's League for Woman Suffrage brought him to political life, turning a languorous womanizer into an energetic activist and intellectual.

As editor of the *Masses*, then, Eastman brought to the job feminist convictions, a humorous, wry temperament, some expertise in contemporary literature, and the sociable skills of a man-about-town well versed in the art of free speech. He made the journal, literally, an open modern space. He took on the typographical version of the crisis of ornamentation—the profusion of florid decoration, the Victorian *horror vacui* that in the old *Masses* resulted in crowded lines with scant margins and heavy, ornate headlines. Much like the modernists in Central Europe who spurned archaic Germanophile lettering, he replaced the clogged format with lean, stripped-down typography, the headlines different in size but not in font. With the help of the downtown artists he recruited—especially John Sloan—he created an elegant layout: clear headlines, generous margins, and widely spaced

The masthead of The Masses

type. He stopped the practice, universal to American magazines at the time, of chopping up columns to make room for advertisements—"ad-stripping"—thereby registering, graphically, the anticommercial values of the journal.

The effect was to liberate the writing and graphics from claustrophobic columns of exposition. The page breathed, functional, efficient, inviting—a space not to burrow into, as with the old paper, but to move about in, free-footedly, free-thoughtfully. Poems, short stories, cartoons were displayed as discrete pieces rather than subordinated to a dominant pedagogical purpose, so that the journal became a collage of offerings rather than a lecture. The images of clenched fists and heroic workers gave way to striking sketches and cartoons. "We wanted each object, whether art or literature, presented as a unit, in adequate isolation, unpecked at by editorial sales talk," Eastman remembered. The arrival of Floyd Dell as assistant editor in 1913 sharpened the magazine's adeptness at appealing to an audience drawn to metropolitan sophistication as well as political ideas; at the *Friday Literary Review* in Chicago, Dell had addressed a less politicized but similar version of this constituency.

Politically, the magazine was a forum for left-wing socialism, allied in practice with the IWW and in theory with Marxism, critical although not denunciatory (as were the anarchists) of the socialist parties. Eastman would always take pride in the journal's militancy, even as in his later years he moved to the right. At the time, though, the *Masses* was known more for its "impertinent" qualities than for political astuteness. The opening statement declared that the journal would have no part of socialism's sectarian debates. For "disputes" the editors would substitute "entertainment, education and the livelier kinds of propaganda," plain talk, revolution, and a literary workers' cooperative:

THIS MAGAZINE IS OWNED AND PUBLISHED COOPER-
ATIVELY BY THE EDITORS. IT HAS NO DIVIDENDS TO
PAY AND NOBODY IS TRYING TO MAKE MONEY OUT OF
IT. A REVOLUTIONARY AND NOT A REFORM MAGAZINE

And downtown *jouissance*:

A MAGAZINE WITH A SENSE OF HUMOR AND NO
RESPECT FOR THE RESPECTABLE; FRANK, ARROGANT,
SEARCHING FOR TRUE CAUSES

The editors signaled their distance from the preachiness that pervaded
both progressivism and the SP. The journal was determinedly free
from

RIGIDITY AND DOGMA WHEREVER IT IS FOUND

The first editor had done the job on his own but under Eastman
and Dell a new method evolved. Once a month, the editorial board of
a dozen or so met along with whoever else might attend to determine
the contents of the next issue. The meetings became another popular
spot of sociability, a demonstration of how conversational community
could accomplish practical tasks. "We had a custom of inviting our
friends to these meetings," Eastman reminisced happily. "Labor people came to it, people who were interested in life," recalled Mary
Heaton Vorse, who was often there. Articles and poems were read
aloud and artwork pinned up to be voted in or out; cartoons were cap-
tioned with one-liners the group invented amid banter and hilarity. "A
good part of New York's intelligentsia turned up one time or
another—and we always urged them to join in the voting."

A newspaper reporter in search of bohemian types found the group
tucked away in their lair: "A cozy room, soft, yellow light, lots of
tobacco smoke, a group of twenty men and women around a table,
much, much talk, noise and excitement. . . . Strewn all over the
room . . . there are papers, manuscripts, drawings, single and in rolls.
[Eastman] sits at the head of the table draped over a chair . . . [and
reads] a poem about some chap who says he is tired of writing. . . .
'Chuck it!' someone calls." Mary Heaton Vorse remembered the badinage: "As Floyd read along, Sloan would give a groan. . . . A voice
would say, 'Oh my God, Max, do we have to listen to this
tripe?' . . . Nothing more horrible can be imagined than having one's
piece torn to bits. . . . On the other hand, there was no greater reward
than having them stop their groans and catcalls and give close atten-

The journal's offices at 91 Greenwich Avenue (Glenn Coleman, "Mid Pleasures and Palaces," Masses, *June 1914)* TAMIMENT INSTITUTE LIBRARY, NEW YORK UNIVERSITY

tion; then laughter if the piece was funny, finally applause." Art Young treasured a memory of Hippolyte Havel, always testy, inveighing against a vote on a poem: "Bourgeois! Voting! Voting on poetry! Poetry is something from the soul. You can't vote on poetry!"

Later in life, Eastman tried to temper the carnivalesque image of the *Masses*. By 1948, when he published his memoirs, the Village conversational community had fallen into low repute on both the right and the left and Eastman was interested in undercutting the reputation of bohemian playboy that had dogged him since his Village years. The real work, he maintained, had gone on between the meetings when the editors made the rounds, pressing the writers to write, the artists to draw, and the radical rich to write checks. But Vorse remembered it differently: "There would arise from the clamor and strife of those meetings something vigorous and creative of which we were all a part." Whatever the role of the meetings, however, the seeming spontaneity of conversational community rather than disciplined editorship set the *Masses* apart from other political journals to its audience, making it and not, say, the contemporaneously published *New Republic* the emblem of the historic moment.

It is no surprise that the editorial group partook of Greenwich Village sensibility. "Bolder and freer," "frank and free": accolades fluttered around the journal, capturing the lyricism—and, not incidentally, the self-congratulation—of free-speech sociability. The more interesting question, though, is how the journal packaged that sensibility to readers outside New York, how it purveyed its iconoclasm to a national audience. How did the *Masses*, once a tedious sheet of party dogma, sell itself? To our eyes, the contents are hardly surprising and never shocking: anticapitalist cartoons, parodies of patriotic rhetoric and Christian belief, strike reporting, and calls for legalized birth control. While the graphic design was unquestionably arresting, the texts and images drew on established traditions of writing and drawing: the invective of European humor magazines, the cartoons of Thomas Nast, the sarcasm of college humor magazines, the sketch artistry of the Sloan/Henri circle, and the literary ramble among the poor, rendered in this case as downtrodden industrial workers.

Yet some readers were shocked. They claimed they had to hide their copies from family members. "Nasty, dirty, smutty, harmful, immoral, blasphemous and destructive," a Williams College student charged. "So loud, so bitter and so lacking in brotherly love," complained a friend to Rose Pastor Stokes. Older progressives chided Eastman directly. "Vulgar beyond anything I have ever seen in an American magazine," protested Oswald Garrison Villard, soon to be editor of the *Nation*. A philanthropist who had bankrolled Eastman's men's suffrage work worried in carefully coded Victorian cadences that the paper would incite immorality: "I think it is distinctly injurious to your great powers," he intoned, "to so deliberately throw away that refinement which is true power. . . . I fear it also invites to careless living both as to care of body and mind."

For these readers, the transgression lay not so much in what was discussed as in the mélange of topics, in the mixture, for example, of anticapitalist polemics with sexually explicit subjects like prostitution and birth control. There was an insouciance to the juxtapositions: "unconditioned freedom of expression," Max Eastman promised Mabel Dodge when he asked her to take over an issue. "Fill all space you can with plays, stories, editorials, verse, articles, suggest cartoons, anything you choose." The journal's defiance of expository conventions was made all the worse because so many women participated— as editors, like Dodge, and also as fiction writers, reporters, essayists, and poets. Their influence sealed the journal's alliance with militant feminism, antagonizing some readers but also making another third space where the sexes seemed to mingle and talk, easefully, in print. The journal constantly discussed issues of equality in marriage, access to divorce, free love, prostitution, and sex discrimination. The editors' unstinting support for legalized birth control in 1916 placed it in the thick of the battle swirling around women's right to speak openly about sex.

Fond readers, on the other hand, found the whiff of modernity tantalizing, even thrilling. They constituted the same market segment, we can guess, that Chicago's *Friday Literary Review* had identified. The editors took for granted the presence of a welcoming public willing to pay for modern work: "We have perfect faith that there exists in America a wide public, alert, alive, bored with the smug procession of magazine platitudes," John Reed declared breezily in his manifesto for the *Masses*. Advertisements on the back pages, one clue to readers' sociology, hint of ambitious working people, shopkeepers and immigrants, the upwardly mobile and self-taught rather than the well-heeled and well-educated. In contrast, say, to the *New Republic* or, later, *Seven Arts*, which addressed a tony liberalism with their ads for literary agents and private schools, the *Masses* featured in its back section sets of the classics (to be purchased on installment), ads for patent medicines to cure hemorrhoids and eczema, guides to "good English," and paeans to a sleep device that would alter the shape of one's nose ("You have a BEAUTIFUL FACE but your NOSE?"). Ads for classics of the literary left—Strindberg, Shaw, Wells, Ibsen—jostled with those for sexual-advice tracts. Self-help and literature converged.

"Most of alert young America," thought a feminist reader, was reading the *Masses*. There must have been something wonderful and inspiring that jumped out from its pages, although it's hard to get a fix on it now. The journal seems to have exported an intangible nexus of bohemian affiliations, some assurance that, even if you were immobilized out in the provinces—or, alternatively, in the depths of Brooklyn—you wouldn't always be stuck there. Georgia O'Keeffe, who must have known about the journal from the time she lived as a student in New York, subscribed when she left for home in Virginia. For the suffragist Sara Bard Field, her subscription kept her spirits up in the dreary months she spent in a Nevada desert town in 1913 establishing residency for her divorce proceedings. But not just young America read the journal. Abraham Cahan pitched the *Masses* in the *Daily Forward;* crusading editor William Marion Reedy, in Saint Louis, reprinted pieces in his *Mirror*. Sherwood Anderson found in it confirmation of Chicago's subordination to Greenwich Village in matters of the new writing. Louise Bryant sold so many subscriptions in Portland that, even before she moved to New York, Max Eastman knew her name.

The *Little Review*, Margaret Anderson's avant-garde literary journal, was the other magazine of the moment and it seems to have attracted a more upscale segment of the modern audience, although here, too, there are the tracks of a crossover readership. Anderson's advertisers, when she could get them, were book publishers, not patent medicine manufacturers, and the *Review* sold at the elegant Chicago department store Carson, Pirie, and Scott. Yet the *Little*

Review was on the stands at plebeian radical bookstores as well: cele-brations of classical music surrounded tributes to Emma Goldman's writings on modern drama. Indeed, it was Anderson's singular genius to mix, for a time, Emma Goldman with Imagist poets, but in doing so she implicitly depended on a readership who would gamely accept the mélange in the name of the new.

Both journals used a form of intimate address that linked the met-ropolitan writer to the reader elsewhere, transforming the Victorian educative paternal/maternal voice of the journal essayist into the voice of a friendly, helpful contemporary. The potpourri of forms, the feuil-leton character of much of the writing, the idiosyncratic editorial voices all implied participation in a community of free speech rather than membership in an audience for educative discourse. Anderson's readers saw themselves as the compatriots of a presence they addressed as "you" in their chatty letters to the editor. The New Yorkers issued an invitation to join them. "You know how Washington Square looks in a wet mist on November nights," begins a *Masses* short story, enfolding the reader into the setting of the journal itself, into an intimacy of bohemian knowingness between the reader and the writer. "From my garret window I look out on Washington Square," a "New York Letter" in the *Little Review* echoed. Thus was ventured, and at least partially secured, a relationship between a Manhattan-based cohort of writers and a national audience that the *New Yorker* capital-izes on to this day.

Reading these publications of the teens, you could find a map to bohemia. The new writing was a literature of invitation to a metropolis not closed in upon itself, a celebrity gala, but opening out toward the rest of the world. People had always read about cities and the young men and women from the provinces who went to them, but mostly as places that were dark and difficult. "Never yet have I entered the city by night, but, somehow, it made me feel both bitter and sad," observes Melville's Pierre. Instead of recoiling from the city, its cruel-ties and terrible solitude (one of Gogol's Petersburg clerks cries, "There is no place for me"), early-twentieth-century writing promised not just intellectual and political affiliation with those who had already arrived—the writers and the urban characters they created—but the sympathy of like-minded spirits in search of the same freedoms. From a small Ontario town a thrilled *Little Review* reader penned a poetic tribute to Margaret Anderson laden with portentous friendship:

> I have just had the January number.
> I feel as if I had found my companions.

From the empathies the printed page engendered, a reading person might mobilize an idealized self, a subject of rich possibilities fated to be joined felicitously with others. Like much modern literature, this writing enacted an estrangement from bourgeois life, but here the estrangement was softened and transformed through the admission it promised into a community of dissenters, into kinships wrought by a culture of letters. Creative spirits, stepping from one life to another, might find themselves in league with others from across the social spectrum who had taken the same steps, eager to weave bonds of politics, ethics, and sex.

6

Writer Friends:
Literary Friendships and the
Romance of Partisanship

The prospects for representing the messy truths of American life in print seemed immensely hopeful in the early 1910s. There was an easy fit between the imaginative work of writers and the analytical work of intellectuals and, in turn, between literary purpose and political alignment. "Every writer I came to know called himself a radical, committed to some programme for changing and improving the world," the literary critic Van Wyck Brooks mused years later. Nonfiction writers were the greatest beneficiaries of the gathering sense of literary importance; novelists and poets, after all, had long had access to a Romantic tradition that cast them as rebels against stifling convention. But nonfiction writers—reporters and essayists—occupied a humbler mental world. The infusion of politics into literary precincts heightened their imaginative prowess, their appeal to varied audiences, and their sense of their work's importance in American letters.

These literary radicals shared certain assumptions about the writer's political power. If, as Mabel Dodge claimed, it was only the separation between different kinds of people that allowed them to have power over one another, then the recognitions that writers activated were ways to bridge that separation on a much larger scale than the colloquies of free-speech salons allowed. In their books, articles, and essays it seemed that writers could not only intervene in particular political controversies but deepen democratic sensibility: through a lively citizenship that developed, ideally, from readers' empathetic responses to honest renderings of American realities—the afflictions, the struggles for decency and justice, the aspirations of their fellows. Books and magazines allowed the free-speech sensibilities of metropolitan intellectuals to pulse through a growing nexus of readers, transformed into compatriots by imagined affinities.

Everywhere, writers wanted to turn literary life into something big, loaded with transformative possibilities, Brooks's "changing and improving the world." One role that emerged from this notion of purpose was the radical "writer friend" of the labor movement, a downtown New York invention. Writers touched in some way by this idea of artistic commitment could differ from one another in important ways—in their precise ideological loyalties, for example (liberal, socialist, anarchist), their stylistic allegiances, the nature of their achievement, the degree of distinction attained. But they shared one key trait: political engagements shaped by bohemian ideals of friendship and conversational community. No doubt friendships have always been important to writers, but they took on added meaning in a moment when the apostles of the new announced that literature must be liberated from the rule of the elders. Friendships among equals, not loyalties to patrons and mentors, would be the vantage point from which one would write about the world.

Mary dear, there never was a time when we needed our writer friends to get busy, more than right now," the IWW organizer and Villager Elizabeth Gurley Flynn implored her fellow Heterodoxy member Mary Heaton Vorse. Flynn wrote in 1916 from the bleak Mesabi Range in Minnesota, where striking iron miners and their families had squared off against an army of U.S. Steel's private police. Since the 1890s, the labor movement had had middle-class friends. Progressive reformers had certainly worked alongside labor leaders for particular aims, but always with a sense that workers represented a limited if necessary constituency in the enterprise of American democracy. A few writers—William Dean Howells, for example—were sympathetic to labor causes, but there was no group of writers who could be depended on to contribute to workers' movements. And labor organizations, for their part, had had no interest in such support and had made no effort to win over writers or shape printed accounts of any of the great nineteenth- and early-twentieth-century strikes—to gain, in our parlance, sympathetic coverage.

The literary enthusiasts for labor, then, were novel figures, synonymous for both detractors and adherents with changes in the culture. As free-speech and censorship battles increasingly encouraged writers to see themselves in league with workers, metropolitan writers found a politically efficacious role for themselves, laced with the pleasures of crossing class lines, the promise of political influence, and the benefits of journalistic prominence. Partisan writers turned workers into a sort of proletarian "folk" endowed with hidden reserves of expressiveness and democratic virtue that could, once tapped, invigorate American society. Realism spiced with picturesque color and vivified by readerly identifications produced a literary politics that mobilized publicity and the media. Ironically, it was the support of the "capitalist press" that made this anticapitalist journalism marketable.

The emergence of the writer friends en bloc can be dated precisely, from the big 1912 strike in the textile mills in Lawrence, Massachusetts. Lawrence was arguably the most successful strike of the Progressive Era (inspiring those Harvard protestors of Lippmann's day, among others, to demonstrate their unity with the strikers). The Lawrence workers walked out in response to a pay cut that equaled the price of three loaves of bread, an intolerable hardship for families subsisting on bread, molasses, and beans. When employers retaliated with a massive show of force, anarchists among the strikers called in the IWW.

Lawrence was a new kind of strike, involving a workforce of recent immigrants—twenty different nationalities—and of women and children as well as men. No one except the Wobblies believed these kinds of workers could be organized into a union, let alone sustain a strike. But the greenhorns and women defied stereotypes, and the presence of women and children alongside male workers roused a previously unimaginable kind of outside support. It was at Lawrence that the

Wobblies, pushed by the brutality of the police against families, decided to send the strikers' children to stay with Boston and New York well-wishers, only to be met at the Lawrence train station by angry police, who attacked the mothers and children and the middle-class women who had come by train to fetch their charges. Beating up grizzled male workers in remote mining towns in the West was one thing, but clubbing women and children in a town in Massachusetts was quite another. The incident ignited protests from the middle-class victims and hooked the newspapers' curiosity. The family maga-zines—*Harper's, Collier's,* the *American*—sent reporters from New York who rallied to the cause. In this banner year of socialism, when Debs won a million votes for president, the writer friends' articles about Lawrence, interspersed with assuring reports of the IWW's repudiation of violence and its doctrinal embrace of "the brotherhood of man," moved even those middle-class readers who balked at the merest hint of literary anarchism. "The Lawrence strike touched the most impervious," an approving Walter Lippmann wrote the next year. "Story after story came to our ears of hardened reporters who suddenly refused to misrepresent the strikers, of politicians aroused to action, of social workers become revolutionary."

Essentially, the strike was a sensation because a pack of sympa-thetic reporters sensationalized its unfolding events. A collaborative creation of writers, IWW leaders, and workers, it was a turning point—the first strike to attract sympathetic coverage from mass-circulation publications—announcing a mutually beneficial alliance. In liberal and left circles, abhorrence of the dirty, savage Wobblies, armed to the teeth, gave way to admiration for their comradely man-liness—their strength, their reckless courage in the face of hopeless odds, their care and solicitude for women. "Gentle, alert, brave men," John Reed called the IWW militants. An aura of picturesque human interest enveloped the organization. Lawrence prompted a shift in the Wobblies' views as well. The union had never experienced anything like this rush of concern set off by shrewd publicity. Since the IWW's founding in 1905, the membership, hard-bitten, ill-educated men from extremely rough sectors of the working class, had viewed intel-lectuals as aliens and enemies. "The working class and the employing class have nothing in common," sternly preached a widely reprinted

IWW manifesto; intellectuals, in this Manichean view of class structure, were deemed patsies of the bosses. The fellow traveling of Emma Goldman and the free-speech lawyers had tempered the distrust, although pure proletarian action was still a premise of Wobbly doctrine. But the presence of such helpful middle-class supporters at Lawrence necessitated softening the line and pointed toward an organizing strategy of coalition rather than proletarian separatism.

The literary turn had further ramifications. The writer friends' influence created the conditions for the cross-class involvements that became a hallmark of radical politics in the decade. For strikers, publicity worked magic on morale, overcoming the terrible isolation that IWW organizers faced in the West. Confidence surged among the leadership and, to some extent, the rank and file. The strikers' success—a full settlement after two months, with pay cuts rescinded and wage increases across the board—was a stunning victory. "It was a wonderful strike, the most significant strike, the greatest strike that has ever been carried on in this country or any other country," Bill Haywood rejoiced.

Elation reigned; notes of rhapsodic fellowship and millennial change rang from Mabel Dodge's salon to union halls. The socialists saluted the strike as "the greatest victory in American history." The jubilation inspired a burst of successful organizing activity and free-speech battles in the West among all sorts of people: lumber workers, hobo migrants, Eastern and Southern European immigrants, Mexicans, Asians, itinerant construction workers, and housemaids. "The question of 'Will the I.W.W. Grow?'" boasted one member, "is now answered in the affirmative by the masters who add, 'and damn it, *Can it be stopped?*'"

Through Lawrence, the left wing of labor came to grasp the potential of the "capitalist" press. The melding of sensation (police brutality), the picturesque (the ethnic variety of the workers), and human-interest detail (children separated from their families by dire necessity) created just the sort of subtly managed sentiment that could float the story in the genial pages of the monthlies. With their story narrated by this sort of writer, strikers became people with whom a certain kind of middle-class reader could feel at home, not menacing proles but resourceful actors in a moving drama worthy of fellow feeling. This new way of telling a strike story domesticated the assault on capital by reframing a story of economic power (and the lack of it) into a narrative of human interest. Lurid versions of the outcast masses and the violent Wobblies faded for the moment, displaced by a plebeian epic in which class differences and political opposition played out against a background of sentimental unity.

Improvising with newly acquired tricks of publicity, labor leaders quickly understood that if journalists could transform highly political, even violent events into affecting stories, writer friends could themselves manufacture events that were precisely suited for human interest. Strikes could become spectacles for readers who liked their politics mixed with excitement and color; they could become living theater, with writers serving as producers and directors. The first effort in this direction was to orchestrate the arrival of the Lawrence children, malnourished and bruised from the police melee, at Grand Central Station. The next came with the silk workers' strike in Paterson, New Jersey, where the IWW moved in soon after they finished up at Lawrence. The proximity of the New York media (Paterson is only a short journey from Manhattan by ferry and car) and Haywood's many friendships in the Village attracted the moderns in droves. Writers and political intellectuals spoke at mass meetings, organized strike support, walked the picket lines, and wrote for the papers back in the city. Mabel Dodge motored out (one imagines her being chauffeured in her limousine because surely Mabel Dodge couldn't drive) and transported workers back and forth from the picket lines. Margaret Sanger organized the picketing. Hapgood wrote about the strike for the New York *Globe*.

Paterson saw a full integration of labor politics with bohemian theatrics. All together, the overlapping of the intellectuals' energies with those of the IWW created "a new field of force," in the phrase of the strike's historian. It was in this context that someone—no one knows exactly who—had the idea to stage the pageant in Madison Square Garden, with strikers acting out their own strike before a New York audience. The pageant was intended to raise funds for the strikers—a goal it failed to realize—and to bring the dire situation of the workers to the attention of New Yorkers. Pageants were enjoying a vogue in community theaters in the United States, but the moderns honed the middlebrow fashion to a sophisticated edge. With a cast of over a thousand workers, Reed's old Harvard chum Robert Edmond Jones, who had studied the new theater in Berlin, staged the drama in the manner of German director Max Reinhardt (in his day, a sort of Steven Spielberg of the stage): a spectacle featuring huge crowds milling around expressionist sets designed by another Harvard comrade, the action moved along by stentorian speeches delivered through bullhorns, all against towering backdrops painted by John Sloan. The pageant pleasingly evoked those modernist forms from the Continent that the Armory Show was displaying at almost the same moment. "In the future we may well find strikers spending their best efforts to get their cause 'staged,'" blithely predicted Mabel Dodge, the pageant's co-organizer along with Reed, her lover at the time. The Paterson Pageant was a financial bust and in the end the strike was lost. But in a sense, Dodge was not wrong, as the success of labor in the twentieth century came more and more to hinge on mobilizing middle-class sympathizers and the media.

After Paterson, metropolitan flaneurs further expanded their compass and authority as interpreters of the aspirations of the "other half." During the miners' strike in Ludlow, Colorado, the writer friends went national; several Village men hopped on trains to investigate the massacre that occurred the same spring as the New York unemployment demonstrations. In 1916, Vorse acceded to Flynn's request from the Mesabi Range and, along with another Heterodoxy woman, traveled to Minnesota on assignment from several New York magazines—an assignment unthinkable for a woman a few years earlier—to try to crack the isolation of the strikers, barred by public and company officials from access to the mails, newspapers, telephones, or telegraphs.

The scenes of industrial violence became places for metropolitan writers to roam, casting the light of human interest on the secrets hidden there. The writers' presence at labor trials had a similar effect, turning local travesties of justice into national spectacles of injustice. In 1911 in Los Angeles, two union leaders, John McNamara and his younger brother James, went on trial for murder in the dynamiting of the *Los Angeles Times* building, bastion of a notorious anti-union publisher. The McNamara brothers were widely believed to have been framed, and sympathizers made the case into a donnybrook as reporters descended on Los Angeles to report the proceedings and the plea bargain. Similarly, during labor leader Tom Mooney's murder trial in San Francisco in 1916 for allegedly setting off a bomb that killed ten people during a war-preparedness parade, writer friends, aided by a national letter campaign organized by Mooney's labor and anarchist sympathizers, magnetized national interest and helped expose what turned out to be perjured testimony and shameless collusion of the authorities.

Although it is possible to identify the role of the writer friends in support of these and other causes, there was no single model for that role. Indeed, three of the better-known writers—John Reed, Margaret Anderson, and Randolph Bourne—exemplify distinct variations of the type. Motivated by the desire to fuse art and life but in very different ways, each sought literary distinction within a context permeated by political friendships. John Reed—the paradigmatic writer friend of revolution—tried to invigorate realist genres with a lyricism born of fellowship, imagined and actual, with his plebeian subjects. Margaret Anderson's iconoclastic career was made possible by unusual relationships with women that lent her a critical edge of authority in an avant-garde literary scene dominated by men. And Bourne fed on his own experience of modern friendships in Greenwich Village—the "beloved community," in his phrase—to develop an ideal of a relationship that bound the metropolitan intelligentsia to the rest of America.

John Reed is surely the best-remembered of the writer friends, the Greenwich Village bohemian who expanded the romance of partisanship into international politics, first in Mexico, then in Russia. In the process he became a tourist of the revolution, literary explicator of faraway insurgencies. The bohemian about town turned into the revolutionary citizen of the world, equipped, as he (and others who followed him) believed, for instant political empathy in distant places, his populist friendships guaranteeing incisive insight. "His understanding of the peon soldiers with whom he marched and slept and went into battle was not the fruit of intellectual processes," raved Jig Cook of Reed's Mexico writing. "He simply felt what they felt." As a writer

Reed was good, but as a master of cultural politics he was extraordinary. Ever the journalist on the make, he used radical politics to bolster his limited talents; ever the Harvard man, he used his literary talents to generate inordinate intellectual authority. His trail of friendships, hearty if superficial, ran from the Lower East Side to Mexico to Petersburg. It was not that his political commitments were spurious. But he did usually manage to use lessons learned in lower Manhattan to turn an outsider's luck to an insider's advantage.

Reed first discovered the romance of partisanship in Paterson. He went out to take a break from work at the *American*, the big-circulation magazine where he toiled after Harvard. Although the trip began as a lark, not that different from a ramble around some poor part of New York, Reed's abiding search for a role to match his collegiate ambitions opened him to the serious possibilities contained in the occasion. The police regime in Paterson was so draconian that anyone on the streets was vulnerable to arrest, and within a few hours of arriving Reed landed in court and then in jail.

Journalistically speaking, Reed dined out on the prison term. Thrown into the fetid, vermin-ridden county jail, he found himself sharing a cell with a man who turned out to be the anarchist agitator Carlo Tresca. The next day he met Bill Haywood, a recent arrival, exercising in the prison yard. The other prisoners thought he was a stool pigeon planted by the police, but Tresca and Haywood knew him from the Village and vetted him with the IWW crowd. "I am a Personage in here," he proudly reported to an old Harvard friend: he was in love with the common men's warmth and courage yet, by virtue of being a journalist, still distinct from the mass. His writing took off; he not only reported the news but *made* the news. A Cambridge crony teased him about his Jack London derring-do: "I see the *American*'s circulation booming. 'Twenty Days in Hell' by Jawn Reed Esq."

None of this could have been predicted before Paterson, when John Reed was one struggling writer in the pack, doing hackwork at the big magazines. Like other Village intellectuals, Reed later recast his arrival in New York as the springing loose of possibilities theretofore only vaguely sensed, the joyful moment he came into his fully adult, fully modern self. But in fact, during his first years in

Manhattan, Reed's writing was prosaic. He wrote snappy potboilers and filler for the magazines. He failed to place his favorite pieces.

His gripping reports from Paterson, published in the *Masses*, alerted the New York editors to Reed's mettle as a reporter. When Carl Hovey, editor of the socialist-tinged *Metropolitan*, asked Lincoln Steffens to recommend a young man to cover the insurgency in Mexico led by peasant rebels Emiliano Zapata and Francisco "Pancho" Villa, Steffens vouched for Reed. Altogether, the *Metropolitan*'s interest in Mexico speaks to the mainstream journals' awareness, since the Lawrence strike, of the appeal of human interest blended with plebeian revolt. Subsidized by millionaire Harry Payne Whitney—at the moment one of the radical rich—the magazine by its very name promised something spicier than family fare; Mexico was just the ticket, with its exotic locale and peasant revolutionaries. And it was just the thing for Reed as well. Trailed by Mabel Dodge, at this point very much in love with him, an eager Reed, clad in a spanking bright yellow corduroy suit, took a train to El Paso. The baking, seamy city proved too much for Dodge (whose idea of roughing it was to bring along a satin-lined tiger-skin hunting jacket). She turned back, and a relieved Reed went on to cross the border to the northern desert town of Presidio, where government troops were encamped.

Revolutionary Mexico proved the making of Reed professionally. His dispatches elevated him to the rank of the finest reporter—even the finest writer—of his generation, an American Kipling (the *Metropolitan*'s ad copy boasted), successor to Richard Harding Davis of Spanish-American War fame. From the border, he set about finding a way to get to the rebels, going one better than the other reporters stuck in Presidio. Defying authorities who forbade him to cross the lines, Reed sneaked away, finally reaching Villa's army. He settled in with a cavalry unit—"La Tropa"—to swelter in the desert heat, dodge bullets, face down drunken threats, drink, and swagger through commandeered haciendas. In Reed's account, his hair-raising journey to get to the real story became as interesting as the battles. It was not just the quality of the writing that invited the comparisons to Davis and Kipling, it was the literary heroism Reed generated, his drive to get the news, his compulsion to test his courage under fire.

Reed made the revolution an adventure. You could even say he colorized it. He used human-interest techniques to touch up—if only lightly—stock peasant types into individual characters, but he also adapted elements of an older Victorian story of travel in primitive places. Reed the revolutionary sympathizer descends from a literary line of intrepid colonial adventurers, narrators both marveling and discerning, who bring readers to what seems to be a wilderness devoid of life only to reveal the human activity perceptible to the practiced eye. In Reed's 1914 *Insurgent Mexico* (the book that eventually grew out of his dispatches), the bleak Chihuahua desert, a trackless waste in the opening passage, soon brims with life and "color," bursts with anecdotes and drama, teems with characters "in all stages of picturesque raggedness." Below the torpor and poverty lurks "pageant material"—just like at Paterson. Reed's Spanish must have been rudimentary—he wouldn't have learned the language either growing up in Oregon or at Harvard—but the language barrier is never acknowledged. His simple peasants, bubbling over with talk and song like sunnier, more zestful versions of Lower East Side Jews, hand their stories over in excited, effusive English, littered with dialect markers (Reed is "Meester") and Spanish phrases (*"pobrecito," "quién sabe, señor"*) for authenticity.

The effect, as in other travel writing, is to enhance the writer's incantatory power over a mysterious countryside that seems like his personal possession, a Mexico according to John Reed:

One could see the square, gray adobe houses of Ojinaga, with here and there the Oriental cupola of an old Spanish church. It was a desolate land, without trees. You expected minarets. By day, Federal soldiers in shabby white uniforms swarmed about the place desultorily digging trenches, for Villa and his victorious Constitutionalists were rumored to be on the way. You got sudden glints, where the sun flashed on field guns; strange, thick clouds of smoke rose straight in the still air.

Toward evening, when the sun went down with the flare of a blast furnace, patrols of cavalry rode sharply across the skyline to the night outposts. And after dark, mysterious fires burned in the town.

Smart Harvard friends commented on how the author's subtly vaunted gifts of insight and empathy substituted for solid reportage. "It's so much Reed that I suspect it is very little Mexico," commented the Village playwright Dave Carb. Leo Stein, who cast a jaundiced eye on the American arts from Paris, was more severe: "I read Jack Reed's Mexico," he dryly informed Mabel Dodge, who was his friend. "He does not give the impression of having much and in order that he should play at the nozzle he must keep on filling up the tank and I doubt whether he can do that for long." Would the Mexican Revolution seem so appealing if John Reed had not had so much fun?

But the writer-adventurer also becomes a friendly political analyst. As daring as Richard Harding Davis or Kipling, he is also more interested in his subjects, more cognizant of the depths of their emotions, hopes, and sufferings. Reed's analysis of the revolution is simple and categorical. He is not especially interested in concrete political issues and maneuvers, which he places far away among bigwigs in Mexico City. What he sees, rather, is a premodern peasant rebellion driven by a spontaneous sense of injustice welling up from the people, prompting them to defy the tyranny of feudal lords. Villa appears as a Mexican Robin Hood. In reality, Villa's army was not made up of "simple" peasants but of workers, small ranchers, storekeepers, and day laborers—the complex class mix of a Western borderland economy comprised of capitalist agriculture, herding, mining, and railways. Villa himself was an operator and sometime bandit whose sense of political justice converged, as sometimes happens, with his self-interest. But Reed, working through Villa's handpicked translators and committed to a particular kind of writing in which his own heroic sympathies are central, sees simple *campañeros*. Reed's soldiers and *commandantes* are naifs, ignorant of or indifferent to the issues that divide the warring sides, gracious rural hosts and blundering commanders who run a slapstick operation, perching dynamite boxes precariously on the backs of balky mules.

Fellow feeling is the core of the analysis. *Insurgent Mexico* is, in other words, an early entry in the literature of revolutionary solidarity. Fashioning that solidarity, Reed focused almost entirely on men's valor, on the transactions of courage between him and his Villatista companions; women (and, by extension, civilians as a group) were unimportant to the story and the political understanding it created. True, the relegation of women to the background is a generic feature of war reporting, but the Villatistas were fighting in a region heavily populated with civilians, and that makes Reed's decision to exclude them particularly telling.

Place Reed's *Insurgent Mexico* alongside a very different text, Isaac Babel's near-contemporaneous (1920) account of another cavalry war, his diary of his experience with the Red Cavalry in the Russian civil war, and it becomes clear that Reed was not only making generic choices but that those choices blinkered him to acute realities. The comparison between Galicia, where Babel fought, and the Chihuahua desert may be a stretch, but it is not far-fetched. The Russian war, like the Mexican, was among the last large-scale cavalry actions in military history. Both were civil wars notable for savagery toward civilians, the commonplace use of rape, pillage, and mass murder to terrorize and punish noncombatants. On the Polish front, where Babel traveled, unarmed Jews bore the brunt of the violence, exacerbated by anti-Semitic terror perpetrated by the Cossacks who made up the Red Cavalry. In Mexico, 10 percent of the civilian population died, probably 1.5 million people, with another million driven into exile. Both Reed and Babel rode with the troops as sympathizers as well as correspondents, although Babel's assignment as a reporter from the Soviet wire service made his capacity official, and his veiled identity as a Jew made his position more painfully complicated than Reed's.

It is true that Reed wrote for a mass audience and Babel wrote for himself, furtively, in a diary. Yet the issue is not the relation to readers but the perspective—what these writers chose to represent—and in this regard, the two sensibilities could not be more different. The terse vignettes of the Babel diary push toward a fully modernist narrative of war as unimaginable horror, while Reed reworks late-Victorian conventions into what was fated to become the reigning left-wing idiom of revolution, shot through with redemptive valor. Babel, like Reed, felt the pull of male affinity, the yearning to join the camaraderie, but unlike Reed, he also saw what happened at the edges of the set pieces of fervor and bravado. The diary, for all its rending complexities of betrayals and loyalties—to the greater humanity of the revolution, to the human beings around him, to his Cossack comrades, and to their Jewish victims—bears witness to a full range of suffering. "A dreadful, an eerie town, Jews in their doorways look like corpses, how much more can happen to you, I think, black beards, bent backs, ruined homes . . . indescribable." For Babel, the story lies outside the epic action, in the silence after the swirl of horses and gunfire and men recedes: stunned faces peering out from ruins, bodies on the ground, shards of possessions everywhere. He records what happens at the edge of the action—careless killings, rape, desperate bargaining: "A painful two hours. . . . The girls run around the wet gardens half-naked and disheveled, importunate lust gets the better of Prishchepa, he falls on the girl engaged to the one-eyed man's son, meanwhile they're commandeering the cart, an unbelievable swearing match is going on, other soldiers are eating meat from mess tins, she: I'll scream, her face, he pins her to the wall, an ugly scene. She does all she can to save the cart, they had hidden her in the attic."

There is nothing like this in *Insurgent Mexico*. For Reed, the story is always with the stomping, shooting, riding, drinking men. The effects of war go unimagined, even if pressures from background characters sometimes intrude. What are we to make of this celebration after a battle, for example? "Everybody was drunk now. Pablo was boasting horribly of killing defenseless prisoners. Occasionally, some insult would be passed, and there would be a snapping of rifle levers all over the place. Then perhaps the poor exhausted women would begin to go home; and what an ominous shout would go up: *'No vaya!' don't go! Stop!* . . . and the dejected procession would halt and straggle back." The episode is quaint and comedic, a bit of ephemera of overflowing spirits.

In the United States, Reed's romance of partisanship met extraordinary acclaim. He had hit upon a lode of human interest. Tourism of the revolution, spiced with a liberal interpretation of peasant wrongs, appealed even to people in the upper echelons of the establishment in 1914. Walter Lippmann praised his old friend: "Your first two articles are undoubtedly the finest reporting that's ever been done. It's kind of embarrassing to tell a fellow you know that he's a genius." Always politically canny, Lippmann was bothered by how easy Reed made it

John Reed in Greenwich Village, c. 1916 CULVER PICTURES

for readers to "sit comfortably at home and know all that we wanted to know. You make it unnecessary for the rest of us to stir." A fan writing from a posh hotel commended Reed on his "pen pictures," which she found "perfect in their simplicity" and delightful in their "treatment of crudities"; she sweetly equated his defense of revolution with a popular account by Robert Louis Stevenson of his travels with a donkey in the remote French countryside. The president of Reed's New York bank found the work on Mexico "a valuable contribution" and reported with a note of bonhomie—just a touch of "chuff-chuff, pass-the-port"—that the men at the Century Club were impressed too, and wouldn't Reed stop by to meet him the next time he was in the bank? Editors vied to publish the reports in book form; Lippmann went public with his ambivalent admiration, at once puffing and twitting the "Legendary John Reed" in the front of the *New Republic*. Reed was a national celebrity, important enough, once he was back in the United

States, to meet with Secretary of State Bryan and President Wilson to discuss American policy in Mexico.

The next step was the war in Europe. The *Metropolitan* sent its smashingly successful reporter directly after the declaration of hostilities. To the New York publishers, watching closely, he seemed the man to produce the great war novel, a writer who could place himself, imaginatively and literally, in concourse with the common soldier. "It seems to us that there should be a real place at this time for a book even of short stories dealing with the soldier not as a fighting machine, but as a 'human man' experiencing extraordinary things under unusual circumstances," wrote a Macmillan editor to Reed, tossing out a lure.

But World War I, which might have capped his position as premier writer of his generation, instead pulled him up short, as he found himself unable to use the usual tricks to transform intractably brutal material. Even in Mexico, he had run into the limits of the writer friend's genre when Villa tightened up tactics and discipline and brought in heavy artillery, machine guns, and trains to move troops around. Reed could not adapt to ineluctably modern warfare. Leached of its "color" and stripped of pageantry, the revolution settled into troop deployments and great torpid movements of masses of people seeking water, food, and rest in the bitter wastes. Desperate mobs of refugees, that quintessential presence of the twentieth century, replaced Reed's robust *campesinos*. "A clamorous, dirty throng stormed the engine of our train, screaming for water," he reported. "Around the twelve immense tank-cars, a fighting mass of men and animals struggled for a place at the little faucets ceaselessly pouring." But such powerful passages are exceptions; mostly, he was "sick with boredom," and he escaped as soon as he could.

The flatness Reed sensed toward the end of the Mexican assignment overwhelmed him in Europe. Like all the other downtown intellectuals in 1914, Reed was a noninterventionist who believed that the armament manufacturers and their allies in government had led Europe into the slaughter, aided by imperialist and nationalist parties. He had counted on discovering similar views among the soldiers and civilians he met and he was badly disappointed. This was not a war that produced the conversational communities he had sketched around the Mexican campfires or that encouraged the hearty friendships that had set off his own empathetic responses so nicely. Rather than human interest, Reed found dreary capitulation to jingoism and nationalist fervor. He knocked around France unable to reach the front. The war was "ghastly," he wrote his editor, Carl Hovey, a "gray and unenthusiastic struggle" devoid of meaning. "I have never done such awful work," he confessed. (And no American did succeed in finding the form and the language until Hemingway.)

Reed encountered a war that could not be shrunk to the scale of human interest. For the first time in his life, he had difficulty writing. Indeed, his only animated dispatch from Europe was a diatribe against Britain, which he believed to be, despite its rhetoric of liberty, as warmongering as Germany. Sympathy for England was an article of faith among the East Coast liberals (although not in the rest of the country); Carl Hovey, alarmed that his star reporter was turning to political analysis outside his expertise, refused to print the piece. No politics, ordered Hovey. Find a front to write about, any front; get back to the proven ground of "experience." Yet when brought to bear on the actualities of trench warfare, Reed's techniques of rendering "experience" were useless. He ended his stint in Europe with a dreary sojourn in Berlin (as an American reporter, he was still a neutral at this point) and traveled courtesy of the German government to the trenches in Ypres. In a dismal moment, he fired a few rounds of artillery into the French line. It was a rote gesture of the writer friend that had worked before to make him part of the action. But now the act of partisanship turned out to be for the wrong side. When Reed's gesture came to light several months later in the States, it confirmed his reputation as anti-British and suspiciously soft on the Germans. The writer friend was persona non grata on the Western Front for the rest of the war.

Back in New York in the spring of 1915, Reed cast about for new material to revive his fortunes. In his personal life, the affair with Dodge was over, leaving a residue of rancor in their shared Village circles. Professionally, his career slumped as all the magazines, even the ones with left-wing sympathies like the *Metropolitan*, backed away from writers known to be strongly antiwar. A stint on the Eastern Front and in Russia, accompanied by a sketch artist Village friend, Boardman Robinson, promised to repair his reputation. Reed hoped the trip would lift his depression and restore the vital psycho-logical/literary connection to combatants that had animated him in Mexico. "I have come to hate Europe," he wrote his mother during the Atlantic crossing. "But of course, it will be different, and better, in the East. The Caucasus is something like Mexico, they say, and I'm sure I'll like the people." At first, the journey went well. He and Robinson landed in Salonika in Greece, a polyglot seaport brimming with the ethnic poverty that always enchanted Reed. He predicted "great stuff ahead" to Hovey. Writing about Salonika suited him: he roamed the city, poked around the poor neighborhoods, conversed with characters in ethnic costume.

Once the two crossed into Serbia, however, this war suited Reed no better than the Western Front had. His vexations bear upon larger limitations of writer friends abroad in the twentieth century, with lit-tle knowledge of the societies they wrote about yet a need to shape their material within the tropes of human interest. Reed's model of meaningful political conflict required a tension between the people and their overlords; he was incapable of grasping more complex divi-sions and antagonisms. So he saw the Serbs as peasants, and when he met urban intellectuals, they were so "saturated with European cul-ture" that they didn't fit into the schema. In his reports, collected immediately into the volume *The War in Eastern Europe* (1916), Reed and Robinson can never find the front, only its remnants: depopulated villages, trenches where the dead lie festering, crowds of numbed refugees. His writing trails through the devastated countryside in a desultory way, now through a typhus zone, past the site of a massacre, then into Galician towns where Jews board up their houses against the Cossacks. One senses the writer's listlessness—not just the deadened response of a traveler in a war zone but disappointment that this field is so barren. Bureaucrats, great-power politics, and anti-Semitism, not insurgent rebels, drive the action and then put a stop to Reed's travels altogether: the Russians, convinced that he and Robinson are Jewish revolutionary spies, put them under house arrest in Chelm.

Precisely because it confronts its own limitations—although unsuccessfully—*The War in Eastern Europe* makes a more interesting book to read now than *Insurgent Mexico*. At the time, however, it fell flat. Sales were minuscule. Back in the States, Reed's speeches across the country against U.S. intervention further constricted his commercial appeal. The author of pen pictures was now an antiwar socialist. Money pressures increased with the arrival in his life of Louise Bryant, the indefatigable *Masses* representative from Portland, Oregon. Right after returning from Europe, Reed had traveled to Portland to visit his mother and there met Bryant, who in short order left her dentist husband and followed him back to Manhattan. He supported them both, because Bryant was as yet earning no steady income. To pay the rent, the American Kipling now took on boilerplate assignments—slice-of-life human-interest and celebrity interviews. And for the first time, he encountered censorship. The *Tribune* assigned him to cover an oil workers' strike in Bayonne, New Jersey, and then rejected his angry account of the strike's suppression. Several stories and articles for the *Masses* and the socialist *Call*, now his only reliable venues, never saw the light of day because the government confiscated the issues for their antiwar sentiments. "How far I have fallen from the ardent young poet who wrote about Mexico," he lamented to Bryant.

Reed's vision of his authority in American society had long been bound up with his writerly ambitions, his politics inseparable from his search for literary eminence. After Mexico this vision seemed momentarily fulfilled: he commanded attention from diverse and sometimes antagonistic audiences, moved confidingly between bank presidents and peons, and spoke with statesmen. To the most gifted of the writer friends, America in 1914 promised, despite the Rockefellers and the Morgans, infinite receptivity and elastic tolerance.

But within two years, that opening was gone. In early 1917, Reed's most pressing need was to get away from the "desperate grind" of newspaper work. How painfully he chafed at his diminished provenance is evident in his self-disparaging complaints to Bryant. "I realize how disappointed and cruelly disillusioned you have been. You thought you were getting a hero—and you only got a vicious little person who is fast losing any spark he may have had." He planned to go with her to China, where Harvard connections in the Foreign Service and business could help him along. China must have seemed a sufficiently strange and vivid locale to make his work safe again for the *Metropolitan*; various warlords and reformers were contending in a bloody contest to preserve the 1911 republic or restore the emperor.

But in June, Lincoln Steffens returned from Russia burning with fervor for the February Revolution.

Reed heated up about the Russian masses. Here might be a "people" and an insurgency to accommodate his method and his gifts. Bryant returned from France in August, having been stymied in her own venture because the French would not allow women correspondents at the front. Reed convinced her to go with him to Russia. Bryant hitched up as a correspondent for a syndicate and several magazines, but Reed's reputation was too sullied for this kind of backing. Village connections, however, made the difference. The *Masses* and the *Call* gave Reed credentials, and Max Eastman and a socialite friend raised the money for the trip from radical rich friends. Shut down and shut out in New York, Reed set off with Bryant at the end of the summer of 1917.

Reed had not always been lucky, despite his Harvard cachet, but he was now. To many travelers at that moment, it was New York that seemed to be, surprisingly but indisputably, the capital of the modern world. But Reed sensed that another city, Petersburg, stood on the edge of transformation into a competing capital of the new. Once there, he worked his older roles—romantic adventurer and man of the people—so successful in Mexico, into a more powerful personage, the revolutionary citizen of the world. *Ten Days That Shook the World*, his impassioned story of the October Revolution, would make him, in the years to come, an icon of the writer friend in a greatly altered world.

There were, however, more idiosyncratic uses of literary partisanship. In the case of Margaret Anderson, editor of the *Little Review*, political engagement released in her a corresponding literary ferocity; for her, the moderns' reworking of the relations of culture and society, life and art also demanded a radical reinvention of aesthetics, the propagation of high modernism in a devoutly democratic context. On the face of it, Anderson and Reed are quite different. While Reed was the literary politico—we imagine him on the barricades, cheering on the comrades—Anderson was first and foremost an aesthete, destined by the zeitgeist, as she saw it, for the heights of the international avant-garde. Yet they both launched their careers from similar places in metropolitan journalism, tapped similar sources of bohemian inspiration, and shared readers. They imagined themselves in league with some of the same people—the IWW, Emma Goldman—and when life got difficult, they faced some of the same antagonists.

Anderson was the oddest of writer friends. Labor journalists and revolutionaries like Reed belonged de facto to the camp, but Anderson, while a supporter of the left, had little interest in realism of any kind and championed instead experimental poetry and fiction. When she first came to Chicago from small-town Indiana, she worked as a human-interest journalist, but the job bored her. Blessed with a temperamental aversion to earnestness and dogma of any kind, she was enchanted by European literature, classical and modern music, and linguistic inventiveness, not by urban types and strike reporting. Yet the political connection was critical to her work: Anderson, more than any other writer friend, demonstrates how, at this early moment, political radicalism could nourish high modernism, before a socialist realism vexed the connection. The equivalences Anderson drew between art, revolution, and a sweeping manner of living, analogies very much in common use, fortified her belief that a heterogeneous modern audience could respond to avant-garde work. The *Little Review*, a journal of poetry, fiction, and criticism that published some of the most eminent modernists of the day, was a testing ground for her faith.

Anderson has often been taken as a girlish art lover who played at politics, not knowing much about what she was doing. The blithe tone of her memoir, *My Thirty Years' War* (1960), contributes to this evaluation: the narrator sashays through pages of history and biography, gesturing breezily toward momentous experiences and influential friends. In her years in America (she expatriated to France in 1922), she garnered a reputation as an adorable enthusiast, an exemplar of what we would now call radical chic. Her looks encouraged the view—she was lovely and always exquisitely dressed. "She was so unbelievably beautiful, so vital, and so absurd," judged Eunice Tietjens, a poet who had pawned her wedding ring to give Anderson money to start the journal. "Margaret could never think, never distinguish one thing from another. She could only feel in a glorious haze." "Life to her was a rapidly taunting mixture of glints, hints, undertones, surface blooms, fleeting tints, portentous shadows . . . and misty heights," wrote the poet Maxwell Bodenheim, whom Anderson helped when he was starting out in Chicago. He repaid her generosity by portraying her, thinly veiled, as a little whirlwind of a ditz in his 1923 confessional novel, putting her in her place with a nasty leer. "He [the Bodenheim stand-in] knew that he wanted her body because it was the only mystery that she seemed to pos-

Margaret Anderson. From the cover of My Thirty Years' War.

sess and because he wondered whether it might not be able to make her thoughts less obvious. Her mind was a stumbling jest."

Like other smart women of the time—Mabel Dodge was another—Anderson fashioned a self-protective pose of splendid obliviousness and it seems to have served her well against the likes of Bodenheim, and more important detractors, too. Yet the facts of her life show a woman both decisive and committed. There was nothing hazy about her painful break with her family, nothing dilettantish about her struggles to support herself as a Chicago journalist, nothing indistinct about her quest to keep the *Little Review* going, and nothing unthinking about her choice to live more or less openly (with a painter, Jane Heap) as a lesbian. Her magazine was, without question, the finest collection of modern writing in the country at the time. True, her political allegiances dropped away after she moved to France and, although she detested the Nazis and fled the Occupation, her American anarchism never led to political antifascism. Yet to see Anderson as an upper-class woman flirting with politics is to miss the real costs her commitments exacted over time.

How did politics come to matter so much to Anderson, a woman raised by her upper-crust family for "the higher joys of country club and bridge," as she mordantly put it? Her intellectual influences can be traced to Emma Goldman, whom she met in Chicago when Goldman was staying there with Ben Reitman. Before Jane Heap entered Anderson's life, this was her most important friendship. From Goldman she learned about anarchism's cultural appeal: defiance of the philistines and the plutocrats, the quest for a capacious life, the political value accorded to "the great emotions" and the animated imagination. In Goldman, too, she encountered politics as a means of self-dramatization, a discovery that proved enormously helpful in pushing the *Little Review* into the limelight and defending it when it was attacked. Politics helped Anderson give greater significance to her personal risk taking and aesthetic daring. "Life is a glorious performance," she rhapsodized in the first issue. "In spite of the kind of 'part' one gets, everybody is given at least his chance to act." At the beginning of her editorial career, the idea of life as performance was an abstract proposition, but Goldman showed her how to turn it into experience.

The magazine itself was a performance, at once discriminating and beautifully eclectic. It spoke, in its very materiality, for Anderson's beloved art. Copies were bound in thick, velvety pearl-gray paper, graced by creamy rectangular slips of vellum, precisely hand-pasted on, with the journal's title printed in a clean, elegant modern type. But, in the manner of the moment, the magazine was "art" unabashedly interspersed with "life," in this case the life of the editor. In the *Little Review*, Anderson let the reader in on her thoughts and feelings, from her enthusiasm for particular classical pianists to her anger about legal frame-ups of IWW leaders to her difficulties in snagging advertisers. All these registered in the pieces she selected and in the diatribes she wrote but also in the pages she sometimes left blank in ironic protest—an essay titled "The War" in 1917 tops an empty page, with a dig at the censors at the bottom—"[We will probably be suppressed for this]"—and the advertisers' pages at the back of the June-July 1915 number contain nothing but a gibe on each page at some retailer who should have purchased the space. Jane Heap, Anderson's lover and coconspirator, once supplied

SUFFERING FOR HUMANITY AT EMMA GOLDMAN'S LECTURES

*Jane Heap. "Light Occupations of the editor,
while there is nothing to edit." From* My Thirty
Years' War.

two pages of funny little mocking
sketches of the editor's life under
duress—practicing the piano, riding a
bony mare. Was she twitting the swashbuckling heroism of the writer friend?

Anderson's editorial voice spoke in the
most intimate of addresses, teasing, defiant, insinuating, inquiring. It was a voice
formed in conversational community. At
first her Jackson Park bohemians carried
the journal along, but she learned to
bring in contributors from farther afield.
Early issues featured Americans writing
on the European avant-garde, and soon
she had Europeans—at least the
English—writing for her as well: Richard
Aldington, John Galsworthy, Clive Bell,
and so forth. In the free-speech manner,
she welcomed discord and peculiar juxtapositions. "Our point of view shall not be
restrictive," she insisted. "We may present the several judgments of our various
enthusiastic contributors on one subject

BREAKFASTING

TAKES HER MASON AND HAMLIN
TO BED WITH HER

in the same issue." Readers encountered sharp disagreements and odd obsessions. In one editorial Anderson criticized a Chicago literary critic for his view that Emma Goldman was a milquetoast revolutionary; in the next issue she gave him the lead to elaborate his complaints—about Goldman and about Anderson's literary taste, too. An essay on British modernism was followed by an appreciation of the Russian revolutionary Catherine Breshkovskaya. A truly incendiary issue in 1915 published after the execution of Joe Hill, the popular IWW troubadour widely believed to have been framed for murder in Utah, began with an outraged list of rhetorical questions: "Why didn't someone shoot the governor of Utah before he could shoot Joe Hill?" Why don't the Chicago garment workers (on strike) set fire to the factories? "For God's sake, why doesn't someone start a revolution?" And then on to "Reflections on the Art of Prsybyszewski," an appreciation of a pianist known for his interpretations of Chopin. After the call to the barricades, the next issue shifted gears to a lovely H.D. poem, "Late Spring":

> We can not weather all this gold
> Nor stand under the gold from elm trees . . .
>
> We can not see:
> The dog-wood breaks—white—
> The pear-tree has caught . . .

For Anderson, essays on Gertrude Stein, manifestos from Filippo Marinetti, paeans to feminism, calls for the release of political prisoners, and feuds over Imagism were all enveloped within a copious notion of Spirit or, alternatively, Feeling, signaling the end of the reign of the dead over American culture. If you'd ever felt poetry was your religion, been stirred by music, watched the flight of some great bird with awe, then, she urged, you should buy her magazine.

The pastiche, slightly madcap, was Anderson's adaptation of Goldman's ideas about art and life. And she plumped endlessly for Goldman in the pages of the journal. But Anderson's espousal of anarchism did not simply come from her infatuation with Goldman. Her rhetoric of revolution cannot be understood apart from her attempts to fend off the power of another, apparently unrelated discourse—the much-discussed "feminization of culture"—and the male condescension that came in its wake. Concerns about the influence of women and their insipid tastes, current in the 1890s, were very much alive in the 1910s, given new life by the emergence of modernism and fears that women would impede the progress of the virile new. Modernism was seen as the antidote to the saccharine and moralizing art of the nineteenth century, a decrepit culture nursed along, supposedly, by female readers, writers, concertgoers, and collectors addicted to its niceties and sentiment. In England, Ezra Pound and Wyndham Lewis and, in Italy, Marinetti—all whom Anderson admired—revived the identification of femininity with bourgeois mediocrity in the arts. And the threat of feminization still lurked at the edges of bohemia, a reserve of deprecation and malediction against women searching for roles of leadership. Thus when female modernists like Anderson fled woman's sphere for the salubrious air of the third space where women and men could mingle, they were running *toward* something—new kinds of work, new relations with men—but they were also running *away* from the designation "woman artist" and the sneers that middle-class women's cultural activity provoked.

The anarchist language of personal emancipation and the revolutionary power of art enabled Anderson to distance herself decisively from the negative influence attributed to other female poets and editors (like Harriet Monroe, her rival at *Poetry*) and to set herself up as a different sort of female presence. Goldman was a "role model" to Anderson in this regard, a female authority who spurned the designations of sex difference. Goldman's presentation of feminine identity, the way she comported herself as a woman who transcended the trappings and limitations that oppressed the rest of her sex, fed Anderson's fantasies of the lofty, ungendered soul. Politics was a means to this grand prowess.

The actual ties she developed within bohemia also sharpened her sense of vocation. As an editor, she saw herself as an avant-garde critic-agitator to a gathering of American moderns, composed not of the cognoscenti, the affluent connoisseurs sought by other high modernists—Ezra Pound, for one—but of readers like the working-class activists and intellectuals, newsmen and middlebrow journalists, obscure painters and sculptors she knew through her Jackson Park world and through Goldman. To be sure, she never lost a certain snootiness. "Everyone who came to the studio smelled either of machine oil or herring," she would boast of her years in Chicago in the vainglorious, faintly anti-Semitic manner of the rich gone slumming. Nonetheless, her indiscriminate socializing nourished in her a sense of creative classlessness that underscored her sense of creative genderlessness (interlaced with her lesbianism), a core self that thrived in a world of peers outside traditional relations of kin and marriage. "I have no place in the world—no fixed position," she would write proudly in her memoirs. "I am not a daughter: my father is dead and my mother rejected me long ago. . . . I am not a sister: my two sisters find me more than a little mad. . . . I am no man's wife, no man's delightful mistress, and I will never, never, never be a mother." Her literary confidence grew in proportion to the distance she traveled from polite audiences, family, and her debutante past.

The *Review* was at first structured along the lines of the "higher journalism," which Anderson had encountered when she wrote for Chicago's *Friday Literary Review*—a movement for noncommercial, taste-inducing nonfiction writing led by genteel critics. But she wanted to take modernism's appeal beyond a cultured audience. Quite early on, she cut her subscription rate from $2.50 a year to $1.50. "A great many of the people whom we wish to reach cannot afford to pay $2.50 a year for a magazine. It happens that we are very emphatic about wanting these people in our audience, and we believe they are as sincerely interested in *The Little Review* as we are stimulated by having them among our readers." The magazine always embodied a religious devotion to high art, with long essays on canonical writers as well as the European avant-garde that assumed readers' knowledge of the oeuvre. Readers on the left were sometimes unschooled, but they were also game to learn and they replaced those scandalized respectable citizens who canceled their subscriptions. More about economics and the class struggle! urged the former. "As for you, haughty young woman, may the Lord have mercy upon your sinful soul!" inveighed the latter. The fights in the letters columns turned the *Little Review* into something of a free-speech soapbox.

Late in 1915, the country began to turn against leftist writers, beginning with antiradicalism at the top. President Wilson's first speech calling for the country to prepare for the possibility of war equated domestic support for socialism, anarchism, and trade unions with a lurking foreign menace. In the rumblings of interventionist sentiment, the left and the unions blended in the public mind into a mass of pacifist quislings, immigrants of shaky loyalties, and anarchist saboteurs. The IWW's steely campaigns for migrant labor in the West, a labor force now badly needed in the mining industry as it geared up for war, met vicious reprisals abetted by state governments. Tom Mooney's prosecution in San Francisco signified an escalation of government activity against the unions.

Anderson felt the effects, but her politics were too grounded in her sense of cultural purpose for her to abandon them. Her political principles matched deep requirements of her temperament. In the end, her allegiance to anarchism in general and the IWW in particular cost her support from her major financial backer, and subscriptions fell also. But Anderson held firm: "I like these IWW people a lot," she declared. "They are not only offering an efficient program of labor; they are getting close to a workable philosophy of life." After the Joe Hill issue, police detectives descended on the *Little Review* offices looking for signs of a revolutionary conspiracy, yet she was undeterred. She continued to publicize Emma Goldman's ideas and travails and took up Tom Mooney's defense. From Boston, poet Amy Lowell offered money on the condition that the *Little Review* purge anarchism from its pages, but Anderson refused. In summer 1916, lacking money for the rent, she set up a tent camp on the shores of Lake Michigan with a retinue of women friends and children, a female mise-en-scène that proclaimed Anderson's stubborn gaiety. Bohemian friends hiked out to free speechify on Schoenberg, Freud, modernist painting, and "group action and socialism" and to pin submissions for the journal on the tent flaps.

Anderson's enthusiasm for Emma Goldman flagged as Goldman, pressured by her own political troubles, retreated to a doctrinaire left-wing position on culture and scorned Anderson's defense of "art for art's sake." The rift began early in 1916, when Anderson fell in love with Jane Heap, whom she cast as an arty rival to Goldman the politico. After summer in the tent camp, she and Heap moved the journal out to San Francisco for the winter, helped by the San Francisco anarchists. In 1917, the pair made a bid to resurrect the journal and catapult into the big time by moving the *Little Review* to New York.

Lesbians, although tolerated in Village circles, were never wholly comfortable in the compulsively heterosexual surroundings, and in New York tension developed between Heap and Anderson and the downtown crowd, many of them also burdened by political worries. The pair was perhaps too ironic for the downtown writers, whose sense of historic mission was increasingly tragic and portentous. "We were considered heartless, flippant, ruthless," she reported later. "Because we could always laugh we were always suspected of being frivolous." The couple lived at the edge of the Village on Fourteenth Street and socialized only sporadically, more often turning inward to their own conversational community of two. But their political interests, if waning, still led them to the Ridgefield colony and Dada in New Jersey, where homosexuality may have found greater acceptance and where free expression had shucked off any adherence to political discipline. Elsa von Freytag-Loringhoven, something of a Dada mascot for Man Ray and Duchamp, became a kind of pet project of living art, to feed, shelter, and encourage. (A vagrant, impoverished German baroness, Freytag-Loringhoven was a proto–performance artist who paraded regularly in the evenings in Washington Square with her hair half shaved and shellacked in vermilion, face smeared with yellow powder, lips painted black, fur coat or Scottish kilt adorned with Kewpie dolls, stuffed birds, flattened tin cans, or cigarette packages. For head wear she sported a coal scuttle, a military helmet, and once a birthday cake.)

These were difficult years. Financial strain plagued Anderson's New York adventure from the start. She and Heap confided their troubles to distant readers: Please renew quickly, Anderson appealed, and "will any of you who are overburdened with money contribute a little? It is so terribly hard to get started in a new city." The consummate self-dramatist found that her sense of narrative in the city failed her altogether. She was too lonely, and there was no lyrical story as there had been in Chicago. "It wasn't like a beginning in New York. It was like an ending in the tomb."

At this low point, she took on Ezra Pound as foreign editor, although retaining control of the journal herself. Pound brought with him a guarantee of money from his friend and backer, John Quinn, the conservative New York lawyer and art collector with a love of the avant-garde; he also promised to bring the *Little Review* "the most creative work of modern London and Paris." Pound, the upstart American in England, had already allied himself with a string of little magazines to promote his aesthetic program. At the moment looking to outmaneuver his rivals in the poetry world, Pound was drawn to the prospect of a Manhattan redoubt. Arrogant and considered by many "unbelievably pretentious" (the words are those of Walter Lippmann, who met him in London) and having burned many bridges in the poetry world, he was hard up for allies. But Anderson was excited about a mainline to Europe. And Pound did not disappoint: the very first issue he edited featured Yeats's "The Wild Swans at Coole."

Pound's relationship to the female avant-garde and, by extension, to Anderson was complicated. He seems a quintessential misogynist, not just a sexist (in our terms) but a man with an explicit repugnance for women. His contempt, however, was mitigated by a tincture of respect for the vanguard feminist, the "freewoman" who upset traditional morality in the name of advancing Life. Still, he believed freewomen were getting out of hand, acquiring too much power in modernist locales—as poets, writers, editors, and patrons. In language redolent of the feminization discussion, he blasted both the "sugar teat optimism" of the women who, in his opinion, overran the poetry world and the emasculated sexuality of the men who let them. If he could have his own review, he suggested hopefully to John Quinn, women writers might be banned altogether from its pages. He had already taken over one English journal edited by feminists. From London, the *Little Review*, run by two women down on their luck, must have looked like an easy mark.

Yet Anderson held her own with the man of genius. Although the manifest content of her leftist politics faded, her free-speech radicalism still fortified her with psychological ballast and a distinct set of bonds and commitments, even if they were increasingly metaphorical. Pound got his pages and the satisfaction of seeing his compatriots' work published in the United States, and for a time he overran the journal with his harangues and hectoring disquisitions. But he failed to take control and, one senses from his letters, even came to respect Anderson's savvy and judgment.

Interestingly, Anderson seems to have been impervious to Pound's contempt for women editors and poets—the "gynocracy" was his term of derision—perhaps because her anarchism had immunized her to slurs on lady art lovers. And her own experiences with modern American audiences, however untenable her democracy of readers finally proved, left her unmoved by Pound's vision of an austere and exclusive society of visionary artists and enlightened patrons. Her readers, in fact, were not satisfied with Pound's exclusive literary offerings and protested that they missed Anderson and the communal spirit of the journal. It was as if they were calling her to account for harming a shared enterprise. "The spirit of the old *Little Review* is dead," a college professor complained. His students, once captivated by the magazine's youth and spontaneity, were bored by Pound. "When I compare the first year of the *Little Review* with the present numbers I feel sad," another reader informed her, and a Ridgefield poet, Lola Ridge, wrote in to complain directly about the foreign editor, "his vituperations," his destructive energy. Pound and Quinn tried to moderate the editors' frankness with readers—stop telling people you're poor, they urged, keep quiet about pawning the ring to put out the issue—but she and Jane Heap refused. She was too fond of those anarchist readers, whose subscriptions saved the journal from penury in the grimmest months. "Vive the anarchists!" she wrote. The women were cheeky, complained Pound. Too damn fresh, expostulated Quinn.

As a cultural position, Anderson's was not unlike Mabel Dodge's: both women were impresarios, Dodge of speech and Anderson of print. Both presided over switching points in modern culture, shunting people, artworks, and movements here and there to unusual audiences in unlikely destinations. Theirs was a milieu where smart women could find power on the margins and then emerge at the center as authorities to be reckoned with. As free speech and free expression buckled under the pressure of war politics, however, Anderson's capacities to preside were stretched thin.

R andolph Bourne's relationship to the partisan role that Reed and Anderson tapped was always ambivalent. A brilliant thinker, gifted in friendship, and like John Reed fated for an early death, Randolph Bourne might be seen as an American member of the doomed generation of golden young men of 1914, a counterpart to Wilfred Owen in England or Charles Péguy in France. Although Bourne did not go to war, his life was suddenly cut off when he died at the age of thirty-two in the terrible influenza epidemic that swept through an exhausted world in 1918. He made his career as a political writer and he ended a political writer, although he often found the cultural politics of the moment depressing and spurious. He, too, wanted to write in ways that would change people's minds and lives, stir them to criticism and action. His search for that enlarged part for the writer led him all around New York, from the liberal mainstream to the downtown radicals and out to the provinces, only to discover his most meaningful political inspiration in the realm of friendship.

When Bourne returned to New York from his postcollege tour of Europe in 1914, he wanted to write, but he had difficulty imagining just whom he could write for. None of the obvious venues suited. The *Atlantic*, where he had published his essays on youth while he was at Columbia, must have seemed prim and pallid to a man charged by the ideas of the European socialists he had met abroad. But neither could he project himself into the milieu of reportage that supported the downtown writer friends. The theatrics of solidarity with the people were not in his nature and the form of his writing was not exactly "new." He favored the short essay and never dabbled in free verse or colorful descriptions of "life." He was analytical and pensive, a fastidious craftsman (a friend recalled him rewriting his essays twenty, thirty times) given to elegantly phrased generalities. So initially he had difficulty finding a place in a literary market that valued writing that was fast, loose, and embellished with social detail.

But the brilliant Columbia graduate would not be allowed to falter, at least not yet. Someone—perhaps his Columbia teacher Charles Beard, perhaps Walter Lippmann—secured him a staff job at the *New Republic*, a position that conferred prestige and a regular salary. In

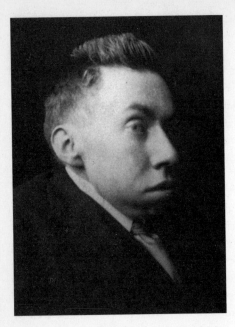

Randolph Bourne, c. 1916
RANDOLPH BOURNE PAPERS,
RARE BOOK AND MANUSCRIPT
LIBRARY, COLUMBIA
UNIVERSITY

accepting the offer, Bourne, a marvelous talker, could look forward eventually to conversing with barons of government, finance, and law. Herbert Croly founded the journal in 1914 to promote a critical role for progressive intellectuals in the nation's affairs. He aimed the *New Republic* at a select slice of the modern audience, the best and the brightest, "a strategic elite" with direct political influence and power, an axis of reform that ran from lower Manhattan to Washington—not from Greenwich Village to the Lower East Side or Paterson, New Jersey.

To Bourne, the gathering of brilliant young men under Croly— the *New Republic* staff writers were all men, although there were a few female contributors—undoubtedly promised satisfactions remembered from his circle of friends at Columbia. This was a very different kind of operation from the *Masses* or the *Little Review*. Financed by millionaire progressives and housed in Chelsea, north of Greenwich Village, the journal's office resembled a gentleman's club: a four-story brick townhouse with an opulent library, a French chef in the kitchen, and a paneled dining room where distinguished visitors chatted with the staff. Such environs were not designed for free-speech sociability, but then, Bourne had never been impressed by free-speech sociability, at least as he had encountered it at the Liberal Club, the derring-do of radicals "who talk with a bravado as if they were doing the most desperate thing in the world to be Socialists at all." His brush with British and French intellectuals had made him long for a "much more direct and definite and intellectual" political life at home, on "a much higher plane." He thought he had found it in a journal that billed itself as at once experimental and devoted to "sound and disinterested thinking."

In 1914, radicals and liberals of Croly's and Lippmann's bent—progressive, sympathetic to labor and social welfare—enjoyed something approaching concord. Certainly there were flash points of disagreement, but overall the conviction that men of goodwill sought "a more spacious order of living" joined in amity people who would, once America entered the war, cross the street in order to avoid speaking. Croly himself was an original thinker with a powerful vision of New York as a capital of ideas; he had been a contemporary of Hapgood's at Harvard and had studied with William James, whose work Bourne revered. The journal's literary editor, Frances Hackett, had been Floyd Dell's mentor at the *Friday Literary Review* in Chicago. And Walter Lippmann, the leading writer and, at age twenty-five, a certifiable "youth" in the group, must also have seemed to Bourne something of a kindred soul. Lippmann at this point in his life still had a certain experimental reputation from passing through the Village. He was, after all, a fellow *révolté* of the Ivy League, he was a friend of Mabel Dodge, he had helped at the Paterson Pageant, and he had even marched with the Ferrer crowd to protest Frank Tannenbaum's arrest.

The magazine's position was set just far enough left of the progressive consensus to be piquant. Bourne, with his socialist background reassuringly vague, a man pleasingly legitimated by his *Atlantic* and Columbia associations, must have promised the magazine a reserve of tactfully modulated irreverence. As it turned out, Bourne could not quite adapt to the expectations. The *New Republic* wanted critical thinking, Croly assured him, absolutely! But criticism in the journal required a dose of patriotism to make it "effective"—that key term of insider politics. "We have got to be thoroughly critical," he allowed, but at the same time there had to be "a positive impulse behind our criticism." Initially, Croly's admonitions did not trouble Bourne. The magazine seemed a charmed circle, an incomparable school of writing where he once again played the student role that had brought him such glory at Columbia.

Bourne, then, like John Reed, began his career as a heavily sponsored Ivy League man slated for considerable achievements. But even golden boys could run into trouble in the New York literary world, trying to outrun the pack. Soon Bourne found himself relegated to the magazine's margins. He failed to garner admission into the journal's inner circle, the select few who chatted with important guests over lunch. He wanted to write about literature, but the choicest books went to more powerful editors and his longer articles were rarely printed. Those essays that were accepted often appeared as humble unsigned contributions. A fairly low-ranking staff member, he found little opportunity to slip his opinions into the cracks of conversations with judges and politicians, and in any case the lure of chatting with the powerful diminished. He was looking for a politics that was populated, dense with intent talkers, not a room of deferential listeners presided over by a tribune of powerful experts.

Shut out of cultural criticism, his forte, he carved out a niche as a writer on progressive educational reform, a line of inquiry that connected his work to his Columbia teacher John Dewey's theory of "learning by doing." Bourne reported on a program in progressive education in the public schools of Gary, Indiana, where the superintendent, a Dewey disciple, was implementing progressive ideas about educating the "whole" child. The Gary schools aimed to be a "preparation for life," divided into components of work-study-play. Some students learned chemistry by testing the town's water while others worked in vocational shops and others played on the playground or in the gymnasium. It all sounds familiar now, but in 1915, movements from one class to another, the principle that learning should be proximate to experience, and even the glass partitions and wide, sunny hallways in Gary's model schools were serious departures from the educational norms, which still depended heavily upon memorization, rote movement, and deadening recitation.

Bourne's excitement about Gary did not just come from seeing his teacher's ideas put into practice. His year in Europe had made him eager to meld ideas with politics; his relationships with Greenwich Village feminists, especially his dear friend Alyse Gregory, made him all the more wistful to join his beliefs to work with others. "It would be so glorious to be 'in' something, or making something go, or at least connect up with something or somebody," he mused. Furthering the cause of educational reform through his writing seemed to provide a way to be something more than a staff writer; it was a way to be " 'in' something" that involved lots of people, not just a tiny elite mulling over the country's problems from the empyrean heights of the *New Republic*. When the Gary superintendent, hired by the New York City school board as a consultant, attempted to bring the system to public schools in the Bronx, furious controversy erupted between reformers in favor of the Gary plan and working-class parents, aided by Tammany pols, who believed progressive schools would deny their children a proper education in the three Rs.

For all his longings to participate, however, Bourne was not comfortable racing around the city from meeting to meeting with Henrietta Rodman (the feminist schoolteacher who had caused such a fracas at the Liberal Club) and Agnes de Lima, an educational reformer who became a new friend. He backed off into his writing, packaging the Gary articles and other essays on education in two books. Disappointment clouded the episode, as the reformers lost the battle in New York. He felt he had been not much help in any case, and the books were, at best, modest successes for a young man who had published his first work in the *Atlantic* when he was a college sophomore. He must have been comparing himself with his literary peers, dashing about the country and the world. There was something dutiful and plodding about the essays on education, for all they provided a longed-for bond between "the experimental life" and politics. Bourne himself judged the education writing "a fearful thing": "I tried to be official and descriptive and to quench all unqualified enthusiasm, with the result that I am duller than the most cautious schoolmarm." The furrow was narrow and monotonous and there was little chance to deviate.

The coolness that developed between Bourne and the *New Republic* has been attributed to the magazine's drift toward a pro-war position, but the problems ran deeper. There was a more general feeling that there was some mark—of responsibility? achievement?—against which Bourne had failed to measure up, a feeling to which Bourne, his confidence shaken, was not immune. The editors refused an essay he wrote for the special 1915 supplement on women's suffrage, even though feminism and suffrage were, through his acquaintance with Alyse Gregory and his knowledge of the British situation, not only passions but specialties with him. He griped ceaselessly to friends about his low status and thwarted ambitions; the proof of the matter, he told Gregory, was when he received his weekly issue in the mail. "Its coming . . . always gives my proud spirit the awareness that I am having nothing to say about its policy, and that I am a very insignificant retainer of its staff. I haven't done anything to deserve the high place I would like, but this only makes the cut all the deeper." Rivalry afflicted him: he compared his old youth pieces, collected in one volume, invidiously to Lippmann's *Drift and Mastery* (1914), "a book one would have given one's soul to have written." After two years, he had written "nothing at all of permanence." He remained merely "a promising young author."

For Bourne, as for other radicals, the liberal shift toward supporting American intervention in the war proved his undoing in the mainstream press. At the same time, the crisis also released him from the tether of polite discourse. As debate over American involvement mounted, Bourne urgently wanted to participate, but Croly and Lippmann kept him on the education beat. Their reluctance—and the "suave and discreet disapproval" of coeditor Philip Littell—signaled that they had sized up Bourne correctly: he could blunt the edge of his radicalism to write on many subjects, but not on war. The editors stoutly favored the Allies, believed that U.S. interests were tied to those of Britain, and saw some kind of engagement—if not outright war, then benevolent neutrality toward the Allies and participation in a settlement—as a chance for America to join the great European nations on the world stage. It was not just the prospect of exercising power that drew these progressives to Wilson but the hope for implementing, within the framework of wartime emergency, the progressive agenda they had long advocated: central economic planning, socializing goods and services, setting aside the profit motive for the greater good. What began with war could end with a grand peace: "We stand at the threshold of a collectivism which is greater than any as yet planned by a socialist party," Lippmann wrote a month before America's declaration of war. To stand aside was unthinkable; both idealism and realpolitik favored intervention.

Bourne saw in all the jockeying for an interventionist rationale a bid to paper over the literal disaster of the war with abstract consolation. Croly and Lippmann, he believed, had fooled themselves into thinking they were leading public opinion, shaping the outcome with reason, when in fact they were acquiescing to the primitive force of nationalism. They were obsessed, he wrote his friend Elsie Clews Parsons, a fellow *New Republic* writer, "with the idea of themselves controlling the war-technique in a democratic manner . . . everything polite, well-bred, humane, enlightened." Edged out of discussions in the magazine, he slipped the leash to write an antiwar essay in *Lippincott's Monthly*, inquiring why a civilization (Germany) that only recently had been held up as a model of culture and learning should now be vilified as warlike and ruthless. He persuaded his old editor at the *Atlantic*, Ellery Sedgwick, to print an essay with which the Brahmin gentleman profoundly disagreed, "Trans-National America," an eloquent defense of ethnic pluralism and open immigration that proposed a benign, nonmilitaristic nationalism based on America's role as the first truly international society. Reluctantly, one imagines, Croly published in the *New Republic* Bourne's piece questioning idealizations of England as a model of democracy. Such opinions pushed Bourne, in readers' minds, beyond the pale of intellectual respectability. Denunciations poured in. "I have become an impious, ungrateful, pro-German, venomous viper," he observed acerbically.

Like John Reed and Margaret Anderson, Bourne was out of favor and nearly out of work by the end of 1916. Wilson was reelected on a shaky peace platform and Lippmann worked openly to influence the president, with whom the magazine had close ties, to enter the war. There was no formal break with the *New Republic*—Bourne continued, in fact, to publish in the journal sporadically until his death—but his salary diminished and then disappeared.

How to proceed? The job had been a costly detour from his intention to work the experimental life into print. The city that had once seemed so voluminous and hospitable now looked mean and pinched. Youthful radicalism, which had propelled him into commercial success, was no longer as attractive as it had once been. "I really thirst for fame, but the minute I begin taking steps for it, it seems so absurd to imagine that I am likely to do much more than I've done." As the year wore on and war sentiment mounted, Bourne shouldered the burden of minority dissent, detaching himself from his customary readers and sources of work. As work at the *New Republic* petered out, he scratched around for other assignments.

The shift demanded an alteration in his literary modus operandi. He could not practice intellectual opposition alone, from on high. A man who had left a tiny, shaky family of origin behind in the New Jersey suburbs, he needed compatriots and a dependable venue for his work. He was not a solitary writer, a gentleman of letters pronouncing from his study, assured of an income from family wealth or a university and succored by a wife and children; he was a modern freelance intellectual, a single man living on his writing fees. In this moment of need, his friends began to take on new value and to expand into a sustaining literary milieu. Friendships became a way to be " 'in' something" at a dispiriting moment when so many political possibilities were blocked.

When Bourne first came back from Europe, he had shared an apartment with his friend Carl Zigrosser in the East Thirties, a place that became a magnet for a crowd composed of old college chums and feminists from Barnard and the Patchin Place group. When the checks from the *New Republic* stopped coming, he moved farther downtown, closer to the alternative milieu from which the magazine had distanced him. In the Village he made new friends: not the illuminati—he was too much of an unknown for the likes of Mabel Dodge or the Hapgoods—but Alyse Gregory's feminist and Liberal Club compatriots and a few *New Republic* stragglers. He was a familiar figure on the streets, rustling about in a long black cape—an attempt to refashion his disfigurement into bohemian mystery. It was among these downtown New Women and the men who circled around them that Bourne found a way to transplant his work.

Bourne first used the phrase "beloved community" in "Trans-National America" in 1916. The term has a long history in America: the philosopher Josiah Royce spoke of the "beloved community" as a model for contemporary life that could be transposed from the Gospel of Paul; Bourne picked it up from reading Royce at Columbia, and from Bourne it passed into left-wing pacifist circles and from thence to militant students in the southern civil rights movement in the 1960s. For Bourne, the beloved community meant a youthful gathering of rational discourse and intimate fellowship, a model for a modern, socially heterogeneous leadership. It would be a community both intricately intertwined, through friendship and love, and outward looking to the advanced currents of thought and culture throughout the world. It would invite emotional connections—he wrote of "the good life of personality lived in the environment of the Beloved Community"—and cosmopolitan, or "trans-national" ties. The beloved community went beyond the *New Republic* paradigm of an educated elite advising and directing the masses. Bourne's "beloved" were self-chosen, equipped to serve by virtue of their youth, not social position, their disposition for closeness and understanding, not their proclivity for mastery. "To make real this striving amid dangers and apathies is work for a younger intelligentsia of America. Here is an enterprise of integration into which we can all pour ourselves." John Dewey's influence is evident in Bourne's belief that democracy could not be separated from the individual's quest for self-realization. But he was not simply returning to the lessons of his student days. He translated Dewey's faith in civic life into something much more personal and playful—even sexy.

There was, of course, a gap between high ideal and modest experience. Bourne's gift—his curse, too—was that he was as stringent in his expectations of life as he was in his expectations of his writing. Bohemia gave elements of what he needed, fostered friendships and conversation, but the Village habits of display and posing militated against the kind of severe integrity he sought in others. A relative latecomer to the scene and handicapped by his disability in the social whirl, Bourne was fascinated by but also wary of bohemian sociability. He was also increasingly alienated by the Village's conflation of culture with politics, which, he believed, weakened any serious opposition to the war. His experience as a onetime "radical pet" of the establishment made him dubious about the political durability of protest based on ephemeral cultural appeal. There was too much bombast on the left, he

Randolph Bourne and friends in New Jersey (left to right): Frances Anderson, Agnes de Lima, Esther Cornell, 1916 RANDOLPH BOURNE PAPERS, RARE BOOK AND MANUSCRIPT LIBRARY, COLUMBIA UNIVERSITY

later argued, too much radicalism that was "merely stagy and blatantly rebellious." Modern audiences were "almost pathetically receptive" to novel ideas and shocking material, but their openness eventually tamed the writers and artists who depended upon them. For Bourne, downtown life seemed bare of intellectual sustenance. "Why in the world do you (and I) fiddle around hectic and unperceptive Greenwich Village?" he grumbled to Alyse Gregory. And, morosely, to Esther Cornell, a young actress with whom he had fallen in love: "I am coming to think of Greenwich Village as a poisonous place which destroys the souls even of super-villagers like ourselves."

Uneasiness and disaffection led him to the time-honored urban fantasy of a simpler bucolic life. Beginning in summer 1915, he tried out different American settings, places where he believed he could find nourishing creative fare. On lecture tours, he imagined himself living in smaller cities, flourishing in fresh intellectual air. "When I get away," he confided to Alyse, "I have an entirely new sense of freedom and command of my own resources. I pick up new acquaintances, and converse with ease." *New Republic* bigwigs who terrified him in New York seemed, in Boston, merely amusing acquaintances. "I lose all that hectic, anxious note of New York." In Boston he could thrive as a suave guest of honor in well-to-do socialist salons; in Milwaukee, too, in winter 1917, he spied another, kindlier life: "This should have been the soil in which I was raised. I shouldn't have my confidence always damped by thickly cynical Columbia and rapid, sure New Republic."

But haltingly a Village community, imperfect but resignedly beloved, materialized. New relationships with women branched out from the old, platonic friendships into flirtations and romance, literary comradeships deepened, and a cluster of fictive kin formed: mostly single friends from Columbia, Barnard, and the *New Republic* and friends of friends, and, most important, a group of writers of both talent and sensibility comparable to his. In *Seven Arts*, a dazzling new journal, he found a place where he joined fully for the first time with intellectual compeers. Begun in 1916 by James Oppenheim and Waldo Frank, young writers, *Seven Arts* was devoted to promoting an American culture purged of chauvinism and puritanism. Backed by one of the radical rich, *Seven Arts'* program was modernist in a utopian, almost mystical vein and implicitly political: the sunny cosmopolitanism of its vision of the "new America" was a dissenter's stance at a moment when xenophobia swept the rest of the country. "The brighter color of a new day" would run through the magazine, Oppenheim insisted. "We bring good news, even if we have to cut our way through some swamps to bring it."

Filled with ruminations on Whitman, lyrical New York sketches, and tributes to the "new" in Ireland, Spain, and Japan, the journal was high-toned, arty, and, until Bourne joined the group, weirdly silent on the war. Bourne was at first dubious: "You wouldn't allow me to say what I want," James Oppenheim remembered him saying. "Try us," they countered. Having read Bourne's "Trans-National America," the editors believed they had spotted a writer of the highest caliber, with a vision of a diverse America similar to their own. And like Bourne, the *Seven Arts* writers repudiated any hint of estrangement from the country; they wanted a "group life" where the claims of American artists were as powerful as the claims of American business. Now the vision seems incredibly implausible, and even then it took considerable uto-pian buoyancy to keep it afloat. But buoyancy was what these writers, for all their differences of temperament and degrees of pessimism, shared with Bourne. Here were writers he could engage in conversa-tion, rather than imposing bigwigs; here he would be an equal, not a "radical pet." The man who had often been on the edges was really "'in' something."

The *Seven Arts* group merged with old friends into a sustaining cir-cle. Mostly unmarried, lovers of gossip and opponents of the war, these gadabouts relied on one another for subleased apartments, meals, companionship, and loans. And for deep-going, unceasing talk, driven hard by Bourne. In this moment of political paralysis, the exer-cise of intellectual passion in talk mattered all the more. Bourne once wrote that "the only way by which middle-class radicalism can serve is by being fiercely and concentratedly intellectual," and in the last months of his life he primed that concentration by engaging with those around him.

A friend described his talk as "a sort of angelic wrestle." His con-versations were the means by which he investigated and formulated his ideas, "that tireless research," she remembered, "into what is fair and good to you and me here and now as the one firm rock on which to rear a life that may be good and fair." Bourne's talk—which was, by his own testament, the heart of his intellectual modus operandi—was best described by Alyse Gregory, and she bears quoting at length:

> Though he was to so large an extent the leader of his generation in education and politics, his chief interest centered upon personal relationships. He was one of the few people I have known who could combine interest in causes with a subtle perception, and per-ception kept at the pitch of passion. He had an inspired, almost Proustian gift for uncovering the motives of human conduct. Nothing was too small or too great to serve him as quarry. His mind moved in every direction, was porous to every atmosphere.

This intensely personal process, concerned both with the "small" in human relationships and the "large" in world affairs, was perhaps what Bourne was thinking of when he observed to Gregory that "having led the experimental life, and sifted and sorted, I feel that I know exactly what I want." The break with the *New Republic* had sprung him loose to sift and sort through a pile of political ideas.

Bourne transmuted the writer friend into an intellectual provocateur among other malcontents, a critic among critics, a friend in a close group of like-minded associates. His experiments in life and mind led him to an intimate community, where relations of searching honesty, he believed, could provide a model for a modern intellectual class given to integrity of purpose rather than to hyperbolic claims of unity with the people.

Reed, Anderson, and Bourne belonged to the first generation of American writers who believed that politics were, in effect, a catalyst for infusing art with life. Left-wing alignments seemed generative, because they opened up to experiences otherwise blocked off. Writers could be the guides, the cicerone to literary meetings with social strangers—angry workers, yearning immigrants, and bristly New Women—in encounters smoothed by political understanding. The sensibility of writer friendliness opened up American prose to a broader range of images of modest people with their own modern desires, images that became, by the 1930s, so vivid in the theater and literature that a historian of the Popular Front speaks of the "laboring" of American culture as an enduring achievement.

But the conflation of cultural achievement with political opposition eventually fell apart, leaving most writer friends, like John Reed and Margaret Anderson, stranded in places both familiar and remote. Randolph Bourne was one of the few to grasp the problem raised by the ongoing debacle of wartime politics: if a modern cultural politics of the left could lay the basis for participatory democracy, it might also come to serve as a substitute for that democracy, a substitute that lacked the strength to withstand reprisals.

Bourne's life and work, taken together, oscillate between lonely polemic and an inward-turning movement toward a treasured group of friends. Some might say that his testament to the powers of friendship, his preoccupation with men's relations with women, and his vision of the beloved community reveal a therapeutic bent that was always hindering the modern cultural left, a floppy psychologizing about relationships, especially men's and women's. "A man like Randolph Bourne brought to the art of friendship all the energies which in another age he might have expended on art and politics," historian Christopher Lasch kindly judges, as if this were a regrettable dispersion of his powers.

But we can understand Bourne's intellectual contribution more exactly, I believe, if we see his espousal of the art of friendship as allied with, not extraneous to, his attempt to make a life as a political critic. For while many elements of the writers' imaginative democracy dissolved in the harsh climate of the war, their attempt to locate a core of democratic practice in their own lived relations—most powerfully, in the negotiations of men and women—proved to be of tougher stuff, indeed, perhaps, the defining achievement of their version of the new.

IV

THE HUMAN SEX

7

Sexual Modernism

Whaen Hutchins Hapgood looked back on the heyday of bohemia, it was the New Women he cast as the movers of history, standard-bearers of the modernist telos. "When the world began to change, the restlessness of women was the main cause of the development called Greenwich Village, which existed not only in New York but all over the country," he elegized. Throughout the left intelligentsia, the emancipated woman stood at the symbolic center of a program for cultural regeneration. Her enactment of destiny was considered a historical spectacle: "The awakening and liberation of woman . . . is not an event in any class or an issue between classes," proposed the *Masses* in 1913. "It is an issue for all humanity." The innovations of the moment benefited all, but they were thought particularly to aid women. Free speech allowed them to break a long taboo against female sexual expression, the new writing invited them to share literary enterprises monopolized by men, and bohemian politics accepted the fundamental premises of women's rights and expanded on them. Indeed, freedom of thought and action and "the removal of the barriers between the sexes" went hand in hand.

Men like Hapgood, Max Eastman, John Reed, and Randolph Bourne saw themselves as coconspirators of the heroines of the day. In their writings, political pronouncements, and friendships with the opposite sex, they articulated fond expectations of the advantages that would accrue to all—themselves included—from women's eventual triumph. "Feminism is going to make it possible for the first time for men to be free," the *Masses* predicted. This was a distinctly American sensibility; it was to prove enormously influential in modern sex relations, more so than the explicit antipathy to women (misogynistic at worst, ill-tempered at best) that wound through high-modernist corridors in Europe. Pound, with his animus toward women editors and patrons, Wyndham Lewis, Filippo Marinetti, T. S. Eliot—these men had variegated relations to women artists and subjects, to be sure, but they were given periodically to overt scorn for the modern woman's quest for self-determination or to muted anxiety that their sex was losing control.

Men of the American cultural left tended rather to extol sexual democracy in the same terms as they extolled the concord of workers and intellectuals. A militant belief in sexual equality was, ostensibly, common ground between men and women, and feminism, like the workers' commonwealth, would liberate society from a gloomy past. The moderns believed that the crippling conventions of their parents' generation had set the sexes against each other by segregating people into separate spheres—the female-dominated home, the male-dominated world. Modernity, with its generative powers of communication, would overcome the division and thereby put an end to the ancient battle of the sexes. A third space of reciprocity would nourish transcendent friendships unimaginable to earlier generations, the "true companionship and oneness" of men and women that Emma Goldman preached in her lectures on love.

The concrete manifestations of the egalitarian élan vital were the agitation for legalized birth control in 1916 and the achievement of woman's suffrage in 1920. A few of the goals of the nineteenth-century woman's movement had already been attained by the early 1900s: the abolition of the worst legal disabilities of married women, an end to some formal sex bars in the professions, less rigid divorce laws, and greater access to higher education. And though in the 1910s inequities of paid work and women's burden of responsibility for children remained severe, a sense of confidence reigned, expressed in ebullient language ("Feminism Will Give—Men More Fun, Women Greater Scope, Children Better Parents, Life More Charm," gushed one article). A peculiarly twentieth-century belief in what might be called willed equality held sway, a conviction that right-minded people in general and brave, iconoclastic women in particular could surmount injustice by force of will.

Men and women drew sustenance for their faith from the availability of work for women in the cities, from anarchist-tinged beliefs in the power of emancipated individuals to transform themselves and others, and from literary representations of New Womanhood. Their premises were not enunciated in tracts or manifestos but, haltingly and fragmentarily, as ethical predispositions: in romantic love, work, political activism, and sociability. In fact, few of these experiments were as successful as the participants billed them. Instead, the structures of sexual modernism proved highly elastic in their ability to accommodate elements of the old sexual hierarchies. The persistence, even the consolidation, of men's privileges within an egalitarian framework would prove a defining feature of twentieth-century American society. Ironically, despite all their good intentions, the bohemians helped construct the fundamental paradox of a sexual modernism that was also a patriarchal modernization. They were the very first generation to live with the promises and perplexities of what came to be seen, much later, as a great change in the lives of girls and women.

Feminism as a synonym for women's rights was a coinage of the 1910s, transposed from the French *féminisme*, a word around since the 1880s. Associated with the newest of New Women, feminism betokened not just a claim to the vote or to making mothers' roles in society more honored but rather to economic independence, sexual freedom, and psychological exemption from the repressive obligations of wifehood, motherhood, and daughterhood—a jettisoning of family duties for a heightened female individualism. The appearance of the term in the urban lexicon signaled the cohesion of a politics—better yet, a sensibility—of equality distinct from the nineteenth-century tradition, which had consistently stressed women's roles within the family and marriage and repudiated any ideas of women's sexual desires independent of making babies. Like other specialties of the metropolitan intelligentsia, feminism was new, "so new that it isn't in the dictionaries yet," an advocate boasted. The mixture of utopianism and advertising hype—"the stir of new life," "world-wide revolt against all artificial barriers," the "complete social revolution"—propelled the term into the limelight. Like so much else that was happening, feminism denoted a world-transforming rupture. "We have grown accustomed . . . to something or other known as the Woman Movement. That has an old sound—it *is* old," another adherent explained. "But feminism!"—*that* was something different. Magazines buzzed, not just the *Masses* and the *Little Review* but the family periodicals, the stodgy *Nation*, the grave *New Republic*. "The word is daily in the pages of our newspapers. The doctrine and its corollaries are on every tongue," marveled the *Century* in 1914.

Feminism drew its adherents and some of its momentum from the women's suffrage movement. "All feminists are suffragists, but not all suffragists are feminists," explained a guide to the terminology. There had been continuous agitation for the vote for women in the United States since the 1870s. Toward the turn of the century, the movement gained strength. In 1890, the two competing middle-class white women's organizations merged to form the National American Woman Suffrage Association (NAWSA). Throughout the next two decades a surge of civic activity among women occurred in the usual middle-class sectors but also among black and working-class women, whom the women's rights movement traditionally had ignored or patronized. Their organizations, based in churches, women's clubs, settlement houses, and labor unions, swelled the suffrage ranks. As a result, in the 1910s women's suffrage commanded a far-flung mass movement, one of the most socially heterogeneous in American history. Working-class women, wealthy women, clubwomen, urban settlement leaders, temperance crusaders, women of the left, and southern community leaders joined forces. "To me it seemed the big fight for freedom in my time," Max Eastman avowed.

New York was a hotbed of suffragism. In 1907, the Women's Trade Union League (WTUL) spawned the Equality League for Self-Supporting Women, led by Harriot Stanton Blatch (a progressive reformer and Elizabeth Cady Stanton's daughter). In the Equality

League, female professionals worked for suffrage alongside labor organizers and workers from the garment trades. The presence of the radical rich in the city meant that wealthy women also helped. "Polite up-town rich ladies mingling . . . with us poor wage slaves of the slums" was Mary Heaton Vorse's ironic characterization of this contingent, but Vorse's stereotype belies the complexity of the extremely broad mobilization of New York New Women. Ettie Stettheimer, for example, the youngest of a trio of sisters who in the late teens would replace Mabel Dodge as leading *salonnières*, was a rich lady, a wealthy uptown German Jew, but she was also an outspoken suffragist and a Barnard graduate who had studied philosophy abroad. Similarly, the tremendous mobilizations of women workers in the garment unions— the high points were great needleworkers' strikes in 1909 and 1913, each involving thousands—overflowed into a militant Wage Earners' League for Woman Suffrage, founded by union organizers and directed toward the specific injustices that the vote could alleviate for workingwomen.

The downtown radicals, men along with women, embraced suffrage as a tenet of democratic politics. Max Eastman's Men's League for Woman Suffrage put men's support into the newspapers and drew contingents of male marchers who braved roars of derision in big suffrage parades down Fifth Avenue. Eastman took his feminism to the *Masses*, insisting that, contrary to socialist doctrine, issues of women's equality were not secondary to the class struggle: "The question of sex equality, the economic, social, political independence of woman, stands by itself parallel and equal in importance to any other question of the day." The Harvard radicals, inspired by Eastman's New York effort, formed their own Men's League for Woman Suffrage in 1911 and fought for the right of suffragists to speak on campus despite President Lowell's revulsion at the prospect of "a mob of women trooping about the Yard." The Cambridge men who made their way to Greenwich Village were thus already well schooled in women's rights; indeed, participation in suffrage was pretty much de rigueur for male intellectuals on the bohemian left. Greenwich Village radicals marched, wrote about women's freedom, and chimed in at the suffrage meetings that were a staple of downtown sociability. Even the middle-aged

Theodore Dreiser shambled along with a new lover in a suffrage parade.

The Congressional Union (CU), formed in 1913 as a rival to the mainstream NAWSA, followed the example set by British suffragists, who were repudiating the tactics of an older, ladylike movement. In London, frustrated by years of stasis, suffragists led by the militant Pankhurst women engaged in sensational melodramatic protests that made international news: public demonstrations, heckling members of Parliament, smashing windows of government buildings, and going on hunger strikes when they went to jail. The CU followed suit, linking the American movement to publicity-grabbing militancy and attracting the loyalties of the Village. Although Americans toned down the civil disobedience, the point was still for suffrage women to mobilize the newspaper publicity by making a spectacle of themselves, flouting NAWSA's taboo on respectable women "displaying" themselves in public. There were huge flamboyant parades and coast-to-coast all-woman suffrage car trips. After Woodrow Wilson became president,

Suffragists in Washington Mews CORBIS-BETTMANN

the militants picketed the White House, a form of protest hitherto unthinkable for ladies. Melees with police and hostile passersby resulted for the picketers in jail sentences, hunger strikes, and force-feeding. Village women found CU politics congenial; the British tactics were quite similar to IWW direct-action tactics, predicated on the permeability between radical politics and the news.

But there was more to feminism than suffragism. Feminism's love of personality, spirit, and eros appealed to women simply drawn to its glamorous vision of female assertiveness and independence. It reached the newspapers. In 1917, one New York paper deemed a cluster of women in Greenwich Village—Margaret Anderson, Jane Heap, zany Elsa von Freytag-Loringhoven, Ida Rauh, Margaret Sanger, Louise Bryant—to represent a vanguard of the sex "half-way through the door into To-morrow." Randolph Bourne encapsulated the myth of this newest of New Woman, the feminist bohemian, in a letter to an adoring fan, Prudence Winterrowd, with whom he had struck up a regular correspondence. To Winterrowd, an awestruck midwesterner, Bourne turned New York feminists into icons of modernity who established the tone and temper of the scene. The tableau of femininity he presented was a lure to all that awaited her should she dare to make the move:

They are all social workers, or magazine writers in a small way. They are decidedly emancipated and advanced, and so thoroughly healthy and zestful, or at least it seems so to my unsophisticated masculine sense. They shock you constantly. . . . They have an amazing combination of wisdom and youthfulness, of humor and ability, and innocence and self-reliance, which absolutely belies everything you will read in the story-books or any other description of womankind. They are of course all self-supporting and independent; and they enjoy the adventure of life; the full, reliant, audacious way in which they go about makes you wonder if the new woman isn't to be a very splendid sort of person.

These "zestful" New Women of New York bore little resemblance to earlier modernist femmes fatales, women who reigned over salons or lived, wrote, and made love at the edges of café society. And male support for the purposeful American feminist was also quite unlike the fin-de-siècle mythologizing of the Eternal Feminine, which was always intertwined with an elaborately masked contempt (woman as both life-giving and death-dealing principle, muse and incubus). On the Continent, perhaps the closest counterparts to American feminists were the brainy young women in the background of Georg Lukács's circle in Budapest and Kafka's Prague. In Prague, many of Kafka's acquaintances were Jewish, but there were also Gentile flouters of bourgeois convention, a group that included Kafka's entrancing lover Milena Jesenká, women who wore clothes that outraged the respectable, experimented with drugs, and slept with men they didn't marry.

The more familiar parallel, though, is with London's Bloomsbury. Virginia Woolf and Vanessa Bell were of the same generation as the fin-de-siècle avant-garde, and one of the many wonders of their self-invention as modernists was their escape from the role of muse. A more exact comparison, though, is with the London generation Woolf and Bell termed (with condescension, envy, and fondness) "the crop-heads," younger, short-haired women tending toward socialism. Much like the New Yorkers, they were convention-spurning, vocationally ambitious, sexually active, and politically serious, convinced they were living at the edge of history. Randolph Bourne, when he stayed in London during his trip, met a few female refugees from stuffy families whom he immediately recognized as the type. He marveled to Alyse Gregory that modernity had reached into the farthest corners of "dingy" England. "The educated daughters obviously hated the place and the wearing ties of family life," he wrote of a tea in Clapton, "and were moving with their souls and interests in realms so unintelligible to the Victorian parents as to make them almost a different animal species."

But nowhere in Europe—or in the world, for that matter—did modern culture orient itself to the New Woman as its defining figure as it did in America. One emblem was the dancer Isadora Duncan, tied to the new in feminism through her Manhattan residence, her suffrage politics, and her friendships with downtown intellectuals. Isadora's long-limbed arcs dividing up space reminded some of the ways feminists seemed to move through daily life—utterly present yet light on their feet. A socialist reviewing Duncan's dancing encapsulated the almost messianic faith in emancipated femininity: "In this age of feminist aspirations, woman as beauty is subordinate to woman as a New Being. Woman is seeking more than beauty—*individuality;* the beauty of a free personality. . . . And woman—the Modern Woman—is striving for all this with an energy . . . peculiarly adaptable to expression in dance."

The Americans thus present the paradox of a modernist intelligentsia that elaborated on, painted in, affirmed, and obsessively detailed the distinct properties of women while at the same time insisting that such distinctions were irrelevant to a human sex in the making. The paradox is visible, lightly, in the beguiling September 1916 "woman's issue" of the poetry journal *Others,* published at the Ridgefield commune. The editors take on the rhetorical question "Why a 'Woman's Number'? . . . Art is surely sexless." Yes, avows the guest editor, a woman, and yet . . . "most of what we know, or think we know, of women has been found out by men. We have yet to hear what women will tell of herself." Women, in other words, have a particular voice to which the audience for revolutionary poetry need attend. "It is time woman played troubadour!" Alfred Kreymborg chimes in. Women were to be heralded—and to salute themselves—for their distinct character (audacious, adventurous, creative) and at the same time to be seen as no different from men.

The paradox has always been embedded in movements for sexual equality. In the nineteenth century, too, women's rights activists stressed the distinctiveness of a collective "we"—women—all the while insisting that discriminatory designations be dropped from education, social custom, and the law. But these nineteenth-century advocates did tend to mobilize the paradox in favor of sexual differences, basing their arguments for the vote and a meaningful place in public life on their particular contributions and strengths as women—and, even more so, as mothers. For the feminists of the 1910s and their male supporters, the Victorian belief that women's moral power and social wisdom derived from their domestic roles was unacceptable, an antiquated remnant of their mothers' generation. Floyd Dell's *Women as World Builders* (1913), a book of essays on major feminists, would have none of this maternalism or its heritage of self-sacrifice: "It is the setting of mothers free" that concerns people now, he states firmly. He ends with a paean to the young English feminist Dora Marsden, editor of the *Freewoman*, a representative of "a band of capable females, knowing what they want and taking it, asking no leave from anybody, doing things and enjoying life."

The preoccupation with the self linked feminism to an incipient twentieth-century cult of personality: ideas of ever-expanding capabilities replaced the Victorian construct of a stable character. Once released from historic constraints, women could become their "whole big human selves." The utopian language of human development seems vapid today, but in the 1910s it was full of meaning. In the sun of modernity, blooming fields of individual personalities would bear a harvest of enhanced humanity—a "human sex," only incidentally differentiated as male or female. A better sort of people was emerging from the ruins of the old system. "Masculine brutalities and egotisms and feminine pettinesses and stupidities have been purged away so that there is left stuff for a genuine comradeship and healthy frank regard and understanding," Randolph Bourne, in his sunnier moments, believed of himself and his friends. As the IWW was to the classless society, so the feminists were to universal fellowship.

The greatest practical demonstration of the vanguard role of feminists was the birth control campaign, perhaps the clearest political articulation of sexual modernism and a lasting achievement of the cross-class coalitions of the teens. The agitation began in radical Manhattan in 1912 and spread across the nation in the next five years through IWW and Socialist Party networks and free-speech conduits. The fight to legalize birth control was in many ways a free-speech battle, because the dissemination of contraceptive information and devices—the pessary (our diaphragm) and the condom—fell under the obscenity provisions of the Comstock laws. In its connections to free speech, birth control called forth democratic enthusiasm for the unhindered circulation of information and ideas. With its ties to the labor movement, the campaign appealed to downtown Manhattan's pleasure in loitering along class lines.

The birth control movement was very much a product of the

human sex, growing practically and theoretically from the relations of feminists and their male supporters. Charismatic Village celebrities— Emma Goldman, Elizabeth Gurley Flynn, and the up-and-comer Margaret Sanger—led the battles; left-wing New Women carried on day-to-day operations. But its lines of support and finances ran through the downtown journals, salons, and clubs and depended upon male interest.

Margaret Sanger and the crusade she led were creations of Greenwich Village, dependent on its mechanisms of advertisement, its literary channels, and its resources for political spectacle. An emigrant from a small place—Corning, New York—Sanger had learned enough about American radicalism from her father (Michael Higgins, a disciple of free thought, the single tax, and women's rights) to look to the left for paths of mobility and sources of energy. With William Sanger, a young architect she married in 1902, she embarked on a life of decorous middle-class socialism. In 1910, they moved to New York and Bill Sanger, a rising star, ran for alderman on the Socialist Party ticket. At first they settled uptown and sent their children to the Modern School; then Margaret Sanger helped Dolly Sloan organize the children's exodus from Lawrence. She found a forum in the socialist newspaper *Call* for writing about contraception, her expertise ratified by her work as a public health nurse. The column, "What Every Girl Should Know," elicited both opprobrium and indifference from the SP faithful. The *Call* on its own was an unpromising venue, since its respectable socialist readers looked at contraception as a Pandora's box of sexual profligacy. But it was Sanger's ironic good fortune to attract the attention of Anthony Comstock, who descended on the paper in 1913 and banned the column.

With Comstock involved, contraception turned into a free-speech issue and all Greenwich Village jumped on board to protest Sanger's right to publish her views. Shortly thereafter, Sanger addressed huge crowds in the Paterson strike on the importance of voluntary motherhood and developed a warm working friendship with Elizabeth Gurley Flynn, who was fearless when it came to raising sexual issues. Strike leader Carlo Tresca tried politely to neutralize Sanger's message by painting, in the macho Wobbly manner, rosy pictures of a working-class future in which women, freed from want, could bear children willy-nilly. But the enthusiasm of the Village intellectuals and the willingness of Flynn, an IWW heavy hitter, to lend her name to the birth control issue soon snapped IWW leaders into line.

In the summer of 1914, Sanger, who had started her own birth control journal, the *Woman Rebel*, was indicted for sending obscene material through the mails. Instead of preparing for trial, Sanger sat down to write a plain, clear manual of instruction on contraception called *Family Limitation*, arranged for an anarchist printer to print 100,000 copies and bundle them for distribution through IWW and labor networks, and hustled off to Europe to avoid prosecution. Her months in Britain and France strengthened her sense of mission by exposing her to ideas about state-sponsored birth control held by French radicals whom she met through Wobbly friends. Meanwhile in New York, Emma Goldman, although personally cool to Sanger, took the measure of the political moment and pitched in. Goldman's interest in contraception was long-standing: she had worked as a midwife on the Lower East Side at the turn of the century and knew well the devastating consequences of unplanned pregnancies. In 1900, she had attended a clandestine neo-Malthusian conference of birth control radicals in Paris but had shied away from taking up the issue in the United States, where it remained too hot to handle, except obliquely in her lectures on love and marriage. With the emergence of a force field of emancipated womanhood in the Village, however, Goldman sensed an opening. She vigorously promoted birth control on her national lecture tour that year and worked to increase the identification of militant labor politics with family limitation that had evolved at Paterson.

A second attack of the forces of Comstockery—this time on William Sanger, entrapped by one of John Sumner's agents for handing out a copy of *Family Limitation*—fully activated Greenwich Village. A Heterodoxy member, Mary Ware Dennett, organized a National Birth Control League that called for the repeal of all obscenity regulations related to contraception. Across the country, the IWW defied censorship to distribute *Family Limitation*. Goldman and Ben Reitman were arrested for distributing contraceptive information. Young feminists and hardened Wobbly free-speech agitators went to jail. Everywhere, popular working-class interest—especially women's—was stirred by the prospect of discovering what was widely regarded as a rich woman's secret, since those with money could already get contraceptive devices from private doctors. A young woman told Elizabeth Flynn that the women workers in the stockyards in Chicago kissed her hands when she distributed the pamphlet; Flynn visited a cigar factory in Tampa where one worker read Sanger's writing aloud while the others worked. By the time Sanger returned from Europe in the fall of 1915, writer friends had broken through into print with an issue once seen as too vulgar to discuss. The big magazines treated birth control mildly, indeed sympathetically, and even the *New Republic* enlisted in the cause.

Generally, birth control proponents pictured the working-class women who were their political troops as women in need—drudges bowed down by poverty and too many children, hardworking wives who stood loyally by their family responsibilities. Now another image glimmered occasionally through portrayals of worn-down wives and mothers, that of the "rebel girl" who might want contraception for her own reasons. The "Rebel Girl" was an IWW sobriquet, the title of a popular song composed by Joe Hill; it was an apt phrase at a moment when militant young workingwomen were becoming politically visible in some of the great strikes and culturally visible every day on the city streets. The rebel girl was a New Woman neologism but with a plebeian edge. Like Elizabeth Gurley Flynn herself, implicitly deemed their representative, rebel girls were sexualized figures, seen as erotically adventurous and disregardful of marriage. They were "girls" not only of the picket lines at Paterson but of the dance halls and nickelodeons, their high spirits captured in John Sloan's *Masses* sketch of a gaggle of friends on their way somewhere after work. Such young women could conceivably want birth control for the same reasons that bohemian women needed birth control—in order to have premarital sex without getting pregnant.

Single workingwomen, however, were not to attain a political presence or a voice in the birth control campaign. It would have been inconceivable. In the big public demonstrations in New York, mothers with babies, not bedizened factory girls, were in evidence. But the rebel girl lingered at the edges of the movement, beckoning toward a sexual democracy of women. Emma Goldman, after all, was pretty

John Sloan. "The Return from Toil." Masses, *July 1913*
TAMIMENT INSTITUTE LIBRARY, NEW YORK UNIVERSITY

much a rebel girl herself, despite her age (forty-six in 1915), and Sanger's first publication when she returned from Europe was called *The Woman Rebel.* Funded by free-loving, radically rich feminists Mabel Dodge and Jessie Ashley, *The Woman Rebel* preached nonchalance and defiance, the duty of the freewoman to "look the whole world in the face with a go-to-hell look in the eyes, to have an ideal, to speak and act in defiance of convention." Echoing the tone of the British *Freewoman,* Sanger spoke for the rights not just of woman but of the rebel woman, an amalgam of bohemian slouch, feminist eros, and Wobbly sabotage. "The right to be lazy. The right to be an unmarried mother. The right to destroy. The right to create. The right to live. The right to love." At the edges, then, and especially in the excited early days, there was mischief in the movement—sexy

Village women confabulating, if only in the feminist political uncon-
scious, with working-class tarts.

With the IWW excited—socialist women, too, joined in—Village
politics reached for the always-hoped-for contacts with the working
classes. As the *Masses* publicized Sanger's case, requests for instruction
in birth control techniques poured in from working-class readers, and
the journal's attention to the cause courted reprisals from the censors.
A luminous Carnegie Hall meeting to welcome back Emma Goldman,
newly released from jail, spilled over into direct action when Rose
Pastor Stokes offered to distribute slips of paper with contraceptive
instructions to anyone in the audience. When Sanger returned from
Europe, she opened a clinic in Brownsville, a very poor immigrant
neighborhood in Brooklyn, and openly dispensed contraceptives to
crowds of patients. When police shut down the clinic and arrested her
once again, neighborhood women flocked to her support. At the next
Carnegie Hall protest meeting, workingwomen packed the cheap
twenty-five-cent seats and Brownsville mothers sat on the platform—
Sanger's suggestion—as a hieratic backdrop of downtrodden women
to the succession of feisty, mostly middle-class speakers. At the subsequent trial, too, Brownsville women came to testify, shlepping bags of
food for themselves and pacifiers and extra diapers for the babies at
their breasts.

But like other emancipationist causes, birth control was not to
remain within bohemia's grasp. Once the United States entered the
war, the government's repression of labor and the left-wing media
weakened the cross-class bases of support. Sanger, who was under surveillance for her part in organizing protest of Emma Goldman's and
Alexander Berkman's arrests for agitating against the draft, was also
threatened with another arrest under the Comstock laws. She began
to distance her cause from radicals and ally herself with the
respectable, a shift in tactics that also made sense in terms of her qualified legal victory in the Brownsville case, in which the appellate judge
had opened the way for doctors to dispense contraceptive information.
In 1917, Sanger was on her way to making birth control "her" cause
and leaving radical Manhattan altogether. She turned toward wealthy
donors and the medical establishment; the eugenics undertow that had
always been there in her thought—the drive to limit the births by

Margaret Sanger outside Brooklyn courthouse, 1917 CORBIS-BETTMANN

mothers she judged to be unfit because they were poor—eventually rose to the surface in the 1920s. She abnegated the free-speech issue altogether, preferring to campaign for doctors' dispensing of birth control information. Goldman, who had been shunted to the wings (literally, at one Carnegie Hall meeting) found the costs simply too high and dropped the issue. Birth control had become Margaret Sanger; when she turned her back on radical Manhattan, she took the battle with her.

Nonetheless, the movement has to be counted as one of the era's— and bohemia's—great achievements. Birth control agitation gave political shape and purpose to a sexual revolution already in motion. Although it did not secure the repeal of the Comstock laws at the time, the public activity and debate had a tremendous effect in legitimating contraception among women who already possessed the means and in endorsing the search for contraception among those who didn't. Its proponents declared that all women, rich or poor, should have the ability to share the bounty of technology that separated sex from reproduction.

The cross-class politics of the movement cast intellectuals as leaders in reforming working-class family life, helping poor parents—especially mothers—become more accountable to one another and their children through limiting and timing their pregnancies. But the image of the rebel girl also occasionally glinted within the language of family responsibility, evoking a different kind of political mission, a concourse of modern women shaping their own destinies, regardless of class. The birth control campaign proved the Village was not just the "hellhole of free love, promiscuity and prostitution masquerading under the mantle of revolution" its critics thought it to be (this one was the disaffected Bill Sanger) but a reserve of erotic enlightenment for the labor movement and, indeed, the country at large. The whole world might benefit: Bill Shatoff, Margaret Sanger's radical printer, translated *Family Limitation* into Yiddish and shipped bundles off to Russia.

Sexual freedom was critical to feminist modernity, but that freedom cannot be understood apart from its twin support for female independence, paid work. Unlike the political activists of the nineteenth-century women's movement—married women whose understanding of women's labor mostly rested on the home—the feminists predicated their politics on women's full access to paid work. They prided themselves on their status as workingwomen and affiliated with other self-supporting women of the working classes, fellow rebel girls such as those they met at Paterson. The movement for the emancipation of women depended, they believed, on the recognition of the huge contribution their sex made to the world's labor and on their ability to find meaningful, remunerative work. "As human beings we must have work," wrote Harriot Stanton Blatch. "We rust out if we have not an opportunity to function on something."

Because feminists recognized that all women needed justly remunerated work to spring them from the indignities of dependence on men, there was real bite to the female writer friends' involvement with labor issues. The labor politics of New York also contributed. It

Cornelia Barns. "My Dear, I'll be economically independent if I have to borrow every cent!" Masses, *March 1915* TAMIMENT INSTITUTE LIBRARY, NEW YORK UNIVERSITY

was a union town, and its labor force was heavily female because of the ubiquity of the garment industries. In 1910, 27 percent of the workforce was female; only Massachusetts had a higher proportion. These workers were mainly Jewish and Italian. The needleworkers' strikes brought them onto the public stage and turned feminist interest toward them. By 1914, when Heterodoxy sponsored mass meetings on feminist topics, female trade unionists were prominent among the speakers and the right to organize was declared a fundamental right of women. Elizabeth Gurley Flynn had been a hardcore believer in the old IWW line that class conflict was the fundamental political division and women's rights a frivolous, bourgeois diversion; before Paterson, she had worked almost exclusively with men and condemned the idea of the sisterhood of women as a sham.

But in the Village she found such congeniality that she, too, became a feminist.

This latest incarnation of New Womanhood—Floyd Dell dubbed her the Freewoman, after the British journal of that name—might seem to belong exclusively to the middle class, but in fact the figure was also alluring to working-class women, a vehicle for self-esteem and self-amplification. The mixture of classes in the women's movement in the 1910s was both cause and consequence of the fluidity. Traditional views held that wage work was only a way station to marriage for working-class women, but the freedoms of the city and the spread of trade unionism undermined this assumption. There were, in fact, plebeian "women adrift" who followed radical causes and found their way into bohemia as artists' models and would-be artists, actresses, organizers, and lovers. There was sometimes only a narrow gap between the peripatetic traveling female labor organizer and the bohemian female vagabond.

Middle-class feminists, for their part, idealized young working-women as heroines, active shapers of their own destinies. And although there is not much evidence from workingwomen themselves, there are hints that this particular generation, many of them trade union militants, shared the assessment. No longer willing to accept labor rhetoric, which pictured them as wage slaves who needed to be rescued by male comrades and sent home, female workers in the garment unions demanded a language that would express "a way of life and a soul." Earning money, being on one's own even if it meant being poor, living loose: these were desires of working-class modernity. "Working girls have a chance to be themselves because they earn their own wage and nobody owns them," proposed a Women's Trade Union League writer to her constituents. "I am pretty sure you are somebody, because you are self-supporting."

Female champions of labor no longer kept themselves at arm's length, as they often had in the nineteenth-century, from the workingwomen who were the objects of their largesse. There could be lyrical identification. Margaret Anderson confessed that in her first year in Chicago, when she worked for the newspapers, she was always fantasizing she was "a poor working-girl"—the imaginative crossover—thereby forgetting that in truth, she "was really poor—also a working girl." Dorothy Day, once she became a workingwoman, convinced her working-class mother to tell her about her own life as a militant factory worker before she married. Like many daughters of later generations who investigated women's history, Day saw her task as reframing the older woman's story, once "hidden from history," as a compelling romance, an imaginative position that made her the powerful interlocutor and reversed the sequence of generational dependency. "She had seen no romance in those few hard years of her life until she saw them through my eyes. . . . To her it was an episode to be forgotten."

Much of the hope for sexual equality emanated from women's success—although success was ambiguous—in entering paid work. Work for women carried with it a galvanic charge, difficult to appreciate now, when women enter the labor force so matter-of-factly. But in the 1880s, Jane Addams, then a recent college graduate, looked up from her breakfast in a plush Chicago hotel to see people bustling to work and yearned with all her heart to join them. By the 1910s, the longing no longer seemed a fantastic dream for which a young woman had to battle. True, there were still exceptions from wealthy, conventional families, daughters like Margaret Anderson who had to fight their way out. And the act of crossing the sex bar was still sufficiently novel to be turned into entertainment extravaganzas of women emulating "masculine" feats. When a woman from Australia, for example, appeared on Broadway in 1910 to dive from a high board into a tank, she was a hit. She intrigued Crystal Eastman, who invited her down to the Village to talk about feminism. But in general, changes that had begun in the 1890s continued apace, hastened by increasing numbers of women with college degrees—nearly half of all enrolees by 1920. Some pushed on after they graduated into formerly male bastions of medicine, the law, college teaching, and the ministry.

The careers of a clutch of women lawyers in the Village—Jessie Ashley, Crystal Eastman, and Ida Rauh—exemplify this movement. Ida Rauh was the daughter of a well-to-do uptown German Jewish Manhattan family. She went to Barnard for a year, grew bored and left, and took the entrance examination for New York University law school. Although there was a separate women's track, she graduated at the age of twenty-five with a regular degree in 1902. At NYU she would have met Jessie Ashley, whose father was dean there, and

Crystal Eastman. The others moved with her into organizing for the WTUL and in 1909 served as leaders of the middle-class "allies" in the shirtwaist makers' strike. Soon after, Rauh traveled to England to throw herself, along with a coterie of other American militants, into the thick of the suffrage battle there. Despite her formidable intellect and infinitely plastic talents, she never practiced law, but devoted herself in the bohemian manner to shifting artistic and political pursuits. Indeed, all female lawyers had great difficulty practicing their profession; Jessie Ashley and Crystal Eastman also made alternative careers for themselves as full-time activists in suffrage work, labor support, the birth control campaign, and (in Eastman's case) peace organizing.

For the most part, however, advanced degrees were rare, perhaps because the higher professions required a certain propriety, especially for a woman, which sat uneasily with bohemian life. The New Women of the intelligentsia were more likely to be employed in fields where training and certification were informal: journalism, book publishing, acting, or advertising. In this respect, they replicated the national pattern: although the numbers of women in the professions climbed from 8 percent in 1900 to 12 percent in 1920, the gains can mostly be attributed to their employment in the lower ranks of professional hierarchies. Formal bars to women's entrance into the professions had fallen, but entire fields divided up along sex lines—female executive secretaries, for example, working for male literary editors. Alyse Gregory, who supported herself in the lower echelons of New York publishing, remembered how hard it was for women. Salaries were so low that being a workingwoman could mean going hungry, even if you were middle-class. Women "could force their way into the professions only against obstacles that prevented all but the most determined and brilliant from keeping up the struggle."

The feminist program for economic independence concentrated on penetrating the realm of paid work rather than criticizing structures of inequality within it. Feminists took heart from women's presence in sectors once designated male, a sign to them of the success of the human sex. The political successes of the women's movement had bequeathed to them a sense of efficacy in the world, of the riches bestowed by living in what was "really for women a golden age," Mary Heaton Vorse thought. "We had the feeling that we were important civic factors who could put a thumb almost anywhere and pull out a plum, ranging from votes for women to a fine new building."

Positions we now see as dead ends for women, ghettoes, were at the time so new that a low place in the hierarchy seemed less important than having a job in the first place. "New York was largely run by women," Mabel Dodge believed. "There was a woman behind every man in every publisher's office, in all the editorial circles, and in the Wall Street offices, and it was the judgment and intuition of these that determined many policies, for they were anonymous women. They didn't seem to mind being so, for the most part." Likewise, what we call sexual harassment could be an unpleasantness to be tolerated as a small price to pay for a much greater benefit. In Margaret Anderson's account of her coming of age, she gave less attention to the sexual overtures of the Chicago bookstore owner for whom she clerked than to his willingness to teach her the masculine art of typesetting.

Feminists were in flight from the nineteenth-century connotations of "woman" and believed that working alongside men ensured they had escaped. "Women" and "mother" were often elided, so much so that the desire for a life different from the mother's was one of the great psychological themes of this generation on both sides of the Atlantic. In that desired state, one would profoundly *matter*, not just in one's family but in the world. "I wanted to go on picket lines, to go to jail, to write, to influence others and so make my mark on the world," recounted Dorothy Day of her young self. In England, we see the drama of rejection in Virginia Woolf's tender repudiations in *To the Lighthouse* (1927), her great novel about a woman artist seeking to separate herself from a powerful maternal figure, a character based on Woolf's own mother. No American writer offered reflections of comparable complexity, although Willa Cather's *Song of the Lark* (1915) bears on similar themes. Nonetheless, eloquent testaments to a need for an identity separate from the mother's run through this generation's published and unpublished materials.

Recall Mary Heaton Vorse's grim description of herself in the 1890s as a soldier in the army of women all across the country "out to hurt their mother, who have to, in order to work." Margaret Anderson claimed to despise her mother and, once she had found the protections of bohemia, developed almost a horror of the older woman writer, Clara Laughlin—a self-appointed mother figure—who had kindly sponsored her when she first came to Chicago. The psychology of disaffiliation spread through feminism, so much so that the disavowal of the mother came to be almost a trademark of female modernism. Maternal disaffiliation was, indeed, more of a leitmotif than antipatriarchalism: antipathy toward the fathers expressed itself less in disdain for particular parents than in a general disdain for the world of the elders. But feelings about mothers were personal, cutting, reproachful. The very stuff of the daughterly self, the "I" so different from the woman her late nineteenth-century mother thought she should be, could represent defiant recantation. "Am I the Christian gentlewoman my mother slaved to make me?" boasted an aspiring West Coast writer headed for Greenwich Village. "No indeed."

The search for a life freed from a mother's burdens could be covert, disguised even to oneself. Margaret Anderson's critical, controlling mother, a pillar of small-town Indiana society, was so destructive that Anderson broke with her family altogether. Other young women, however, groped to retrieve some strengthening identification: a plucky aunt, perhaps, or a revered grandmother, or even a beloved mother one exempted from the general condemnation. Dorothy Day had grown up in the Chicago tenements closely allied with her mother through love and labor: as one of the older girls in a large family, Day was her mother's helper and raised her youngest brother. Indeed, her first memories of strolling about Chicago were of pushing a baby carriage, a little sister toddling alongside—a peculiarly female form of the flaneur. Yet Day remembered her mother not as a drudge but as a woman of gaiety and fortitude who in her low moments went shopping and came home with some cheap treat for the children or a new hat for herself. It was not from her mother but rather from her mother's life of endless housework and child care that Day fled. Even as a scholarship student at the University of Illinois, she couldn't escape housework completely—laundressing was her first job. It was only when she struck out on her own as a journalist, modeling herself on her father and older brother, that she completed the separation.

In later years, Dorothy Day wrote lyrically about the poverty she endured after she graduated and moved to New York to work for the *Masses*. The reverie is peculiar, since deprivation was no novelty to her. But a metropolitan writer's poverty was different from that of a working-class daughter. She could romanticize a life without money once she lived apart from tired women, dirty kitchens, and fussy children. Day's poverty was now worthy of the bohemian plot. Meals snatched on the fly from pushcarts after work or shared with fellow reporters in cheap restaurants (soup and bread for a dime), a cigarette smoked on the sly since it was still illegal for women to smoke in public—this was the stuff of fond memories. She moved from a room on the Lower East Side to share a spacious Village apartment with two men. But men as friends did not exact the domestic services from women that brothers and fathers did: Day's roommates' expectations were so relaxed that housekeeping itself became a model of cooperation. "The rooms were large and well furnished and there was a good kitchen so that we could have supper parties, and even breakfast parties, everyone chipping in for the stew and the breakfast brioche."

Buoyed by an ingenuous faith that sexual inequality could be willed away by virtue of courage, hard work, and alliances with well-meaning men, such women were not drawn to the separate women's world that had provided succor to earlier generations of pioneering professional women. They intended, rather, to build up the human sex. As historians have noted, the feminists paid a price for their lack of interest. Abandoning the supports and compensations of woman's sphere, they were thrown into male-defined work situations where they ended up second-best. They failed to see that "they lacked the real economic and institutional power with which to wrest hegemony from men and so enforce their vision of a gender-free world," judges the historian Carroll Smith-Rosenberg.

But such assessments are anachronistic, framed in the context of our own knowledge, not theirs. None of these women had an experience of an even faintly integrated world. They had no basis from which to foresee the traps of inequality that willed equality could harbor. They only knew the cold comforts of their mothers' sphere; it was this experience they acted on. Our shrewdness is indebted to their naïveté.

For the feminists, work and romance with men were ideally and, one could say, ideologically, entwined. In this they differed not only from their Victorian predecessors but from the preceding generation of New Women in the 1890s. For Anglo-American daughters like Jane Addams, who came of age determined to leave woman's appointed sphere, work was the object of desire, the redemptive force that would save them from their mothers' fate, and heterosexual passion was a treacherous lure away from one's chosen destiny. For those not inclined to "Boston marriages" with other women that combined love and work, the practical choice seemed either celibacy or marriage without a sexual charge. But with the supposed emergence of a sphere where men and women mingled in all sorts of meaningful ways, work no longer obviated the possibility of heterosexual love. Rather, the release of female expression in work, feminists believed, could create playful, inventive partnerships.

Bohemia was rife with such partnerships, relations that broadcast (often self-consciously) the importance and pleasure of sexual cooperation. The list is long but interesting. Writers were especially prone to form couples: Neith Boyce and Hutchins Hapgood, Mary Heaton Vorse and Joe O'Brien, Louise Bryant and John Reed, Susan Glaspell and George Cram Cook. Then there were more evanescent literary pairings: Floyd Dell and Edna St. Vincent Millay, Eugene O'Neill and Louise Bryant (who liked to move around). The art world, which bordered on bohemia, produced more conventional marriages structured by nineteenth-century expectations (female art students who married male mentors and gave up their careers), but here, too, there were exceptions, such as Marguerite and William Zorach, fauve painters and set designers for Village plays. Alfred Stieglitz would tap into the spirit of the bohemian couple when he set up his lover, Georgia O'Keeffe, as archetype of female creativity and sexuality, both as a painter at 291 and as a subject in his photographs. Common political work created duos: Elizabeth Gurley Flynn and Carlo Tresca, Jessie Ashley and Bill Haywood, Emma Goldman and Ben Reitman. Even the conventional marriage of John and Dolly Sloan—he the gifted artist and man of the world, she the adoring wife and dependent—changed slightly when the Sloans moved from Philadelphia to the

Village, where Dolly Sloan found work as a busy organizer for the Socialists and the birth control movement.

Shared artistic or political labor became a requirement of love; people structured their affairs around it. The appeal was so strong that when lovers did not share a vocation, they invented something to do together, like the Liberal Club plays or the Paterson Pageant, which John Reed and Mabel Dodge cooked up in the heat of their ardor. Shared work was a metaphor for erotic intimacy. In 1915, the artist Man Ray and his lover, a poet whom he met at the Ferrer School, printed up two books of her poems with his illustrations on the press in the Ridgefield commune and billed them as productions that "concreted" their affair, "an epitome of work since their partnership." Such was the romance of bohemian partnership that the pair actually made money hawking the books around Manhattan.

The proliferation of professional couples can be understood as a chapter in "the invention of heterosexuality," as one historian terms it. An institution once seen as a practical arrangement, undergirded by religious dictates, was elevated in the twentieth century to a relation imbued with psychological significance. The shift may seem counterintuitive—have not heterosexual relations always been with us? But it is true that in the twentieth century, sexual relations between men and women assumed unprecedented significance as conduits of mutual understanding, a preeminent form of companionship.

Not everyone worked at refurbishing heterosexuality, but the fascination with men's and women's intimacies was the dominant discussion of the day. There was a muted gay life in Greenwich Village for both men and women, although even now little is known about it except for manifestations in a few bars and tearooms. While not exactly closeted, homosexual preferences had little place in semipublic life. Later, the Village's reputation for unconventionality and sexual experimentation made it a mecca for gay people across the country. But in the teens, mentions of gay and lesbian sexuality were heavily coded: Mabel Dodge delicately described her friend Carl Van Vechten, for instance, a man who cheerfully hearkened in behavior and appearance to the "pansy" (one gay stereotype of the day), as capable of "warm friendships for other men . . . dead sweet affectionateness that had run over." Friends more easily accepted Van Vechten in the context of his marriage to Fania Marinoff, a Russian-born actress. Claude McKay, who followed Hubert Harrison in the generally thankless task of serving as the Village's liaison to Harlem, seems to have had affairs with men, but also used his relations with women to create an acceptable persona. McKay, a poet emigré from Jamaica, liked to pose as a naive child of the countryside blessed with an Afro-Caribbean peasant simplicity that elevated him above the complicated sexual dilemmas of urban white New Yorkers (and later Parisians), the happy "primitive" trumping the neurotic moderns. "Sex was never much of a problem to me," he wrote in his autobiography. Margaret Anderson and Jane Heap were the only gays of either sex in these circles who seem to have acknowledged the truth of their relationship. Homosexuality, if elliptically allowed, did not signify in the new sexuality.

Marriage and love affairs, however, were loaded with expectations. To be sure, middle-class marriage in the nineteenth century had incorporated ideals of romantic love (less compelling among the working classes, where marriage retained its practical basis well into the twentieth century). Nonetheless, although romance was a prerequisite of courtship, after marriage the psychological worlds of husbands and wives could well diverge. But in the twentieth century, it was not enough for spouses to form functional households, bear and raise children, do their part in common tasks, and treat each other with love and respect. Sophisticated people aimed to share work as well as innermost thoughts, an exchange smoothed by a steady effusion of eros. "I could not imagine a love affair which was not a sharing of every phase of intellectual life as well as the emotions," Sara Bard Field—a feminist cheating on her husband—wrote her lover C. E. S. Wood, a married man himself, in the first plummy days of their affair.

As so often with these people, it is difficult to peer through the effusive rhetoric to discern the truth of everyday life. Ever aware of an audience, the moderns dramatized sex and love as another act in the metropolitan spectacle. Louise Bryant, for instance, having set up with John Reed in Provincetown in 1916, preened herself on how the two of them appeared to Hippolyte Havel, their cook that summer. The romantic Czech was impressed by the harmony of their relationship, so different from his Continental expectations of Sturm und Drang.

"He is quite inspired by us," reported Bryant. "He told me that he always thought people had to quarrel just to stir themselves up to keep on loving each other. 'But it's not so . . . and dis is so lovely—you and Jackie.'" The bohemians' stories of love often turn upon such charming anecdotes of sweet equality. To see the ambiguities and conflicts, we need to peer more closely at the texture of particular relationships.

Like a number of other bohemians, Louise Bryant came from a family teetering on the line between working-class toil and middle-class security. She was born in San Francisco in 1885. Her father was a newspaperman who, like Dorothy Day's father, seems to have bequeathed her intellectual ambitions, despite a wandering and no doubt impecunious upbringing. Bryant gained middle-class credentials at the state universities of Nevada and Oregon. In 1909, she plunked herself down in the midst of the Portland, Oregon, bourgeoisie; it was then she married her dentist, albeit a dentist with bohemian flair. Scraps of bohemian radicalism had been floating about Portland for a while: the young married set indulged in risqué drunken parties in the woods, plans were afoot for a Ferrer School, and the Northwest was hopping with IWW activity. Bryant was sufficiently inspired by all this to stake herself as an artist with her own little studio on Portland's waterfront, peddling subscriptions to the *Masses* and firing off articles to Alexander Berkman's *Blast*. Reed, on a visit to his mother in Portland after he returned from reporting on the war in Europe, met a young woman who was straining to outstrip her provincial limitations.

Glistening with the patina of Harvard, exotic travels, and the *Masses*, Reed embodied a metropolitan splendor that must have beckoned to Bryant as the chance of a lifetime. The proportions of romance and opportunism in her affair with him are unclear. Mabel Dodge, Reed's earlier lover, was obviously not an unbiased observer, but her tart judgments of character are still interesting. "The girl was clever with a certain Irish quickness," Dodge sniffed, "and very eager to get on. I think Reed was a stepping stone, and through him she met a lot of people she never would have known otherwise. It had not seemed to me that she cared very much for him." Sara Bard Field, who grew close to Bryant in Portland, was perhaps more discerning: "She asks for life not stagnation." Field was suspicious of Reed's overtures to her friend. But Ida Rauh, who also came to know Bryant, assured Field that, in a sense, John Reed was beside the point: "It is experience she is seeking."

Because the professions were opening up to women, this was the first generation to use alliances with men as an avenue of mobility toward something other than marriage. Greenwich Village was, of course, teeming with people "eager to get on" and longing for life and experience, including Mabel Dodge herself. Bryant's was perhaps a balder means of utilizing love to get from some small place to a big one, but she was not unique. Whatever she felt about him, Reed was a ticket out of town into a remote and glamorous world where provincial writers like Bryant were crossing over into the upper reaches of the literary marketplace. She followed him back to New York, determined to set up housekeeping with him and become a writer.

In Greenwich Village, Reed and Bryant threw themselves into a life shaped by ideals of heterosexual intimacy. Passion did not seem to animate them so much as mutual dependency with a touch of the sibling relation. For a moment, their needs meshed: Bryant was a vulnerable newcomer to New York, but Reed, too, reeling from his bad time in Europe, had his own vulnerabilities, his professional status shaken, his emotional reach constricted. A childlike language of cozy attachment runs through their letters, quite different from the erotically saturated language that, say, Neith Boyce or Emma Goldman used in writing their lovers. A telling comment of Bryant's was embedded in a typically grandiloquent letter to Sara Field shortly after Bryant arrived in the Village. "Sarah, our relationship has been so beautiful and free! I don't know why Jack and I should ever quarrel. We don't interfere with each other at all—we just sort of supplement, and life is very lovely to us—we feel like children who will never grow up."

The sibling connection generated strong loyalties, despite the short time Reed and Bryant had known each other. Their actual families were deemed irrelevant, especially by Louise, who felt that "my people are in no way a part of me." Theirs was a life without father *or* mother. "I only want my honey for a family," she gushed. "We," the dyad, fused their common labors into a political and emotional whole, despite the vast differences in experience and fame. Reed was Bryant's great supporter, generous with his earnings and contacts. He provided the financial cushion that allowed her to launch herself, as she worked up from unremunerative pieces for the *Masses* to a modest assignment in 1916 for the wire services in France. He attentively criticized and edited her writing and made plans for assignments they could share— his China trip, spun out of his Harvard contacts, was from the start to be their joint venture. "China is going to be a splendid thing for both of us," she rejoiced. Championing Bryant must also have affirmed Reed's own sense of professional authority even as his position as America's hottest young journalist was crumbling.

Which is not to say that the affair and the marriage (in 1916) were always amicable. But it was, tellingly, professional rivalry rather than sexual angst that caused conflict. In the free-love mode of the Village, each had running sexual involvements with others—Reed with unknown women, Bryant with Eugene O'Neill and Andrew Dasburg,

Louise Bryant, Provincetown, 1916 HOUGHTON LIBRARY, HARVARD UNIVERSITY

a painter. But sexual jealousy was muted. Reed possessed an extraordinary equanimity about O'Neill, so much so that his letters to Bryant touching on the matter seem almost anesthetized. When Reed was in Johns Hopkins Hospital in Baltimore for major surgery, O'Neill moved in with Bryant. Bryant wrote Reed chirpy, encouraging letters interlaced with homey references to O'Neill's presence. She always referred to Reed's sexual adventures only obliquely.

Bryant's sense of their difficulties was dominated rather by issues of professional advancement and competition. "Just wait until we get well," she brightly assured Reed after both had been ill. "We will both do *things*—even *I* will—that will be really good." She allowed the specter of professional jealousy out of the bag by mentioning another literary couple, Will Irwin and Inez Haynes, who were "so *jealous* of each other's work." But immediately she flapped it away: "We won't *ever* do that anyway. That is just one thing that I love about our being together. You want to see me do my best and I want you to—*at any cost!*" She affirmed her commitment to their shared life not in conventional longings for children, sex, or leisure time together but in concern that, together, they maximize their literary gifts. Thus their second summer in Provincetown promised the chance they needed "to keep close to each other and I want to be very close." A lazy idyll was not what she had in mind: "It will be so fine to do *work* out here uninterrupted, and play in town. We can't put off real work year after year."

Bryant's wire assignment to the war in France seemed at the time the break she had been waiting for. Like other women, she took the press's need for reporters as the opportunity to fling herself across the gender line. The act hummed with rivalry, despite (or perhaps because of) Reed's support. Because Reed was barred from the Western Front, it was the first time she was the one with the glamorous and dangerous assignment, he the one relegated to hackwork back home. Although the job came through his contacts, it offered the prospect of loosening her dependence on him and, perhaps, shaking her free from the dyad. For a time Bryant in France had the upper hand, the knowing insider dishing out advice to the unwitting dupe. "*Be careful* what you *write now*—not because you might get into trouble . . . but because you might be *terribly mistaken!*" she urged. "If I could only *tell* you my dearest dear what the situation is. . . . Don't write anything that is untrue better a thousand times silence."

But despite Bryant's coy boast that "soldiers, civilians, all have taken me strangely into their thoughts," the job amounted to little. She never got out of Paris, since the French barred women reporters from the front. A partnership, in fact, turned out to be the only way to circumvent the regulations. (Inez Haynes, Bryant's nemesis, got behind the lines by accompanying Will Irwin, now her husband.) In fact, the boom for women writers would not occur till after the armistice, when travel became possible through the war zones. The moment when a disappointed Bryant returned to the States in early 1917 was probably the closest the two ever came to professional parity, since Reed's career was simultaneously at a low ebb. The chance to go to the Russia was, for the two of them, one of those huge pieces of luck for which downtown Manhattan was fabled.

In France, Bryant, along with other women reporters, had tried to become a daring citizen of the world, the literary identity that Reed had invented. She failed there, but the trip to Russia, a far more open journalistic situation, began to work transformations that war reporting could not. Armed with credentials from a news syndicate and Reed's old magazine, the *Metropolitan*, she, too, became a writer to be recognized and a cosmopolitan nomad, that charismatic personage of modernity. As one of a handful of American reporters, she acquired precious contacts, a thorough familiarity with the arcana of revolutionary politics and factions, and knowledge of a cast of characters still unknown to the American public. She found a place within a floating transcontinental milieu of Russians, European and American socialists, and Russian expatriates, brigades of sympathizers rolling in and out of Moscow and Petersburg. She traveled back and forth to the United States, with Reed and without him: it was a commuter marriage between Russia and Croton-on-Hudson.

Reed and Bryant's marriage was fully within the mode of the modern partnership, but the bond had a different valence for each of them. For Reed, at a low point in his life, the relationship became a sanctuary, a triumphant little stake in some brave new world. In a melancholy summation of his young life, a short memoir written in the doldrums of 1917 before they set off, he made his relationship with an unnamed

Bryant the culmination of his life. He toted up his balance sheet in the elegiac cadences of the men of 1914, the catastrophe of the war a pall over everything: "I am twenty-nine years old, and I know that this is the end of a part of my life, the end of youth. Sometimes it seems to me the end of the world's youth too; certainly the Great War has done something to us all." Pluckily he evoked the persistent dream of a democracy to be born of a diminished world, "richer, braver, free, more beautiful." There was little to hold on to, except what he had created with Bryant. The association with a New Woman glowed, a precious remnant of large ambitions. "I've had love affairs, passionate happiness, wretched maladjustments; hurt deeply and been deeply hurt. But at last I have found my friend and lover, thrilling and satisfying, closer to me than anyone has ever been. And now I don't care what comes."

To Bryant, the partnership was a launching pad. Yet the spring mechanism was faulty. For all her New Womanhood, she remained financially, emotionally, and professionally dependent on her husband. The working partnership was, ostensibly, a mark of her independence but in fact she exercised her independence most vigorously as she tacked on other love affairs, thus multiplying her dependencies. With Eugene O'Neill, too, Bryant created a partnership, in their case through a shared involvement with the Provincetown Players. Her modest success at playwriting and acting in Provincetown encouraged her to toy with a second career in drama; O'Neill became a mentor, critic, and backer. She sought to propel herself beyond romance to creative work, yet in doing so, she continually entangled herself in romance. There were, in the short run, enormous benefits to be garnered from such associations with successful men; a novice to journalism in 1916, Bryant rose in ten years' time to become a handsomely paid foreign correspondent for Hearst. The ease with which she accomplished this is evidence of the efficacy of heterosexual partnership and male sponsorship. But in the long run the conflation of love and work created its own problems; autonomy and a conviction of her professional worth, separate from powerful lovers, forever eluded Bryant. In the late 1920s, her career destroyed through the combined effects of alcohol, illness, and devastating divorce from a third husband, she would, in fact, try desperately to resurrect her role in the old

Reed/Bryant partnership by re-creating herself as professional widow and keeper of his flame.

Even at the time there were liabilities. For Bryant, as for other women of her generation, creative work and heterosexual drama were easily confused. Were love affairs her job? Or was journalism? play-writing? She applied herself almost as assiduously to keeping her romantic triangles moving (the one with Reed and O'Neill, another with Reed and Andrew Dasburg) as she did to her writing. It took work to maintain an equilibrium between her requirements and their needs, her cloudy dreams and their solid attainments, her ambitions and their triumphs. The requirements of these partnerships weighed differently on men and women. For men like Reed and O'Neill, the connection, albeit rich in rewards, was an embellishment on a career with multiple supports. The problem for women like Bryant was that the partnership was the foundation itself.

The celebration of equality did not reach into the home. The iconographic power of feminism, the way its language resonated on a public stage on which women "moved freely up and down the earth in such large numbers" (an eloquent phrase of Mary Heaton Vorse's), was less suitable for the mundane spaces of everyday life, where meals were cooked, beds made, children dressed and sent to school. Any political culture is blinkered in one way or another, but it is striking that feminists virtually ignored this particular problem. Around 1900, Charlotte Perkins Gilman and a few other thinkers, inspired by the socialist ideal of cooperative labor, had developed an analysis of women's relegation to housework and child rearing as a sig-nal source of female subordination. Gilman believed that sexual equal-ity could be achieved only when women were relieved of their labor at home, through cooperative housekeeping and public care for children (we would call it child care); then they could thrive in the world. But except for apartment house living, which faintly replicated Gilman's scheme of households grouped around common facilities, cooperative housekeeping remained a utopian dream for evangelists like Henrietta Rodman, who tried to use her Liberal Club connections to start such a facility in the Village. In comparison with free-love thought, which was once the ideological property of dreamy splinter groups but swept modern America by storm in the twentieth century, the cooperative feminist critique of housework never secured a mass following.

This meant there was tremendous disparity between the putative third sphere of sexual equality and a domestic life that was traditional in all but superficialities. In Village brownstones and Jackson Park storefronts, the ponderous Victorian furniture of the parents was gone, replaced by brightly painted castoffs, and sprightly disorder reigned. But as the Victorian furniture disappeared, so did Victorian servants, a staple of home life for all but the poorest working-class women of previous generations. After 1910, the percentage of women in domestic service began to decline everywhere in the country except the South (where alternative jobs were lacking for African American women). This was the first generation of urban middle-class women to do some of their own housework and raise their children without the benefit of full-time help. The irony is that the material burdens of domesticity increased at the moment when feminist women rejected domesticity altogether and embraced work in the world instead.

A few nonchalant eccentrics simply rejected domestic conventions. Grace Mott Johnson, a sculptor married to painter Andrew Dasburg, insisted on a strict division of labor at home, but her zealotry eventually led to an amicable parting of the ways. A woman friend who shared a studio with her claimed that, on principle, Grace Johnson would never even make anyone a cup of tea. Floyd Dell claimed that he and Margery Currey always divided up the housework; his is a self-serving memory but plausible, since Currey was a follower of Charlotte Perkins Gilman. And the frequency of divorce in bohemia when it was still rare in the nation—in Heterodoxy, the divorce rate was 33 percent, exponentially higher than the national average—indicates a widespread disaffection expressed de facto.

Crystal Eastman, after her second marriage and the births of two children, was sufficiently troubled by the problems of cohabitation to write an essay calling for the separation of heterosexual love from cohabitation: spouses could set up separate residences, she suggested, and preserve some of the excitement and intimacy of a love affair. Yet tellingly, her reasoning had nothing to do with equilibrating the work of child rearing but rather with criticizing how marriage can deaden sexual feeling. Children would naturally remain with the mother, she believed. But spouses, by living separately, could avoid the regimen of daily irritations that threatens to strangle romance. "For the usual modern type, the complex, sensitive, highly organized city dweller, man or woman, marriage can become such a constant invasion of his very self that it amounts sometimes to torture."

Eastman's frank admission of problems was rare. The difficulties these particular modern women experienced in keeping egalitarian partnerships afloat as they juggled the demands of what we now call the double shift of work and family were not discussed in any public forum. As long as a couple was childless, fecklessness in domestic life was still possible. Downtown, the implicit ideal was two adults unencumbered by children, a vision of marriage made possible, of course, by birth control. The rarely articulated but implicit understanding was that motherhood all but disqualified most women from an active role in the drama of New Womanhood. Margaret Sanger was exceptional in her success in clambering into the feminist spotlight while she cared for young children, but like Mary Heaton Vorse, who left her children for months at a time when she was on writing assignments, she did so only by casting them aside in a pinch. When Sanger bolted for Europe in 1914, it was women friends in the Village, not Bill Sanger, who looked after their three children. Once she began her rise to birth control stardom, Sanger, for all purposes, never lived with them again.

As a rule, children undid whatever reciprocity a couple had achieved in a work partnership. This is not to say that men decided to dump their offspring on the mothers or even that they necessarily enjoyed the imbalances that parenthood brought on. Many of these men had, indeed, thrived on vocational involvements with wives and lovers. William and Marguerite Zorach, for instance, worked habitually and happily with each other. The Zorachs designed sets for Village plays and even showed paintings together at the Armory Show. But the birth of two children changed things. "Up to this point," an art historian notes, "they had been considered artists of equal importance and worked in similar styles." Now William Zorach's reputation grew while Marguerite's declined. Despite his willingness to help with the children, she lacked the uninterrupted time to paint and retreated to needlework tapestry, a traditionally feminine form that she turned into expressionist composition. Although earnings from her needle-work pieces, which were almost immediately picked up by prominent collectors, supported the family for long periods of time, she was inevitably demoted from the status of avant-gardiste to that of the woman artist dabbling in crafts.

The Hapgood/Boyce marriage provides unusual and exhaustive documentation—an archive's worth, in fact, of exasperated, angry, frustrated, loving letters—of the devolution of a feminist-inspired partnership into a tense marriage between an aggrieved woman, her ambitions thwarted by family life, and a freewheeling man uncompre-hending of his wife's complaints. Because the pair were slightly older than many in the Village, their decline into chronic animosity set in early, while friends and comrades were still in the midst of egalitarian self-congratulation. In 1899, Boyce could write jauntily to her hus-band that "I begin to feel that we are a couple of sports," the couple-about-town having replaced Hapgood's man-about-town. Meet me at the Astor Hotel, she enjoined in a note anticipating an evening's plea-sure. "We can go and see high art or loaf around by our two selves." But by 1905, after two babies, Boyce saw her literary ambitions not as their collective property but as hers alone, to be defended. "I wonder if putting as much energy into marriage as I have done . . . has not been against me, so far as success in writing is concerned. . . . I think I'm less buoyant—& that counts for a lot! And I do want success. . . . I want it horridly, and money—and I want some gayety, too—*now!*"

Did the marriage and children undermine her professional stand-ing? She broached the question to her husband with a bluntness that would have been impossible two decades earlier. Her situation wors-ened when the family moved out of the Village to a house in Westchester County so as to give the children the benefit of country air and themselves more room. Because Hapgood traveled so much for his writing and commuted to his news desk in the city, she took care of the four children and huge (twenty-room) house mostly by herself. The shop talk of writers—a publisher's response to a manuscript, the prospects for an advance—gave way to anxious, defensive conversa-tions about the size of doctors' bills and the price of children's shoes. "She has no high shoes—you know she has been barefoot till lately," Boyce wrote her husband. "I would not buy *much* for her—the shoes

& rubbers I believe will be all she needs" . . . "Yes, I will bring your shaving soap" . . . "I will write you tomorrow about the jerseys & underwear for the children which I need." Her immersion in household matters would have seemed, to the women of her mother's generation, unremarkable. But unlike them, she derived no sense of social worth or power from her position as matron of a large household. Rather, she continued to judge herself as a writer—an identity she had once fully shared with her husband—and when she did, she came up short. Her husband, too, found her wanting and threw himself into affairs to regain the vital contact he had once experienced with her.

The limitations of willed equality are easily visible now but were hidden to the principals then. Despite everyone's good intentions, and despite the piquant pleasures of children, work in the home could turn into an abandoned field of old female grievances where radical women, bereft of the male companionship they had learned to prize, trudged in the same ruts their mothers had ploughed, despite all their resolution not to live like their mothers. The third sphere did not encompass households. The irony was that feminist discussion—determined to ease differences between the sexes—could not acknowledge the problem but, rather, implicitly proposed that, as if by some magic of the modern age, a free female spirit could banish the intrusions of children and the demands of housekeeping. Consequently, the demands of family life became matters for New Women to manage covertly. Feminism kept domestic difficulties apart from its demonstrations of winsome adventurousness.

The assertion of an older pattern of men's privileges and women's subordination was a result of the lack of attention radicals gave to domestic life and the constant—one could say compulsive—attention accorded heterosexuality. But psychological dynamics between men and women were also at work—more precisely, men's needs, however subliminal, to get a leg up on the heroines of the day, to reassert their ascendancy at whatever cost.

The Eastman/Rauh marriage was another fabled Village partnership, fabled because of the magnetism of each partner, its charmed beginnings, and its calamitous disintegration. Husband and wife were both prominent downtown, Eastman as *Masses* editor, Rauh as a WTUL supporter and a brilliant actress in the Provincetown Players. Initially, gifts so evenly parceled out promised to make theirs a blessed match. Both were charismatic, but if anything, Ida Rauh was the more accomplished and popular partner at the beginning, possessing just enough extra ballast in accomplishments and friends to counterbalance Eastman's big ego. Yet there was no equilibrium in the marriage. The logic of reversal (how he rose, how she sank) and their rationalizations of the failure (how he justified his aggression, how she explained it away) provide a glimpse into the intimate costs of being a New Woman and the covert anxieties of being her male partner.

Most of what is known about Rauh comes from Max Eastman's 1948 memoir, and he is an undependable, although still useful, witness. They met in 1907. Eastman was a newcomer to New York, dependent on his sister and her friends; Rauh was a Manhattan native, an insider, trailing wisps of uptown money and a mysterious liaison with a man of great distinction. He met her at the Village apartment of Madeleine Doty (Crystal Eastman's friend and a journalist who later married social activist Roger Baldwin). She is, in his evocation, a slightly spoiled, indolent poseur in perpetual high dudgeon:

> Ida was a truant from a family of rich Jews who lived uptown behind a brownstone front, and she had renounced so hotly all the frills and luxuries of bourgeois life that she lived almost like a pauper. She would bring one informal garment, a simple, self-made, unobtrusively becoming garment, and lie in Madeleine's room reading or sleeping all day long. She had the voice of a great actress and would come to life sometimes at table and converse with brilliant intelligence and rebel emotion about everything under the sun. . . . I was told afterward that she was in love, or hate, with a famous personage, and that a private grief, or grievance, combined with her revolt against bourgeois society to make her into such a decorative negation.

There are no biographical facts to flesh out Eastman's portrait, except that Rauh was a recent graduate of law school with little hope of practicing law, so closed was the profession to her sex. It is not hard to look more sympathetically than Eastman does at this talented young woman, plainly stymied for the moment yet waiting for a life to commence. Costumed in that plain dress—felicitously becoming—she keeps to herself and then, when the spirit moves her, rises to glide to center stage. Poignantly and understandably, she wants onlookers to see she is a person destined for big things in this world.

Eastman at this early point was directionless, indifferent to the reform zeal that drove his sister, interested in the philosophy courses he was taking at Columbia but not enthralled by them, and recuperating from a painful love affair. What Rauh made of him at first is impossible to tell, since she left no traces from those years. What he made of her is more readily available in the pages and pages he devoted to their broken marriage, more than thirty years after the fact. Once roused from her melancholy, she became, at least in retrospect, a "dramatic and exciting" instructor in a political seriousness he felt he lacked, a true militant who enticingly challenged his own ennui. Initially, he emulated her. She tutored him in the fine points of Marxism, of which he knew nothing, and supervised his reading of *Capital*. She helped him separate from his straitlaced Protestant past "with its pagan prayers and Emersonian moralism." The relationship was made up not from the romantic transports he had concocted with other loves but from the stuff of "factual, familiar, everyday, indubitable reality, giving the mind as well as the senses vital pleasure."

From the beginning, the Eastman/Rauh marriage was cast as a paradigm of emancipated partnership. Joseph Pulitzer's *World*, ever on the prowl for scandal, picked up from the labels affixed to their Village mailbox the fact that Rauh had kept her name. Headlines announced the radical couple worthy of a public curiosity otherwise devoted to murderers and thieves: NO 'MRS.' BADGE OF SLAVERY WORN BY THIS MISS WIFE. "I do not want to absorb my wife's identity in mine," Eastman affirmed to the *World* reporter. "I want her to be entirely independent of me in every way—to be as free as she was before we were married." The publicity provoked a torrent of hate mail; in Eastman's home town of Elmira, New York, where his parents were both ministers, it unleashed a storm of abuse. Virtuous province denounced the black sheep. Separate names were the first step on a slippery slope that led to feckless wives of loose morals, easy divorce, and free love. EASTMAN DISCLOSURES SHOCKING, declared the Elmira papers, followed by a flurry of appalled opinion pieces that concurred that Max Eastman and his sluttish paramour were personae non grata among civilized people.

Yet subtly, the terms of the marriage, which had begun with Rauh in a strong position, were reversed. The sticking points, according to Eastman years later, were her indolence and dilettantism. Rauh skipped through a succession of enthusiasms: first sculpting, then acting, interspersing her artistic work with agitation for the WTUL and women's suffrage. A family inheritance obviated the need to support herself—and helped support her husband in the bargain. Eastman reproached her for her meandering and for the lack of life force that he required from a woman to restore his own sagging energies. She cared too little for domestic affairs, he claimed; true, she was beautiful and brilliant—"noble-looking, like a lioness," Mabel Dodge, who did not often praise other women, paid her tribute—but to her husband she was too grave, too moody, too lazy, too soft, too hard, too volatile, too rigid.

With the birth of a son Rauh's life force spluttered all the more, although it ignited intermittently in anger at Eastman, in political involvements, and, as even he acknowledged, in episodic "feats of brilliant vigor" at the Provincetown Theater (she was fondly called "the Duse of Macdougal Street"). She raged at him for his affairs, including one with the baby's nanny and another with a dear friend of hers. For a time, they managed separate residences. In an arrangement like the one his sister advocated, Eastman settled into a nearby apartment and visited his wife and baby every day. But the ménage fell apart when Eastman moved in with Eugen Boissevain, who had just lost his wife, Eastman's old lover Inez Millholland, to a freak illness incurred from overwork on the suffrage circuit. The two reverted to bachelor mode, squiring Isadora Duncan's young dancers about in Boissevain's luxurious motor car. Eastman, on the advice of his new psychoanalyst, walked out on Rauh and the baby. He had no connection with his son until twenty-three years later.

Reading Eastman's account of the end of the marriage, a narrative at once ostentatiously generous toward his ex-wife and cruelly undermining, one wonders about the force the marriage still exerted on him many years later. Eastman's lighthearted, urbane prose mutes the continual carping and whining of a wronged man who lays his own fallibilities at the door of an old antagonist. Take his failure to make good as a war reporter. What went wrong? Embroiled in a "state of negation" that Rauh communicated, he could find nothing interesting about World War I. When the memoir was published, she objected to his autobiographical harassment. "Why not refer to our marriage (if you feel you must refer to it) as an experiment which did not result in a permanent relationship? Is it necessary to justify yourself to the public? or blame me?" At the time, though, the dissolution was devastating. Her heterosexual ideals ran toward a life force burning steadily on a stage both public and intimate, not a conflagration. She left the theater and slowly moved away from the women's movement. She threw herself into raising their child and finally left New York for New Mexico.

Rauh's confessions to her friend Sara Bard Field and Field's replies are the only record of Rauh's experience of the divorce. She "talks so tragically of 'the buried life,' the cruelty of Nature in fashioning women to want so much and get so little return from men," Field reported to her lover, C. E. S. Wood, piggybacking her own grievances on Rauh's. "Why is it that there seem to be so many more intellectual attractive women in the world to-day than men?" she mused. It was as if the laws of natural selection were out of kilter, with the superior species threatened with extinction. "Women of evolved personality cannot find enough mates of their own kind to go around." The proof, in Field's view, was that women still swarmed around the detestable Max Eastman. The disappointments of the third sphere produced a view of sexual difference as extreme in its own way as that of the Victorians.

Yet were the needs of the "evolved personality" really so rarefied? Did women really "want so much"? Field's judgment, seemingly critical of men, bespoke a deeper discomfort with female desire, longings that the women themselves sometimes viewed as inordinate and overwhelming. Plainly put, Rauh seems to have wanted companionship in parenthood, a husband's belief that her talents would develop and bear fruit despite the interruptions of child rearing, some assurance of sexual fidelity. In a milieu that celebrated other forms of female desire, such mundane longings were often ignored. Perhaps this was an inevitable outcome of a historical moment that put so much stock in youth and embraced so uncritically assumptions about the unbounded capacities of the present. But it is also true that delusions infected men and women differently, souring domestic negotiations, even between well-meaning partners. The gravity of the charge—women want too much, men give too little—slipped into the century's stream of heterosexual progress, an undertow of mutual suspicion in an era that authorized, in theory, an enlightened amity between the sexes and women's right to the world's bounty.

Paradoxical, self-deluding, sometimes harmful: without question there was a dark edge to sexual modernism. Yet the concord of bohemian relationships, however fragile, must be acknowledged, too, the full range of "suppleness, inventiveness, erotic ambivalence, misunderstandings, estrangements, and even the occasional tenderness," as literary scholar Maria DiBattista notes of the moderns more generally. Among the most beguiling of New York relationships willing itself into equality is the friendship of Randolph Bourne and Alyse Gregory. Any community in which Bourne imagined himself beloved had to begin with her. True, they were not lovers and thus avoided some of the meaner snares of heterosexuality. But they were best friends, and the platonic bond of the Columbia man, primed for greatness, with the poet suffragist counts as a high achievement of the experimental life. They ate their evening meals together, gossiped, plotted, moaned, and chuckled; to Alyse Gregory more than to anyone else, Bourne confided his dearest hopes, his hurts in love, his professional despair, and the sad state of his finances. "Please don't leave me in the lurch, and make me feel like a precarious incident," he teased her once when she contemplated leaving New York.

No less than a love affair, however, their closeness required negotiating the tensions resulting from his obscure feeling that she had what he lacked, an assignment to lead or, at the very least, inspire the culture. Bourne idealized her participation in the suffrage movement and Alyse became a compelling model of an American political intellectual. "You cannot think how I envy you with all your hustle and adventure of work, your crowds of interesting friends, and your ostensibly—though you do so often hint differently—so easy command of life." Against Gregory's example he counted himself the loser. He longed for her kind of activity and connections, the integration of thought and life. "As I read over your letter I am struck with the artificiality of my life and ideas. . . . Writing without contact of some definite movement, some definite demand, some definite group, must lack real vitality as I feel all mine does."

Like other bohemian men, Bourne labored to express his admiration but also bridled at his subsidiary part. By 1915, Bourne and Gregory were close enough to be openly irritable with each other over their respective roles as ardent feminist organizer and thwarted male genius. He wrote her curtly when she was off on the suffrage trail: "I don't like to hear your tales of overwork and discouraging drudgery any more than you like to hear about my sickness. I am well again, but your labor goes on. People must pay the penalty of their efficiency by overwork, I suppose. You ought not to envy me who no sooner got into a movement or group than I am thrown off by the roadside." Bourne was referring to his brush with activist politics in the Gary schools controversy; although he lent his time and writing skills to the progressive educators who defended the plan, he seemed to have no stomach for the day-to-day political defense work, meetings, and speaking. "I shall give up clamoring to be 'in' things and 'do' things, and accept my fate as a lonely spectator, reserved from action for contemplation." His dolor was in part personal, a reserve of loneliness that fed a tendency to solicit pity from those close to him. But his sense of estrangement also hints at a deeper, culturally induced jealousy.

Wistfulness about women's heroic role could turn into aggression. As women gushed in the newspapers and journals about the human sex, men issued a line of overtly sympathetic and covertly critical meditations on their female counterparts. Bourne's first effort in this direction was a 1915 article on a French woman he met in Paris on his European tour, the unnamed "Mon Amie." At first glance the piece might seem a formulaic tribute to a New Woman—the heroine is ecstatically described—but a closer reading reveals that the lovely French friend serves as a foil for her American sisters: the good feminist set up against the bad. In Bourne's account, this Parisian feminist poses a man no problems; she is a free spirit who bounds over obstacles with good spirits and nary a reproach. An implicit comparison hovers between the "uncomplicated and happy march" of French women toward equality and the truculence of the marchers at home. "Mon Amie" is delightfully self-sufficient; "the glory of being a woman in the modern world was enough for her," as it could not have seemed with those irritating American suffragists he knew. His contrast of the Parisian's "luminously expressed" ideas with those of American female friends—"how strangely inarticulate they sometimes were, and, if they were articulate, how pedantic and priggish they seemed to the world about them!"—surely recalls his spats with Alyse Gregory.

As the political climate in New York worsened with war fever, Bourne's frustration and anger spilled over into his views of feminism. His later essays on modern women are exercises in backstabbing from a writer typically so generous that the spiteful tone has baffled his biographers. His veiled portraits of women he knew are tinged with cunning, precise nastiness. The extended, beautifully turned psychological observations remind one of Henry James's portraits of American girls (and Bourne mentions James) but they lack James's amplitude of discrimination. The women are brightly idealistic, determined to choose their destinies, partisans of feminist ideas and solutions. But feminism, which he so prized in Gregory, is now "a queer distorted thing." Take "Karen," given to mannish shirtwaists, determined to set up, should she marry, separate domiciles for herself and her future husband, hell-bent on economic independence and convinced of the woes of women. When Bourne has finished with her, she stands exposed as infinitely misguided, warped by distorted ideas, stupid ideas, really. Her conversation, for example:

Karen's notes were always a little more brightly intimate than her personal resources were able to support. She seemed to start with a plan of the conversation in her head. If you bungled, and with her little retreats and evasions you were always bungling, you could feel her spirit stamp its feet in vexation. She would plan pleasant soliloquies, and you would find yourself in a fiercely cross-examinatory mood.

Her relations with men are always troubled, and the trouble is her own fault. She expects too much, gives too little, plays on too high a plane. She sees herself as the center of attention, the heroine of the tale (or the conversation). "She was much interested in men, but it was more as co-actors in a personal drama of her own devising than as lovers or even as men." The result? Spinsterhood, the old antifeminist outcome. "Men could not be crowded into her Jamesian world and she has solved the problem by obliterating them. She will not live by means of them. Since she does not know how to live with them she lives without them."

Yet what was so troubling about a woman who demanded to be the center of attention, who insisted on speaking freely and being listened to? What was wrong with "pleasant soliloquies," a form that, we know from his friends, was a favorite pastime of Bourne himself? For these offenses, Bourne implies, she must end up alone. Here again is the charge that lingered about sexual modernism: feminism was fine, but women—*some* women, anyway—wanted too much.

At its inception, sexual modernism required of men rhetorical enthusiasm, political loyalty, and fellow feeling for the cause of the New Woman, a willingness to be folded into the one big humanity that feminism heralded. But bohemian men had come of age in a time in which the depleting effect of feminization on the nation's cultural and intellectual life was taken as fact. One of the risks they seemed to take as adults was to deny these supposed perils and invest in the ascent of women.

Yet then they faced the question of how to be culturally potent at a moment when women seemed to be the bearers of change. Bohemia had always hinted at sexual ambiguity: historically, the trick had been to keep at bay the strains of effeminacy. In the 1890s, bohemians had done so by invigorating the figure of the man-about-town with the swagger of the colonial traveler and the western explorer. But in the 1910s, bohemia presented the problem in a more aggravated form, since its men were not always cast in a leading role in the theater of the new. The stage belonged, above all, to the self-proclaimed heroines in the story of emancipation, the rebel girls, the Emma Goldman fans, the writers of racy vers libre, "all of the girls [who] felt that they were young women of genius condescending to enjoy life among this gypsy rabble."

These perplexities really could not be expressed in the enthusiastic clamor for the "human sex." The very extravagance of women's involvements demanded an explosion of New Manhood but who could talk about men's needs to lead when everyone knew that the big fight of the time was the women's? In the end, the search for a liberal, replete masculinity, independent of ties to New Womanhood, took the moderns into some odd byways.

One recourse was to idealize the manhood of the proletariat. The writer friends' Wobblies, daring, hardy, rough (yet caring and gentle, too), suggested a less troubled masculinity, rooted in a more stable system of sex roles. Reed's Villatistas and his Petersburg streetfighters live in a world pretty much free of women, where they uninhibitedly exercise their revolutionary derring-do. Even the peculiar character of the tramp took on interest. In Britain, there was an earlier vogue among writers for disguising oneself as an itinerant laborer and taking to the road, and the fashion passed to America, where riding the railroads made it feasible to travel long distances without real danger. Max Eastman, for one, right after he graduated from college, disguised himself as a hobo and rode the rails across country with a college chum. Hardened, untouched by domesticity, the tramp presented an intriguing emblem of primitive masculinity isolated from women, a wandering hero of the American spirit; sometimes a Wobbly served as well, since the IWW was renowned for organizing just this sort of migrant laborer. A despised figure from the depths of the underclass became imaginatively available to middle-class men, not only as protagonist of death-defying labor organizing and free-speech battles but, in Charlie Chaplin's brilliant silent film *The Tramp* (1914), as the hero of a picaresque narrative in which the impulses for adventure and serving others overcome the miseries of capitalism.

These imaginative fraternities never deepened into the "homoerotic humanism" that literary historian Paul Fussell notes in the work of Wilfred Owen and that infused the generation of young men in Europe who went off to the war. But in John Reed's dispatches from the barricades—and in Hemingway's later writing from the Spanish civil war, as well as in the literature of the American Popular Front—we can see the lasting power of masculine energies swirling around the plebeian heroes and their sources in ambivalence toward women.

If women were at the center of the culture, active subjects in making their own stories, were men reduced to being docile interlocutors? As Randolph Bourne aired his affront at being cast as a listener to feminist monologues, so Floyd Dell touched on his discomfort at being the object of the New Woman's inquiring gaze when he modeled for a Jackson Park sculptor. "I shall never forget the sensation of sitting on a model stand and being stared at by a handsome sculptress. A man is used to having a prolonged meeting of his eyes with a girl's mean something; and it is hard to get used to meeting a girl's wide-eyed, impersonal stare." The habit of a masculine lifetime bridled at looking at a woman with sexual interest and receiving nothing in return. "I became uneasy and almost afraid—I wanted to look away, but that seemed cowardly and evasive."

Retrospectively, Dell was perhaps tracing his discomfort at being placed in a position that left him squirming for some years before the appraising gazes of talented, active, demanding women. To look away seemed timid, cowardly, perhaps unmanly; the imperatives of the day demanded that men meet the New Women in an equally searching gaze. Indeed, Dell and some of his male counterparts would eventually learn to shore up their manhood with close observation. From an admiring, exasperated, and not infrequently resentful audience, feminists' sponsors would become critics, impresarios, and, ultimately, judges.

8

Talking about Sex

Free love was the raffish accomplice to free speech and free expression, a variant of the new played out in flirtations, seductions, fallings-in-love, fallings-out, carnal delight, and despair. Women were at the center, known for sleeping with men to whom they weren't married, living openly with their lovers, and conducting multiple love affairs, all in the name of high ideals. In the 1920s, elements of free-love ethics—a faint tolerance of premarital sex for both men and women, the acknowledgment of female sexuality, and the acceptance of birth control—slipped into mainstream culture, to be heralded as a sexual revolution. Yet the origins of this revolution belong to downtown New York and the enclaves it spawned in the rest of the country. The bohemians were leaders in recasting sex, both inside and outside marriage, as an expression of the developing self and a means toward a better life. They abandoned marriage as the locus of legitimacy and upheld instead a principle of honesty among equals: the acknowledgment of sexual interests among a community of freely participating partners. Truth telling and equality, not a church ceremony, became the basis of morality, signs that distinguished honorable from immoral sexuality, whoever the parties and whatever the context.

Older women's rights leaders had been formed by nineteenth-century notions of sex as fundamentally dangerous to women and were repelled by the new ideas. But for the feminists, male and female, free love was a critical assault on the old dogma that the sexes were essentially different beings, formed from incommensurate sensuous materials. Once that shibboleth had been swept away, free love could exercise its political force, bringing men and women together, creating more space for affinities to develop. Erotic freedom became one basis for making the human sex. This was especially true for women since men, it seemed, were already endowed with so much sexual freedom that they were more or less prepared for their historic role. But now women, too, could be stimulated by a variety of experiences, romantic and erotic, comparable to those of men.

The suppositions of free love are now so much a part of American life that the shock value is difficult to retrieve. But in the early twentieth century, the assault on sexual respectability took on the "nature of a crusade," according to Lawrence Langner, an impresario of Village theater. The "spirit of revolt," of unimpeded expressiveness between the sexes, was evident even in the dancing: at the Liberal Club—perhaps in the Turkey Trot—"as you clutched your feminine partner and led her through the crowded dance floor . . . you felt you were doing something for the progress of humanity, as well as for yourself and, in some cases, for her." Love without marriage was seen as infinitely superior to conventional partnerships, moving the world "night by night, a little nearer to freedom and Utopia," Floyd Dell observed wryly. "One's sexual impulses were indulged, not impulsively or at random, but in the light of some well-considered social theory." This was so much the case that John Reed and Louise Bryant, who had been living in a free-love arrangement for some months, joked that they would hush up their marriage lest they lose face with their friends.

Free love involved sex, of course, but it also signified talking and writing about it, a lively discourse of sexual conversation and revelation. In books, salon discussions, letters, and plays, the intelligentsia made their attempts to create different sexual arrangements the subject of intense articulation. Indeed, talking publicly about sexual matters—erotic exchanges, configurations of partners, and the attendant emotions of passion, jealousy, humiliation, rapture—became seen as political in itself. This might simply be a private matter, the stuff of love letters in which partners spoke of their intimacies and women experimented with an emboldened vocabulary of desire.

But sex talk also went public. Bohemia, where, long before, dandyish young men took refuge from women, became a hotbed of sex talk. Theatricals at the Liberal Club and the Provincetown Playhouse dwelt on erotic matters, comically at the former, darkly at the latter, where the involvements of the players became material for portentous dramas of psychological depth. The campaign for legal birth control swept the Village up in sexual politics, and cerebral interest in sexual questions spilled over into personal disclosures in the cafés. The exposure of matters once deemed private appalled conservatives, especially when women were involved. No sensible person could dispute the right of women to enjoy sex, insisted one writer, striving for open-mindedness, but you certainly could deplore women who insisted on bringing up sex in common conversation. Yet it was just this—lobbing sex into the middle of common conversation—that thrilled the moderns.

It was not that no one before them had ever talked about sex. There were nineteenth-century precedents for this sort of revelatory conversation and writing, particularly a tradition of European Romantic confession, mostly male. American Victorian culture had bustled with sex talk in its own segregated, covert ways. But nineteenth-century women's ability to speak as sentient sexual beings had been limited by a melodramatic vision of decent women's victimization by men's lust. Outside pornography, the words were literally lacking to speak of female desire. Now, the garrulous exponents of free love broke with the asymmetrical pattern by according women a voice and transforming the male soliloquy into a conversation between the sexes.

The transformation of sexual mores was thus linked to literary and conversational dialogue. The authority of European sexual science (which reached America in the 1890s) helped: on the simplest level, Havelock Ellis and Krafft-Ebing gave license to the previously unused term "sex," as in "sex hunger" and "sex instincts." Even the more progressive sponsors of moralistic social-purity campaigns to combat prostitution, male promiscuity, and venereal disease sometimes advocated more honest discussion, on the grounds that education would decrease, not increase, young people's erotic drives.

Free love and its enactment in conversation and writing became a distinguishing feature of modernity. In Britain, where similar currents were at work, D. H. Lawrence implicitly invoked the connection when he introduced in *Lady Chatterley's Lover* (1928) two young women of advanced views, leaning left politically, educated on the Continent and tramping about with men. "They were free. Free! . . . free to do as they liked, and—above all—to say what they liked. It was the talk that mattered supremely: the impassioned interchange of talk. Love was only a minor accompaniment."

Since the moderns saw themselves as a shocking avant-garde, they were oblivious to free-love precursors. But in fact their elevation of sex outside of marriage to a point of principle derived from a long political and intellectual tradition, going back to utopian socialists in France and England in the early nineteenth century. The free-love movement may seem an obscure and dusty byway of history, but its ideas, crackpot at the time, are actually important to our understanding of sex in the twentieth century. Its disciples maintained that sex was a precious human capacity that, by its very nature, stemmed from voluntary attachment—from freely given love. To subject that love to the control of church or state stifled, indeed desecrated it, which is why legal marriage was wrong. For men, the loss of personal liberty in marriage spawned possessiveness and tyranny; for women, marriage ended up in subjection and enslavement.

From the beginning, then, free love was allied with women's rights. Practitioners wanted to replace marriage with an ethic of sexual responsibility that, they believed, would lead to a nobler monogamy. The ideal of the "higher love" was incredibly useful at a time when sex outside marriage was seen by most people as depraved; it gave free-love adherents a way to view themselves as superior to married couples and lifted them far above libertines, since free lovers, too, saw profligate sex as licentious. Except for a few communitarians on the fringe, the very early free lovers did not condone multiple partnerships or promiscuity, what they called "varietism." Their radicalism rather lay in their views of women's sexuality, their faith that sex was critical to the well-being of society, and their belief in the moral claims of sex outside marriage.

There was an unbroken thread of free-love thought in the United States from the 1830s through the turn of the century, intertwined with other kinds of iconoclasm, especially free thought, or religious doubt. But before the 1910s, free love was a marginal movement, hardly worth noticing in terms of its historical effects (except for its contributions to the cause of birth control). Mostly free lovers clustered in little knots of true believers, sectarian, distinctly odd, and, by 1900, elderly, with leading practitioners in their seventies. At the turn of the century, the movement was concentrated in the Pacific Northwest, with an anarchist/free-love commune on an island in Puget Sound—Emma Goldman dubbed it the "anarchist graveyard"—and a newspaper published in Vancouver. The devotees, who were also adherents of nudism, vegetarianism, and the simple life (one resident lived year-round in a stump) were working-class native-born radicals, with a smattering of Russian Jews and middle-class eccentrics. Outside the Northwest, the most important center of the tradition was New York City, where a few freethinking physicians championed contraception and sexual activity as health measures. Their writings in medical manuals and popular health magazines brought them afoul of Anthony Comstock, whose harassment led to an alliance with the free-speech movement.

While free lovers were a tiny minority, they were also great talkers and inveterate proselytizers. Isolated believers scattered throughout the country were fortified by small newspapers that expounded the faith, and various Village explainers in the late nineteenth century liked to impress their opinions on others, especially the inquiring young. Some of the bohemians had learned about free love in their youths from older people among the faithful. Elizabeth Gurley Flynn's high school sweetheart was the son of a New York free-love physician, and Djuna Barnes's father was a zealot who bicycled around the countryside from one tryst to the next, taking pains—reportedly—to display his wet crotch to passersby. The typical free-love intellectual exchange around 1900 was probably between a wide-eyed acolyte and some freethinking man of society, prone to weighty philosophical reflections on marriage and love within the privacy of his study. This was, for instance, the character of Floyd Dell's first encounters with Jig Cook in Davenport in the early 1900s. Cook's sexual radicalism—like his incarnation as Tolstoyan chicken farmer—was part of his assault on provincial convention. While he held forth to his young friend on Nietzsche, he also talked about the oppressions of marriage and the sanctity of eros and plotted to woo Mollie Price, then a young anarchist actress in Chicago.

In this manner, the noble claims of free love turned adultery into intellectually justified revolt against bourgeois life. The romantic involvements of C. E. S. Wood, who was much older than his feminist lover, Sara Bard Field, show how a man who spent much of his adulthood in the nineteenth century could graft a critique of monogamy onto the long-standing privileges of a Victorian gentleman. Wood was a well-heeled Portland radical—a lawyer, a writer of warmed-over free verse, and an inveterate adulterer. He graduated from West Point and came west in the 1870s to fight in the Indian wars, and he was so appalled by the brutality that he became a philosophical anarchist. In the 1880s, he settled in Portland where he acquired a grand house, a lucrative law practice in land claims, a well-born and devoted wife, and many children, all the while crafting a counterpersona as lonely rebel of the provinces. He dressed in bohemian garb—a long flowing cape and broad-brimmed hat—and turned his wife's society gatherings into masques and poetry readings tinted with sedate decadence.

Wood's proximity to the Puget Sound colony put him in touch with an active free-love tradition. After 1900, he defended labor radicals on the side and became friendly with Emma Goldman and other working-class free lovers. The audiences for his ideas were local ladies he seduced; by 1915, there were enough of them to comprise a veritable harem. Louise Bryant, who knew him well, mocked his passé tactics in a letter to John Reed, poking fun at his propensity to recite Walt Whitman on the body electric and dedicate his poems to his latest "Sappho." The Sapphos trail forlornly through Wood's papers: his secretary, fellow members of the Socialist Party branch, a young New Woman physician, his wife, and then Sara Bard Field, who would become his longest running, longest-suffering lover (she outlasted all the competition and finally became his second wife).

For Wood, free love justified excursions outside marriage and at the same time allowed him to hold on to marriage's safeties. In a distinctly fin-de-siècle manner, Wood mixed anarchist tenets of personal liberty with Romantic sonorities about Truth and Beauty and paeans to female sexual mystery (Sara Field was "Circe" to his "Ulysses"). Principle prompted him to avow honesty about his involvements but in fact principle usually failed at the mark. Both Sara Field and his first wife, Nannie Wood, made dreadful discoveries, slopping through puddles of indiscretion, the byproduct of his "great love," the measure of "the pulsing thought of modern man."

Although Wood's promiscuous career gained momentum after the turn of the century, he began his extramarital forays earlier and experienced little difficulty in finding partners. Memoirs of the fin-de-siècle sometimes hint at a vast moral wreckage beneath the surface of late-Victorian family life, dark sexual secrets. This was especially true of the men—polygamous fathers, philandering uncles—but the women, too, could carry on as lesbian aunts and adulterous mothers. In their childhoods, the early moderns encountered Victorians who were not very Victorian in their sexual lives but seeking, however surreptitiously, a loosening of the system.

B y the turn of the century, Eastern European Jews were infusing new life into this meager American free-love tradition, even loosening the strictures on varietism. Russian anarchists introduced free love into the ferment of immigrant bohemia and into the left wing of labor, opposing the socialists' conservatism on sexual matters by insisting on a connection between revolution and erotic emancipation. In Russia, notions of free love dated back to the 1860s, when Nikolai Chernyshevsky had electrified the intelligentsia with *What Is to Be Done*. The book was, among other things, a free-love tract; it considered women's subjection in legal marriage to be the basis of other social tyrannies. Chernyshevsky's ideas commanded the allegiance of generations of Russian radicals and circulated throughout Eastern Europe as well, following the paths of exiles, refugees, and expatriates.

Political young men and women who emigrated, whether to London, Paris, New York, or Chicago, carried free love in their ideological baggage. Konrad Bercovici's partner, Naomi, for instance, was a Jewish socialist and economics student who stopped over in Paris around 1900, in flight from pogroms and antisocialist repression in Romania. She and Konrad moved in together and started a family with apparently no thought of marrying (although she did take his name), their union unremarkable in the bohemian student life of the Left Bank. In Chicago, Edgar Lee Masters, a young and curious lawyer, got to know a circle of Russian Jewish intellectuals. "When I went there," he recounted, "we all talked free love, sex and every imaginable thing." The young woman to whom Masters was drawn insisted to him that marriage was wrong and "that a man and woman who truly loved each other should live together." When Emma Goldman and Alexander Berkman first met in the early 1890s, they set up their apartment with a similar lack of scruples, sharing it with another young man and woman, with whom they were also sexually involved. The foursome lived in a feverish state, sharing everything, avoiding closed bedroom doors, and arguing incessantly about revolutionary ethics.

Such arrangements were not for the pious or fainthearted but neither were they flatly ostracized on the immigrant left. In the Yiddish press, poets warned young women to beware the funereal dirge of the wedding march and journalists translated the works of European sexual emancipation—Ibsen, Strindberg—before they were available in English. Historians know nothing about this kind of radical thought. Perhaps free-love discussion flowed into a more general rebellion against traditional family restrictions. Shorn of its overt politics, the affirmation of voluntary love may have appealed, if only for a moment, to high-rolling daughters. Might Jewish rebel girls have flung Chernyshevsky at their dismayed parents when they stomped out the door to kick up their heels in the dance halls?

An intriguing example comes from an out-of-the-way source, the memoirs of Ariel Durant, who married the philosopher-pundit Will Durant (they would coauthor the multivolume *The Story of Civilization* and he wrote *The Story of Philosophy*). Born Chaya Lebe to a grocer's family in the Ukraine, Ariel took her Shakespearean name at the age of thirteen when she married Will, her teacher at the Modern School.

The interest is not, however, in Ariel's story, unusual as it is, but rather in her mother's. Already married when she came to the United States, Ethel Lebe plunged into Lower East Side bohemia and came out a New Woman. To her children she talked about Chernyshevsky and Whitman and to her husband she alluded meaningfully to Ibsen's Nora. Her family harangued her; neighbor boys smashed a bust a sculptor had made of her; and she finally left the house and the neighborhood, unrepentant. Untroubled by the niceties of legal marriage, she never made a move for divorce but supported herself and the children on her own, entertaining a succession of lovers.

In the minds of radical intellectuals, immigrant free love created a link between proletarian assertion and sexual freedom. While socialists saw workers as virtuous upholders of sexual morality and monogamy who struggled valiantly against the morally debasing effects of capitalism, radicals thought working people were blessed with a sexual largesse that was scarcely imaginable to the middle class. In part their understanding came out of an old tradition of erotic voyeurism across class lines. Middle-class Victorians had also believed the laboring classes to be immune to bourgeois sexual morality; the difference was they judged them harshly for this. The departure of the moderns lay in their belief that working-class sexuality was a distinct alternative that could inspire and invigorate the culture.

Hutchins Hapgood, accustomed since the 1890s to crossing the class boundary, played a role in putting the idealization of plebeian free love into play. In 1905, after publishing two books about his Lower East Side rambles (*The Spirit of the Ghetto* and *Autobiography of a Thief*, a "human document" of a pickpocket), Hapgood found himself at a loss for new material. Always under financial pressure to publish and looking to escape the constraints of the feuilletonist sketch, he set off to Chicago to write a full-length study of an American workingman, leaving Neith Boyce and the children at home in Westchester County. Chicago was at the moment a city brimming with literary potential, lots of "bully material," Hapgood assured his wife, sure to yield the "original and corking point of view."

It was a promising moment to make the move. In 1905, Chicago emerged as the capital of the labor movement's left wing when the founding congress of the IWW met there that summer. The city was, to Hapgood's mind, more sensational than New York, "the hot-bed of the Middle West, the place where labor is most riotous, most expressive, where the workingman abounds in his own sense and has formed an atmosphere of democracy extending far beyond his own class." The months he spent with working-class anarchists, as well as labor progressives at Hull House and the University of Chicago, were momentous, he felt, changing him from a genial man-about-town to a seasoned supporter of the labor movement. The sojourn resulted in two books. *The Spirit of Labor* (1907) is a biography of an anarchist union leader, Anton Johanssen. *An Anarchist Woman* (1909) is an account of a love affair between two people in Johanssen's circle: Terry Carlin, a working-class bohemian (later to be Eugene O'Neill's crony and drinking partner), and his companion, Marie, a former prostitute.

Hapgood's subject was, supposedly, the spirit of labor. But the writing kept slipping into sex talk, despite his vows to his fretting wife that he was staying clear of the temptation to write a "sex novel." The Chicago anarchists turned out to be committed free lovers with none of the old nineteenth-century compunctions about varietism. Men and women slept around and changed domiciles when partners no longer suited them. As Margaret Johanssen, Anton's sweet-tempered wife, cheerfully assessed the situation, "the need to work and love and have pleasure among many men and women" brought interest and life back into marriage. While the book managed to establish Johanssen's political trajectory as its central concern, sexual adventures threatened to derail the action, enticing readers with allusions to the hero's picaresque encounters and the titillating, changing combinations of the other comrades.

Much of Hapgood's exposition of life among the "other half" was familiar from magazine articles and social investigations. But while his treatment of labor and urban hardship was formulaic, his discovery of proletarian free love undoubtedly provided an "original and corking point of view." *The Spirit of Labor* eroticized the subject of labor and the figure of the radical workingman, striking a connection between working-class life and sexual license. Hapgood had set out to describe the "expressiveness" of the American worker and that expressiveness turned out to be, in good measure, a superabundance of sex. The democracy that beckoned across the class line was erotic as well as industrial, a liberalized regime of heterosexual love.

What is striking in Hapgood's book is how profligate workers, once the depraved others of the Victorian literature of poverty, figure as positive points of reference, the erotic avant-garde. "Very anarchistic ideas about all have their birthplace in the laboring class," he lectured Boyce: educated gentlemen like him, however well-meaning, were at best apprentices to their proletarian mentors. Hapgood was quite a sexual adventurer himself (he suspended his affairs for only a brief time after he married), yet the sophisticated New Yorker felt himself something of a naif in the fast-paced Chicago set. The psychoanalytic vocabulary of repression was not yet available to him to articulate his own awkwardness, but notions of Comstockery and puritanism were and he judged himself the lesser before his working-class friends, exemplars of emancipation.

In the next book, *An Anarchist Woman*, the sexual subplot curtailed in the Johanssen book took over. Purportedly another human interest study, the book turned out to be the "sex novel" that Neith Boyce feared was in the works. The sexual narrative subsumes the sociological material on poverty and working conditions, joining a Victorian story of women's fall and redemption to a modern exploration of the extremities of heterosexual feeling—a New Womanish study of psychological depth. Marie, the heroine, is an innocent daughter of a Chicago immigrant family, forced as a girl into exploitative labor that drives her to the temptations of the fast life. She ends up a prostitute. The premises were familiar, even hackneyed, since there were many fictionalized versions of such stories. *Sister Carrie* was an especially subversive instance of these morality tales of vulnerable women who fall prey to sexual vice and are rescued by benefactors, suitors, or settlement house workers.

Hapgood, however, was not a hack but an ambitious literary writer interested in escaping formulas, not recycling them. *Anarchist Woman* pulls the rescue tale out of a Victorian framework by making free love, rather than marriage, the agent of redemption. Terry Carlin, a wild-eyed worker, saves Marie from the streets. The two form a proudly bohemian ménage in a crummy little flat, reading poetry, poring over

Nietzsche, chain-smoking, and, in the evenings, presiding over an anarchist salon. Both have lots of love affairs, and free love at once reclaims Marie from a life of debased appetites and turns her into an anguished modern heroine, torn by erotic turmoil, living on the psychological edge.

Hapgood's work on the Lower East Side had taught him about the pungency a writer might create by reminding readers of his proximity to the strange lives he described. In Chicago, he at first adopted a disguise to insinuate himself into his subjects' milieu, donning workingmen's clothes to present himself as just another fellow on the road looking for work. But as it turned out, Hapgood needed no clothes, only sexual energy, to blend into the anarchists' world. He became something of a free lover himself, on equal footing with the others in mixing and matching bed partners, including Marie.

In these encounters, a habit of womanizing he had once denounced in himself as libertine when he was courting Boyce took on positive meaning. Sex became the means to escape his "leisure class" psychology and propel him into a heartfelt identification with the working class. Here was vital contact! Here was experience! "These last two months have meant a great deal to me," he confided to the increasingly anxious and lonely Boyce.

> They have made me see the real sadness of things more deeply than I ever did before and they have removed almost the last vestige of snobbishness of the "class" feeling that I had. My relations in past years with thieves, vaudevillists etc., etc., seem now to me quite unimportant, socially. But these working people and the radical atmosphere in which the thought of the working class results—this seems significant to me in a tremendous almost terrible way, and the personalities—many of them—fascinate, please sadden and excite me.

Lofty rhetoric whose code of sexual involvement—the key words "fascinate," "please," and "excite"—would have been discernible to the practiced eye of a fearful wife.

Through free love, Hapgood also claimed to have gained an understanding of women that transcended social convention and male condescension. Having lived with tense, conflicted Neith Boyce for some years, Hapgood seems to have been puzzling in his own way over the question of the day, "What does woman want?" Free love provided him with the answers: in his emancipated affairs, he was doing his part to encourage his partners to untrammel themselves from the double standard of sexual morality. The logic will seem self-serving, but it is important to see that Hapgood was a liberal, in his own terms a radical, since in these early years of the century, before feminism gained real momentum, any equanimity on the subject of female sexual desire was still rare.

Anarchist Woman was tricky to publish in 1909, with Comstock prowling around. In the text, Hapgood protected himself by invoking the position of the realist writer obliged to tell the truth despite any offense he might give. Yet in his private relations, he was feeling his way toward another role, that of champion of his amoral heroine and, by extension, of the eroticized modern womanhood she represented. His persona of literary champion of a heterodox heroine anticipated the position taken by male supporters of feminism, all those applauding onlookers to the restless women shortly to appear. In life, he became his subject's lover and, as the authoritative man on the scene, made Terry Carlin, the working-class hero, move over.

But the more significant triangle he organized was between himself, Marie, and Neith Boyce. Throughout the months of her husband's absence, Boyce maintained a jaunty, devil-may-care tone about Hapgood's relationships, although occasionally it cracked with anxiety or admonition. "Varietism," she ventured, was so "crude & unlovely—and besides it takes all the zest out of sinning!!" Hapgood assured her she was primary in his affections by sending her the letters Marie had written to him, a revelation that elicited not just jealousy from Neith Boyce but also a shiver of sexual feeling. She imagined herself, alongside Marie, as Hapgood's mistress; Hapgood fantasized he lay in Neith's arms. So what began as an exercise in human interest ended up as a program of intimate democracy. Preparing to leave Chicago, he bubbled with exuberance to his wife about the benefits of knowing other women. "What haven't I got to say to you! But the important thing is that I love you! And I know it all the better after meeting and knowing other women."

Like his male peers, Hapgood was caught between a late-Victorian mentality of learned privileges that he consciously rejected and expectations of women's deference and availability that he unconsciously retained. Free love provided a view that was in line with the emancipations of the time yet still allowed a man to rule a little roost. It was a complex balancing act turning adultery into a feminist gesture, love triangles into political solidarities. The baroque curves and loops of Hapgood's confessions were his own, but his habit of erotic truth telling was more widely shared.

The interest in working-class sexuality also heightened the intellectual appeal of the prostitute, who was the most eroticized working-class woman imaginable. Victorians had made the prostitute the negative referent of the virtuous wife, but a loosened dichotomy between the good women and the bad led the moderns to conceive her within a spectrum of female figures—bachelor girls, bohemian girls, New Women, free women—all connected by their independence, unorthodox behavior, and sexual expressiveness. The prostitute, by virtue of her defiance of gender norms, was seen at moments as a version of the rebel girl. Talking about sex linked the ultimate female victim with the heroine of the moment, lifting the prostitute out of her old lowlife niche and holding her up as a figure of the revolutionary age.

Collectively, prostitutes endeared themselves to radicals as a potential constituency. For the IWW, prostitutes were simply exploited workers, to be defended from moralizers; the Wobblies had even organized a prostitutes' union in New Orleans. Emma Goldman, never one to shy away from extreme formulations, went over the top by turning the old relation of wife and prostitute upside down. In "The Traffic in Women," a lecture that denounced sexual-purity crusades, she turned prostitutes into virtuous, independent sex workers and married women into lackeys of male lust. Quoting Havelock Ellis, Goldman proposed that "the wife who married for money, compared with the prostitute, is the true scab. She is paid less, gives much more in return in labor and care, and is absolutely bound to her master. The prostitute never signs away the right over her own person, she retains her freedom and personal rights, nor is she always compelled to submit to man's embrace."

The prostitute became a symbol of modern female ambiguity. Fiction and poetry about prostitutes proliferated, so much so that the *Masses* editorial board, inundated, vowed to reject anything at all on the subject. Billowing with desire to walk the city streets, she brought plebeian energy to ruminations on the restlessness of women. Subversive, a little romantic, she allowed intellectuals to identify her transgressive desires with their own. And in her willingness to open up her life to sympathetic writer friends, she demonstrated how sincere women and empathetic men could turn once debased sexual bonds into understanding—free love into free speech.

In a group of short stories, John Reed used the theme to explore a variety of perplexing encounters between men and women. Reed was an inveterate roamer who liked to chat up streetwalkers and regale his then-lover Mabel Dodge with tales of their "strange purity" ("I shut him up hard," she later boasted). For Reed, the walks were as much literary as sexual. In his fiction, John Reed follows the tradition of the urban flaneur, but the moral certainties of identifying lowlife types, along with the geographical boundaries that once contained their activities, are gone. A paid dancer in a tacky dance hall tells one narrator she bolted from a luxurious trip to Europe paid for by a "Count" to wing it back to New York for the summer opening of Coney Island. A "girl" loitering outside the Harvard Club explains to George, a skeptical gentleman interlocutor, that she is a tourist from Ohio. She is penniless, she readily admits, but she claims she survives by picking out some pleasant-looking house each night and asking for shelter. George sees a vagrant who needs a train ticket home and gives her money, but then she pops up in New York again. Confusion adds to confusion. "The poor fellow's impatient curiosity consumed him bodily. What would she say? How would she explain it? Or would she simply own up to the fraud? Or would she tell as marvelous and incredible a story as before?" Was she one of the deluded down-and-out? Or was the whole concoction a street hustler's scam?

In the nineteenth century, the need to fend off the imputation of prostitution ruled women's comportment in the public world: no less, in their own way, than women in orthodox religious societies, Victorian women covered their bodies, hands, and heads on the streets, walked with companions, and avoided looking directly at male passersby. A strict bearing, bred in the bones of respectable women, designated their distance from prostitutes. But now the code of conduct buckled, and for onlookers it could be as hard to pin down the truth about women as it was to grasp the verities of the modern city, which itself shimmered with seductiveness. "Girls" are no longer in their niches in the shadows, Reed implies; they are everywhere, sauntering through a city that is their stage, "as if it had all been created to set them off." Who were they, these creatures who met a man's stare so readily? Appearances were deceptive. Reed's stories mull over the difficulties—and the pleasures—of deciphering female types once easily identified. A "girl" drifting about the street outside a gentleman's club might be a prostitute or a con artist but she might also be a virtuous waif from the Midwest.

The freedoms of women with which the city abounded caught the artist's look. How many stories might accrue to what he glimpsed? John Sloan's sketches and paintings of women on the New York streets from the same years also play with the ambiguity that hovers around female independence. Women sashay down the street, easy in their bodies, hatless, gloveless. Are they streetwalkers? Is the bold pair in *Sunday Afternoon, Union Square, 1912* intending to draw the interested glances of the men? What is it about the two that provokes the less obtrusive pair of women on the bench to whisper?

Sloan and Reed probed a world in which women's surfaces, and their conversation, were insufficient to fix them in one's mind. "Whether the girl was straight or not, George doesn't know yet," we learn when Reed's narrator first spots his subject. "It's a thing you can usually detect in a five minutes' conversation"—but he finds this no longer to be the case. Consider the conversational community in which Reed moved, where female self-invention was central. Women speaking freely about themselves, their relations with men, their innermost needs and desires: it could make a man uneasy, despite his manifest enthusiasm. A fellow could be had. Reed's girls, it seems, had stolen the male narrator's prerogative to explain their lives; these women had the power to make up their own stories.

John Sloan. Sunday Afternoon, Union Square, 1912. *Oil on canvas.*
BOWDOIN COLLEGE MUSEUM OF ART

   Women writers must have felt ambivalent about the prostitute's prominence. No matter how au courant were idealizations of the streetwalker, for women abroad—out of the home, on the streets, acting in public—the stigma hovered at the edges of female independence. Especially for those who lacked the inner conviction of blameless ladyhood born of white middle-class status, the threat could be dreadful. Police tactics of harassing women often turned on taunting them as prostitutes. Black women were especially liable, criminalized simply for being out on the streets without male escorts, but white workingwomen, too, were vulnerable and so were their female writer friends. In the New York needleworkers' strikes, the police intentionally threw arrested strikers into holding cells with prostitutes and sometimes charged them with prostitution as well, knowing what it would mean to them when they went back to their families. Dorothy Day remembered with shame being charged with prostitution in a police raid on an IWW house in Chicago where men and women were sleeping.

The reverberations must have made lyrical renderings of prostitution problematic for women. The oversimplifications of a streetwalker's life—the "strange purity" admired by Reed—had more to do with male fantasy than with women's realities. In the end, the stories did not so much relax the hold of conventional morality on modern women as displace men's anxieties, sublimating worries about the potentially thwarting powers of the women who were more surely their equals.

It is worth turning once more to the Hapgoods, who left such a stunning record of their intently ethical sexual transactions. Through the layers of published books, love letters, and erotic transactions that made up Hapgood and Boyce's marriage, literature commingled with sex, the writing inextricable from the eros it sought to represent and comprehend. The remarkably open and explicit record of their relationship mixes confession, narration, print, and drama into a distinctly modern relationship, in which an outward show of equality obscured a deeper reconfiguration of male privilege and female acquiescence.

An ideal of open discussion and frankness wound through the correspondence, injecting into the marriage the stimulation of sexual transgression and erotic triangles—honesty as aphrodisiac—but mostly to Hapgood's advantage. Over the years he increased his own freedoms while retaining an ostensibly protective control over Boyce's. At the same time, free-love talk helped him become something of a literary authority on the vagaries of modern love. Politics provoked sex; sex produced writing and also garnered publishers' interest. The sequence, despite its origins in feminist intentions, ended up strengthening Hapgood's position, turning him, in the name of feminism, into a new kind of patriarch.

Love letters such as theirs are, admittedly, difficult historical documents to use. They seem to float in a timeless realm of attachment and need. The world exists at their margins; indeed, love letters mostly belong to those moments of life when lovers create, in the writing, a world of their own. In a time that saw world war, revolutions, and tumultuous labor battles, there was scant mention of current events in Boyce and Hapgood's voluminous correspondence. Rather, they used the letters to adjudicate practical matters about children's shoes and doctors' bills, publishers' advances and repairs on the house—and to enact their erotic connection. But however private the genre may seem in these most intimate moments, their confidences about desire took shape from historical and psychological materials at loose in the world at large.

Hutchins Hapgood CULVER PICTURES

Although Hapgood had never been one for sentimental effusions, even when he was passionately courting Boyce in the 1890s, his encounter with working-class sexuality in Chicago moved him to an epistolary language that flaunted what still must have been the reigning romantic imagery of hearts and flowers. Often traveling for his work or spending the night away from home in Manhattan, he scribbled late at night from hotels and rented rooms, reproducing the rhythms and verbal exhortations of sex. "I am naughty tonight," he began. "Why are you not here? I'd try to give you a good time. Did I ever give you a good time? Did any other man ever do as well? better? Do you love me? will you always love me? Well, why don't you say so? Kiss me. Hug me. Closer, closer. ah! ah! ah! I'm quite wild. I don't dare go to bed." The phrasing was colloquial, with just a hint of the play with which a man might whip up a "good time" with a prostitute—"Did any other man ever do as well?"—or at least an easygoing workingwoman like Marie or others with whom he became involved. The letters mimic bedroom conver-

Neith Boyce Hapgood
COURTESY NEITH BOYCE SOUZA

sation, sometimes laced with a touch of pornography: the sly proposition, the naughty wink. "I wish you could be with me now! I want to sleep with you tonight! Is it allowed?"

When he was away, Hapgood's favorite strategy to thicken erotically the atmosphere between himself and his absent wife was the free-love triangle he first set up with Marie in Chicago. Initially, his was a literary rationale for disclosing to Boyce his attractions to others and demanding she do the same. As sex became writing for Hapgood and writing became sex, he construed sharing material as a benefit of a partnership of two writers, both working on New Woman themes. So he sent her Marie's letters as a "document" that could aid in her own work. As his free-love relations progressed in the years after Chicago (which he and Boyce spent living with the children in Europe, the Midwest, and then back in New York in 1914), the letters and stories about his affairs became more frankly erotic. He invited her to join in. "Tell me you love me and also tell me about the flirtations you are having," he teased. "Have you been unfaithful? Have you sinned? Did you like it. . . . Do you like me better than ever? What shall we do when we meet so as to take another step?" "Come and hug me and confess it all," he begged. Disclosure was the turn-on. "I am full of lust and love and desire to talk and hear you talk."

Conversations about sex were reported on both sides; letters were exchanged between the partners but also handed around among other sexual talkers. In Chicago, Hapgood chatted with Emma Goldman about her sex life with Ben Reitman and with Reitman about a prostitute Reitman knew; Reitman, who was himself enjoying a heavy-breathing epistolary relationship with Goldman, gave Hapgood the letters of the prostitute, which Hapgood then sent on to Boyce. He invited the confidences of Ruby Darrow, a woman embittered by Clarence Darrow's years-long affair with Mary Parton (Sara Bard Field's sister and a San Francisco labor radical), and contrasted Mrs. Darrow's monogamous martyrdom with Neith Boyce's pleasing willingness to venture outside the marriage. "You say you are sensitive to the interest and attraction of other men," he commended her. "I think that this is true, and I am very glad of it. You would not be the interesting woman you are, if you were not."

Boyce gamely struggled to keep up, although her heavy responsibilities for their four children and the difficulties of doing her own writing sometimes overwhelmed her. In gay moments, however, she also wrote about sex, though more euphemistically and allusively than her husband. In Florence, where she stayed for a time with the children in 1907 while Hapgood was in Paris, she blossomed in the humid atmosphere of the exile colony, where a lingering decadence rather than boisterous American free love permitted discreet adultery and same-sex liaisons. She lightly conversed about sex with Bernard and Mary Berenson, the art collectors, reported a serious kiss with a young woman whom her husband had also fancied, and sportingly passed on accounts of her flirtations with men. "She is so pretty and gay," she confided about the woman. "I have often wanted to do it before—& I daresay *you* have??" True, her determined gallantry sometimes failed her: of Hapgood's lover of the moment in Paris she declared flatly that "she is the one person in the world I hate." Mostly, however, she abided by the principle that their sexual involvements were common property, equity for the marriage. She had few affairs in comparison with her husband's many—only one was serious—but after some resistance she agreed to make the letters available to Hapgood in exchange for the documentation from his own contemporaneous amour.

In its nobler moments, free love aimed to subvert the marriage system, but in its more earthbound aspects it edged into voyeurism. The circulation of letters and revelations of relations with others created keyholes through which each partner in turn might peek. The idealistic, feminist imprimatur of free love sanitized these "low" elements, removing sex talk and writing from the venues of the brothel and the leatherbound volumes of Victorian pornography and making the explicit discussion of adultery, for example, fit stuff for a woman of letters like Neith Boyce.

The raunchiest performance of free-love talk comes from Emma Goldman, who produced an intensely revelatory and detailed account of her sexual life with Ben Reitman, her working-class "Hobo." Her wild language often outstripped free-love elocution to reach for a pitch of erotic abandon. "[I] would devour you, yes," she avowed, "I would put my teeth into your flesh and make you groan like a wounded animal." The two wrote each other in code, naughty allusions echoing pornographic euphemisms: her "t-b" ("treasure-box") longed for his "Willy"; he wanted to put his face between her "joy mountains," "Mt. Blanc" and "Mt. Jura."

The letters became a paramount form of not just emotional connection but sexual performance, since the lovers were often separated. Goldman strived to outdo herself, narrating the carnal particularities of past meetings and drumming up anticipation for the future: "The day seems unbearable if I do not talk to you. I would prefer to do something else to you, to run a red hot velvety t over W and the bushes, so Hobo would go mad with joy and ecstasy. . . . Oh for one S—— at that beautiful head of his or for one drink from that fountain of life." Like Hapgood, Goldman recorded the throbbing of desire: "Lover, Hobo you have never really loved me enough, nor the t-b, nor the m, no, you have not. But I know how to induce you, and if I could draw, you would see, but this way you wait until Oh let it be soon, please, please, come right on." The sexual rhythm was intended to stimulate a response, seeking an autoerotic compact in the space between meetings.

Goldman's letters are extraordinary both in what they say—it is unusual to come on such sexually explicit language outside pornography in the early twentieth century—and for who wrote them. We are fascinated by the great champion of women's freedom making a spectacle of herself before gamy Ben Reitman, a man on the make with any woman who crossed his path. The juxtaposition of language in the letters heightens the incongruities, as pornography jostles a confessional idiom befitting a romantic heroine: "pour your precious life essence

into mine and let me forget that I have neither home nor country. If I
have you, I have the World. . . . Darling lover, champion f—— just 4
more days and then and then. Every nerve is tense, my t—— is hot and
burning with the desire to run it up and down W. My m—— scream
in delight and my brain is on fire." Treasure-box, mountains, and
Willy mix indiscriminately with talk of souls thirsty for love and flowers opening to the sun, the roar of the ocean, the surge of the waves,
and the omniscience of the great, good, and beautiful.

It is easy to discern the sources of Goldman's rhapsodic language
in European Romanticism. The greater difficulty is understanding
how a woman who prided herself on her refinement in all matters
political and cultural came to occupy the role of pornographic narrator. Goldman was one of the few Americans to be acquainted with
Freudian thought—she may have heard Freud lecture when she studied midwifery in Vienna in 1899 and she traveled expressly to hear his
American lecture at Clark University in 1909—yet her eroticism
depended not on the terms of the fin-de-siècle sexual science that was
Freud's context but rather on colloquial conventions. The key to
Goldman's persona as a smutty conversant lay in the way she glamorized Reitman as a working-class primitive endowed with supranormal
sexual appetites that had developed unchecked in his vulgar lowlife
upbringing; her projection was kin to others' fantasies at the time of
African American "primitives." She was his "Hobo lover," unable to
resist, despite her better instincts, "the call of the wild" (Jack London's
book of that name came out in 1903).

There was a trace of Russian literature in her portrait of Reitman as
social outcast, a Dostoyevskian cast to the wounded psyche she
ascribed to him. But mostly she saw him through an American lens, a
type of the urban shadows flickering with lust. And Reitman indeed
trailed salacious associations, which he took pains to advertise: as a boy
he had worked in brothels, his mother was probably a prostitute, and in
his years of riding the rails as a hobo he was in contact with a subculture known to the cognoscenti for its homosexuality. In his plebeian
person he embodied forbidden power that released a carnal self within
her. In an exchange suggesting the one between Hapgood and his anarchist woman—although the roles were reversed—the working-class
man revealed to the intellectual woman the powers of desire.

Ethnic and racial primitivism were bound up with notions of sexual licentiousness. The racialist thought that was ubiquitous at the time held the darker, poorer "races"—Eastern European Jews, Italians, and above all, African Americans—to be animalistic and uninhibited in their sexual excesses. We are accustomed to thinking of blacks as the paramount hypersexualized beings in American culture, but the stereotypes were more complicated. Certainly the black poor could signify, even in Manhattan, a sexual license beyond the province of tolerant people: think back to Mabel Dodge's mortification at the black blues performers whom Carl Van Vechten brought to stir up her salon. And soon, with the migration of African American music and dance into northern white culture, the association of blacks with sexual expressiveness would spread. But in the 1910s, working-class sexuality also served that role for northern intellectuals. For Goldman, a Russian Jew herself, excitement was bound up not so much with skin color or ethnic origins but with the delectable smack of lowlife. In Reitman, Goldman believed she had found a man inoculated against middle-class decorum.

For Almeda Sperry, a working-class friend of Goldman's who had once been a prostitute, Reitman's call of the wild held no charms. To her he was more like a common john. If Goldman knew what she knew, Sperry chided her friend, she would find the man intolerable. "For a woman of your knowledge you are strangely innocent," Sperry told her. Sperry, a lesbian, wanted to sleep with Goldman when she came to visit Goldman in New York. Reitman, sensing a primitive after his own heart, tried to draw her into a triangle, inquiring when he met her at the train station (as she described the encounter to Goldman) "how many men there are in this town that I had not fucked yet" and then sketching a pornographic scenario she could act out with him and Hutchins Hapgood. But Sperry, impervious to the thrill of male lowlife, gave back as good as she got. "He tackled the wrong woman when he tackled me," she boasted to Goldman. "I used the same language he did." A veteran of the roughest working-class sexual politics, Sperry held no truck with Reitman's self-aggrandizing plebeian masculinism and judged his " 'fuck' talk" by the lights of a hardened sexual realpolitik.

Goldman and Reitman's stories, like Hapgood and Boyce's, constitute a world unto itself. Hapgood and Boyce, married with children, surrounded their sex talk with consultations about domestic matters. Goldman and Reitman, responsible as lovers only to each other (although as public figures they moved amid a huge cast of characters), remained in an exclusive, closed epistolary circle. Hapgood and Boyce employed an allusive language of carnality, conjuring up the elements of an encounter but never setting them in motion in stories or remembrances. Goldman and Reitman staged detailed erotic anecdotes.

Yet for all their differences, the letters exist in the same universe of sexual ethics, emotions, and sensations. The pairs were actually joined in conversation and possibly in bed. When Hapgood was in Chicago, he had elicited Goldman's confidences about her enslavement to the hot hobo. His curiosity piqued, he then struck up a friendship with Reitman, who showed him the letters of the prostitute they had discussed. Possibly these were seductive letters that Almeda Sperry had written to Goldman and that Goldman had passed on to Reitman. And when Reitman proposed to Sperry a sexual threesome with Hapgood, the fantasy was all the more alluring because, as he acknowledged to Goldman, he himself was attracted to Hapgood. Intrigues with others were a medium that held the erotic dyads in a suspension of other affinities. Both couples looked to erotic conversation to heighten attraction. And both Goldman and Boyce saw sexual talk as an equalizing force for women, opening up a space of reciprocity where jealousy, hurt, and humiliation could be banished to a bygone era of women's powerlessness.

Revelations that were habitually confined to conversations and letters also took place in public and semipublic. Sexual revelations—gossip about others, admissions about oneself—were self-conscious acts whereby the radicals stretched the faculties of conversational community for friendship, tolerance, understanding, free speech, and expression. Hurtful secrets, hypocrisy, the sexual double standard—those were atavistic habits. Recounting a sexual tale conferred a sensation of community: "the relief of telling the story . . . [of the] last unhappy love affair to a sympathetic listener," Floyd Dell wrote.

Dorothy Day took a less benign view of Village confessions, however, at least as practiced by men. His love affairs, she commented of Dell, "should have taken place on the stage of the Hippodrome before a packed house."

Day touched on the ways in which sexual conversations served as a boast of potency. Women might play a leading role in their own intimate dramas but they seldom put those dramas onto a bigger stage. Rather, they used the act of disclosure to create supports for themselves. Talking helped untangle and control sexual complications. Sometimes opening up a conversation could even rein in a free-loving man. Thus Mabel Dodge, an experienced practitioner of free-love tactics, took matters in hand conversationally when she sensed warmth between her then-lover John Reed and one Babette, a seductive German radical who had come to town in 1913 and was going around pretending to be a prostitute. Dodge didn't bother to negotiate with Reed but went straight to Babette. "I immediately wrote her a note and told her . . . that she could stop right there." Babette took the occasion to pour her heart out—Mabel Dodge prided herself on being a good listener—about her lack of particular interest in Reed but also her general problem of uncontrollable "desire for the male." The potential love affair was aborted and Dodge had gained an admirer. "Oh, how we were all intertwined!" Dodge marveled.

The feminist Sara Bard Field negotiated her way for years through C. E. S. Wood's multiple involvements by weaving conversational relations with other women: her sister Mary (involved in the affair with Clarence Darrow); Margaret Johanssen, the willing wifely heroine of *The Spirit of Labor*; Ida Rauh. All shared the travails of loving promiscuous men. Field also spoke with and wrote to as many of Wood's lovers as would reciprocate, although the circle was always widening and she never quite kept up with his involvements. New candidates appeared whom she failed to rope in but she did manage to develop confessional relationships with a few. Wood was another who circulated love letters women wrote him, but Field accomplished something of a flanking action by developing her own relations, actual and epistolary, with his lovers. A mutual accord with Kitty, Wood's stoic, depressed anarchist lover/legal secretary, pleased her greatly. To Wood himself, she preened herself on the achievement their friendship represented: "two women who love *one* man . . . not a speck of that jealousy with which the story books teem."

These women put sex talk to therapeutic rather than aphrodisiacal uses. Female conversation helped Field cling to the high ground of her "soul affinity" for Wood while externalizing what were, in the schema of free love, base reactions of jealousy and rage, evils Field detested herself for entertaining. She reported back to Wood other women's criticisms and condemnations of his actions, taking care to present herself as his defender. Field had been raised in a rigid midwestern Baptist home and, despite her adult agnosticism, her defiance of convention in her extramarital affair with Wood cost her in self-esteem. Sometimes, she confessed, she felt "smutty." She fought such internal judgments by holding herself aloof in her sacred passion and distinguishing their liaison from mere bohemian promiscuity, "not lovely to me even if done by good looking intelligent people who call it high sounding."

As she situated herself in a coterie of unorthodox women, she comforted herself with the knowledge of what they shared—having sex outside marriage—but also with the conviction that she was different. The old dichotomy between good and bad women may have blurred, but still, she drew lines. Florence Deshon, a beautiful and talented actress who had taken up in the Village with Max Eastman, came in for a gibe when Field visited New York in 1917: "a bit shop-worn, I fear, sexually speaking," she wrote Wood pityingly, "having been handed about among a number of men in Washington Square." The confiding Kitty, who admitted to Sara Field a "sex hunger" that led to other affairs besides the one with Wood, served as a foil for Field's single-minded devotion. "I cannot conceive of such a thing *for myself*," she gloated, "as divorcing my physical love from my soul affinity." In a mental game of king of the hill, she clambered to the top, where she might know all, elbowing aside her rivals. There, at the pinnacle, she might have a power that could rival that of Wood, the person who really knew all. Or did he? Women's sex talk might illuminate corners where even he hadn't visited. Had he known before Sara mentioned it, for example, that Kitty had other lovers?

This was not the sustaining, diffusely sensuous "female world of love and ritual" that historian Carroll Smith-Rosenberg believes to have gently encompassed Victorian women. It was rather an adjunct to heterosexual relations, a combination of training ground and retreat for recuperation. But haven't women always complained about men to each other? The answer is complicated. The confessions of Sara Field and her friends did echo women's ancient plaints about men's propensity to roam. Bringing back a straying husband, exterminating a rival: these were reasons women for hundreds of years consulted conjurors and prayed for help to the divine. But the terms were new, partly in the women's compulsion to distance themselves from traditional expressions of female sadness. The modern touch came in their intense effort—in words, not prayer or magic—to transcend jealousy and hurt, repudiate an emotional vulnerability they associated with female weakness, and forge, teeth gritted, an alliance with male sexual adventure in the name of the human sex. Confessions to friends drew off some of the power of anger, reminded the women of the ethical system to which they had pledged fealty, and staked out the ground of psychological authority. They fortified themselves for the next round.

Sometimes there was a more robust inheritance of women's historical care for the collective female welfare. Sometimes, in the tenderness of a friend's bracing encouragement, a woman tapped into a clear-running spring of well-being. Margaret Johanssen, a woman with her own troubles to bear but endowed with great optimism and generosity, was such a friend to Sara Bard Field. "I never had anyone believe in my possibilities as she does," Field wrote. In the overheated world of radical heterosexuality, love letters fell into the hands of readers intended and unintended; spectral posses of rivals hovered outside bedroom windows; love, for all its promise to bring into balance two distinct beings, threatened to swamp the boundary between self and other. It was good in such a world to see herself reflected in another's eyes, sufficient just as she was, her integrity and gifts intact. Not a thrilling love—no transports of passion. Something more ordinary: the love of a woman friend.

With sex talk so widespread and extravagant, dramatists could easily adapt it for the theater. Heterosexual exchanges, keyed to angst and discord, became a fund for dramatic experiments, culminating in the depth dramas of the Provincetown Players. Partners in sexual dialogue, negotiating with each other or with a third party in a triangle, moved onto an actual stage. Indeed, these "he said, she said" one-act plays, structured around psychological action with virtually no plot and performed on a bare set, were the beginning of "serious" theater in New York, the first modernist alternative to the light musicals and melodramas of Broadway. There is a direct connection between the Provincetown Players and Eugene O'Neill, who produced his first plays with them. Through the new theater, the radical ethos of heterosexual dialogue and disclosure became implicated in notions of psychological insight just gaining currency in American culture.

In 1913, Floyd Dell formed the Liberal Club Players. Newly arrived from Chicago and brimming with purpose, Dell gathered a group of eager amateurs and professionals and set about staging monthly one-acts at the Liberal Club. From his days in Jackson Park, he was familiar with the ideas of the Little Theater—a movement that sought to displace the trashy, elaborate commercial dramas that dominated American theater with serious plays, produced on a shoestring—but he wanted to do something that was less grave and less European. He thought that in the Village, theater could draw from the living material eddying around its players, a community enacting itself. So Dell took lovers' quarrels, men's promiscuity, women's resentments, and the difficulties of marriage and staged it all at the Liberal Club, mostly as farce. Some of the plays were thematic and ideological, fleshed out with speeches on the inevitable failure of monogamy and the death of love in marriage—not so different from an Emma Goldman lecture. Others were self-mocking treatments of what Dell referred to as "everybody's private affairs." Wryly, he set himself up as the Village Ibsen.

The "he said, she said" format of the plays replicated the openness and purported symmetry of the free-love dialogue. Two actors performed on a set designed as a psychological space with minimal scenery and props. But the plays also spoofed free love's pretensions to high-mindedness and honesty. A man and woman, each believing the other is married, fall into a free-love passion, but the attraction fizzles when they discover that neither is married and there are no third parties to make up a triangle. The self-dramatics of free love turn out to be as flimsy as Liberal Club productions: a bohemian who presents himself to his new lover in the Village as a gallant refugee from a stultifying bourgeois marriage turns out to be a compulsive liar who uses the story on every new woman he picks up. Heterosexual honesty, the great shibboleth, becomes in its feints and evasions the force that drives the plot. *Enigma* (dedicated to one of the troupe's stars, the glamorous Chicago actress Kirah Markham, and her notoriously promiscuous lover Theodore Dreiser) circles around lovers' lies, never achieving a resolution. The stark confrontations of the heterosexual dialogue double back on themselves; honesty creates its own circumlocutions.

The theater of sex had little to do with Freud. Historians have left the impression that psychoanalysis arrived in force soon after Freud's 1909 visit to the United States, but American habits of talking about sex were, at their inception, derived from other sources. Among the downtown moderns, there *were* physicians who treated what we would now call emotional problems, especially women's problems, but they did so within an older model that mixed gynecology with advice. There was a doctor who performed abortions and pronounced upon marital problems (he was the man who advised Max Eastman to stay away from his wife and child). But medical practice still relied on the diagnosis of hysteria to explain women's depression, anger, and paralysis. Before 1920, neither men nor women turned habitually to Freudian theories of the inner life and there were only one or two trained analysts in downtown New York with as yet, it seems, only a few male patients. To adjudicate the pressures and problems of modern heterosexual relations, the earliest of modern intellectuals turned rather to the relief available within conversational community—its books, plays, and talk.

So in 1916, a group of Liberal Club players summering among the Portuguese fishermen in Provincetown, on Cape Cod, decided to replicate their Manhattan venture but with a greater degree of seriousness. Their purpose had much to do with the presence of Jig Cook, who loved Greek drama and believed something of equal import could be done for the modern age, and with the presence of the dissolute but undeniably talented Eugene O'Neill, who agreed to write plays for them. Other actors and actresses arrived from New York. Ida Rauh had come, trying to recuperate her self-image as independent woman after her bruising separation from Eastman. Hapgood, Boyce, and Mabel Dodge were there, Dodge having possibly slept with Hapgood and certainly having had an affair with John Reed, who was also present with Louise Bryant. When Reed left to cover the Democratic convention, Bryant took up with Eugene O'Neill, who was living in a shack with Hapgood's one-time literary subject Terry Carlin. Sara Bard Field passed through to visit Ida Rauh. Polly Holladay and Hippolyte Havel, owner and cook respectively of Polly's Restaurant in the Village, provided what passed for comic relief with their violent and abusive fights over Havel's indiscretions.

In such a heated atmosphere, with the European war raging in the background and American intervention imminent, bohemian banter gave way to psychological probing. One of the first plays the group staged in an old fish house was Boyce and Hapgood's *Enemies*. The piece followed the light Liberal Club formula of "he said, she said" but its heterosexual dialogue strained for painful honesty. The characters remain the nameless allegorical figures of He and She, speaking to each other across a great divide. No one in the audience could fail to recognize, however, the account of the authors' own conflicts from the references to Her bad housekeeping and His drinking, His affairs and Her reserve. Although both partners were credited with authorship, textual evidence indicates that *Enemies* was primarily Boyce's work. The dialogue is firmly disciplined in its symmetry—my point of view, your point of view, give and take, tit for tat—but it is Her speech that indisputably crowns the piece. "You, on account of your love for me, have tyrannized over me, bothered me, badgered me, nagged me, for fifteen years. You have interfered with me, taken my time and strength, and prevented me from accomplishing great works for the good of humanity. You have crushed my soul, which longs for serenity and peace, with your perpetual complaining." Pent-up energies were at work, an alternative understanding of the marriage and Boyce's own role in it that had long been suppressed by the pressures of bohemian ideology, the sheer volume of Hapgood's talk, and the prolixity of his relations. The historian who has followed the long saga of the marriage inwardly cheers. At last! Did anyone in the audience at the fish house feel the same way?

The enterprise of reconciling free love with commitment to a talented, prideful woman eventually provided literary material for a number of male bohemians. Hapgood was at the forefront of the confessional genre. In 1919, he published under his own name a first-person narrative of his marriage with Boyce, *Story of a Lover*. Boyce goes unnamed again, denoted simply as the allegorical "she," antagonist to the narrator. The book follows the births of the couple's first three children and recounts Boyce's one serious love affair, with an old Harvard friend of Hapgood's, that took place some years earlier, around the time they lived in Europe.

In the 1920s and 1930s, other male veterans of bohemia, including Max Eastman and Floyd Dell, would slip their own free-love experiences—by this time underwritten by psychoanalysis—into meditations

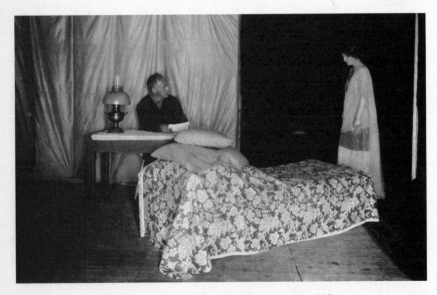

Hutchins Hapgood and Neith Boyce in Enemies. *Provincetown, 1917.*
YALE COLLECTION OF AMERICAN LITERATURE, BEINECKE RARE BOOK AND
MANUSCRIPT LIBRARY

on the problems of modern heterosexual love. *Story of a Lover* was a first entry in the line. The book is purportedly a sympathetic tale of the psychological and sexual development of a New Woman, a fond account in which the husband ostentatiously takes a back seat. But in truth, it effectively signals a revanchist turn in sexual politics. It is a complicated testament to masculine resentment, its feminist trappings serving to embellish the narrator's enlightened tolerance of his wife's inordinate demands and to heighten readers' sympathies for his grievances. Explicit antifeminism is altogether absent; to the contrary, the narrator insists on his loyalty to principles of sexual equality— women's work, their economic independence, their sexual freedom. *Story of a Lover* thus represents an important break with customary attacks on women's rights, late-nineteenth-century polemics that championed men's rightful prerogatives. It is rather an early contribution—perhaps the first—in what would become a vigorous, long-lasting tradition of male complaint founded on psychological wounds rather than political objections.

Although *Story*'s grievances center on the woman's affair with another man, her faithlessness is really an expression of a more profound betrayal of the narrator's sexual and emotional needs. The indifference he ascribes to her begins with her first pregnancy and continues with more babies, domestic cares, and her own writing. She is an allegorical figure of mystery, aloof and remote—"she had no soul," Hapgood writes at one point—an icon of withdrawal through which an imaginably actual woman occasionally peeks out in the text. The book is extraordinary in many ways, not least in the feat of describing in detail the actions of a depressed woman without ever acknowledging she is depressed. Boyce's debilitating state after the birth of their first child, for example, "a time of weeping sensibility," is enfolded into the mysteries of her mute nature; her difficult second pregnancy, when they are living in a small New York walk-up apartment, elicits the narrator's wonder at how "beautifully exhausted" she is, so filled with a "wonderful sufficiency" that by the time she clambers to the top of the stairs she wants only to lie in bed and read.

Like John Reed's stories, Hapgood's book questions the credibility of the female voice. His heroine is so remote that she barely speaks, and when she does speak it is better if she hadn't: "Because it was unnatural for her to express herself in sound, when she did so, the sounds, if those of exasperated discomfort, were peculiarly irritating." A book about a woman writer works hard to construe her as an inarticulate object, very much like Hapgood's anarchist woman of 1905. Yet Hapgood insists throughout on his enlightened stance. He is a man who respects women, supports women, admires women; so much so, in fact, that he really wants to be one. "Is it not a crime for a man to want to be pregnant?" But the show of admiration actually disguises theft, literary and actual, the obliteration of the heroine's subjectivity in the name of the narrator's superior powers to elucidate her character, analyze her dilemmas, and criticize her, to tell her how she is bearing up and where she is falling short—in short, the usurpation of her story as his story.

Hapgood's challenge in the book is to justify to readers his conviction that he has been done a terrible wrong despite what he admits inter alia to be his own lively adulterous career. He solves the problem by making himself into a supplicant and contriving a heroine who is withholding, uncaring, and self-involved. The problem with the marriage thus becomes his commitment and her lack of it, despite the fact that he is the compulsively unfaithful one. Her affair hurts him not because of his jealousy or possessiveness, those outmoded artifacts of a bygone age, but because she refuses to disclose the details to him. The book ends with an ambiguous reconciliation. "She" suffers a nervous breakdown and emerges chastened and accepting, more or less, of her husband's need for other women. Having acceded to his womanizing and broken off her own affair, she allows him to rekindle his attraction to her through a fantasy of free love: the two meet in a French restaurant where they impersonate adulterous lovers, retiring to a back room to make love as participants in an imagined triangle.

This was a sleight of hand possible at a moment when a comparatively broad-based feminist consensus required a new justification for men's resentments. The man of feminist principles nods toward the female voice at the same time he suppresses it. He applauds the New Woman and blames himself for his traditional expectations of her, even as he posits those expectations as normal and unobjectionable. In elevating her to a position of spiritual power and cultural allure, he manages to make himself the vulnerable one, thus ignoring the very real differences in power and status between the two. Talking about sex, as conceived by a male pundit, ended up as a genre we might call male feminism with a vengeance.

The destiny of sexual talk followed the trajectory of free love in the culture at large over the next twenty years. Talking about sex originated in the 1910s as an amalgam of feminism, cross-class fascination with working-class mores, and a belief in the power of honesty between the sexes. In the 1920s, the political aura dissolved. The sexual liberalism that had flourished in the cities passed into the realm of commercialized eros, denuded of feminism: flappers replaced New Women, packaged youth culture ousted bohemia, and romance magazines, with their true confessions, brought to popular culture a depoliticized version of the bohemians' fascination with disclosure.

Yet this narrative of declension misses what was problematic in talking about sex all along, the optative character of the supposed equal exchange of views, the willed equality. Bohemian sex talk can be seen as an early contribution to the annals of "men talk, women listen," a chronicle that has played a large part in our understanding and experience of sexual modernism. The fusion of modernity with emancipated femininity simplified both, assigning the New Woman an overweening symbolic role that promised power but in reality imprisoned. The sexually free woman became a frame for propositions about the modern and the feminine that reduced both to a matter of their effect on male authority. It was left for women to display their spiritual and erotic riches and others—men—to speak for them.

The play of feminism had paradoxical effects. The positive outlook and putative towering self-confidence of the free-loving woman became a seductive model of action, will, and sexual agency, but these ascribed powers left women little room to address their actual needs and difficulties. It was rare for women to give back as good as they got when they talked about sex. One prizes the moments when someone spoke her mind. A Village feminist ended up heaving Theodore Dreiser off her one evening—he got mean when he suspected she was trying to get on top during sex—and told him he talked like a thug. And there was Goldman's tough friend Almeda Sperry putting foul-mouthed Ben Reitman in his place. But such evidence is rare. Glamorous representations of free womanhood, so attractive to women deprived of the idealizations of Victorian culture, seem to have cramped women's ability to speak for themselves. At the same time, ironically, talking about sex gave men status as liberal commentators with a speciality in the "modern woman." Theirs was a critique of patriarchal values that ended by sacrificing its most compelling practitioners.

V

FORMER

PEOPLE

PREVIOUS PAGE: *Emma Goldman, Prisoner No. 38. Deportation photograph, Ellis Island, 1920.*

9

Loving America with
Open Eyes

For the bohemians, the First World War had begun, as had other political crises, as a feast of opportunities. "Don't worry about the war," Carl Van Vechten, who was traveling with Mabel Dodge in Europe in July 1914, assured his wife. "It is tremendously exciting here—but not dangerous—at least not for Americans—and I can always get away." Writers, facing as yet no danger of conscription, saw the hostilities as a fund of good assignments. The journalists flocked to Paris that fall, "excited, pleased, happy," remembered Dodge.

In the States, the war set off a burst of left-wing activity. There were articles to be written, protests to be organized. The war posed an intellectual challenge, troubling dearly held pieties of the times. There were pressing questions for the left: whither international solidarity? For believers in the power of youth, it was a puzzle: how could a transatlantic band of brothers be turned to slaughter one another in an old men's war? Initially, these were abstract problems, not cries of the heart, but they were enough to keep people busy. No one could have predicted that by the war's end the glamorous protagonists of the new would be well on their way to being passé, not just former radicals but "former people," in the damning judgment of Malcolm Cowley, a member of the younger generation.

Henry James, we've seen, divided Americans into the satisfied and the swindled. In a sense, the war shoved the moderns into the camp of the swindled, a territory of dispossession they had visited, observed, and written about but never actually lived in. The war ousted them from cultural ascendancy; it robbed them of their relevance. It destroyed friendships and alliances, institutions and conversations—it even did them out of their own neighborhood. In the United States, the war was not the titanic, illimitable catastrophe it was in Europe, but for the bohemians it was a debacle all the same.

In the fall of 1914, no one—and this was true in Europe as well—was prepared for catastrophe. No Euro-American person in the prime of life, literary historian Paul Fussell points out, had experienced a major war, although plenty had lived through the carnage of colonial expansion (in Africa, India, the Philippines, and Cuba). But a major war in the heart of Europe had not occurred in living memory. In the United States, the horror of the Civil War was already swathed in commemorative platitude. Contemporaries in 1914 imagined war to be a stately affair of great marches and battles, occurring within a purposeful historical stream, to be quickly ended.

Early on, although the ghastliness of trench warfare dispelled that illusion, the war still seemed very much a European matter. Political sentiment in the United States was overwhelmingly against intervention. There was animus against German Americans, to be sure, and Anglophilic conservatives, especially East Coast elites, raged about the atrocities of the Hun and the world's debts to English democracy. But across the country pro-war politics ran into stolid indifference, strengthened by workers' and socialists' denunciations of the war as serving only the interests of the armaments manufacturers and by Irish American hatred of the British.

So even as war raged in Europe, modern America still seemed bound up with feminism, birth control, rebel girls, and insurgent manly workers, not the unimaginable horror of the trenches and shell shock, the nightmare of reason that rendered language impotent to describe it. In Europe, words proved inadequate; in the United States, the language of the new continued to issue forth in a stream of voluble adjectives and superlatives. The *Masses* mixed slashing attacks on the war with vignettes of the urban poor and defenses of a birth control battle at its pitch. "Pictures and poetry poured in," mused Floyd Dell. "So much good humor, sweetness, happiness." Writer friends were busy with the IWW, which in 1914–15 scored impressive victories in the West, where manufacturers of arms and equipment for the European belligerents were leaning heavily on workers in the mining and timber industries.

But as the country shifted course toward intervention, right-wing suspicion mounted, "a psychic complex of panic, hatred, rage, class arrogance and patriotic swagger," as Randolph Bourne described it. The labor situation was volatile, perhaps explosive. Indeed the IWW successes were part of growing worker militancy everywhere in the country. The cutoff of immigration meant that employers found themselves unable to replace strikers, and workers responded with concentrated energy; in 1916–17, there were more work stoppages than at any other time in U.S. history. Despite European socialists' support for the war, the SP remained opposed to U.S. entrance and drew in thousands of new members, predominantly immigrants, on the basis of its position. To pro-war Americans, socialists, militant workers, and immigrants merged into one abhorrent pacifist mass.

After the declaration of war in April 1917, violence escalated against the antiwar opposition. People were beaten, tortured, threatened with death, even shot and hung by fellow citizens, police, soldiers, and various combinations thereof. Wobblies were favorite targets but people of German descent as well as radical speakers were also fair game: Max Eastman was nearly lynched in North Dakota on an antiwar lecture tour, saved only by the timely intervention of some local Wobblies and old populists. A terrific official repression of civil liberties ensued, intended to suppress dissent and labor militancy and at the same time quell unregulated mob violence. The federal Espionage Act, passed in 1917 shortly after America entered the war, and the Sedition Act, a companion law that followed a year later, set long prison terms for anyone convicted of obstructing the war effort, including expressing antiwar opinions that might conceivably reach soldiers and affect their willingness to fight. Journals that published writing to this effect were denied mailing privileges. The Justice

AMERICAN MODERNS

Department and its newly formed branch of enforcement, the FBI, as yet lacked the personnel to ferret out offenders, so the attorney general actively solicited the aid of volunteer spy catchers, who coalesced into a network of superpatriots dedicated to surveillance of their neighbors, colleagues, and coworkers.

Prosecutions and convictions proceeded at a clip. Early roundups of dissenters occurred mainly in the Midwest and West, but after the October Revolution in Russia in 1917, the dragnet moved toward the East Coast, with its great population of Russian immigrants. The vendetta against "aliens," at first directed at supposed German spies, now elided with fears of an internal Bolshevik menace. By the war's end, conservative fears had come to rest on pro-Russian radicalism to the exclusion of other concerns. Labor militancy, strong already, increased phenomenally in 1918–19 as workers suddenly faced high inflation and layoffs. In 1918, Congress authorized the deportation of foreign-born advocates of revolution. Beginning with a general strike in Seattle—to conservatives a harbinger of an American soviet—a tremendous wave of strikes moved across the country in 1919. In New York that summer, some fifty thousand workers were out on strike each month. The crusade against radicalism—now known as the Red Scare—culminated in January 1920 with the Palmer raids, when Attorney General Mitchell Palmer organized a Justice Department sweep that led to some ten thousand arrests of alleged Bolsheviks.

Despite the bellicose urgings of its financial elites, New York had initially been an antiwar stronghold. It was, in its inimitable way, a haven for insurrectionaries: among the huddled masses in the immigrant districts in 1916 were the Russians Alexandra Kollontai, Nikolai Bukharin, and Leon Trotsky, biding their time; and there were Indian, Dutch, Japanese, Italian, and Finnish radicals, too, plotting various revolutions. This Red menace was obscure, however, hidden away in the tenements; what really alarmed conservatives was a strong showing by the Socialist Party in the municipal and state elections of 1917. Mob violence and spying cropped up in the city. Passersby picked up "seditious" pamphlets on the streets and turned them over to the authorities. Soldiers and sailors based in New York led roving mobs

314

looking for radicals to intimidate. Columbia University turned into a nest of patriotic zeal as the autocratic president, Nicholas Murray Butler, restructured schools and departments along military lines and announced that faculty debate about the wisdom of intervention was "intolerable . . . what had been folly was now treason." Firings, dismissals, and resignations of antiwar faculty followed.

For the first time, radicals encountered physical danger in New York. For Emma Goldman and Alexander Berkman, the organizers of a No-Conscription League, the meetings to encourage conscientious objection were tests of physical courage. During a suffrage protest against President Wilson, who was still vacillating on votes for women, angry soldiers attacked marchers of both sexes. The playing of the "Star-Spangled Banner" was a flash point: Fred Boyd, a British socialist and a habitué of the Village scene, was beaten up in a New York restaurant for remaining in his seat during the anthem; he was lucky to escape since someone in Washington, D.C., had been killed for the same reason.

The Justice Department was at first stymied in its efforts to penetrate New York, but in 1918, aided by the broadened powers of the Sedition Act, zealous Red-hunting agents and their civilian helpers turned their sights on the city and increased the number of prosecutions from 378 in 1917 to over two thousand the next year. Spying seeped into intellectual life. In Greenwich Village, the festive performances of free speech were unthinkable. The Liberal Club disintegrated. The Heterodoxy group continued meeting in semiclandestine fashion, changing the spots each week to outwit spies supposedly alerted by a patriotic club member. Heterodoxy members with family connections to antiwar progressives were shadowed and picked up for questioning. Agents tapped phones and intercepted telegrams.

There were arrests, indictments, and trials. Goldman and Berkman went on trial in 1917 for conspiring to obstruct the draft, the *Masses* editors in April 1918 for conspiring to cause mutiny in the military with antiwar articles, then again in October on similar charges. Big troubles with the law precipitated the collapse of liberal/radical affiliations that had been the stock in trade of downtown politics. "Neither a middle ground nor ambiguity fared well in the crisis of war," observes historian Thomas Bender. Yet the problem was that the middle ground was precisely where moderns were accustomed to operating. Ambiguity—a fuzziness about where one thing left off and another began—was one of their most valuable political resources, allowing them to create otherwise incomprehensible analogies and identifications. The drawing of lines between "them" and "us"—most especially between "America" and "us"—was not a familiar political skill. Drawing lines would become more of a habit after the Manichean dichotomies of Communism had infiltrated the political culture, but in 1917 it was a skill of the right, not the left.

The America the downtown moderns had investigated, exhorted, and cajoled seemed a capacious place, for all its shortcomings. They could not have foreseen the greatest threat to American civil liberties since the Alien and Sedition Acts of the 1790s. Politically, there was no room to maneuver once Wilson had convinced left-leaning liberals at the *New Republic* and elsewhere that entering the war would bring about much-needed changes in nationalizing resources and social benefits. Once liberals identified the national good with the war effort, dissenters' outcries over individual rights seemed callow and self-serving, whiny nay-saying to a wholesome, if strenuous, enterprise. Even John Dewey, the great elucidator of democratic possibility, remained silent about the destruction of civil liberties, including the repression on his own Columbia campus. Willing to entertain—if only at a distance—the commotion of free speech when it promoted harmony across class lines, the progressives drew back when it meant tolerating irreconcilable disagreement. By the armistice, "freedom of speech" had come to seem to the public "a license for Bolshevik thuggery," a legal historian writes.

The crackdown in New York terminated the felicitous relationship downtown radicals had enjoyed with the press. Publishing was seriously hampered by the threat, both implied and actual, of the Espionage and Sedition Acts. Between 1917 and 1918, the forces of decency in print let loose, and there was no slackening after the armistice. Within five months after the Espionage Act took effect, every major left-wing publication in the country had been barred from the mails at least once, some for weeks at a time. The postmaster denied mailing privileges to more than four hundred publications by the end of the war. The *Masses* and *Mother Earth* went under, driven into bankruptcy by repeated confiscation of their issues and the legal travails of their editors. After the armistice, when the worst censorship subsided, Max and Crystal Eastman, aided by the canny Claude McKay, pulled together the *Liberator*, a short-lived successor to the *Masses* hauled up in 1919, like many other left or liberal journals, before the Lusk Committee, a state legislative body created in the midst of the Red Scare to ferret out seditious activity.

The old moral censorship bolstered the new political censorship, and vice versa: "political" literature was virtually guaranteed to be prosecuted under the Espionage Act and "art" that was not liable to suppression under the Espionage Act was vulnerable to obscenity prosecutions under the Comstock laws. An official at the Post Office Department observed stoutly of his censorship duties, "I know exactly what I am after. I am after three things and only three things—germanism, pacifism, and high browism." The Post Office troops gave renewed authority to John Sumner, Comstock's successor: Margaret Anderson, for example, ran afoul of Sumner when the *Little Review* published a Wyndham Lewis short story that was about sex but also about pacifism. The commercial publishers who prided themselves on sponsoring new work faced intensifying harassment. Writer friends who had been operating in a seller's market found their work virtually unprintable: strike reports, antiwar essays, and above all writing sympathetic to the Russian Revolution were anathema to editors worried that their issues could be confiscated and that they could be indicted.

Despite the stringent repression, however, the effects of the crisis varied, depending on luck, connections, temperament, and situation. Some memoirs of the period mull over shattered lives; others, in the spirit of the fizzy decade to come, marvel over the gay nonchalance of those who landed on their feet. The *Masses* editors maintained a front of devil-may-care rebelliousness despite the grave charges against them. Even in the second trial, when the legal assault on the political opposition was most ferocious, they staged a collective performance that became legendary for its free-speech insouciance, poking fun at the charges, teasing the judge, ridiculing the notion of espionage. People with the means and the money left town: in 1919, for example, a literary colony started up in Taos when Mabel Dodge and *New*

Republic writer Elsie Clews Parsons moved to New Mexico. After the armistice, more journalists flocked to Europe, where the papers needed correspondents so badly that John Dos Passos observed that "every man and woman in the U.S. who could read and write had wrangled an overseas job."

More vulnerable were working-class activists and intellectuals, both native- and foreign-born, whose appeals to the Constitution prompted sneers from prosecutors. But even here experiences varied. Some Ferrer principals—the printer for Margaret Sanger's birth control pamphlet, for example—were able to skip town, to join the action in Petersburg or Moscow. Leaders of the IWW were less fortunate. Their success in organizing the mines and timber fields led to a huge indictment on Espionage Act charges of conspiring to obstruct the war effort, effectively smashing the union; one hundred Wobblies were convicted in Chicago and sent to prison for up to twenty years. But the New York leaders, with the exception of Bill Haywood, managed to escape the fate of the Chicago comrades, having used their connections to influential liberal friends to sever their cases from the mass indictment.

The people in jail or facing trial or being dogged by spies, however, were in the minority. Most downtown people lay low, fulminating at the government and at neighbors, friends, and former coconspirators who had joined the government's cause, making do in a situation that oscillated between extremes of high drama and banality, paranoia and real danger. Some straggled off into irrelevance; others marched straight into history. To trace the defeats, fallings-out, defections, expatriations, and retreats, consider once more four figures—John Reed, Emma Goldman, Margaret Anderson, and Randolph Bourne—and the paths that led them away from an American modernity they helped create.

John Reed arrived with Louise Bryant in Petersburg in the fall of 1917. The czar had abdicated six months earlier; power was still divided between a provisional government and the popularly constituted soviets, organizations of workers and peasants led by socialists. The city was feverish with fears, plots, and counterplots; organizers, demonstrators, troops, and armed militants wended their way among crowds of shoppers and concertgoers attending to business as usual. Only a handful of American reporters were on the spot and none spoke Russian. Reed and Bryant, however, knew many Russians from downtown New York who, in a reverse emigration, had returned to join the revolution. Through these contacts the two quickly became privy to deliberations inside the Smolny Institute, the stronghold on the outskirts of town where the Bolsheviks over the next few weeks prepared for their decisive coup.

The revolution was Reed's story of a lifetime, set in a city not unlike his own rather than on the baffling military front that had stymied him in his war reporting. Indeed, some of his strongest writing captures the peculiarly metropolitan paradoxes of those October days, like when the Bolsheviks seized the Winter Palace while several blocks away trams ran on schedule, movie marquees blazed, and theater audiences hurried to their shows. He scribbled maniacally in notebooks and transcribed on his portable typewriter at night: the words of speeches and proclamations hastily paraphrased by acquaintances from the Lower East Side, his visual impressions of orators, crowds, and street battles. From these piles of notes, Reed dashed off the exuberant *Ten Days That Shook the World* when he returned to New York in 1918. At first, politics blocked him: the State Department confiscated his papers at the dock and no journal except the *Liberator* would publish him. But once he recovered his papers, he was back in stride, despite worries about money and the turmoil around him. The golden boy from Harvard had repositioned himself.

As he had always sublimated his political choices in the search for an adequate genre, Reed now embraced the revolutionary epic, a form that elevated him to a position as narrator of "the greatest story of my life, and one of the greatest in the world." The story is unflagging, the momentum relentless—people declaim thunderously and hurtle about; grandiloquent proclamations are issued, guns fire. It crackles with zest, echoing American soldiers' cheerful, peppy accounts of the "big fight" in Europe. But for all the swoosh of crowds, the book is curiously bare of locations where life is trapped. Protagonists materialize not from concrete situations but from a nexus of ideological equivalencies, pushed to the foreground to serve exemplary purposes.

Lenin represents the cunning of revolution, Kerensky stands for the puerility of bourgeois liberalism, and nameless workers make speeches and analyze events in a manner that demonstrates the proletariat's unerring comprehension of the imperatives of class struggle. While Reed's Mexico had been a "mysterious, romantic country" of expressive gestures, charming rags, and sweeps of unknowable desert, his Russia is a tidily delineated cartography of groups—peasants, liberal intellectuals, aristocrats, workers—the masses nicely arrayed in ranks ready to revolt. The book closes with a triumphal session of the Bolsheviks, now ensconced in state power, their victory conveyed by explosive images of firestorms and apocalypse. "The old world crumbles down, the new world begins."

Ten Days became a paradigmatic text, perhaps *the* text of twentieth-century Marxist revolution. Reed hit on a literary formula that coincided with an institutionalized political agenda—the Bolshevik vision of international revolution on the Soviet model, soon to be dictated to the new Communist parties of Europe and the United States formed at the Soviets' behest. For all its spirited sympathy, the book emptied insurgency of its particular, local complexities and singular sufferings. In line with the Soviet vision, Reed made revolution exportable, a literary commodity on the world market adaptable to different national settings. *Ten Days* demonstrated to readers, Irving Howe dourly remarks, "*this is how it happened; this is how it's done.*"

Boni and Liveright published the book in 1919; its appearance at the height of the Red Scare was something of a miracle. "Bolshevik," an obscure reference only months earlier, had by now become a powerfully expansive term on both the left and the right. Reed was known in the papers as a Bolshevik sympathizer, maybe even an agent, from his testimony before a Senate committee investigating the Red menace. No longer a congenial figure to the wealthy and powerful, he was persona non grata in the press, at the Harvard Club, and with his bank. Nonetheless, reviews and sales were respectable and Reed forged a more intimate kinship than ever before with those readers who stayed loyal, an audience that included socialist and anarchist partisans, Russian-born workers, and IWWs in federal prison in Leavenworth, Kansas. They responded with an urgent sense of engagement, seizing the story as their own; the armchair tourism Reed had always played to now inspired readers' desire to jump into the narrative themselves, to lay plans to travel to the Soviet Union and offer their help. Did Reed think the Russians could use a railroad man who knew how to manage things? inquired one correspondent. Might he pass along a few tips to Lenin and Trotsky?

In downtown Manhattan, events in Russia acquired an immediacy almost unimaginable today. The Soviet Union was a momentous fact, "capable of extension through space, becoming an almost tangible part of intellectual life in New York," notes Thomas Bender. Reed's voluble, bounding excitement, unloosed in lectures across the country and proselytizing in his old haunts, helped shift the collective sense of possibility toward a scarcely industrialized agrarian society with no substantial democratic traditions. Blocked at home, many poured their considerable faculties into endowing the new Soviet Union with an imaginative democracy that stretched across the world to include them. Reed, the American outsider turned Russian insider, seemed to embody that double citizenship. No one knew much about the Bolsheviks yet, but from the reports of Reed, Bryant, and other fellow travelers who had been on the spot, they seemed admirable enough, pretty much like Wobblies, only Wobblies with state power.

The identification with the Soviet Union was an odd sort of cosmopolitanism for people who, for all their knowledge of Europe, had always focused their efforts at home. To be sure, the bohemians had modeled themselves, unwittingly and half-consciously, on European prototypes. A number were born in Europe or grew up there and others traveled abroad; they prided themselves on familiarity with European art and thought. Nonetheless, Europe remained essentially remote, even for the immigrants. France, Germany, England, Austria, Italy—these were countries for inspiration and delectation, by turns awe-inspiring and off-putting in the brilliance of their new, the massive grandeur of their old, the fecundity of their paintings and books, the destructive power they had wielded over the entire world in their war. But outside the left-wing parties, close working relationships with the Europeans and a sense of common enterprise were the province of the older generation, progressives looking to Europe for models for municipal housing, sewage facilities, and child labor laws. The bohemians, for all the analogues they drew with European modernism, kept their transatlantic peers at a remove, as if no one could doubt that Europe was sufficient unto itself.

But Russia, that was another matter, a place where one could imagine a role for oneself. The belief that Russia was the beacon for a new era of world democracy spread through the ranks of labor and the Socialist Party and to every center of modern culture. In 1919, there were Communist uprisings and coups in Munich, Berlin, Vienna, and Hungary; general strikes in Seattle and Winnipeg; left-led strikes throughout Europe and in the steel industry at home. To some on the left—Reed and Bryant among them—a worker's revolution, the dream of social democracy long deferred, seemed imminent.

Reed's partisanship deepened; the writer friend turned Communist organizer. The articles he published in America in 1919, all in the left-wing press, were boilerplate expositions of Marxist doctrine. He had never before been a man for party politics; *Masses* editorial sessions were the closest he had come to long meetings and intricate parliamentary maneuvers. But in the United States, following orders from Moscow, he jumped into Socialist Party affairs, engineering the ascendancy of the pro-Bolshevik faction through internecine splits and purges. In the fall he once again made the dangerous trek to Russia, this time spirited across borders by a Communist underground. In Moscow, he served as a delegate to the second congress of the Communist Third International, or Comintern. Although he worked with others from the West to loosen the Russians' iron control of the proceedings, the opposition was quashed and Reed's demands for democratic process denounced as "petty bourgeois" by hard-liner Grigory Zinoviev. Whatever Reed's reservations about the Bolsheviks, thereafter he was publicly loyal to party orders and the party line.

The revolution must have seemed at once ominous and marvelous that fall when the Comintern sent him by train across thousands of miles to a gathering in Baku, on the Caspian Sea, to help woo restive Asiatic leaders whom the Soviets were courting. Before an audience whipped to a frenzy by Zinoviev's calls for a "holy war" against the West, Reed detailed America's ill treatment of its own native peoples as an illustration of imperialist iniquities. Back in Moscow and reunited with Bryant, who had just arrived in what proved the last trek of their marriage, he fell sick with typhus contracted on the trip and died a few days later. The Bolsheviks buried him in state in the Kremlin. In New York, people soon began to argue about whether or not Reed, on his deathbed, had expressed any doubts about his political choices. Speculation and rumor continued through the 1920s. In 1929, the American Communist Party settled the matter: Reed was a devoted Communist who had sacrificed his life and his gifts for the cause; his memory would undergird a network of writers' organizations, the John Reed Clubs, to serve as the organized vanguard of the party's cultural front. The Harvard cheerleader, man-about-town, and chronically hungry writer entered history as an icon of sacrifice, an emblem of the ideologically disciplined imagination.

E mma Goldman rode out the first wave of political difficulty with phenomenal energy, trusting her hold on her accustomed audience. When she went on trial with Berkman in June 1917, optimism still reigned even as war hysteria surged. Even if they were convicted, she assured a friend, "it will be our gain. People will see what crimes and injustices are committed in the name of democracy." The two, coached by their free-speech attorney, conducted the defense themselves, a compelling improvisation of cagey equivocation, precise arguments, and rousing declarations of principle. Goldman was at her best, so stunning that even the hostile judge acknowledged her magnetism. Witty, scathing, and spellbinding, she won converts even in the mostly unfriendly courtroom crowd from which her supporters had been barred.

In a beautiful summation before the jury, she spoke of an American patriotism that she believed was consistent with her life's work. Being Emma Goldman, she found her simile in a love affair. What kind of patriotism did she represent? That of "the man who loves a woman with open eyes. He is enchanted by her beauty, yet he sees her faults." Before a jury of middle-class businessmen, she called for an accommodation between the country and its critics, an American accord that she entered in good faith:

> Gentlemen of the jury, we respect your patriotism. We would not, if we could, have you change its meaning for yourself. But may

there not be different kinds of patriotism as there are different kinds of liberty? I for one cannot believe that love of one's country must needs consist in blindness to its social faults, in deafness to its social discords, in inarticulation of its social wrongs. Neither can I believe that the mere accident of birth in a certain country or the mere scrap of a citizen's paper constitutes the love of country.

Even a dissenter, she held, could love America with open eyes. But in a dismayingly short thirty-nine minutes, the jury was back with a guilty verdict. The judge returned the maximum sentence of two years in federal prison. Supporters were aghast: the full dimensions of the wartime legal regime were only becoming apparent. Yet Goldman was defiant. She insisted her love affair with America was not over, only troubled, poised on the brink of an anguished but necessary revelation of truth. "Nothing better could have happened. . . . From now on no one will dare maintain in any public meeting that we have free speech and free press."

In prison Goldman, too, read *Ten Days That Shook the World*. Like the incarcerated politicals at Leavenworth, she warmed to Reed's world of action and idealism and inserted herself into the text. Here was one more story to inhabit with the ardor of her being. "I felt myself transferred to Russia, caught by her fierce storm, swept along by its momentum." She would have comforted herself, too, with the elated news of the people's triumph that filtered back to the States from returning radicals, their jubilation making its way from Russia to New York to Chicago and eventually to the jails, so that in Leavenworth, prisoners gravely debated exactly which features of American reform programs to preserve, come the U.S. proletarian revolution: should they, for example, institute the single tax once they seized state power? "Every once in awhile, long ago we made them listen," a prisoner joyfully assured Roger Baldwin, then in Manhattan's Tombs for conscientious objection. "Now we have them standing up to attention, all the time. The flags of Europe are all flying 'Red' so when we get out, this world may be a fit place to live in."

Released in the summer of 1919, Goldman was promptly tailed by agents from the Justice Department. No longer accused of being

German spies, Goldman and Berkman—also freed—were now suspected of being Russian agents, and under the antiradical immigration provisos of 1918 they were candidates for deportation. Immediately they were embroiled in hearings, petitions, and consultations with lawyers. Amidst the turmoil of the Red Scare, Goldman turned into a celebrity scapegoat, symbol of a foreign menace still on the loose. The *New York Times* led the cry to ship her out. In December, immigration authorities ordered Goldman and Berkman, along with 249 other radicals, to Ellis Island to be sent on a "Red Ark" to Russia.

Publicly, she embraced her destiny as providential: hers was not the tragic narrative of persecution and loss but a victorious story of the exile's return. She ordered her attorney to stop all appeals and inform the immigration authorities that she *demanded* to be sent to Russia. She would join the Bolsheviks, a group she then thought of as splendid liberators. Never could she in 1919 have foreseen her fate, that until her death twenty years later she would be, in her haunting phrase, "nowhere at home," exiled from the Soviet Union for her denunciation of authoritarian Communist rule and drifting about Europe on temporary visas. No, she was an international revolutionary spirit, called to join the "glorious work." Goldman had never been one to preach the abnegation of the self that grounded the old Russian anarchist politics, but now she had lost so much that she needed to make something of what remained, turn desolation into renunciation. In joining the revolution, she could subsume her particular tragedy in historical generality.

Privately, however, the grief was almost unbearable. With a humility that did not come easily, she drew up final accounts with friends—most movingly in a letter to Ben Reitman, newly settled into marriage with a young wife—taking stock of the costs and gains, toting up balances. She mulled over her ambivalent, profound devotion to America and the severed dreams of the work she still wanted to do there. The land that had cost her so much suffering had also, she confessed, given her great joy. She had, despite all, been rich in love.

Yet even in the miserable circumstances of the day of departure—the prisoners, who had been awakened abruptly before dawn on a freezing February morning, stumbled through the rooms of Ellis Island clutching their belongings like any dazed, fearful bunch of immigrants—Emma Goldman pulled off one last American performance. She had to know the onlookers were hostile but she must have trusted there were admirers to marvel, as there always had been, even in the worst crowds. On the dock stood a few federal officials who had braved the cold and the hour to gloat (young J. Edgar Hoover, then an up-and-coming bureau official, was among them). As the boat pulled away, it is rumored, one of them called out a taunting farewell. And Emma Goldman, it is said, stood at the rail and thumbed her nose at the lot.

In Greenwich Village, Margaret Anderson was immune to the romance of Russia. But though she was increasingly cut off from left-wing support, her passionate modernism was still sufficiently unorthodox to link her in official minds to the internal menace. Abandoned by other radicals and under siege from the censors, Anderson lived in a sort of internal exile, more isolated in her fight to save the *Little Review* than were the politicals in their battles.

After 1917, Anderson remembered, "there was almost never a week when the morning coffee was assured." Advertisers and newsstands were wary of radical publications; the radical rich were not returning calls; the censors were voracious. The subscription base eroded as readers turned away from a literary revolt that had once looked psychologically tantalizing but now seemed too close to political danger. Bursts of activity and determined resistance alternated with listlessness and waiting for disaster. "It is a great thing to be living when an age passes," Jane Heap observed sardonically in 1917. "There is a beautiful poetic vengeance in being permitted to watch that age destroy itself."

In 1918, Pound, the foreign editor, perched in London and oblivious to what was happening in New York, suggested that the *Little Review* publish installments of James Joyce's *Ulysses*. It was without question a dangerous proposition, possibly a disastrous one. Joyce was virtually unpublished in Europe, eliciting publishers' responses that ranged from prudish to frightened; in the United States, only *A Portrait of the Artist as a Young Man* had appeared, from the publisher Ben Huebsch (Emma Goldman took a copy to jail in 1917). Now

Joyce was finishing off great chunks of *Ulysses* and his publishing prospects seemed, if anything, dimmer. Even John Quinn, who was Joyce's patron as well as the *Little Review*'s, was leery. He hated all the passages about bodily fluids and saw an inevitable ruckus with the police looming. But Anderson and Heap thrilled to the manuscript. They found an immigrant printer, a Serbian whose lack of English and love of literature combined to make him indifferent to the threat of being shut down. In the spring they went to press. They published, over the next three years, twenty-three installments of the novel.

The censors descended, seizing one issue after another for burning—four thousand copies at a swoop—thereby driving the journal's finances into the ground. Anderson and Heap found themselves alone. Left-wing writers were too focused on the trials and the war to care about the strange book; the New York literary critics were cold and condemnatory; the new publishers looked the other way. Finally, in 1920, the vice squad brought the pair up on criminal charges of purveying obscenity through the mails. The offending matter was the "Nausicaa" episode of *Ulysses* in which Leopold Bloom engages in "some erotic musings"—Anderson's delicate phrasing—and masturbates while watching Gerty MacDowell lean back and bare her legs.

A few years earlier, the *Little Review*'s troubles would have been a cause célèbre for free-speech lawyers and enthusiasts intent on defending sex talk, in art and outside art. The case would have drawn the support of downtown Manhattan—one imagines Carnegie Hall rallies, outraged conversations at parties, polemics from the *Masses*. Yet in 1920, those connections between the literary world and the political one had disappeared. The one durable free-speech institution to emerge from the war years, the American Civil Liberties Union (ACLU), scorned Comstock law litigation. John Quinn was thus the only ally within reach, a man who disliked women in general and particularly despised Anderson and Heap because they were lesbians. He agreed to represent them, but if it had not been for his devotion to his fellow Irishman Joyce, Quinn took care to tell them, he would have had no truck with what he called "sex literature."

Anderson, familiar with free-speech tactics of publicity and theater from her days with the radicals, insisted on going to trial rather than entering a plea. In the *Little Review*, she published a running denunciatory account of the proceedings accompanied by diatribes against the suppression of free speech. Quinn, however, who had his own covert sympathies with censorship, insisted on sticking to the narrowest possible grounds and ordered his clients to keep quiet. He brought in a panel of male experts who testified variously that *Ulysses* was incomprehensible, not obscene; loathsome and disgusting, not obscene; and Freudian, not obscene. Yet the editors refused to be entirely subdued. In a pretrial hearing, Jane Heap aggravated Quinn by standing up to give a speech, defiant in its lovely matter-of-factness, on the relations of art and life, a kind of paean to the ubiquity of Freewomen. "Girls lean back everywhere," Heap observed lyrically of the example of Gerty MacDowell, as if she were reciting a slip of impromptu free verse, "showing lace and silk stockings, wear low-cut sleeveless blouses, breathless bathing suits; men think thoughts and have emotions about these things everywhere—seldom as delicately and imaginatively as Mr. Bloom—and no one is corrupted."

The verdict was, not surprisingly, guilty. The editors were fined fifty dollars and taken off to police headquarters to be fingerprinted. The trial provoked only mild interest in the press and brought no outcry whatsoever from New York literary critics. Anderson returned to publishing the journal, but its financial and intellectual health was broken. The *Ulysses* trial was really the end of the American venture for Anderson; the disinterest of both the New York critics and what remained of the radical press made it clear that there was no support for her particular high-handed orchestrations of art and democracy. In 1922, Anderson emigrated to Europe, to become an elegant grande dame of the Parisian lesbian salons. Her migration was an early sign of a general retreat of the American avant-garde from a politics that had grown too narrow to interest them.

Randolph Bourne, too, living in the Village, was aware that an age was destroying itself. A political person, not an aesthete, yet only mildly interested in Russia, Bourne was still embroiled in the affair with America that others were abandoning. He was incapable of expatriation, literal or psychological. So while other writers celebrated the Soviets, embraced "life" shorn of politics, or made themselves oblivious to the crisis, Bourne kept on thinking, hard, about what modern intellectuals could and could not do to influence their country.

The first step, as he saw it, was to make the strongest case possible against the war. Beginning in June 1917, Bourne published one searing essay each month in *Seven Arts*, surpassing even the *Masses* in his excoriation of the slaughter and the folly of the liberals who supported it. For years Bourne had longed for faith from his editors; now the journal's confidence pushed him to reach beyond the boundaries of his previous achievements. One magnificent piece followed another. The penchant for generalizing that had always threatened to turn his work into delectations for the genteel now fused with actual enemies and intense emotion to make his writing take fire. Together, the *Seven Arts* pieces join a group of political essays—one thinks of Karl Marx's "Eighteenth Brumaire" or Zola's "J'Accuse"—in which literary power turns political protest into an artistic tour de force.

Once Bourne had fretted that his writing was marginal to the participatory democratic movements he idealized. But now the writing itself carved out a space where the thinking mind could join with others. At the time, to think differently from one's countrymen was so difficult it could be said to constitute an act of protest. Bourne was critical in helping people to do so. He skewered the smug certainties and the puffed-up egos of his old mentors, reserving his opprobrium for the liberals who prided themselves on having gotten the country into a war that, by virtue of their patronage, was going to be better than anyone could hope, the "cosmically efficacious and well-bred war":

> A war made deliberately by the intellectuals! A calm moral verdict, arrived at after a penetrating study of inexorable facts! . . . An alert intellectual class saving the people in spite of themselves, biding their time with Fabian strategy until the nation could be moved into war without serious resistance! An intellectual class gently guiding a nation through sheer force of ideas into what the other nations entered only through predatory craft or popular hysteria or militarist madness!

And so on: passage after passage skewering a political elite's capacities for smug self-delusion. "Only in a world where irony was dead

could an intellectual class enter war at the head of such illiberal co-
horts in the avowed cause of world-liberalism and world-democracy."
Outrage expressed bluntly, immoderately, furiously, yet never collapsing into rant: the reader's excitement builds as each piece gains in
momentum. "A man must glow, writing like that," observes the political theorist Michael Walzer of the *Seven Arts* polemics.

A man must also worry, writing like that in 1917. Bourne lived in
chronic fear of going to prison, not an unreasonable fear given the fact
he was publishing indictable essays. He believed he was under surveillance, also not unreasonable given the ubiquity of spies in the city. A
trunk of his writings mysteriously disappeared (a serious loss in an age
before photocopy). Agents from the Justice Department inquired after
him at the *New Republic*; Bourne suspected his old teacher John Dewey
had put them on his trail. A Columbia English professor savaged
Bourne's *Seven Arts* essays as the product of a deformed mind in a
deformed body; another young English professor, an outspoken pacifist, was fired when he came to Bourne's defense. In the summer of
1918, when Bourne took a break from the heat in the city to hike up
the Connecticut shore with two women, naval anti-espionage police
detained and questioned them. The interrogation turned on whether
his lover Esther Cornell's bursts of Isadora Duncanesque dancing on
the sand might be semaphoric signaling to German submarines, a
comical interpolation of rituals of the new into the grim wartime language of sedition. Bourne, however, feared that the real purpose of the
exercise was to keep him under observation.

Yet nothing really happened. *Seven Arts* folded when its wealthy
backer, appalled by the antiwar politics, pulled out. Among the downtown moderns, aimlessness, thwarted hopes, and premonitions of disaster yielded to torpor, a mood Bourne described memorably as the
supreme peacefulness of being at war, all dissent quelled. He scratched
around for work; he was sometimes only days away from being flat
broke. Once *Seven Arts* collapsed, possibilities for sustained antiwar
criticism were blocked. But Bourne, while depressed and fearful, was
too practical to indulge in jeremiads. Elsewhere on the left, the drift
was toward martyrdom and elegy. "The big game is over," Bill
Haywood wrote John Reed after the Chicago verdict. "The other fellow had the cut, shuffle and deal all the time, personally we didn't lose

much just a part of our lives." Bourne would have no renunciations. He had begun, rather, to think about postwar society and consider what could be retrieved from the battered romance of moderns with America.

With rare (in those days) enthusiasm he imagined a band of "malcontents" who would supplant the compromised alliance of the old idealists who rationalized the war effort and the eager young technocrats who implemented it. Not unlike Emma Goldman's brace of severe but loving critics, Bourne's malcontents would have no stomach for what had occurred in America, yet their very disaffection would make them hope for what might yet transpire. "Irritation at things as they are, disgust at the continual frustrations and aridities of American life, deep dissatisfaction with self and with the groups that give themselves forth as hopeful—out of such moods there might be hammered new values." Such people would have "a taste for spiritual adventure." "They will take institutions very lightly." "They will be glad if they can tease, provoke, irritate thought on any subject." And in the long run, they might engender "a tang, a bitterness, an intellectual fiber, a verve" out of which might still come fresh ideas, artistic vigor, intelligence suffused by feeling. It was the malcontents, bad-tempered and mocking as they could be, who were still the country's best hope for substantive, considered answers to the question that would inevitably arise after the war: "What shall we do with our America?"

By 1918, Bourne even proposed a coherent program, strikingly original at a time when friends on the left either rolled out the old panaceas of socialism or turned to the newfound religion of the Bolsheviks. He was not a manifesto maker, so he expressed his ideas piecemeal, in book reviews and short essays, but from these can be culled his thoughts about postwar society. He stresses the urgency of liberating the creative rather than the acquisitive powers, holds up individuality as the defining political ideal, condemns the pursuit of property and power as a dominating ethic, preserves a hope for some kind of democratic socialism and a new international order, calls for guarantees of the rights of minorities, decries the elevation of national security over the well-being of persons, criticizes abstract juridical rights as adequate guarantees of liberty. Big ideas, all—one could even say a laundry list of ideals. Yet deeply felt ethical preoccupations make them into something more than a ragbag of contemporary causes: Bourne's respect for culture and the needs of the imagination, his refusal to subordinate the individual to the state, his emphasis on economic cooperation, and a disbelief in liberal guarantees of rights as an end in themselves.

Whether Bourne could have actually developed this vision in the world of the 1920s is not clear. Certainly those malcontents who now came onto the scene revered his memory. Stories of his death—in Greenwich Village, surrounded by loving friends—evoked the loss of some fabled generational treasure. "It was the good fortune of American society to produce this man. We must not toss that luck away," Lewis Mumford wrote in 1930. But despite his memorialists, his work receded into the domain of academics, perhaps because it was so difficult to get hold of what exactly the man had meant. Referring to Bourne's care for what he called the "abounding vitality and moral freedom" in the lives around him, his *Seven Arts* colleague Waldo Frank ventured that Bourne's politics "took into account the content of the human soul." His elevation of quotidian elements to a level of intellectual and political significance was an approach very modern and very American. A woman friend, trying to pin down his mysterious power, traced its sources to his everyday comportment with others, his concern for his friends, his curiosity about them, his need to discuss and interrogate ideas and personalities and elucidate the sources of confusions. He was, she testified, "a resonant instrument of certain strains of thought and feeling" consciously rooted "in the American scene."

From the edges of the country he wrote for all who longed to be at the center, elucidating an optimism that ran clear beneath a pervasive sense of ill. Shunted aside by his culture, he never resorted to the dubious compensations of the lonely, doom-laden prophet but insisted on seeing himself firmly placed among his own, a band of comprehenders in a sociable American tradition of intellect going back to the Transcendalists. He was a friend among friends, a writer among writers, a man among women. He found a nucleus of thoroughgoing democracy in his beloved community. It was not modernism's grand theater of self-importance, but it was still a sanctuary for promise, tucked away in "this blundering, wistful, crass civilization we call America."

For Bourne, as for others of his world, feminism had been a—perhaps *the*—preeminent source of those fresh and true ideas, of the tang, verve, and intelligence laced with strong emotion that he equated with cultural and political vitality. After the war, this transforming ethos faded. In gender life as in politics, soft lines were out, hard edges in: snappy suits for men, straight flapper shifts for women. The men who took over the conduct of forward-looking arts, letters, and politics in New York continued to pronounce modernity and modernism to be genderless; they accepted the premises of women's rights. But they saw no artistic, political, or cultural gain in expanding on feminist premises, and therein lies the difference in the two eras.

The attenuation of feminism during the next two decades followed ironically on the heels of its great triumph, the winning of the Nineteenth Amendment for woman suffrage in 1920. But the leaders who emerged after the victory distanced themselves from messy definitions of sexual equality and narrowed the movement into a women's campaign for legal equality—what would become the Equal Rights Amendment. Partly because of the Red Scare, the links of feminism to a broader range of left-wing reforms disappeared. The downtown feminists, who were by 1920 engaged in a wide variety of causes—pacifism, trade unions, birth control, the Soviet Union—had little voice in what became a single-issue, single-sex movement. Activists like Dorothy Day and Crystal Eastman found themselves stranded. They wandered away or outright defected from the ERA campaigners who now led the movement. Culturally and politically, feminism was no longer an impetus for spirited conversation or a moving principle.

Among the intelligentsia, women were no longer nominated to lead the culture into the future. Feminism, stripped of its iconography of general emancipation, its vision of life without father, could not engage the brothers and sisters in dialogue. While the New Woman and her variants were still magnets for anxieties and meditations after 1919, they became a devalued subject matter, taking on the intense passivity of the obsessively observed. Across the culture, one has only to look at the finest writers—Hemingway, Fitzgerald, Faulkner, Dos Passos—to see that female characters retained their charge of modernist disruption yet operated at a great distance from women's historical energies.

In the 1920s and 1930s, some of the downtown men, looking about for new niches in the culture, reworked their experiences of the 1910s into autobiographical novels and memoirs. Literary authority became elegiac, foreclosing the resolution of dramas of sexual equality, relegating nervous and self-destructive female characters to the past, to a story that had ended. Neith Boyce, Ida Rauh, Emma Goldman, Mabel Dodge, Crystal Eastman—these creators of a modern life in high relief were re-created as unfortunates too preoccupied with outmoded concerns to take the leap into a newly authorized era of contemporaneity.

Suddenly the civilization the moderns had denounced as philistine and soul-crushing was not somewhere else in America, some small place left behind, but right there in New York, albeit in a merrier guise. Downtown, wartime repression had occurred against the backdrop of a real estate boom and tourist influx, an efflorescence of commercial bohemia capitalized upon by landlords (who profiteered by subdividing row houses into "artists' studios") and also by some Villagers who enacted their bohemian personae for the benefit of tourists. Eager crowds—tourists and uptowners—spilled out of the new subway stop in Sheridan Square with wartime dollars to spend on quaint apartments and spicy fare in Gypsy tea shops, guided to insiders' hideaways by "authentic" bohemian guides. While some moderns had been in court, others were turning into marketable copies of bohemians. Or perhaps a now-marginalized radicalism even fueled commerce, lending a hint of voluptuous adventure to basement eateries like the Café Russia, exotically Slavic but evoking nonetheless the noir of Bolshevik plotting. Sleazy Guido Bruno, an untalented hanger-on, impersonated Hippolyte Havel, the intemperate anarchist (Havel seems to have gone underground during the war), and charged admission to arty evenings in a candlelit garret frequented by down-and-out women he paid to impersonate poets and artists' models.

On the newsstands, slim Village fly sheets replaced the socialist and anarchist papers and the modern monthlies, now banned: *Pagan* and *Quill* advertised tearooms, gift shops, and real estate. The neighborhood's reputation for free love made it a hospitable milieu for middle-class sexual adventurers and a mecca for gay men and lesbians. A neighborhood joker spoofed the scene:

> Way down South in Greenwich Village
> Where the spinsters come for thrillage,
> Where they speak of "soul relations,"
> With the sordid Slavic nations,
> 'Neath the guise of feminism,
> Dodging social ostracism,
> They get away with much
> In Washington Square.

> Way down South in Greenwich Village
> Where they eat Italian swillage,
> Where the fashion illustrators
> Flirt with interior decorators
> Where the cheap Bohemian fakirs
> And the boys from Wanamaker's
> Gather "atmosphere"
> In Washington Square.

Bohemia had always been susceptible to *embourgeoisement*, but in the war years this tendency redoubled. Initially devoted to criticizing, even opposing, bourgeois culture, bohemia turned out to be a reserve of inspiration for renovating middle-class life in the great shift from a nineteenth-century work-oriented ethic to a consumerist, leisured society. "The American middle class had come to the end of its Puritan phase; it had its war-profits to spend, and it was turning to Bohemia to learn how to spend them," observed Floyd Dell, who deplored the phenomenon but, as a pundit of the new morality in the 1920s, would learn to make a living from it.

"It was a bitter thing." Dell was speaking not of the political defeat that marked his generation but of the indignity of seeing himself cast as an old-timer, displaced from the cultural center by people pretending to be him and his friends. Suddenly the moderns were no longer "youth" but another "generation" to be superseded as they had once pushed aside their own predecessors. There was a touch of homophobia to their unease: they were skittish of the gay newcomers flooding the neighborhood, especially the "boys" who embodied both avant-garde sophistication and the ambiguous sexual identity they had worked so hard to banish from their bohemian manliness. But they especially rued the arrivistes who tarted up the masquerade balls and tearooms with parodies of bohemian personae. Bohemian sociability, its unusual combinations, its acceptance of women's freedoms—shorn of political associations, these all devolved into simulacra of what had been vital forms.

In 1919, Malcolm Cowley, a young writer from Pittsburgh, arrived in the Village and discovered a conquered country. He and his crowd of young men, newly demobilized from the army, were youthful revolutionaries eager to seize the cultural space from the dispirited, discredited old guard: "former anarchists . . . former Wobblies about to open speakeasies, former noblewomen divorced or widowed, former suffragists who had been arrested after picketing the White House, former conscientious objectors paroled from Leavenworth," and so forth. "The Village had a pervading atmosphere of middle-agedness," Cowley judged. "There were defeats to be concealed." Cowley's view had some truth to it, and poignancy, too, The "middle-aged" of 1919 were, after all, only slightly older than they had been in 1915, when they reigned unchallenged in the capital of the modern world. The moment they had sponsored lasted less than a decade, a sharp contrast to the decades-long rule of the entrenched elite they had tried to oust.

Nonetheless, if their achievement was invisible to the newcomers, it was still substantial. They had negotiated a transition into a new order, undermining the faith that arts and letters were the domain of the well-born and tasteful and immeasurably broadening in the process the provenance of American culture. Background characters moved to the foreground; literary and painterly subjects once seen as

A tour guide to bohemia, c. 1920 MUSEUM OF THE CITY OF NEW YORK

lowlife outcasts now appeared to contain energies to be tapped. Once the bohemians began to assemble modern collage from the corners of the society, the game of representing the new was open to all comers. From this point on, America—and especially New York—would never lack for critics, artists, and audiences who prided themselves on democratic curiosity, on spotting precisely those forms that lay outside cultivated taste. The crossovers of the Villager became embedded in the culture, laying down channels between high and low culture, outsiders and insiders that made the American avant-garde peculiarly susceptible to vagrant influences and exchanges. Indeed, the bohemians' fascination with the Lower East Side, its stock types, vivid folk, and native explicators set many of the terms (at once helpful and imprisoning) for the African American crossover from Harlem in the 1920s.

The bohemians set out to influence, to shape, and, in their wildest moments, to create the new century. The world did change, inalterably, but not in the ways they anticipated. Placed against the substance of what actually came to pass—the previously unimaginable afflictions and catastrophes of modernity—their presumptions look self-involved, callow, and flimsy. The new turned out to include another world war, mass murder, dictatorships, and countless minor bloodbaths, some of them in devilish league with various ideologies of emancipation that had once seemed pristine.

And yet the bohemians' version of a modernism that is democratic and quotidian endures, a reserve of fresh ideas, artistic vigor, and intelligence suffused with feeling, as Randolph Bourne saw the matter. America, for all its fits and starts of memory, never quite forgets those who hold the country to its most encompassing possibilities. The moment of the 1910s retains a hold on the country's imagination that is more than nostalgic, a promise of ethical abundance allied with art and artful living, a guarantee of a skepticism at once relentlessly questioning of America and entirely embroiled in its future. Enough of its legacy is woven through the society to make the now antique yearnings of the century's beginnings still plausible. The moderns' style of unbounded conversation, their belief that the culture was that much the richer for infusions from outsiders, their faith in the leavening powers of honesty in personal relations, and their adherence—however ambivalent—to equality between men and women: these elements are still familiar.

The connections that these smart, idealistic, self-involved people made between freedoms on many fronts—political, sexual, literary, artistic—are more than a product of naïveté. They give us some clues to modern promises and modern perplexities that are tangled in our very nerve systems, our deepest feelings, our most mundane communications. The bohemians believed they stood at the beginning of an arc through American time. Searching for the place that arc touches down, we can spy a modernity still desirable and absorbing, if necessarily chastened.

Notes

PROLOGUE

page

1. **"The world has changed less"**: Péguy, quoted in Robert Hughes, *The Shock of the New* (New York, 1991), p. 9.

   "On or about December 1910": Virginia Woolf, "Character in Fiction," *The Essays of Virginia Woolf*, vol. 3, ed. Andrew McNeillie (New York, 1988), p. 421.

   "something was in the air": Floyd Dell, *Homecoming* (New York, 1933), p. 217.

   "the revolutionary pot": *Industrial Worker* (1912), quoted in Melvin Dubofsky, *We Shall Be All: A History of the IWW* (New York, 1969), p. 260.

2. **"Whether in literature, plastic art, the labor movement"**: Hutchins Hapgood, "Art and Unrest," *New York Globe and Commercial Advertiser*, Jan. 27, 1913.

   The outlines of the Villagers' story: "Who does not know the now routine legend in which the world of 1910–17 is Washington Square turned Arcadia, in which the barriers are always down, the magazines always promising, the workers always marching, geniuses sprouting in every Village bedroom, Isadora Duncan always dancing. . . . No other generation in America ever seems to have so radiant a youth, or has remembered it in so many winsome autobiographies written at forty." So Alfred Kazin sighed in 1942, and there were still decades of legend-making to come (*On Native Grounds* [New York, 1942], p. 134).

4. **"something considerable may happen"**: Herbert Croly, "New York as the American Metropolis," *Architectural Record* 13 (Mar. 1903): 205.

5. **artistic capital of the modern world**: "French Artists Spur on an American Art," *New York Tribune*, Oct. 24, 1915, sec. 4.

6. **"an architecture conceived in a child's dream"**: Loy, quoted in Carolyn Burke, *Becoming Modern: The Life of Mina Loy* (New York, 1996), p. 211.

   "More than any other city": Trotsky, *My Life: An Attempt at an Autobiography* (New York, 1930), p. 270.

7. **"life without a father"**: Thus Stein described her alliance, "a very pleasant one," with her brother Leo. Quoted in Martin Green, *New York 1913: The Armory Show and the Paterson Strike Pageant* (New York, 1988), p. 67.

   "new temper of mind": Walter Lippmann to Max Eastman, Apr. 2, 1913, Max Eastman Papers, Lilly Library, Indiana University, Bloomington.

8. **One story of modernism**: I have in mind the paradigmatic modernist writer in Raymond Williams, *The Politics of Modernism: Against the New Conformists* (London, 1989). The literature on modernism and modernity is dense and vast; Williams is unusual both in his scrupulous historicization of the aesthetic issues and in his pan-European (although not transatlantic or transcontinental) reach. The omission of the United States in Williams's interpretation is common: accounts of modernism in the American context usually begin in the 1930s and 1940s, not at the fin de siècle. The study of social modernity in the United States has been subsumed by the study of the commodity aesthetic and mass culture, the study of early modernism by the study of discrete intellectual trends. See, for example, Richard Ohman, *Selling Culture: Magazines, Markets, and Class at the Turn of the Century* (London, 1996); John Higham, "The Reorientation of American Culture in the 1890's," *Writing American History: Essays on Modern Scholarship* (Bloomington, 1970), pp. 73–102. Studies of American modernism, broadly considered, are Malcolm Bradbury, "The Nonhomemade World: European and American Modernism," *American Quarterly* 39 (Spring 1987): 27–36; Daniel Joseph Singal, "Towards a Definition of American Modernism," *American Quarterly* 39 (Spring 1987): 7–26; see also the wide-ranging review by Dorothy Ross, "A Sampler of Modernisms," *Reviews in American History* 21 (1993): 121–25. Among works on Europe that have shaped my ideas are Thomas Crow, "Modernism and Mass Culture in the Visual Arts," *Pollock and After: The Critical Debate*, ed. Francis Frascina (New York, 1985), pp. 233–66; Mark M. Anderson, *Kafka's Clothes: Ornament and Aestheticism in the Habsburg Fin de Siècle* (Oxford, 1992); Marshall Berman, *All That Is Solid Melts into Air: The Experience of Modernity* (New York, 1982); Andreas Huyssen, *After the Great Divide: Modernism, Mass Culture, Postmodernism* (Bloomington, 1986); *The Gender of Modernism: A Critical Anthology*, ed. Bonnie Kime Scott (Bloomington, 1990); Sandra M. Gilbert and Susan Gubar, *No Man's Land*, 2 vols. (*The War of the Words* [New Haven, 1988], and *Sexchanges* [New Haven, 1989]); Michael North, *The Dialect of Modernism: Race, Language, and Twentieth-Century Literature* (New York, 1994). A useful compendium of approaches can be found in *Modernism, 1890–1930*, ed. Malcolm Bradbury and James McFarlane (Atlantic Highlands, 1976).

1/BOHEMIAN BEGINNINGS IN THE 1890S

11. **certain places that suddenly vibrated**: *New York Interiors at the Turn of the Century: 131 Photographs by Joseph Byron*, ed. Clay Lancaster (New York,

1976); James Huneker, "A Sentimental Rebellion," *Visionaries* (New York, 1905), p. 237; *Paintings Watercolors and Drawings by George B. Luks*, auction catalog, Parke-Bernet Galleries (New York, 1950), pp. 24, 26.

13. **"other kinds of men and women":** Hutchins Hapgood, *A Victorian in the Modern World* (New York, 1939), p. 138.

   "I am part of the avant garde": Vorse, quoted in Dee Garrison, *Mary Heaton Vorse* (Philadelphia, 1989), p. 24.

   "impossible and forbidden things": Ibid.

   "In New York, as in Paris": James Huneker, *Steeplejack* (New York, 1920), vol. 2, pp. 9–15.

14. **"So cheerful, and so full of swagger":** Adams, quoted in Kazin, *On Native Grounds*, p. 53.

   the satisfied classes and the swindled: Henry James, *The Princess Casamassima* (1896; Harmondsworth, Eng., 1977), pp. 284, 292.

15. **Indeed, the distance:** Useful treatments of the tenor of the nineties can be found in Lewis Mumford, *The Brown Decades: A Study of the Arts in America, 1865–1895* (New York, 1931); Irwin Yellowitz, *Labor and the Progressive Movement in New York State, 1897–1916* (Ithaca, 1965); Nell Irvin Painter, *Standing at Armageddon: The United States, 1877–1919* (New York, 1987); Robert Wiebe, *The Search for Order, 1877–1920* (New York 1967); Matthew Frye Jacobsen, *Whiteness of a Different Color* (Cambridge, Mass., 1998); T. J. Jackson Lears, *No Place of Grace: Antimodernism and the Transformation of American Culture, 1880–1920* (New York, 1981); Alan Trachtenberg, *The Incorporation of America: Culture and Society in the Gilded Age* (New York, 1982); Alan Dawley, *Struggles for Justice: Social Responsibility and the Liberal State* (Cambridge, Mass., 1991). For New York in particular, see Edwin G. Burrows and Mike Wallace, *Gotham: A History of New York City to 1898* (New York, 1998); for the progressives, Daniel T. Rodgers, *Atlantic Crossings: Social Politics in a Progressive Age* (Cambridge, Mass., 1999).

   "The Social Gulf": Addams, quoted in Dorothy Ross, "Gendered Social Knowledge: Domestic Discourse, Jane Addams, and the Possibilities of Social Science," *Gender and American Social Science: The Formative Years*, ed. Helene Silverberg (Princeton, 1998). Compare Wiebe, *Search for Order*, ch. 4, on the political and cultural stalemate of the 1890s.

16. **bohemias sprouted in other places:** Albert Parry, *Garrets and Pretenders* (New York, 1933), chs. 11–20; Douglass Shand-Tucci, *Ralph Adams Cram: Life and Architecture*, vol. 1 of *Boston Bohemia, 1881–1900* (Amherst, 1995); Kevin Starr, *Americans and the California Dream, 1850–1915* (New York, 1973); Stephen Schwartz, *From West to East: California and the Making of the American Mind* (New York, 1998), part 2; Esther Lanigan Stineman, *Mary Austin: Song of a Maverick* (New Haven, 1989); Robert M. Crunden, *American Salons: Encounters with European Modernism* (New York, 1992); "The Discovery of Bohemia," *Literary History of the United States: History*, 3rd ed., ed. Robert E. Spiller et al. (New York, 1963), pp. 1065–79.

   a long tradition that cast the city: See Irving Howe's lucid account of anti-urbanism, "The City in Literature," *The Critical Point: On Literature and Culture* (New York, 1973), pp. 39–58; on realism's relation to anti-urbanism, see Amy Kaplan, *The Social Construction of an American Realism* (Chicago, 1988), p. 141.

17. **an optics of pleasure:** Philip Fisher, "Appearing and Disappearing in Public: Social Space in Late-Nineteenth-Century Literature and Culture," *Reconstructing American Literary History*, ed. Sacvan Bercovitch (Cambridge, Mass., 1986), pp. 155–88; William R. Taylor, *In Pursuit of Gotham: Culture and Commerce in New York* (New York, 1992), ch. 1.

By midcentury the word had acquired: Henri Murger, *Scenes from the Life of Bohemia* (London, 1888); the original French edition was published in 1849. See Jerrold Siegel, *Bohemian Paris: Culture, Politics, and the Boundaries of Bourgeois Life, 1830–1930* (New York, 1986), ch. 1; a contrary assessment of bohemia as the "absolute refusal of bourgeois society" can be found in T. J. Clark, *Image of the People: Gustave Courbet and the 1848 Revolution* (London, 1973). See also Joanna Richardson, *The Bohemians: La Vie de Bohème in Paris, 1830–1914* (New York, 1969), pp. 102–05; Louann Faris Culley, "Artists' Life-Styles in Nineteenth-Century France and England: The Dandy, the Bohemian, and the Realist," Ph.D. dissertation, Stanford University, 1975; Malcolm Easton, *Artists and Writers in Paris: The Bohemian Idea, 1803–1867* (New York, 1964); Robert Michels, "On the Sociology of Bohemia and Its Connection to the Intellectual Proletariat," *Catalyst* 15 (1983): 5–25. The term must have reached London from Paris quickly, for in 1858 a writer mused that "bohemia" had already traveled from London to New York (*New York Times*, Jan. 6, 1858).

the runaway best-seller: On the *Trilby* craze, see Parry, *Garrets and Pretenders*, ch. 9, and the original by George Du Maurier (New York, 1894).

stock "types": Gareth Stedman Jones points out that the urban typologies complemented the Victorian statistical investigation, with the point of inquiry being not economic conditions but ethnographic peculiarities; see "The 'Cockney' and the Nation, 1780–1988," *Metropolis: London. Histories and Representations since 1800*, ed. David Feldman and Gareth Stedman Jones (London, 1989), p. 300. Mark Anderson analyzes "a signifying system of cause and effect, surface and ground" in nineteenth-century urban fiction (*Kafka's Clothes*, p. 171).

18. **explorations of faraway lands:** On urban exploration, see Deborah Epstein Nord, "The Social Explorer as Anthropologist: Victorian Travellers among the Urban Poor," *Visions of the Modern City*, ed. William Sharpe and Leonard Wallock, Proceedings of the Heyman Center, Columbia University, c. 1983; Christopher Herbert, *Culture and Anomie: Ethnographic Imagination in the Nineteenth Century* (Chicago, 1991). On urban strolling and spectacle, see Taylor, *In Pursuit of Gotham*, ch. 3.

symbiotic relation to bourgeois culture: Bohemia also became over the course of the nineteenth century a term for a slightly racier version of gentlemen's clubbiness. *Harper's Weekly* featured "Bohemian Walks and Talks," a column of amiable editorial musings, beginning in 1858. The San Francisco Bohemian Club, founded in 1872 for the city's elite, featured annual retreats and hijinks that brought businessmen into contact with successful artists. See *Bohemian Club Certificate of Incorporation and Constitution, By-Laws* (San Francisco, 1939); William G. Domhoff, *The Bohemian Grove and Other Retreats* (New York, 1974). John O'Reilly's poem

"In Bohemia" (1886) became a recitation piece at those men's clubs that defined themselves as less stodgy than their more traditional rivals (James Jeffrey Roche, *John Boyle O'Reilly* [New York, 1891]). Discussions of the filtering of bohemia into respectable male joviality can be found in Parry, *Garrets and Pretenders*, passim.

the behemoth newspapers: Michael Schudson, *Discovering the News: A Social History of American Newspapers* (New York, 1978); Christopher Wilson, *The Labor of Words: Literary Professionalism in the Progressive Era* (Athens, Ga., 1985). On the *Commercial*, see Lincoln Steffens, *The Autobiography of Lincoln Steffens* (New York, 1931); Hapgood, *Victorian in the Modern World*, chs. 5–7; Stanford E. Marovitz, *Abraham Cahan* (New York, 1996), pp. 41–48.

19. **"the beauty in the mean streets":** Lincoln Steffens, *Autobiography*, p. 317.

Neith Boyce: There is a short biography of Boyce in *Intimate Warriors: Portraits of a Modern Marriage, 1899–1944*, ed. Ellen Kay Trimberger (New York, 1991). Boyce describes her literary apprenticeship with her father's magazine, the Boston *Arena*, in her unpublished fictionalized "Autobiography," typescript in Hapgood Family Papers, Beinecke Rare Book Library, Yale University.

"New Yorkers might see": Steffens, *Autobiography*, p. 311.

20. **"he's a great crook":** Ibid., p. 312.

"that the reader will see himself": Ibid., p. 317.

A toddler falls to her death: *Commercial Advertiser,* June 17, 1899.

The genre of the gentleman's ramble: Instances are the sketches of Brander Matthews, an influential professor of English literature at Columbia, and of H. C. Bunner. See Matthews, *Vignettes of Manhattan* (New York, 1894); *The Stories of H. C. Bunner, 1st ser.* (New York, 1916). The genre is discussed in Trachtenberg, *Incorporation of America*, p. 187.

21. **"what a world of horizons":** Randolph Bourne, "Vanishing World of Gentility," rev. of Brander Matthews sketches, *Dial*, Mar. 4, 1918, p. 234.

The floating milieu: Huneker, *Steeplejack*, vol. 2, pp. 72–73; Arnold T. Schwab, *James Gibbons Huneker* (Stanford, 1963), chs. 4–9; Parry, *Garrets and Pretenders*, pp. 66–75; Nicole Sackley, " 'All Out on Union Square!': City Space and the Rebuilding of the American Left, 1927–1935," seminar paper, Department of History, Princeton University, Spring 1998; Rion James, *Dining in New York* (New York, 1930), pp. 150–51; John W. Frick, *New York's First Theatrical Center: The Rialto at Union Square* (Ann Arbor, 1985), pp. 98, 102, 106.

the most populous Jewish city: Ronald Sanders, *The Downtown Jews* (New York, 1969), p. 351.

"the fabulous East Side": The title of an essay in Huneker, *New Cosmopolis* (New York, 1915).

22. **Bercovici:** Konrad Bercovici, *It's the Gypsy in Me* (New York, 1941), p. 25 and chs. 1–2 passim.

"students, journalists, scholars": Jacob Epstein, *Epstein: An Autobiography* (New York, 1955), pp. 2–3. Epstein, later a renowned sculptor in England, was a Russian-born child of the Lower East Side whose father made enough money to move the family uptown and allow them to live like well-off German Jews. Epstein, however, once he went to the New York Art

Students League, was so mesmerized by the old neighborhood that he spent all his spare time there.

"modern-minded European working class": Sanders, *Downtown Jews*, p. 330.

The grave and precise debate: David Hollinger, "Ethnic Diversity, Cosmopolitanism, and the Emergence of the American Liberal Intelligentsia," *American Quarterly* 27 (May 1975): 133–51.

Bercovici remembered a concert review: Bercovici, *It's the Gypsy in Me*, p. 58.

23. **Cahan squired them around the ghetto:** Marovitz, *Abraham Cahan*, pp. 40–48. The procession of bohemians was not without its critics. An aggrieved writer for the *Jewish Daily Forward*, for one, found the tourists insultingly voyeuristic and viciously attacked Konrad Bercovici for his role: "He brings his friends to look at us as if we were animals in a zoo. Let him get a job with a sight-seeing car and wear the uniform and cap of a guide" (Bercovici, *It's the Gypsy in Me*, pp. 53–54). Bohemians' pleasure in their guided tours of the picturesque ghetto echo the excitement of Americans on the European Grand Tour with their native cicerone. "It's the ideal," thinks a Henry James character in Italy, "strolling up and down on the very spot . . . hearing out-of-the-way anecdotes from deeply indigenous lips" (*Roderick Hudson* [New York, 1875], p. 202).

a period of rising anti-Semitism: Leonard Dinnerstein, *Anti-Semitism in America* (New York, 1994), ch. 3.

a language of biological racialism: See the many books by Sander Gilman; here I have relied on *Franz Kafka: The Jewish Patient* (New York, 1995).

"objectionable races": Prescott Hall of the Immigration Restriction League, quoted in Dinnerstein, *Anti-Semitism*, p. 44.

Scholars disagree: Cf. Dinnerstein, *Anti-Semitism;* John Higham, *Strangers in the Land: Patterns of American Nativism, 1860–1925* (New York, 1972); Higham, *Send These to Me: Jews and Other Immigrants in Urban America* (New York, 1975); Jacobsen, *Whiteness*.

24. **anti-Semitism . . . in Europe:** On officially sanctioned violence, see Gilman, *Kafka;* on anti-Semitic political parties and boycotts, see Marsha L. Rozenblit, *The Jews of Vienna, 1867–1914: Assimilation and Identity* (Albany, 1983). On the Paris community during the Dreyfus affair, see Nancy L. Green, *The Pletzl of Paris: Jewish Immigrant Workers in the Belle Epoque* (New York, 1986).

a trickle of philo-Semitism: Howe, *World of Our Fathers*, pp. 405–08; Richard Wheatley, "The Jews in New York," *Century*, Jan. 1892, pp. 323–42. On the openness of late 1890s newspapers to Jewish material, see Moses Rischin, "Abraham Cahan and the New York *Commercial Advertiser:* A study in Acculturation," *Publication of the American Jewish Historical Society* 43 (Sept. 1953): 26. Zangwill's publications include *Children of the Ghetto* (New York and London, 1899) and *Dreamers of the Ghetto* (New York and London, 1899). James Huneker wrote so often, and so sympathetically, about the immigrant Jews that he was assumed to be Jewish (Schwab, *James Gibbons Huneker*, p. 97). By 1909, this strain of philo-Semitism had sufficiently entered the mainstream to make Zangwill's stage melodrama *The Melting Pot* a Broadway hit. The play revolved around the trope of "God's Crucible, the great Melting Pot" of the United States—a cliché now, a novelty then—"where all the races of Europe are melting and re-forming." *The Melting Pot* opened in Washington, D.C., in 1908; President Roosevelt attended the opening performance and raved (Neil Larry Shumsky, "Zangwill's *The Melting Pot:* Ethnic Tensions on Stage," *American Quarterly* 28 [Mar. 1975]: 29–41).

25. **Cahan's name propelled the *Commercial:*** Steffens, *Autobiography*, p. 319. Indeed, one of the *Commercial*'s Harvard men, Robert Dunn, got himself fired for his anti-Semitism toward Cahan (Ibid., pp. 325–26).

feuilleton then fashionable on the Continent: Allan Janik and Stephen Toulmin, *Wittgenstein's Vienna* (New York, 1973), pp. 46, 79–81; William M. Johnston, *The Austrian Mind: Austrian Intellectual and Social History, 1848–1938* (Berkeley, 1972), pp. 122–23; Carl E. Schorske, *Fin-de-Siècle Vienna: Politics and Culture* (New York, 1980).

"queer and repulsive": Hutchins Hapgood, *The Spirit of the Ghetto* (New York, 1902), p. 5.

the Tenderloin: Keith Mayes, "'The Railroad and Its Terminus': Pennsylvania Station, Commercial Capitalism, and the Politics of Building in Greater New York, 1901–1910," seminar paper, Department of History, Princeton University, Spring 1998. Seventh Avenue from Twenty-third to Fortieth Street was known as "African Broadway." See also Gilbert Osofsky, *Harlem: The Making of a Ghetto*, 2nd ed. (New York, 1971), ch. 1.

Stephen Crane: Christopher P. Wilson, "Stephen Crane and the Police," *American Quarterly* 48 (June 1996): 273–315.

26. **Nightlife catered to:** James Weldon Johnson, *The Autobiography of an Ex-Colored Man* (New York, 1912), chs. 6 and 7. For a geography of New York entertainments, see Lewis A. Erenberg, *Steppin' Out: New York Nightlife and the Transformation of American Culture, 1890–1930* (Westport, 1981).

women were cast as grisettes: See Culley, "Artists' Life-Styles," for an exposition of the female "types" of European bohemias. In early American usages, heterosexual associations were muted: the earliest representatives of bohemia, Poe and the painter James McNeill Whistler, were known for their dandyish sexlessness—Poe for his neurasthenic devotion to his "child-bride"—rather than for any passionate sexual involvements with women. On the masculine character of bohemian Paris at the turn of the century, see Michael Wilson, "'Sans les femmes, qu'est-ce qui nous resterait?': Gender and Transgression in Bohemian Montmartre," *Body Guards: The Cultural Politics of Gender Ambiguity*, ed. Julia Epstein and Kristina Straub (New York, 1991), pp. 195–222.

27. **a few demimondaines hovered about:** These included the writer Ada Clare (veteran of a scandalous romance with a celebrity pianist) and the daring Adah Menken, who in 1860 appeared on the New York stage as a man clad in a flesh-colored body suit that simulated nudity and astride a live horse. On Clare, see her autobiographical novel *Only a Woman's Heart* (New York, 1860); Charles Warren Stoddard, "Ada Clare, Queen of Bohemia," *National Magazine*, Sept. 1905, pp. 637–45; Parry, *Garrets and Pretenders*, passim. On Menken, see Bernard Falk, *The Naked Lady: A Biography of Adah Isaacs Menken* (London, 1934); Richard Northcott, *Adah Isaacs Menken: An Illustrated Biography* (London, 1921). On the question of

women at Pfaff's, see my "Whitman at Pfaff's: Commercial Culture, Literary Life, and New York Bohemia at Mid-Century," *Walt Whitman Quarterly Review* 10 (Winter 1993): 107–26. The earliest American novel of bohemia, Charles De Kay's *The Bohemian* (New York, 1878), conceived it as a refuge from women.

a token female artist or two: Berthe Morisot and Mary Cassatt (both respectable ladies, not bohemians) played this role among the Impressionists, as did Suzanne Valadon, a model from Barcelona but also a painter in her own right. The painter Lluisa Vidal had much the same function in the Els Quatre Gats bohemian circle in turn-of-the-century Barcelona. See Anne Higonnet, *Berthe Morisot* (New York, 1990), ch. 14; for Valadon and Vidal, John Richardson, *A Life of Picasso, vol. 1 (1881–1990)* (New York, 1991), pp. 133–34. In London, a few women writers moved within the orbit of the Decadents, making their accommodations as they could with the men's misogyny (Introduction, *Keynotes*, by George Egerton, ed. Martha Vicinus [London,1983]; Elaine Showalter, *Sexual Anarchy: Gender and Culture at the Fin de Siècle* [New York, 1990], ch. 9). Gertrude Atherton, an American writer in London during the Wilde trial, encountered some of these women. Emily Wortis Leider, *California's Daughter: Gertrude Atherton and Her Times* (Stanford, 1991), ch. 8.

"woman of the streets": On the propriety of women's presence on the streets, see Deborah Epstein Nord, *Walking the Victorian Streets: Women, Representation, and the City* (Ithaca, 1995), and my *City of Women: Sex and Class in New York, 1789–1860* (New York, 1986), chs. 3–5.

The phenomenon of artistic professionalism: The available statistics support this view. In 1870, the presence of women in any federal census category associated with artistic employments was small, in some cases tiny: 412 female artists compared with 3,669 men, for example; 35 women journalists compared with 5,251 men; 159 female "authors" against 820 male. In 1900, men still outnumbered women in almost all categories; music/music teaching and authorship were the exceptions. But the female increases in all fields were phenomenal: 13,875 male artists, 11,027 female; 27,905 male journalists, 2,193 female; and so forth. The numbers come from compendia of the federal censuses, 1870–1920 (Ninth to Fourteenth).

"scribbling women": Hawthorne, quoted in Ann D. Wood, "The 'Scribbling Women' and Fanny Fern: Why Women Wrote," *American Quarterly* 23 (Spring 1971): 3.

28. **"There are ... more would-be *prime donne*":** Clara Louise Kellogg, *Memoirs of an American Prima Donna* (New York, 1913), p. 320.

"There are today thousands upon thousands": Candace Wheeler, quoted in Kathleen D. McCarthy, *Women's Culture: American Philanthropy and Art, 1830–1930* (Chicago, 1991), p. 94.

New Woman: For a comprehensive essay, see Carroll Smith-Rosenberg, "The New Woman as Androgyne," *Disorderly Conduct* (New York, 1985), pp. 254–96; for the British version of the New Woman, see Ruth Brandon, *The New Women and the Old Men: Love, Sex, and the Woman Question* (New York, 1990). Spurred by idealistic educations at women's institutions and a zeal to escape what Jane Addams called "the family claim," the first two generations of college graduates succeeded in establishing a visible presence (while still numerically small) in what had been exclusively male occupations. Addams's phrase is from a passionate diatribe against the cloistering of educated daughters (*Twenty Years at Hull House* [1910; New York, 1974], p. 94).

New Woman illustrators, art students: Increasingly, artistic work occurred within the sphere of commercial culture—to use William R. Taylor's term—rather than that of patronage or artisanal work, its economic basis greatly expanded by new technologies and forms of mass consumption. The development was most marked in the print media. A boom in magazine publishing fueled a market for short stories, poetry, and feature writing; the magazines also created a brisk demand for illustrations, sketches, and, by the turn of the century, photojournalism. Similarly, in publishing, once organized around a genteel ethos of patronage, the old family-based firms began to be restructured or replaced by organizations dedicated to aggressive marketing, vigorous promotion of longer lists, and internal specialization. The huge newspapers of the era—Pulitzer's *New York World*, Hearst's *New York Journal*—expanded beyond the traditional editorial room, where one editor supervised all the work, into specialized structures with separate departments (sports, local, foreign and national, society, theater and music, police, editorials, business, circulation and advertising). Surging circulations in all the print media brought a demand for writing of all sorts, some of which women had done since before the Civil War (sentimental fiction, poetry, family features, fashion and society reporting), some of which they had not. These specializations opened employment for women as copywriters, headline writers, advertising writers, and sometimes editors.

Magazines and books were heavily illustrated and put out work on assignment. In the theater, the growth of the vaudeville circuit and the proliferation of light musicals created work for singers, actresses, and female dancers. See Wilson, *Labor of Words*, chs. 1–3; Taylor, *In Pursuit of Gotham*, pp. 81–82; Barbara Belford, *Brilliant Bylines: A Biographical Anthology of Notable Newspaperwomen in America* (New York, 1986); Albert Auster, *Actresses and Suffragists: Women in the American Theater* (New York, 1984). See also my "Women Artists and the Problems of Metropolitan Culture: New York and Chicago, 1890–1910," *Cultural Leadership in America*, ed. Wanda Corn (Boston, 1998), pp. 25–38.

29. **"the army of women all over the country":** Vorse, quoted in Garrison, *Mary Heaton Vorse*, p. 21.

commissions for illustrations, busts, and paintings: The involvement of women artists in producing images of the New Woman can be seen in the account of the commissions given to women artists in *Godey's* 132 (Jan.–June 1896), pp. 68–76, 356–61, and 133 (July–Dec. 1896), pp. 356–60. See also Neith Boyce, "The Bachelor Girl," *Vogue*, May 5–Nov. 3, 1898.

30. **"When I speak of a person":** Boyce, "The Bachelor Girl," *Vogue*, June 16, 1898, p. vii. Vorse, too, wrote about variants of the New Woman; see "The Art Student and Successful Work," *Delineator*, Nov. 1905, pp. 940–43; "The Truth Concerning Art Schools," *Delineator*, Oct. 1905, pp. 706–10.

"they live in a great measure": Henry James, "The Future of the Novel" (1899), *The Art of Criticism: Henry James on the Theory and the Practice of Fiction*, ed. William Veeder and Susan M. Griffin (Chicago, 1986), p. 243.

"convince the world that she is possible": Boyce, "The Bachelor Girl," *Vogue*, June 16, 1898, p. vii.

"an escaped bird": Vorse, quoted in Garrison, *Mary Heaton Vorse*, p. 21. From an article in *Munsey's*, a popular magazine, we can observe how the identifications took shape within a geography of metropolitan center and margins, a process that we might see as one of collaborative feminine readings. In truth, the article's author argued, the bachelor girl was simply a single woman of small means "pursuing an art or earning a living." But once the descriptive halo conferred by the press surrounded her ("jaunty, winsome, mischievous, gay . . . and—God forgive us all!—bohemian"), she assumed inordinate interest, and those who knew her discovered in her "the corroboration of all they had read—never dreaming that she was but a product of the same reading" (Winifred Sothern, "The Truth about the Bachelor Girl," *Munsey's*, May 1901, p. 282).

31. **only the hardiest, most intrepid defenders:** Charlotte Perkins Gilman was one. See *Women and Economics* (Boston, 1898). Cf. the defensive terms Mary Augusta Jordan, a Smith College professor, used to argue timidly for women's preparation for a profession ("The College Graduate and the Bachelor Maid," *Independent*, July 20, 1899: 1937–40).

Rather, writers updated an old Victorian morality tale: Emilie Ruck de Schell struck the dominant chord in the title "Is Feminine Bohemianism a Failure?" (*Arena* 20 [1898]: 68–75). This literature of anxiety includes Henry Harland, "The Bohemian Girl," *Yellow Book* 4 (Jan. 1895): 12–43; Sothern, "The Truth about the Bachelor Girl"; Du Maurier, *Trilby*; and the novels discussed below.

the cult of the "strenuous life": E. Anthony Rotundo, *American Manhood: Transformations in Masculinity from the Revolution to the Modern Era* (New York, 1993), p. 228.

32. **anarchic sexual modernism:** On Britain, see Showalter, *Sexual Anarchy*; Patricia Stubbs, *Women and Fiction: Feminism and the Novel* (New York, 1979); Linda Dowling, "The Decadent and the New Woman in the 1890s," *Nineteenth Century Fiction* 33 (1979): 434–53; Introduction, *Keynotes*; Richard Dellamora, *Masculine Desire: The Sexual Politics of Victorian Aestheticism* (Chapel Hill, 1990). On the United States, see Michael Kimmel, "The Contemporary 'Crisis' of Masculinity in Historical Perspective," *The Making of Masculinities*, ed. Harry Brod (Boston, 1987), pp. 121–54; Lears, *No Place of Grace*, pp. 108–110; Gail Bederman, *Manliness and Civilization: A Cultural History of Gender and Race in the United States, 1880–1917* (Chicago, 1995).

In truth, there was little substance: McCarthy, *Women's Culture*, p. 150.

the "feminization of American culture": The idea is usually attributed to Harvard philosopher George Santayana, in a 1902 lecture, "The Genteel Tradition in American Philosophy," reprinted in *The Genteel Tradition*, ed. Douglas L. Wilson (Cambridge, Mass., 1967). Santayana was picking up, however, an opposition that had been around for some time, as one can see from William Dean Howells's formulation several years earlier and from even earlier diatribes against "the Iron Madonna who strangles in her fond embrace the American novelist" and the "lady-like" character of the magazines. Compare a sample of sophisticated, Decadent-tinged misogyny quoted by James Huneker, from a magazine he coedited in 1898: "Woman . . . what a damnable noise she makes at this century's end! . . . In letters, painting, science, music, sculpture—nothing. When with simian—the feminine is nearer the simian than the masculine—ease they imitate the gestures of an artist one must always look in the background for a man." Huneker attributes the passage to his colleague Vance Thompson (quoted in Huneker, *Steeplejack*, vol. 2, pp. 192–94). See also "Women—Wives or Mothers, by a Woman," *Yellow Book* 3 (Oct. 1894): 11–18. In 1917, H. L. Mencken still attributed the "imbecility" of American writers to the supposed stranglehold of "women in pantaloons" in the publishing houses (Tom Dardis, *Firebrand: The Life of Horace Liveright* [New York, 1995], p. 51). See also Lears, *No Place of Grace*, pp. 104–10; Kazin, *On Native Grounds*, p. 26.

The phrase gains descriptive and explanatory credence and its misogyny becomes more overt. See, for example, Thomas Beer, *The Mauve Decade: American Life at the End of the Nineteenth Century* (New York, 1926), on "the Titaness," and Larzer Ziff, *The American 1890s* (New York, 1966). See also Ann Douglas, *The Feminization of American Culture* (New York, 1977), a later, feminist treatment that still takes the notion at face value. Joseph Horowitz, *Wagner Nights: An American History* (New York, 1994), pp. 229–34, criticizes the feminization thesis. A subsidiary of the feminization problem was the "*jeune fille*" problem, caused by adolescent girls who, as major consumers of literature and the theater, were supposedly forcing artists into producing sentimental slop. On *les jeunes filles* and the theater, see Auster, "Actresses and Suffragists," pp. 16, 31, 41. For feminization in Chicago, see Carl S. Smith, *Chicago and the American Literary Imagination, 1880–1920* (Chicago, 1984), pp. 40–56.

"a little off, a little funny, a little soft!": William Dean Howells, "The Man of Letters as a Man of Business," *Literature and Life* (New York and London, 1902), pp. 6, 21.

the association with European decadence: The Decadent tinge is evident in the circle of visual artists around the New York artist William Merritt Chase. See Constance Eleanore Koppelman, "Nature in Art and Culture: The Tile Club Artists, 1870–1900," Ph.D. dissertation, State University of New York at Stony Brook, 1985. See also the series on Tile Club bohemian antics: W. Mackay Laffan, "The Tile Club at Work," *Scribner's*, Nov. 1878, pp. 401–09; Laffan and Edward Strahan, "The Tile Club at Play," *Scribner's*, Feb. 1879, pp. 457–78; "The Tile Club Afloat," *Scribner's*, Mar. 1880, pp. 641–70; "The Tile Club Ashore," *Century*, Feb. 1882, pp. 481–98. See also the collector's edition of *Book of the Tile Club* (New York, 1886). The literature on decadence is extensive; useful considerations can be found in Showalter, *Sexual Anarchy*; Linda Dowling, *Language and Decadence in the Victorian Fin de Siècle* (Princeton, 1986); Jean Pierrot, *The Decadent Imagination, 1880–1900* (Chicago, 1981). American adoptions of European decadence were sunny, mostly oblivious to the dark play of morbidity, nihilism, and misogynyny, preferring a commercially viable identification with sophisticated badinage and refined taste.

"tea-drinking" artists of the establishment: John Sloan, one of the dissenters, echoed Howells's language of "a little off, a little funny" when he
scorned the effeminate "five o-clock tea drinking" necessary for succeed-
ing as an artist with wealthy patrons. Sloan was mocking William Merritt
Chase, who fashioned a lucrative career that combined portraiture and
landscape painting, sojourns in lovely beach resorts, charm with well-to-do
female clients and students, and aristocratic bohemianism. Quoted in
Ronald G. Pisano, *A Leading Spirit in American Art: William Merritt Chase*
(Seattle, 1903), pp. 98–100.

33. **Lincoln Steffens mused:** Steffens, *Autobiography*, p. 244.
   novels about bohemia: Others include De Kay, *The Bohemian;* George Alfred
   Townsend, *Bohemian Days* (New York, 1880); L. H. Bideford and Richard
   Stillman Powell, *Phyllis in Bohemia* (Chicago, 1897); Albert Bigelow Paine,
   The Bread Line: A Story of a Paper (New York, 1900); Charles Warren
   Stoddard, *For the Pleasure of His Company* (New York, 1903). Henry
   Harland picked up the theme in "The Bohemian Girl." See Lisa Tickner,
   "Men's Work? Masculinity and Modernism," *differences* 4 (Fall 1992),
   pp. 5–7, on the popularity in Britain of the *Kunstlerroman*, or artist novel,
   between 1895 and World War I.
34. **Jewish Women:** Annelise Orleck, *Common Sense and a Little Fire*
   (Chapel Hill, 1995), pp. 20 ff.: Naomi Shepherd, *A Price below Rubies:
   Jewish Women as Rebels and Radicals* (London, 1993).
35. **"They sit in an atmosphere":** Quoted in Howe, *World of Our Fathers*, p. 243.
   For Russian feminism and Chernyshevsky, see Richard Stites, *The Women's
   Liberation Movement in Russia: Feminism, Nihilism, and Bolshevism
   1860–1930* (Princeton, 1978).
   Emma Goldman: Emma Goldman, *Living My Life* (New York, 1931), vol. 1,
   chs. 1–2; Alice Wexler, *Emma Goldman: An Intimate Life* (New York, 1984),
   chs. 1–3.
36. **"revolutionary mystery":** Wexler, *Emma Goldman*, pp. 23–27.
   "I was twenty years old": Goldman, *Living My Life*, vol. 1, p. 3.
37. **"The door upon the old":** Ibid., p. 25.
38. **Justus Schwab's saloon:** The artists and critics included the writers Ambrose
   Bierce, the Decadent Sadakichi Hartman, and James Huneker (Wexler,
   Emma Goldman, p. 72).
39. **"For many, individual identities":** Lears, *No Place of Grace*, p. 32.

2/JOURNEYS TO BOHEMIA

40. **"Life was ready":** Mabel Dodge Luhan, *Movers and Shakers* (New York,
   1936), p. 151.
41. **"Everywhere . . . barriers went down":** Ibid., p. 39.
   "low houses, transformed bakeries": Max Eastman, *Love and Revolution: My
   Journey through an Epoch* (New York, 1964), p. 4. The earliest reference to
   Greenwich Village as an artists' quarter is Thomas A. Janvier's novel *Color
   Studies* (1885).
   "very largely manufactured and imposed": Caroline F. Ware, *Greenwich
   Village, 1920–1930* (Boston, 1935), pp. 93–97.

"the life that flowed there": Max Eastman, *Enjoyment of Living* (New York, 1948), pp. 266, 418.

42. **varied demographics:** Ware, *Greenwich Village*, passim; on black residential patterns, see Osofsky, *Harlem*.

43. **a fictive community:** Amy Kaplan, quoting Raymond Williams, calls such urban groupings a "knowable community"—knowable, that is, through literary representations (*Social Construction of American Realism*, p. 47). The mutual recognition of members within these fictionalized communities is always alleged and always involves the selection and exclusion of others.

"intellectual": Thomas Bender, *New York Intellect* (New York, 1987), p. 228.

44. **Critics sneered:** *Dial*, Oct. 1, 1914, pp. 239–41.

"Instead of a world": Lippmann, quoted in Arthur Frank Wertheim, *The New York Little Renaissance: Iconoclasm, Modernism, and Nationalism in American Culture, 1908–1917* (New York, 1976), p. 6.

"Whenever a group of individuals": Hapgood, *Victorian in the Modern World*, p. 318.

"I first loved, and I first wrote": John Reed, "Almost Thirty," *Adventures of a Young Man* (San Francisco, 1965), pp. 139–40.

"The only place for me": Harold E. Stearns, *The Street I Know* (New York, 1935), p. 87.

45. **Rural artists' colonies burgeoned:** Alf Evers, *Woodstock: History of an American Town* (Woodstock, 1987), ch. 33; Parry, *Garrets and Pretenders*, ch. 20; William Brevda, *Harry Kemp: The Last Bohemian* (Lewisburg, 1986), pp. 25–27 (on Roycroft); Esther Lanigan Stineman, *Mary Austin: Song of a Maverick* (New Haven, 1989), ch. 4 (on Taos); Gui de Angelo, *Jaime in Taos: The Taos Papers of Jaime de Angulo* (San Francisco, 1985); Wilson, *Labor of Words*, p. 7.

"A richly blended politico-aesthetic ambience": Lisa Tickner, *The Spectacle of Women: Imagery of the Suffrage Campaign, 1907–14* (Chicago, 1988), p. 27.

46. **"good time coming":** This was a socialist slogan. See Mari Jo Buhle, *Women and American Socialism* (Urbana, 1981), p. xiv.

Davenport, Iowa: Federal Writers' Project, *Iowa: A Guide to the Hawkeye State* (New York, 1938); Harry E. Downer, *History of Davenport and Scott County*, vol. 1 (Chicago, 1910); Michael J. Bell, " 'True Israelites of America': The Story of the Jews of Iowa," *Annals of Iowa* 53 (Winter 1994): 85–127; Chip Deffaa, "Bix Beiderbecke," *Voices of the Jazz Age* (Urbana, 1990), p. 56; Charles H. Wareling and George Garlick, *Bugles for Beiderbecke* (London, 1958), pp. 7–8. Lawrence W. Levine, *Highbrow/Lowbrow: The Emergence of Cultural Hierarchy in America* (Cambridge, Mass., 1988), p. 20, mentions the theatrical scene. Population statistics are from *Iowa Official Register for the Years 1911–1912* (Des Moines, 1911).

48. **the Red City of Iowa:** Statewide, Iowa gave Debs only about 3 percent of the returns. Election results are reprinted in *Iowa Official Register for the Years 1913–1914.*

Mollie Price Cook: Robert Humphrey, *Children of Fantasy: The First Rebels of Greenwich Village* (New York, 1978), pp. 97–101; Dell, *Homecoming*, pp. 172–74.

Floyd Dell: Douglas Clayton, *Floyd Dell: The Life and Times of an American Rebel* (Chicago, 1994); Humphrey, *Children of Fantasy*, ch. 6; Dell's autobiography, *Homecoming*, and his autobiographical novel, *Moon-Calf* (New York, 1920). Market day is mentioned in Fred Feuchter (the socialist postman) to Mrs. Floyd Dell, Nov. 14, 1933, Eunice Tietjens Papers, Newberry Library, Chicago.

49. **"My destiny was to be a factory hand":** Dell, *Homecoming*, p. 157.
"manufacturing a Bohemia for myself": Ibid., pp. 147–48.
"He is slight": Jig Cook to Charles E. Banks, n.d., George Cram Cook Papers, Berg Collection, New York Public Library.

50. **regional spheres:** See Wiebe, *Search for Order*, p. 2.
New York had dominated: William Charvat, *The Profession of Authorship in America, 1800–1870*, ed. Matthew J. Bruccoli (Columbus, 1968); Ezra Greenspan, *Walt Whitman and the American Reader* (Cambridge, Eng., 1990); David S. Reynolds, *Beneath the American Renaissance* (Cambridge, Mass., 1989); Frederick Baekeland, "Collectors of American Painting, 1813 to 1913," *American Art Review* 3 (Nov.-Dec. 1976): 120–66; W. G. Constable, *Art Collecting in the United States* (London, 1964); Peter Watson, *From Manet to Manhattan: The Rise of the Modern Art Market* (New York, 1992).
pulled into New York's gravity: For an example of this process in San Francisco, see Starr, *Americans and the California Dream*, pp. 261–62.
"Cattle, hogs, sheep, iron ore": Carla Cappetti, *Writing Chicago: Modernism, Ethnography, and the Novel* (New York, 1993), p. 11.
Chicago: General treatments are Perry Duis, *Chicago: Creating New Traditions* (Chicago, 1970); David Lowe, *Lost Chicago* (Boston, 1978); Neil Harris, "The Chicago Setting," *The Old Guard and the Avant-Garde*, ed. Sue Ann Prince (Chicago, 1990), pp. 3–22; Dale Kramer, *Chicago Renaissance: The Literary Life of the Midwest, 1900–1930* (New York, 1966); Bernard Duffey, *The Chicago Renaissance in American Letters* (East Lansing, 1954); Henry May, *The End of American Innocence* (New York, 1959), pp. 101–06; Kenny J. Williams, *Prairie Voices: A Literary History of Chicago from the Frontier to 1893* (Nashville, 1980); Paul DiMaggio, "Class, Authority, and Cultural Entrepreneurship: The Problem of Chicago," Institution for Social Policy Studies Working Paper 2155, Yale University, 1990.

51. **impossible to describe the city:** Carl S. Smith, *Chicago and the American Literary Imagination* (Chicago, 1984), p. 2.
"enchanted ground": Margaret Anderson, *My Thirty Years' War* (New York, 1969), p. 13.
***American Hunger*:** Properly, *American Hunger* is the second section of *Black Boy*. This section, first published in 1977, was part of the original manuscript. For the publication history and the restored edition, see Jerry W. Ward, Introduction, *Black Boy (American Hunger)* (New York, 1993).

52. **"First Impressions":** Dell, *Homecoming*, pp. 181–82.
Little Room: Members included Harriet Monroe, a poet and editor; her sister Lucy, an editor at a leading publishing company; Anna Morgan, a drama coach and aspiring director; Elia Peattie and Clara Laughlin, both influential editors in the popular press; Jane Addams; the publishers

Herbert and Melville Stone; sculptor Lorenzo Taft; and several wealthy female followers of the Arts and Crafts movement.

On midwestern literary societies, see the Chicagoan John M. Stahl's memoir, *Growing Up with the West* (London, 1930). On the Little Room, see Steven Watson, *Strange Bedfellows: The First American Avant-Garde* (New York, 1991), pp. 13–15; Herma Clark, "The Little Room," *Townsfolk*, May 1944; Rufus F. Chapin to Herma Clark, July 11, 1943, Herma Clark Collection, Chicago Historical Society. Fictional renditions of the scene are in Henry Fuller, *Under the Skylights* (New York, 1901), and Maxwell Bodenheim, *Blackguard* (Chicago, 1923), ch. 10. On the middle-class black establishment, see Allan H. Spear, *Black Chicago: The Making of a Negro Ghetto, 1890–1920* (Chicago, 1967).

53. **Jackson Park**: Dell, *Homecoming*, pp. 232–37; Harry Hansen, *Midwest Portraits* (New York, 1923), pp. 95–107.

"What the 'ell": Arthur Davison Ficke to Floyd Dell, Apr. 14, 1913, Floyd Dell Papers, Newberry Library, Chicago.

"I have stepped back": *Vassar Bulletin* (1914), courtesy of Special Collections, Vassar College Library. Other information on Currey and her family comes from the Evanston Historical Society. A bluff, hearty farewell letter to Dell, undated, is in the Tietjens Papers.

She attracted established artists: These included the newsman and poet Carl Sandburg, Theodore Dreiser, the lawyer and poet Edgar Lee Masters, Sherwood Anderson, and his wife, Cornelia.

"Why does all of sharp and new": Arthur Davison Ficke, quoted in Watson, *Strange Bedfellows*, p. 26. For Dell and Currey in Chicago, see Dell, *Homecoming*, pp. 192–232, and passim.

54. *Little Review*: Anderson, *My Thirty Years' War*, pp. 36 ff.; Dell, *Homecoming*, p. 237; Susan Noyes Platt, "*The Little Review*: Early Years and Avant-Garde Ideas," *The Old Guard and the Avant-Garde*, ed. Prince, pp. 139–54.

55. **the defining cultural journey of the country**: See Kenneth Lynn's observations on patterns of mobility in "The Rebels of Greenwich Village," *Perspectives in American History* 8 (1974): 335–77.

San Francisco's bohemia: Starr, *Americans and the California Dream*, ch. 8; Parry, *Garrets and Pretenders*, chs. 18–20.

college life: Helen Lefkowitz Horowitz, *Campus Life* (New York, 1987), chs. 3 and 4.

56. **Some well-to-do progressives**: See Orleck, *Common Sense*, p. 44.

Intercollegiate Socialist Society: *Encyclopedia of the American Left*, ed. Mari Jo Buhle, Paul Buhle, Dan Georgakas (New York, 1990), pp. 362–63; Mina Weisenberg, *The L.I.D.: Fifty Years of Democratic Education, 1905–1955* (New York, 1955), pp. 5–11.

At the women's colleges: Freda Kirchwey quipped that "you can't go through Barnard without knowing the principles of socialism" ("Socialism's Edge Dulled on Dinner," *New York Tribune*, Dec. 31, 1913).

"more thrilling than the idea of an education": Dorothy Day, *The Long Loneliness* (New York, 1952), pp. 40, 44; William D. Miller, *Dorothy Day: A Biography* (New York, 1982), chs. 2–3.

57. **repressive intellectual politics**: See Kathryn Kish Sklar, *Florence Kelley and the Nation's Work: The Rise of Women's Political Culture, 1830–1900* (New

Haven, 1995), pp. 294–95; Rodgers, *Atlantic Crossings*, pp. 103–04. For the tone at Harvard in the 1890s, see Joan D. Hedrick, " 'Harvard Indifference,' " *New England Quarterly* 49 (1976): 356–72.

a distinguished group of professors: Leaders were Charles Copeland in English, George Pierce Baker in drama, Graham Wallas in social thought. For those who follow Harvard lore, the point is complicated. James had retired in 1907, but he was still very much a presence on campus, taking the trouble, for example, to stroll over to Walter Lippmann's dormitory room to meet him when he came across a newspaper piece of Lippman's he admired. Wallas, a British Fabian, was only at Harvard for one year, but the fact that he taught there at all is significant. The philosopher George Santayana was the other intellectual luminary. Although Santayana's thinking was deeply conservative and is conventionally counterposed to that of James, the seriousness of his engagement with philosophy and aesthetics was in itself a challenge to Harvard traditions of education as a moralizing polish to gentlemen. See Ronald Steel, *Walter Lippmann and the American Century* (New York, 1980), ch. 2; Robert A. Rosenstone, *Romantic Revolutionary: A Biography of John Reed* (New York, 1975), ch. 4; May, *End of American Innocence*, pp. 52–62; Granville Hicks, *John Reed: The Making of a Revolutionary* (New York, 1936), p. 25; John Reed, "The Harvard Renaissance," unpublished typescript, John Reed Papers, Houghton Library, Harvard University (bMS Am 109[1139]). For James's influence, see Kim Townsend, *Manhood at Harvard* (New York, 1996).

fashionable dilettantism: Hedrick, " 'Harvard Indifference,' " pp. 356–72.

58. **"Some men came with allowances":** Reed, "Almost Thirty," p. 135.
   "their fling at those people": Quoted in Dubofsky, *We Shall Be All*, p. 245.
   "real culture lives by sympathies and admirations": William James, "The Social Value of the College-Bred," *McClure's* 30 (1908): 422.
   an annex of Harvard Yard: The dissidents who migrated to New York after graduating included Lippmann, Reed, the poet Alan Seeger, the playwrights Lee Simonson and David Carb, and the set designer Robert Edmond Jones.

59. **"What happened at Harvard":** Reed, "Harvard Renaissance," p. 3.
   "the rich splendor of college life": Reed, "Almost Thirty," pp. 134–35.
   "The manifestation of the modern spirit": Ibid., p. 136.
   "It all comes down to this": Reed, quoted in Rosenstone, *Romantic Revolutionary*, p. 59.

60. **The ease with which they took center stage:** One gets a hint of how they lorded it over others in the wistful recollection of Alfred Kreymborg, the child of New York cigar-store owners, a poet and dramatist. Kreymborg, a modest man, never went to college. He found the Village hospitable to his talents but he couldn't help longing for what he lacked: training in literary "good form" at Yale, or Princeton, "or, best of all, Harvard" (*Troubadour: An Autobiography* [New York, 1925], p. 119).

   progressive politics: Progressivism is a notoriously difficult phenomenon to describe, although it is a staple of twentieth-century historical studies. Historians use the term to unify an assortment of reform groups that arose during the two decades of the Roosevelt, Taft, and Wilson administrations. Trustbusters, advocates of protective laws for women and child workers, women's suffragists, opponents of sweatshops, critics of Democratic machine politics, and consumer protectionists all fall under the rubric. Yet these people did not share a consistent ideology, political orientation, or party affiliation. Progressives were both Republicans and Democrats; on certain issues they included socialists. In our own parlance, they were both conservative and liberal, differing on issues of women's suffrage, the rights of labor versus the rights of capital, and direct democracy in city government. Progressives are described variously as bourgeois self-promoters, upper-class elitists, conservative defenders of capitalism, and liberal predecessors of the New Deal. Daniel Rodgers proposes that what distinguished progressives was an interest and fluency in negotiating among three nodes of discontent: the distrust of monopolies, the reification of social efficiency, and the belief in the redemptive powers of social cohesion. Progressivism's left wing was concentrated around the last orientation. Supporters of labor—the groups and reformers concerned with wages, work conditions, housing, education, public health, and poverty— elaborated a rhetoric of the organic solidarity of all American citizens (Rodgers, "In Search of Progressivism," *Reviews in American History*, Dec. 1982, pp. 113–32). See Rodgers's summa on the progressives, *Atlantic Crossings;* also James T. Kloppenberg, *Uncertain Victory: Social Democracy and Progressivism in European and American Thought, 1870–1920* (New York, 1986); Theda Skocpol, *Protecting Soldiers and Mothers: The Political Origins of Social Policy in the United States* (Cambridge, Mass., 1992).

61. **But especially in Chicago and New York:** Chicago and New York settlement houses were advocates of protective legislation, labor mediation, and in some cases strike support and public health and safety measures (Sklar, *Florence Kelley*, pp. 174, 369, n. 6). On the New York settlements, see Harry P. Kraus, *The Settlement House Movement in New York City, 1886–1914* (New York, 1980); Yellowitz, *Labor and the Progressive Movement*, pp. 50, 73–74; Lillian D. Wald, *Windows on Henry Street* (Boston, 1934). On the national movement, see Allen F. Davis, *Spearheads for Reform: The Social Settlements and the Progressive Movement, 1890–1914* (New Brunswick, 1984).

"Vital contact": the phrase originated with the Harvard dissident Lee Simonson (quoted in Reed, "Harvard Renaissance," p. 8).

62. **"Their convivial atmosphere":** University Settlement (New York), *Fifteenth Annual Report* (1901), pp. 23–24.

"a brittle jabber": Howe, *World of Our Fathers*, p. 395.

63. **"Few have had material":** Ernst Poole, *The Bridge: My Own Story* (New York, 1940), p. 74. Poole was a resident at the University Settlement. He turned a report on boy street workers written for the Child Labor Commission into a series of magazine articles and then into fiction.

Randolph Bourne got into a nasty row with a friend over the settlements' do-goodism. Beulah Amidon recalled the argument in a letter to Alyse Gregory, Oct. 4, 1948, Randolph Bourne Papers, Manuscripts Room, Butler Library, Columbia University.

"doing good *with* people": Frieda Fligelman to Randolph Bourne, Sept. 8, 1911, Randolph Bourne Papers.

WASP prohibitions: Dinnerstein, *Anti-Seminism*, ch. 4.

wealthy little colony of mixed political marriages: On the Stokes marriage, see Arthur Zipser and Pearl Zipser, *Fire and Grace: The Life of Rose Pastor Stokes* (Athens, Ga., 1989), p. 51.

64. **William Dean Howells lent his support:** Clara Marburg Kirk, *W. D. Howells, Traveler from Altruria, 1889–1894* (New Brunswick, 1962), ch. 3.

Hull House staff organized relief: Jane Addams expressed her labor sympathies through a firm and principled call for mediation, ill-received by an obdurate George Pullman and other Chicago business leaders. See Victoria Brown, "Advocate for Democracy: Jane Addams and the Pullman Strike," *The Pullman Strike and the Crisis of the 1890s: Essays on Labor and Politics,* ed. Richard Schneirov, Shelton Stromquist, and Nick Salvatore (Urbana, 1999), pp. 130–58.

ideas about cross-class collaboration were so strong: Robin Miller Jacoby, *The British and American Women's Trade Union Leagues, 1890–1925* (New York, 1994), p. 15.

first Russian revolution: Mary Heaton Vorse, *Footnote to Folly* (New York, 1935), pp. 22–23; Poole, *The Bridge,* p. 103; Wald, *House on Henry Street,* p. 283; Frederick F. Travis, *George Kennan and the American-Russian Relationship, 1865–1924* (Athens, Ohio, 1990), ch. 5.

65. **"The radical East Side lived in a delirium":** Goldman, *Living My Life,* vol. 1, p. 372.

the more staid realms of reform: In comportment, the older settlement house reformers, even the most liberal, were defined by late-Victorian mores of propriety. Among a younger generation, however, involvements in working-class life could lead to breaking the rules. Some settlement residents embraced socialism; others, most notably young women, used the comparative freedom they enjoyed in their living quarters to experiment with novel sexual arrangements. (Hull House and Henry Street harbored quiet long-term liaisons between women that were probably sexual; see Blanche Wiesen Cook, "Female Support Networks and Political Activism," *A Heritage of Her Own,* ed. Nancy F. Cott and Elizabeth H. Pleck [New York, 1979], pp. 412–44.) It seems, though, that some young women from Hull House also practiced free love with men, at least if we are to believe Clarence Darrow, who was prowling around for lovers in the world of Chicago reformers in which he operated. Darrow separated from his wife and lived at the Langdon Apartments, where some Hull House residents also resided. For speculations about the sexual activity in the place, see Arthur Weinberg and Lila Weinberg, *Clarence Darrow: A Sentimental Rebel* (New York, 1980), pp. 72–73.

The A Club: Garrison, *Mary Heaton Vorse,* pp. 36–39; Vorse, *Footnote to Folly,* pp. 32–35. The association of a number of the men is mentioned in Eastman, *Love and Revolution,* p. 134.

66. **"Everybody a Liberal":** Vorse, quoted in Garrison, *Mary Heaton Vorse,* p. 36.

Some traveled to Russia: Anna and Rose Strunsky went to report on the situation and offer their help; it was in Petersburg that Walling and Anna fell in love and decided to marry. Arthur Bullard, writer and former University Settlement resident, reportedly fought on the barricades in Moscow. See Leon Fink, *Progressive Intellectuals and the Dilemmas of Democratic Commitment* (Cambridge, Mass., 1997), pp. 123–24, 153–55; Vorse,

Footnote to Folly, pp. 33–34; James Boylan, *Revolutionary Lives: Anna Strunsky and William English Walling* (Amherst, Mass. 1998), chs. 14–16.

Maxim Gorky: Because anticzarist sentiment was widespread in the United States, Gorky was initially a feted guest. He appeared to his hosts not as a socialist revolutionary—despite his open adherence to Lenin's wing of the Social Democrats—but as an honored victim of czarist repression, much like Breshkovskaya. Gorky was to be welcomed in New York with a celebrity literary dinner. The Russian embassy, working hard to sabotage the visit, finally succeeded in hooking the *New York World* into an exposé of his supposed illicit relations with his common-law wife, Madame Andreeva, widow of a prince and star of the Moscow Art Theatre. Gorky's marital situation was well known by the reading public of Europe and America, so much so that the embassy had no success in drumming up a scandal until Gorky signed an exclusive contract with the Hearst papers; it was then the rival *World* went to press with the so-called news of his sexual wrongdoing. Virtually overnight, the media-induced scandal turned the czarist martyr into a "wicked, dissolute man," and the Gorkys were evicted from their hotel and refused rooms in every other hotel they tried. The New York dinner was canceled and President Roosevelt withdrew his invitation to the White House. See Filia Holtzman, "A Mission That Failed: Gor'kij in America," *Slavic and East European Journal* 6 (Fall 1962): 227–34.

the crossover of immigrant Jews: David Hollinger, *Science, Jews, and Secular Culture: Studies in Mid-Twentieth-Century American Intellectual History* (Princeton, 1996); Hollinger, "Ethnic Diversity, Cosmopolitanism, and the Emergence of the American Liberal Intelligentsia."

67. **"New Negro":** Henry Louis Gates, Jr., "The Trope of a New Negro and the Reconstruction of the Image of the Black," *Representations* 24 (Fall 1988): 129–55.

W. E. B. DuBois: Hutchins Hapgood had met DuBois in Berlin, where they both studied after Harvard, and apparently approached him in New York to ask if he could write "a series of attractive articles on Negroes" for the *Crisis*. DuBois turned him down (Hapgood, *Victorian in the Modern World*, p. 344). In 1914 DuBois worked with Mabel Dodge and other habitués of the Village on a citizens' group trying to influence the Commission on Industrial Relations.

"colored Bohemians": Johnson, *Autobiography of an Ex-Colored Man*, p. 76; Rebecca Zurier, *Art for the Masses: A Radical Magazine and Its Graphics, 1911–1917* (Philadelphia, 1988), p. 187, n. 70.

Hubert Harrison: Kevin K. Gaines, *Uplifting the Race: Black Leadership, Politics, and Culture in the Twentieth Century* (Chapel Hill, 1996), ch. 9; J. A. Rogers, *World's Greatest Men of Color,* vol. 2 (1947; New York, 1972), pp. 432–42; Wilfred D. Samuels, *Five Afro-Caribbean Voices in American Culture* (Boulder, 1977); Claude McKay, *A Long Way from Home* (New York, 1937), p. 109.

68. **Richard Wright encountered bare bigotry:** Margaret Walker, *Richard Wright: Daemonic Genius* (New York, 1988), p. 200.

James Baldwin was assaulted: Dan Wakefield, *New York in the 1950s* (New York, 1992), pp. 140–41.

"trans-national America": Randolph Bourne, "Trans-National America," *The Radical Will: Randolph Bourne. Selected Writings, 1911–1918*, ed. Olaf Hansen (New York, 1977), p. 248.

3/INTELLECTUALS, CONVERSATIONAL POLITICS, AND FREE SPEECH

73. **"a sense of universal revolt and regeneration"**: Eastman, *Enjoyment of Living*, p. 399.

74. **Free speech was self-conscious, flashy:** For a critical view of free speech, see Rochelle Gurstein, *The Repeal of Reticence: A History of America's Cultural and Legal Struggles over Free Speech, Obscenity, Sexual Liberation, and Modern Art* (New York, 1996).

    "free-thought talk": Eastman, *Enjoyment of Living*, p. 399.

75. **The struggle for free speech turned into a concerted battle:** John W. Wertheimer, "Free Speech Fights: The Roots of Modern Free-expression Litigation in the United States," Ph.D. dissertation, Princeton University, 1992, ch. 1; see also David M. Rabban, *Free Speech in Its Forgotten Years* (Cambridge, Eng., 1997). On IWW involvement, see Dubofsky, *We Shall Be All*, ch. 8.

77. **The Socialists in Davenport**: Dell, *Homecoming*, p. 237.

    "In view of the economic tyranny": Jig Cook, "Public Aspects of the Library Board Controversy," Cook Papers.

    "broken-hearted transactions": Eavan Boland, *Object Lessons: The Life of the Woman and the Poet in Our Time* (New York, 1995), p. 61.

    In Spokane: Dubofsky, *We Shall Be All*, ch. 8.

    In San Diego: Ibid., p. 192; Goldman, *Living My Life*, vol. 1, pp. 495–503.

78. **"polite old-fashioned believers"**: Dell, *Love in Greenwich Village* (New York, 1926), p. 18.

    "This time, however, the affront": Goldman, *Living My Life*, vol. 1, p. 452.

79. **An earlier incarnation of the Liberal Club:** Keith Norton Richwine, "The Liberal Club: Bohemia and the Resurgence in Greenwich Village, 1912–1918," Ph.D. dissertation, University of Pennsylvania, 1968.

    Percy Stickney Grant: Grant's first parish was in Fall River, Massachusetts, where he came to know the troubles of working people and to believe that more was needed from a ministry than the condescending philanthropy characteristic of Episcopalianism. See the entry on him in *Dictionary of American Biography*. On Hapgood's proposal of Goldman, see Hapgood, *Victorian in the Modern World*, p. 277; for Lippmann's of DuBois, see Steel, *Walter Lippmann*, p. 39. DuBois and Lippmann worked together on the *New Review* (Leslie Fishbein, *Rebels in Bohemia: The Radicals of* The Masses, *1911–1917* [Chapel Hill, 1982], p. 21).

80. **"She couldn't even do so conventional a thing"**: Dell, "The Rise of Greenwich Village," *Love in Greenwich Village*, p. 19; Rodman appears as "Egeria" in this sketch. She also appears pseudonymously in Harry Kemp, *More Miles: An Autobiographical Novel* (New York, 1926), p. 188. See also Wertheim, *New York Little Renaissance*, p. 89.

    the affair of H. G. Wells: Ruth Brandon, *The New Women and the Old Men: Love, Sex, and the Woman Question* (New York, 1990), pp. 183–205;

Deborah Epstein Nord, *The Apprenticeship of Beatrice Webb* (Amherst, 1985), p. 255, n. 8. Things were made worse by the fact that the distraught parents of the young woman, Amber Reeves, were also Fabians.

dismayed progressives bolted: The Rodman scandal is recounted in Richwine, "Liberal Club," pp. 95–103, 154–56. On progressives' notions of sexual respectability see Christopher Lasch, *The New Radicalism in America, 1889–1963* (New York, 1965), p. 149.

The decor stressed the difference: Anderson, *My Thirty Years' War*, pp. 152–53.

81. **"girls who had run away":** Alyse Gregory, *The Day Is Gone* (New York, 1948), p. 99.

"all the tin pot revolutionaries": Mencken, in a letter to Theodore Dreiser (a member), quoted in Richwine, "Liberal Club," p. 116.

82. **People began to gather in the late afternoon:** Lawrence Langner, *The Magic Curtain* (New York, 1951), pp. 67–73; Dell, *Homecoming*, p. 258.

a long infatuation of American writers and artists: See Alfred Kazin, " 'The Giant Killer': Drink and the American Writer," *Commentary*, Mar. 1976, pp. 44–50; Ann Douglas, *Terrible Honesty: Mongrel Manhattan in the 1920s* (New York, 1995), pp. 23–26.

"An elemental thing like the sea": Floyd Dell, "Alcoholiday," *Masses*, June 1916.

"But it was a very superior kind": Luhan, *Movers and Shakers*, p. 484; see also her uneasiness about Hapgood's drinking, pp. 231, 236–38.

"The idea that anybody would drink too much": Dell, *Homecoming*, pp. 201, 256. There were a number of famous drunks in the Village, almost certainly alcoholics, including Hutchins Hapgood, eventually Neith Boyce, Hippolyte Havel (a notoriously mean drunk), George Cram Cook, Louise Bryant, Max Eastman, and, more famously, Eugene O'Neill and his various drinking companions.

"The women worked quite regularly": Luhan, *Movers and Shakers*, p. 484. My speculations about the shame of morphine addiction come from Garrison, *Mary Heaton Vorse*, pp. 184–95. David Musto confirms that there was a substantial morphine problem at the turn of the century (*The American Disease: Origins of Narcotic Control* [New Haven, 1973], ch. 1).

"The most energetically wicked freeloving den": Louis Untermeyer, quoted in Humphrey, *Children of Fantasy*, p. 25.

83. **The extensive cast of characters:** There is a reconstruction of the membership of the Liberal Club in Richwine, "Liberal Club," pp. 117–18, which I have supplemented with information from the *Dictionary of American Biography*. "The most astonishing group of people I had ever met," Roger Baldwin characterized the group ("A Memo on My Love Life," typescript, box 1, folder 8, Peggy Lamson Collection, Seely Mudd Library, Princeton University).

"conversational communities": Lisa Tickner, "The 'Left-Handed Marriage': Vanessa Bell and Duncan Grant," *Significant Others: Creativity and Intimate Partnership*, ed. Whitney Chadwick and Isabelle de Courtivron (London, 1993), pp. 65–82.

Bloomsbury was too elite and tiny: While reacting against the exclusivity of the English class system, Bloomsbury's bohemians nonetheless created their own "best circle" of people largely connected through intertwined family allegiances. See Hermione Lee, *Virginia Woolf* (New York, 1997), pp. 54–55.

"Civil society": Jürgen Habermas, *The Structural Transformation of the Public Sphere* (Cambridge, Mass., 1989).

84. **"hours of glorious fighting":** Reed, "Harvard Renaissance," pp. 15–16. Note that the Harvard rebels—and no doubt the men at Columbia, too— saw their all-night conversations as a rebellion against the drunken revelry of their peers.

"one could listen": Gregory, *Day Is Gone*, p. 99.

heterogeneous elements assembled without connectives: Roger Shattuck, *The Banquet Years: The Arts in France, 1885–1918* (New York, 1958), p. 260.

85. **vaudeville:** Jeffrey S. Weiss, "Picasso, Collage, and the Music Hall," *Modern Art and Popular Culture: Readings in High and Low*, ed. Kirk Varnedoe and Adam Gopnik (New York, 1990), pp. 82–115; also Robert Rosenblum, "Cubism as Pop Art," *Modern Art and Popular Culture*, pp. 117–32; Dowling, *Language and Decadence*, p. 234. In New York, one of the advanced publishers, Mitchell Kennerley, brought out a book on vaudeville in 1915 illustrated by Marius de Zayas, an exhibitor at Stieglitz's 291 gallery who was also on the fringes of Dada (Caroline Caffin, *Vaudeville* [New York, 1915]).

Oscar Hammerstein: See Goldman, *Living My Life*, vol. 2, p. 526.

"characters": Marybeth Hamilton, *"When I'm Bad, I'm Better": Mae West, Sex, and American Entertainment* (New York, 1995), pp. 29, 40–43; Robert W. Synder, *The Voice of the City: Vaudeville and Popular Culture in New York* (New York, 1989), pp. 90, 149. Bill Haywood, too, received offers from vaudeville producers after his acquittal for the murder of Idaho's former governor in 1907 (William D. Haywood, *Bill Haywood's Book* [New York, 1929], p. 223).

The Dill Pickle Club: See the Dill Pickle Papers, Newberry Library, Chicago; Frank O. Beck, "The Dill Pickle Club," *Hobohemia* (Rindge, N.J., 1956), pp. 78–83; Parry, *Garrets and Pretenders*, ch. 17; Emmett Dedmon, *Fabulous Chicago* (New York, 1981), p. 282; Henry Justin Smith, *Chicago: A Portrait* (New York, 1931), p. 244; Alson J. Smith, *Chicago's Left Bank* (Chicago, 1953), pp. 12–15; Joyce L. Kornbluh, *Rebel Voices: An I.W.W. Anthology* (Ann Arbor, 1964), p. 16. The founder and impresario was Jack Jones, who was briefly married to Elizabeth Gurley Flynn. On Jones, see Sherwood Anderson, *Sherwood Anderson's Memoirs*, ed. Ray Lewis White (Chapel Hill, 1969), pp. 356–59; Rosalyn Fraad Baxandall, *Words on Fire: The Life and Writing of Elizabeth Gurley Flynn* (New Brunswick, 1987), p. 13. Jones can be seen as a Chicago master of the same "culture of pastiche"—the jumble of urban types and experiences— that immigrant songwriters and movie and vaudeville producers were learning to package commercially in New York (Taylor, *In Pursuit of Gotham*, ch. 5).

86. **"a Spanish spiritualist":** Beck, "Dill Pickle Club," p. 82.

"A brilliant Negro": Quoted in Parry, *Garrets and Pretenders*, p. 204.

Chaplin and Eastman invented a game: Eastman, *Love and Revolution*, pp. 173–74; Eastman, "Charlie Chaplin: Memories and Reflections," *Great Companions* (New York, 1959).

"lot of twaddle that goes on": The phrase comes from Glaspell's poetic eulogy to Joe O'Brien, Mary Heaton Vorse's second husband, *Masses*, Jan. 1916, p. 9.

"most of the people": Randolph Bourne to Alyse Gregory, Jan. 13, 1915, *The Letters of Randolph Bourne: A Comprehensive Edition*, ed. Eric J. Sandeen (New York, 1981).

87. **"directly by, for, and of the workers themselves":** An IWW pamphlet, quoted in Kornbluh, *Rebel Voices*, p. 35.

88. **The police hauled him off to jail:** Hapgood, *Victorian in the Modern World*, pp. 285–87; Luhan, *Movers and Shakers*, pp. 47–48.

"swiftly developing ability": Edna Kenton, "Feminism Will Give—Men More Fun," *Delineator*, July 1914, p. 17.

89. **"He would never have spoken":** Anderson, *My Thirty Years' War*, p. 37. On the general situation of women in Greenwich Village, see Sandra L. Addickes, *To Be Young Was Very Heaven: Women in New York before the First World War* (New York, 1997); June Sochen, *The New Woman in Greenwich Village, 1910–1920* (New York, 1972).

"the easiest of clubs": Irwin, quoted in Judith Schwarz, *Radical Feminists of Heterodoxy* (Lebanon, N.H., 1982), p. 13. Heterodoxy's membership is reconstructed in Schwarz, *Radical Feminists*, pp. 85–94.

90. **"fine, daring, rather joyous":** Luhan, *Movers and Shakers*, pp. 143–44.

"We're sick of being specialized": Howe, quoted in Schwarz, *Radical Feminists*, p. 25.

Patchin Place: See Kemp, *More Miles*, p. 347. Djuna Barnes, Alyse Gregory, and Louise Bryant all lived there at various times.

91. **"the atmosphere had been rather stiff":** Carl Zigrosser, "Florence King," *My Own Shall Come to Me: A Personal Memoir and Picture Chronicle* (Haarlem, Neth., 1971), pp. 94–105; Frank McLynn, *Carl Justav Jung* (New York, 1996), p. 215.

"learned something of the fine art": Zigrosser, "Florence King," p. 101.

the Frog Prince: Louis Untermeyer, *Bygones: The Recollections of Louis Untermeyer* (New York, 1965), p. 39. Bourne's editor friend James Oppenheim wrote: "I shall never forget how I had first to overcome my repugnance when I saw that child's body, the humped back, and the longish, almost medieval, face, with a screwed-up mouth, and an ear gone awry. But he wore a cape, carried himself with an air, and then you listened to his marvelous speech . . . holding you spellbound" ("The Story of the *Seven Arts*," *American Mercury*, June 1930, p. 163).

92. **"beloved community":** The term is first used in Bourne's "Trans-National America," *Atlantic Monthly*, July 1916, reprinted in *The Radical Will: Randolph Bourne. Selected Writings, 1911–1918*, ed. Olaf Hansen (New York, 1977), p. 264.

"Thinking cannot be done": Randolph Bourne, "In a Schoolroom," *New Republic*, Nov. 7, 1914, reprinted in *The Radical Will*, ed. Hansen, p. 187. It was a pragmatist's point, and Bourne was a student of John Dewey and a devoted reader of William James.

"Fair and serious and life-denying woman": Bourne to Alyse Gregory,

Nov. 19, 1916, *Letters*, ed. Sandeen, p. 385. Relevant writings on feminism are "Karen: A Portrait," *New Republic*, Sept. 23, 1916, pp. 187–88 (concerning Frances Lundquist, a Patchin Place writer); "Suffrage and Josella," unpublished essay reprinted in *Radical Will*, ed. Hansen, pp. 443–47 (concerning, most probably, Alyse Gregory); "Mon Amie," *Atlantic Monthly*, Mar. 1915, pp. 354–59; "The Later Feminism," *Dial*, Aug. 16, 1917, pp. 103–04. For a general discussion of Bourne's feminism, see Bruce Clayton, *Forgotten Prophet: The Life of Randolph Bourne* (Baton Rouge, 1984), ch. 9.

93. **"It is the glory of the present age"**: Randolph Bourne, "Youth," *Atlantic Monthly*, Apr. 1912, reprinted in *Radical Will*, ed. Hansen, p. 104. "Youth" was a response to Cornelia Comer's sententious "A Letter to the Rising Generation," *Atlantic Monthly*, Feb. 1911, pp. 145–54.

"It is only the young": Bourne, "Youth," p. 99.

94. **generational consciousness**: The idea that each era had its distinctive qualities, walled off from what came before and after, went back to the American and French Revolutions. In the United States, the experience of the Civil War, shared across age groups, did not engender any sharp ideas of generational divisions in the nineteenth century, but in Europe the rhetoric of a divide escalated as *die Jungen* in Austria and Germany and the Populists in Russia honed it to an edge of antipathy toward the older generation. See Carl E. Schorske, "Generational Tension and Cultural Change: Reflections on the Case of Vienna," *Daedalus* 107 (Fall 1978): 111–22; Annie Kriegel, "Generational Difference: The History of an Idea," *Daedalus* 107 (Fall 1978): 23–38; Robert Wohl, *The Generation of 1914* (Cambridge, Mass., 1979), p. 204.

When the world was divided: Michael Walzer, *The Company of Critics* (New York, 1988), p. 49.

"It made me very blue": Bourne to Alyse Gregory, July 30, 1914, *Letters*, ed. Sandeen, p. 263.

Maurice Barrès: Barrès has been called the French "bard of anti-Semitism" (Pierre Birnbaum, *Anti-Semitism in Modern France: A Political History from Léon Blum to the Present* [Oxford, 1992], p. 262).

95. **Seven Arts**: Van Wyck Brooks, "Young America," *Seven Arts*, Dec. 1916, p. 144; Seichi Naruse, "Young Japan," *Seven Arts*, Apr. 1917, p. 616. See also Edward Abrahams, *The Lyrical Left: Randolph Bourne, Alfred Stieglitz, and the Origins of Cultural Radicalism in America* (Charlottesville, 1986).

96. **the Modern School**: On the Modern School and the Ferrer Center, see Paul Avrich, *The Modern School Movement: Anarchism and Education in the United States* (Princeton, 1980); Laurence R. Veysey, *The Communal Experience: Anarchist and Mystical Counter-Cultures in America* (New York, 1973).

Robert Henri and George Bellows taught painting: Watson, *Strange Bedfellows*, p. 196. For connections of the Ferrer artists to other New York artists, see Kent Smith, *Abraham Walkowitz Figuration, 1895–1945*, exhibition catalog, Long Beach Museum of Art (Los Angeles, 1982); Sheldon Reich, "Abraham Walkowitz," *American Art Journal* 3 (Spring 1971): 72–82.

"Free expression of opinions": Harry Kelly, quoted in Avrich, *Modern School Movement*, p. 131.

Notes

Escuela Moderna: Ferrer made the school, which he founded in 1901, a beacon for a libertarian workers' education movement. The school included, at its peak, adult classes, a teacher training institute, and a publishing house and was planning to add a popular university. Ferrer was executed in 1909 during a republican uprising in Barcelona; his martyrdom prompted mass protests across Europe and, in America, the founding of schools to honor his memory. See Avrich, *Modern School Movement*, ch. 1. On the London anarchist school, see William J. Fishman, *East End Jewish Radicals, 1875–1914* (London, 1975), pp. 265–69. There are references to the Université Populaire in the early sections of Bercovici, *It's the Gypsy in Me*, and in Goldman, *Living My Life*, vol. 1, p. 266.

"motley collection": Bourne to Henry W. Elsasser, Jan. 20, 1914, *Letters*, ed. Sandeen, p. 211. Bourne also attended lectures at the Université Populaire (Bourne to Arthur Macmahon, Mar. 15, 1914, *Letters*, ed. Sandeen, pp. 233–34).

97. **Benzion Liber:** Liber set up a prosperous practice in Brooklyn, where he was a beloved pediatrician. He published many books, among them *The Child and the Home* (1922), which was translated into French, German, and Romanian. See also *A Glance into People's Lives* (n.p., 1954) and *A Doctor's Apprenticeship* (New York, 1957).

"a kind of amateur Nietzsche": Will Durant and Ariel Durant, *A Dual Autobiography* (New York, 1977), p. 40. Other biographical information is in Veysey, *Communal Experience;* Avrich, *Modern School Movement;* Rion Bercovici, "A Radical Childhood," *Scribner's*, Aug. 1932, pp. 102–06; Konrad Bercovici, *Crimes of Charity* (New York, 1917). Bercovici mentions his publishing coups in *It's the Gypsy in Me*, pp. 106–07, 121, 133–34.

"Romany Marie": Obituary in *New York Times*, Feb. 23, 1961; restaurant review in James, *Dining in New York*, pp. 194–96.

98. **Hippolyte Havel:** Hapgood, *Victorian in the Modern World*, pp. 198–99, 317–19, 327–31; Kemp, *More Miles*, p. 283; Joel Pfister, *Staging Depth: Eugene O'Neill and the Politics of Psychological Discourse* (Chapel Hill, 1995), p. 153; Day, *Long Loneliness*, p. 84; Wertheim, *New York Little Renaissance*, p. 50; Goldman, *Living My Life*, vol. 1, pp. 260–61. Havel also became involved with Gallery 291. See Havel's cheerful endorsement of Stieglitz as "bombthrower . . . in the foremost rank" in *Camera Work*, July 1914, p. 67. Avrich provides a thumbnail biography in *Modern School Movement*, pp. 121–24.

99. **Margaret Sanger:** Sanger used her Ferrer connections to habituate herself to the European scene, too; lonely and adrift in Liverpool in 1914, she located one of Ferrer's leading disciples and began an affair—sexual and political—with him. See Avrich, *Modern School Movement*, pp. 184–89; Ellen Chesler, *Woman of Valor: Margaret Sanger and the Birth Control Movement in America* (New York, 1992), pp. 100–02, 107–10.

a colony in Ridgefield: During the summer of 1907, a group of young garment workers from the Lower East Side who had been laid off and were facing eviction moved to the Palisades and set up a tent encampment for the summer (Orleck, *Common Sense and a Little Fire*, p. 15). For New York Dada, see Frances M. Naumann, *Making Mischief: Dada Invades New York*, exhibition catalog, Whitney Museum (New York, 1997); *Women in Dada:*

363

Essays on Sex, Gender, and Identity, ed. Naomi Sawelson-Gorse (Boston, 1998). On Man Ray, see Neil Baldwin, *Man Ray: American Artist* (New York, 1988); *Conspiratorial Laughter. A Friendship: Man Ray and Duchamp*, exhibition catalog, Zabriskie Gallery (New York, 1995), esp. p. 66, for Man Ray's political radicalism. Havel, too, hooked up with Dada. A snatch from Juliette Roche's typographical collage *Brevoort, Demi Cercle* reads, "Havel un Personnage Officiel Vive l'Anarchie," with the line "Vive l'anarchie! Vive l'anarchie! Vive l'anarchie" shooting off at an angle from "Hippolyte." Naumann, *Making Mischief*, p. 141. The poets are described in Dickran Tashjian, "Authentic Spirit of Change: The Poetry of New York Dada," Naumann, *Making Mischief*, pp. 266–71; Watson, *Strange Bedfellows*, pp. 300–01.

100. **Mabel Dodge's evenings:** Luhan, *Movers and Shakers*; Lois Palken Rudnick, *Mabel Dodge Luhan: New Woman, New Worlds* (Albuquerque, 1984).
"The essence of it all": Luhan, *Movers and Shakers*, p. 39.

101. **a "lovely frame":** Rudnick, *Mabel Dodge Luhan*, chs. 2–3. Dodge is quoted on the picture frame on p. 57.

102. **John Sloan compared it:** *John Sloan's New York Scene: From the Diaries, Notes and Correspondence, 1906–1913*, ed. Bruce St. John (New York, 1965), p. 633 (entry for Jan. 6, 1913).
"epoch making": Quinn, quoted in Milton W. Brown, *The Story of the Armory Show* (Greenwich, 1963), p. 26.
"The implicit assumption": Harold Rosenberg, "The Armory Show: Revolution Reenacted," *The Anxious Object: Art Today and Its Audience* (New York, 1964), pp. 188–89.
"disrupt, degrade, if not destroy": "Cubists and Futurists Are Making Insanity Pay," *New York Times*, Mar. 16, 1913, sec. 6.
"smoke two pipefuls of 'hop' ": *Chicago Record-Herald*, quoted in Watson, *Strange Bedfellows*, p. 170.

103. **The circulation of the "Portrait":** "Portrait of Mabel Dodge" was reprinted in Stieglitz's journal *Camera Work* (June 1913).
"I suddenly found myself": Luhan, *Movers and Shakers*, pp. 36, 140. See Rudnick's account of the episode in *Mabel Dodge Luhan*, pp. 67–71.
"in an unaccustomed freedom": Luhan, *Movers and Shakers*, p. 83.
"exchanged a variousness in vocabulary": Ibid.

104. **"a number of people (most of whom you know)":** Ibid., p. 143.
serious habitués vowed to purge: Carl Van Vechten to Mabel Dodge, Dec. 24 [1913], *Letters of Carl Van Vechten*, ed. Bruce Kellner (New Haven, 1987), p. 10.

105. **"An appalling Negress danced":** Luhan, *Movers and Shakers*, p. 79. This gathering occurred around the time Van Vechten became interested in African American theater in Harlem. His review of *The Darktown Follies* for the *New York Press* in 1913 was, his biographer Bruce Kellner claims, the first serious criticism of black entertainment offered in a white paper. Van Vechten was a critic of classical music but had encountered African American jazz and ragtime performers as a college student in Chicago (Van Vechten, "Reminiscences, 1960," Oral History Research Library, Columbia University; Van Vechten to Fania Marinoff, Nov. 30, 1913, *Letters of Carl Van Vechten*, ed. Kellner, p. 9).

106. **the tone the Arensbergs would set:** Molly Nesbit and Naomi Sawelson-Gorse, "Concept of Nothing: New Notes by Marcel Duchamp and Walter Arensberg," *The Duchamp Effect*, ed. Martha Buskirk and Mignon Nixon (Cambridge, Mass., 1996); Naomi Sawelson-Gorse, "Marcel Duchamp's 'Silent Guard': A critical study of Louise and Walter Arensberg," Ph.D. dissertation, University of California at Santa Barbara, 1994; Watson, *Strange Bedfellows*, pp. 277–78; Burke, *Becoming Modern*, pp. 212–33; Kreymborg, *Troubadour*, p. 219.

The Wobblies: Margaret Sanger, *Autobiography* (New York, 1938), p. 73. See also Ralph Chaplin, *Wobbly: The Rough-and-Tumble Story of an American Radical* (Chicago, 1948), p. 138, and Jessie Lloyd O'Connor, Harvey O'Connor, and Susan M. Bowler, *Harvey and Jessie: A Couple of Radicals* (Philadelphia, 1988), pp. 24–26, on the attractions of New York bohemia for Wobblies all across the country.

"I wanted to try": Luhan, *Movers and Shakers*, p. 83.

"I saw quite soon": Ibid., p. 59.

"long, bald room": Henry James, *The Bostonians* (1886; New York, 1956), p. 31.

The unusual guests: Luhan, *Movers and Shakers*, pp. 81–83.

107. **"Women that smoke":** The letters are reprinted in Luhan, *Movers and Shakers*, pp. 151–70.

"Mabel Dodge / Hodge podge": Leo Stein, quoted in Rudnick, *Mabel Dodge Luhan*, p. 69.

108. **"a new era of self-amplification":** Taylor, *In Pursuit of Gotham*, p. 129.

"were all unconsciously freed": Luhan, *Movers and Shakers*, p. 88.

"You've got enough endowment": Lippmann to Mabel Dodge, Jan. 20, 1915, quoted in Steel, *Walter Lippmann*, pp. 52–53.

109. **"Parlor Discussion, Parlor Artists, Parlor Socialists":** William Sanger, quoted in Chesler, *Woman of Valor*, p. 91.

"a rich woman amusing herself": Vorse, quoted in Garrison, *Mary Heaton Vorse*, p. 63.

Politically, she leaned far to the left: Steve Golin, *The Fragile Bridge: Paterson Silk Strike, 1913* (Philadelphia, 1988), p. 143; Green, *New York 1913*, p. 60. The Commission on Industrial Relations episode is discussed in Luhan, *Movers and Shakers*, pp. 144–50. The standard history of the commission is Graham Adams, Jr., *Age of Industrial Violence, 1910–1915: The Activities and Findings of the United States Commission on Industrial Relations* (New York, 1966).

the "radical rich": including the lawyers Amos Pinchot and Jessie Ashley, Mary Dreier and Helen Marot of the Women's Trade Union League, Anne Morgan (daughter of J. P.), the oil heiress Aline Barnsdall of Los Angeles, who out of the blue sent a check to the *Masses*, and Alva (Mrs. O. H. P.) Belmont.

110. **"liked to conceive of herself":** Eastman, *Enjoyment of Living*, p. 404; for Amos Pinchot, see pp. 455–63. The tight-fisted rich man was single-taxer Bolton Hall (Liber, *A Doctor's Apprenticeship*, p. 591).

"Dangerous Characters": Luhan, *Movers and Shakers*, p. 88.

"Emma and her bunch": Ibid., p. 59.

"I think she expects to find General Villa": Reed, quoted in Green, *New York 1913*, p. 219.

111. **enactment of the Paterson silk workers' strike:** Linda Nochlin, "The Paterson Strike Pageant of 1913," *Art in America* 62 (May-June 1974): 64–78.

112. **"We have your first case":** Vorse tells the story of the unemployment demonstrations in *Footnote to Folly*, ch. 4.

"Vivid": Goldman, *Living My Life*, vol. 2, p. 523.

the unemployed demonstrations: Carlo Tresca, "The Unemployed and the IWW," *Retort*, June 1944, pp. 23–24; Philip S. Foner, *History of the Labor Movement in the United States*, vol. 4 (New York, 1965), pp. 444–50. The outlines of Tannenbaum's earlier life can be traced in his papers, Frank Tannenbaum Collection, Butler Library, Columbia University.

114. **"drew people to it":** Vorse, *Footnote to Folly*, p. 70.

"were unequalled in this country": Charles Plunkett, quoted in Avrich, *Modern School Movement*, p. 188. Plunkett was from a middle-class Irish family, a Cornell scholarship student who had dropped out to organize with the IWW.

"I was sick at heart last night": Steffens, quoted in Avrich, *Modern School Movement*, p. 190. See also Vorse, *Footnote to Folly*, p. 72.

Jig Cook, for one: "New York Letter," *Chicago Evening Post*, Apr. 17, 1914.

"that winter was a sort of welding process": Vorse, *Footnote to Folly*, p. 61.

115. **"Anyone who has ever been involved":** Stephen Minta, *On a Voiceless Shore: Byron in Greece* (New York, 1988), pp. 216–17.

a ferocious conflict: George McGovern, Leonard F. Guttridge, and Howard Zinn, quoted in Avrich, *Modern School Movement*, pp. 192–93.

116. **an unrepentant terrorist:** Paul Avrich's scrupulous historical detective work has established Berkman's involvement in the bomb plot (*Modern School Movement*, pp. 196–202).

demanded a dramatic reenactment of 1892: Avrich, *Modern School Movement*, p. 199.

great loads of books: Tannenbaum's reading can be traced in the letters of his supporter "A." See A. to Tannenbaum, May 13, 1914, in B File, Tannenbaum Collection.

117. **the school wing of Ferrer:** The June events proved the school's undoing: in 1915, it moved out to an old farm in New Jersey to become a rural commune and children's boarding school (Avrich, *Modern School Movement*, p. 212).

"Comrades, idealists": Goldman, *Living My Life*, vol. 2, p. 536.

"I had always tried": Ibid., p. 538.

118. **"intense personal intercourse":** Lasch, *New Radicalism*, p. 108.

4/EMMA GOLDMAN AND THE MODERN PUBLIC

120. **"Bohemian Greenwich Village":** The minister was discouraging people from attending a lecture of Max Eastman's (Eastman, *Enjoyment of Living*, pp. 477–78).

121. **Goldman's ideas:** Samples of Goldman's concerns can be found in two anthologies, *Red Emma Speaks: Selected Writings and Speeches by Emma Goldman*, ed. Alix Kates Shulman (New York, 1972), and Goldman, *Anarchism and Other Essays* (1917; New York, 1969).

123. **"that terrible name":** a friend to Goldman, quoted in Wexler, *Emma Goldman*, p. 99.

     facial and massage parlor: Such parlors were a means for entrepreneurship in the early century for immigrant women like Goldman (and Helena Rubinstein). See Kathy Peiss, *Hope in a Jar: The Making of American Beauty Culture* (New York, 1998), ch. 3.

     The older generation of leaders: On the inbred character of the anarchist movement in the 1890s, see Burrows and Wallace, *Gotham*, p. 1090.

     the Orlenev troupe: Goldman, *Living My Life*, vol. 1, p. 373; Gavin Lambert, *Nazimova* (New York, 1977), pp. 117–31.

124. **There Miss E. G. Smith mingled:** Goldman, *Living My Life*, vol. 1, pp. 373–76.

     no immigrant Jewish woman had yet done: Mary Antin would not publish her memoir, *The Promised Land*, until 1912.

     "subdivided as a chessboard": Henry James, "The Question of Opportunities" (1898), quoted in Trachtenberg, *Incorporation of America*, p. 195. James went on to lament the absence of any taste establishing itself as "general." It was exactly this—the "general"—that Goldman was after.

     "that would combine my social ideas": Goldman, *Living My Life*, vol. 1, p. 377.

125. **She kept up a grueling schedule:** Wexler, *Emma Goldman*, p. 165.

     "They had never been able": Goldman, *Living My Life*, vol. 1, p. 469.

126. **"New York Jew":** Alfred Kazin, *New York Jew* (New York, 1978).

     Jews became the reigning intellectuals: Paul M. Buhle, *A Dreamer's Paradise Lost: Louis C. Fraina/Lewis Corey (1892–1953) and the Decline of Radicalism in the United States* (Atlantic Highlands, N. J.,1995), p. 70.

     immigrant Jews . . . in New York's entertainment industry: Taylor, *In Pursuit of Gotham*, p. 89.

     the transpositions Jewish songwriters wrought: Ibid.

127. **"scarcely one physically fit":** C. E. S. Wood, Diary, June 22, 1915, Sara Bard Field/C. E. S. Wood Collection, Huntington Library, San Marino.

     Helen Marot: Orleck, *Common Sense*, pp. 67–68; Nancy Schrom Dye, *As Equals and Sisters: Feminism, the Labor Movement, and the Women's Trade Union League of New York* (Columbia, 1980), pp. 54, 116.

     European circles where anti-Semitism penetrated: Anthony Julius, *T. S. Eliot, Anti-Semitism, and Literary Form* (Cambridge, Eng., 1995), pp. 1–40.

128. **Eugene O'Neill was the master of this shift:** Pfister, *Staging Depth*.

     She later turned up: Winifred Frazer, *E. G. and E. G. O. Emma Goldman and The Iceman Cometh* (Gainesville, 1974).

129. **"veritable battle encampments":** Goldman, *Living My Life*, vol. 1, p. 426.

     doctors, lawyers, judges: Wexler, *Emma Goldman*, p. 207.

     Harvard socialist Samuel Eliot: Reed, "Harvard Renaissance," pp. 61–62; Hicks, *John Reed*, p. 74.

     Bayard Boyesen: Avrich, *Modern School Movement*, pp. 69–70; Goldman, *Living My Life*, vol. 1, p. 475.

130. **William Buwalda:** Goldman, *Living My Life*, vol. 1, pp. 428, 448; see Shulman's additional notes in *Red Emma Speaks*, p. 39.

     the execution of a Japanese anarchist . . . the Easter Rebellion: Goldman, *Living My Life*, vol. 2, p. 519.

When she did: "National Atavism," *Mother Earth*, Mar. 1906, pp. 49–57.

131. **In Europe:** Mary Gluck, *George Lukács and His Generation, 1900–1918* (Cambridge, Mass., 1985), p. 70.

"the race of transcendental idealism": Hippolyte Havel, Introduction to Goldman, *Anarchism and Other Essays*, p. 4.

Rosa Luxemburg: See Hannah Arendt, *Men in Dark Times* (New York, 1968), pp. 33–56, and J. P. Nettl, *Rosa Luxemburg*, vol. 1 (London, 1966), especially on Luxemburg's Polish Jewish peer group and its free-love predilections (ch. 3). There was no similar female anarchist celebrity in Europe.

132. **She spoke to thousands:** Wexler, *Emma Goldman*, p. 166.

listeners marveled: Ibid., pp. 167–71.

"rather like a severe": Luhan, *Movers and Shakers*, p. 58; Avrich, *Modern School Movement*, p. 148.

Her genius lay in the polyvalence: See Arthur Redding, "The Dream Life of Political Violence: Georges Sorel, Emma Goldman, and the Modern Imagination," *Modernism/Modernity* 2.2 (1995): 1–16, on Goldman's interest in performance.

"something cosmic in the air": Anderson, writing in *Mother Earth*, Dec. 1914; quoted in Wexler, *Emma Goldman*, pp. 166–67.

133. **"the most important encounter":** Miller, quoted in Richard Drinnon, *Rebel in Paradise* (Boston, 1961), p. 202. See also Jay Martin, *Always Merry and Bright: The Life of Henry Miller* (Santa Barbara, 1978), pp. 137–39.

Almeda Sperry: Wexler, *Emma Goldman*, pp. 182–83; on Christine Ell, see Frazer, *E. G. and E. G. O.*, p. 103. The examples of she-changed-my-life stories could be compounded. See, for example, Drinnon, *Rebel in Paradise*, p. 202. Van Wyck Brooks claimed that "no one did more to spread the new ideas of literary Europe that influenced so many young people in the West" (*The Confident Years: 1885–1915* [New York, 1952], p. 375).

134. **Colorado miners who heard her speak:** Goldman, *Living My Life*, vol. 1, p. 493.

"More and more": Field to C. E. S. Wood, July 24[1914], Field/Wood Collection.

135. **Ben Reitman:** Roger A. Bruns, *The Damndest Radical: The Life and World of Dr. Ben Reitman* (Urbana, 1987).

"drainage basin": *New York Times* (1907), quoted in Bruns, *Damndest Radical*, p. 38.

an eccentric heir to a railroad fortune: The philanthropist was James Eads How, a Harvard and Oxford graduate who became a Fabian and eventually gave away all his considerable fortune to the poor (Bruns, *Damndest Radical*, p. 21).

136. **enumeration of the different species:** Ibid., p. 28.

Reitman's alliance with the "anarchist queen": A comprehensive treatment of the relationship is Candace Serena Falk, *Love, Anarchy, and Emma Goldman* (New Brunswick, N. J., 1990).

137. **a man whom Margaret Anderson described:** Anderson, *My Thirty Years' War*, p. 70.

"he could not understand": Goldman, *Living My Life*, vol. 1, pp. 432–33.

Isadora Duncan: Ann Daly, *Done into Dance* (Bloomington, 1995), pp. 103, 116.

138. **"pitiful efforts to amuse the public":** Goldman, *Living My Life*, vol. 2, p. 526.

139. **anarchism tinged the avant-garde:** Avrich argues that "between 1890 and 1920, it is probably no exaggeration to say anarchism became the favorite doctrine of the literary and artistic avant-garde, in America as well as in Europe (*Modern School Movement*, p. 137). See also Patricia Leighton, *Re-Ordering the Universe: Picasso and Anarchism, 1897–1914* (Princeton, 1989); Donald Drew Egbert, *Social Radicalism and the Arts: Western Europe* (New York, 1970); Richardson, *Life of Picasso*, vol. 1; Shattuck, *Banquet Years*. On Hasek and the question of anarchist influence on Kafka, see Ernst Pawel, *The Nightmare of Reason: A Life of Franz Kafka* (New York, 1984), pp. 69, 151–53, 368. Pawel describes how Kafka's anarchist ideas later merged with his dream of joining a kibbutz.

140. **There were unacknowledged tensions:** Most of Goldman's chroniclers note this, but Redding is adept at characterizing the paradoxes ("Dream Life of Political Violence," pp. 8–9).

"spiritual hunger and unrest": Goldman, quoted in Wexler, *Emma Goldman*, p. 207.

"too cumbersome": Manuel Komroff, quoted in Avrich, *Modern School Movement*, p. 134.

141. **"I could never listen to the socialists":** Anderson, *My Thirty Years' War*, p. 149.

the Marxist theory of class struggle: Fink discusses the problem in *Progressive Intellectuals*, ch. 4.

"builds not on classes": Goldman, quoted in Wexler, *Emma Goldman*, p. 206.

"a movement for individual self-expression": Harry Kelly, quoted in Wexler, *Emma Goldman*, pp. 205–06.

"respectable audiences": De Cleyre, quoted in Wexler, *Emma Goldman*, p. 206.

142. **"unnatural" subjects:** For an example of the anarchists' squeamishness about homosexuality, see Benzion Liber's cautionary views in *The Child and the Home*, p. 192.

"his dream world of 1892": Goldman, *Living My Life*, vol. 1, pp. 392–93.

Psychological undercurrents: These can be best seen not in Goldman's memoirs, which report only her side of the relationship, but in the stunning collection of letters between the two while they lived in exile, *Nowhere at Home: Letters from Exile of Emma Goldman and Alexander Berkman*, ed. Richard Drinnon and Anna Maria Drinnon (New York, 1975).

143. **"a square little solid block":** Eastman, *Enjoyment of Living*, p. 423.

"the vigor and passion of her personality": Hapgood, *Victorian in the Modern World*, p. 203.

144. **"a mixture of wonder, horror, and admiration":** Luhan, *Movers and Shakers*, p. 59.

"I wanted these people to think well of me": Ibid.

5/ART AND LIFE: MODERNITY AND LITERARY SENSIBILITIES

147. **"The artist does not run counter":** Burke, quoted in Jack Selzer, *Kenneth Burke in Greenwich Village: Conversing with the Moderns, 1915–1931* (Madison, 1996), p. viii.

 culture of letters: Richard H. Brodhead, *Cultures of Letters: Scenes of Reading and Writing in Nineteenth-Century America* (Chicago, 1993).

148. **skirmishes to be fought . . . over writing about sex:** For a critique of the push toward exposure, see Gurstein, *Repeal of Reticence*, ch. 5.

149. **as the first painters of modern life:** Philip Nord, *Politics and Impressionism: From the Salon des Refusés to the Dreyfus Affair* (London, 1999).

 a readiness to turn on its own certainties: Berman, *All That Is Solid*, p. 23.

150. **a liberal metropolitan elite:** Joel Pfister has made this argument, pointing to the "literary agents, editors, publicity people, reviewers, buyers of hardbound novels, taste-making intellectuals, critics, professors, most of the students who took literature courses, and . . . the writers . . . themselves" who were rooted in the downtown milieu (*Staging Depth*, p. 72). I would not go so far as Pfister to argue, though, that this moment saw corporate liberalism joined to cultural liberalism.

 never claimed their work: Howells was the exception, but while sympathetic to labor, he did not produce writing that was tied to the movement.

151. **Picasso . . . in workers' overalls:** Watson, *Strange Bedfellows*, p. 41.

 "I have lived like an artist": "To the People of Utah," *International Socialist Review*, Oct. 1915, pp. 222–23.

 Bill Haywood: Hapgood, *Victorian in the Modern World*, pp. 291–93; "Greenwich Village," *Dial*, Oct. 1, 1914, p. 240.

 "I have never known a people": Anderson, *My Thirty Years' War*, p. 133.

152. **more than three hundred socialist publications:** Zurier, *Art for the Masses*, p. 30.

 Louise Bryant: Mary V. Dearborn, *Queen of Bohemia: The Life of Louise Bryant* (Boston, 1996), p. 37.

 "What cause could be more asinine": O'Neill poem, reprinted in Pfister, *Staging Depth*, p. 106. Examples can also be found in Chaplin, *Wobbly*, p. 101; Clarice Stasz, *American Dreamers: Charmian and Jack London* (New York, 1988), p. 144.

 "Everyone on the city desk": Day, *Long Loneliness*, p. 53.

153. **"All of us were going to write novels":** Dell, *Homecoming*, p. 223.

 "Girl poets": Dell's description of the women he met when he edited the *Friday Literary Review*, a group that would have included Margaret Anderson (*Homecoming*, p. 228).

 Djuna Barnes: See the interviews reprinted in Djuna Barnes, *New York*, ed. Alyce Barry (Los Angeles, 1989), and *Interviews*, ed. Barry (Washington, D.C., 1985); also "Confessions of Helen Westley," reprinted in *Gender of Modernism*, ed. Scott, pp. 40–45. Barnes was a resident of the Village, a habitué of its cafés, salons, and meetings, and a principal in the Provincetown Players (Mary Ann Broe, "Djuna Barnes," *Gender of Modernism*, ed. Scott, pp. 21–24).

 the journey from the ghettos: See, for example, Norman Podhoretz, *Making It* (New York, 1967), p. 3. In Alfred Kazin's *Walker in the City* (New

York, 1951), the subway ride from Brownsville to Manhattan becomes the quintessential immigrant's trek from margins to center.

Official prewar American culture: An influential explicator of this view is May, *End of American Innocence.*

154. **family magazines:** Wilson, *Labor of Words;* Ohman, *Selling Culture;* Hicks, *John Reed*, p. 65. A perusal of *Everybody's* magazine for 1912 turns up a muckraking piece on the coal industry graced with sprightly graphics, a melodrama of a Polish worker's tragedy in the steel mills by social worker (and Village resident) Ernst Poole, an essay on the plight of immigrants by the A Club resident Miriam Finn Scott—all mixed with "family fare" fiction and articles on baseball. The placid pages of *Harper's* in 1913 included an article on the general strike in Venice by Mary Heaton Vorse. Art Young illustrated an article on Trotsky on the Lower East Side for *Collier's* (Young, *On My Way* [New York, 1928], p. 163).

Louise Bryant's career: Dearborn, *Queen of Bohemia*, ch. 5; Virginia Gardner, *"Friend and Lover": The Life of Louise Bryant* (New York, 1982), chs. 17–19.

"Before 1914": Alfred A. Knopf, *Some Random Recollections: An Informal Talk Made at the Grolier Club, New York* (New York, 1949), p. 36. On the established publishers, see Alice Payne Hackett, *60 Years of Best Sellers, 1895–1955* (New York, 1956); Roger Burlingame, *Of Making Many Books: A Hundred Years of Reading, Writing, and Publishing* (New York, 1957); Charles A. Madison, *The Owl among Colophons: Henry Holt as Publisher and Editor* (New York, 1966), pp. 188–90.

155. **"a closed universe":** Schuster, quoted in Dardis, *Firebrand*, p. 50.

genial skepticism about the existence of God: As late as 1926 at Scribner's, Hemingway's editor, Maxwell Perkins, urged him to substitute the tamer "goddam" for "God damn" (Burlingame, *Of Making Many Books*, pp. 87–88).

Anglo-Saxonist fears: North, *Dialect of Modernism*, pp. 13–18.

Holt published a few left-leaning books: Holt published Henri Bergson (a best-seller in 1912), John Dewey, Romain Rolland, V. G. Simkhovitch's *Marxism and Socialism*, and, in 1918, Trotsky's *Our Revolution.* But these choices were pressed on Holt by his young protégé Alfred Harcourt and he made them grudgingly (Ellen D. Gilbert, *The House of Holt, 1866–1946: An Editorial History* [Methuen, 1993]). A discerning view of the complications of the genteel tradition can be found in Joan Shelley Rubin, *The Making of Middlebrow Culture* (Chapel Hill, 1992), pp. 26–27. The best study is Marc H. Aronson, "Democratic Standards: William Crary Brownell, Literary Culture, and the Marketplace," Ph.D. dissertation, New York University, 1994.

156. **"all of us had lived":** Oppenheim, "Story of the *Seven Arts*," pp. 156–57.

"the literary sansculottes": Dell, *Homecoming*, p. 191. See also Van Wyck Brooks, *Days of the Phoenix: The Nineteen-Twenties I Remember* (New York, 1957), ch. 2.

A group of independent publishers: Eastman, *Enjoyment of Living*, pp. 540–41; Richard Lingeman, *Theodore Dreiser* (New York, 1986), vol. 2, p. 90; Dardis, *Firebrand*, pp. 51–52; Brevda, *Harry Kemp*, pp. 66–67, 114; *Alfred A. Knopf: Quarter Century* (New York, 1940); Walker Gilmer, *Horace*

Liveright: Publisher of the Twenties (New York, 1970); Daniel Boice, *The Mitchell Kennerley Imprint: A Descriptive Bibliography* (Pittsburgh, 1996); Matthew J. Bruccoli, *The Fortunes of Mitchell Kennerley, Bookman* (New York, 1986).

157. **"I feel so *pained & hurt*"**: Hattie to Rose Pastor Stokes, Feb. 10, 1917, Rose Pastor Stokes Papers, Tamiment Library, New York University.

158. **Anthony Comstock**: Nicola Beisel, *Imperiled Innocents: Anthony Comstock and Family Reproduction in Victorian America* (Princeton, 1997); Gurstein, *Repeal of Reticence*, pp. 125–33; Heywood Broun and Margaret Leech, *Anthony Comstock* (New York, 1927); Anna Louise Bates, *Weeder in the Garden of the Lord: Anthony Comstock's Life and Career* (Lanham, 1995).

159. **Hagar Revelly:** Bruccoli, *Fortunes of Mitchell Kennerley*, pp. 68–72.

legitimate publishers with resources: Lingeman, *Theodore Dreiser*, vol. 2., pp. 90–162; see also Robert Bremner's introduction to Anthony Comstock, *Traps for the Young* (1883; New York, 1967).

"ignorant postal clerks": George Soule, "New York Letter," *Little Review*, Apr. 1914, pp. 46–47.

The *Masses* editors: Sumner threatened them for advertising a book that supposedly advocated sodomy (*Masses*, Mar. 1916, p. 16; Nov. 1916, p. 11).

When Dreiser's *The Genius* went to court: Lingeman, *Theodore Dreiser*, vol. 2, pp. 111–70. Sumner's threat forced the publisher, John Lane, to take the book off the market. H. L. Mencken helped organize a letter of protest with an unprecedented 458 signatories; he wanted to keep the "red-ink boys" from the Village out of the campaign but Dreiser insisted they be included. Dreiser then brought a friendly lawsuit against the publisher for breach of contract, but it was dismissed since, the court ruled, obscenity law was not salient because there had never been any formal charge from Summer.

160. **"Words, words"**: Burke, quoted in Selzer, *Kenneth Burke*, p. 60.

The formative context . . . was reading and writing: Carl Schorske notes that there are other means besides transformative historical events that bind generations together ("Generational Tension," pp. 121–22).

long lists of the books: Hapgood, *Victorian in the Modern World*, p. 20; Day, *Long Loneliness*, pp. 25–26; Dell, *Homecoming*, pp. 39, 55–57, 73; Helen C. Camp, *Iron in Her Soul: Elizabeth Gurley Flynn and the American Left* (Pullman, 1995), pp. 6, 10–11; Randolph Bourne, "History of a Literary Radical," *Radical Will*, ed. Hansen, pp. 421–23; Elizabeth Stuyvesant, "Staying Free," *These Modern Women*, ed. Elaine Showalter (New York, 1979), p. 93; Brevda, *Harry Kemp*, pp. 20–21; William Innes Homer and Violet Organ, *Robert Henri and His Circle* (Ithaca, 1969), p. 15; Eastman, *Enjoyment of Living*, pp. 189, 225.

161. **A renovated realism:** See Carl Van Vechten, who as late as 1922 encouraged Mabel Dodge (then Sterne) to read *Ulysses* for its realism: "The Irishmen (Boyd, Colum, etc.) tell me that it isn't symbolic or anything like that at all—that it's a sordid *realistic* catalogue of everything and everybody in Dublin—done à la Zola" (*Letters of Carl Van Vechten*, ed. Kellner, p. 44).

162. **Henri Bergson:** Nathan G. Hale, *Freud and the Americans: The Beginnings of Psychoanalysis in the United States, 1876–1917* (New York, 1971), pp. 242–43.

The Irish Renaissance: Robert McAlmon wrote in the *Little Review* that Djuna Barnes's plays for Provincetown were both Russian and "Synge-Irish" (quoted in Phillip Herring, *Djuna: The Life and Work of Djuna Barnes* [New York, 1995], p. 122). See also Pfister, *Staging Depth*, pp. 30–31. Jean Starr Untermeyer reminisces about the vogue for the Irish in *Private Collection* (New York, 1965), pp. 56–59.

163. **The reception of Berkman's book:** Goldman quotes positive reviews from the mainstream press in *Living My Life*, vol. 2, p. 506.
"Berkman becomes so near": *Little Review*, Dec. 1914, pp. 13–14.

164. **"The new poetry *is* revolutionary":** *Life*, quoted in *Others* 1 (1915), p. 74a. I am not suggesting that free verse was the only poetry in fashion. Harry Kemp, for instance, a well-known Villager without previous literary connections, won acclaim in the teens as the "Tramp Poet"—his IWW, revolutionary credentials bandied about—publishing conventionally rhymed verse (Brevda, *Harry Kemp*, pp. 106–08). Amy Lowell and Harriet Monroe (Chicago editor of *Poetry* magazine) were avid popularizers; Lowell went on stage to promote Imagism (presenting herself not just as a reader but as an act, a cross between chautauqua and vaudeville), and Monroe consciously set herself the task of "gathering together our public" (Monroe to John Reed, Sept. 28, 1912, Reed Papers [bMS Am 1091{617}]).

"Are you writing poetry?" a fellow journalist inquired of Reed, who had not been writing due to illness. The assumption was that any kind of literary production could turn into poetry (Paul Marriett to Reed, June 9, 1911, Reed Papers [bMS Am 1091{617}]). Joseph Freeman, later a Communist Party ideologue but in 1916 a young modern at Columbia, would in his later, doctrinaire years judge the campus poetry discussions to be an outcropping of the "faith of the middle classes," so easily did they square with the sensibilities of privileged young men at the time (Freeman, *An American Testament: A Narrative of Rebels and Romantics* [New York, 1936], p. 84).

of rhyme and meter: Maxwell Bodenheim, "The Decorative Straight[s]-Jacket: Rhymed Verse," *Little Review*, Nov. 1914, p. 22. On Bill Haywood's anthology, see "Editorial," *Little Review*, Oct. 1914, p. 37. For examples of Wobbly doggerel, see Kornbluh, *Rebel Voices*, p. 271. I'm indebted to the poet James Richardson for explaining to me how baggy was the term "free verse."

vers libre contest: *Little Review*, June-July 1916, p. 45. See William Carlos Williams's blast against popular vers libre, "Belly Dancing," *Others*, July 1919, pp. 25–32.

The *New York Times* linked: "Cubists of All Sorts," *New York Times*, Mar. 16, 1913. Margaret Anderson, arguably the most serious and intelligent purveyor of modern poetry in America, thought free verse "an adequate and distinctive poetical medium" for the revolutionary consciousness of the workers ("Editorial," *Little Review*, Oct. 1914, p. 37). The connections of New York Dada to the radicals, on the one hand, and free verse, on the other, deserve an essay in itself. Once the impish Duchamp arrived at the Ridgefield colony, quivering, elliptical Imagist short lines gave way to Dada antics on the page—typographical, metrical, syntactical, etc.

165. **"free footed verse":** Margaret Johns, "Free Footed Verse Is Danced in Ridgefield, N.J. Get What Meaning You Can Out of the Futurist Verse . . . It's as Esoteric as Gertrude Stein Herself," *New York Tribune*, July 25, 1915, sec. 3, p. 2

 Amy Lowell: Watson, *Strange Bedfellows*, p. 301. "All the questionable and pornographic poets are trying to sail under the name just now," she wrote.

 a revolt against "decency": "Cubists of All Sorts," *New York Times*, Mar. 16, 1913.

 "It is easy to forget": Helen Vendler, "The Truth Teller," *New York Review of Books*, Sept. 19, 1996, pp. 59–60.

 "They burn with hot fire": "Margins," *Masses*, Jan. 1916, p. 11. The novel is *Violette of Père Lachaise.*

166. **luring into type:** Bender, *New York Intellect*, p. 310.

 every up-and-coming writer of the day and some established ones: Those whose work is known today include Walter Lippmann, Djuna Barnes, Carl Sandburg, Vachel Lindsay, Amy Lowell, William Carlos Williams, John Reed, and Sherwood Anderson.

 New York's bid to capture: Kazin, *On Native Grounds*, pp. 169–70.

 The *Masses*: Accounts of the journal's history are in Young, *On My Way*, pp. 274–89; Zurier, *Art for the Masses; Echoes of Revolt: The Masses, 1911–1917*, ed. William L. O'Neill (Chicago, 1966); Eastman, *Enjoyment of Living*, chs. 48–65; Margaret C. Jones, *Heretics and Hellraisers: Women Contributors to* The Masses, *1911–1917* (Austin, 1993).

167. **Circulation increased:** Zurier, *Art for the Masses*, pp. 32, 49.

 "The whole scene and situation": Eastman, *Enjoyment of Living*, p. 399.

168. **antagonisms broke out:** A succinct account of the split in the Socialist Party is the entry on the party in *Encyclopedia of the American Left*; see also James Weinstein, *Ambiguous Legacy: The Left in American Politics* (New York, 1975), pp. 6–19.

 Eastman: The best sources on Eastman are the two volumes of his autobiography, *Enjoyment of Living* and *Love and Revolution*. A complementary perspective on the family background comes from Crystal Eastman, "Mother-Worship," *These Modern Women*, ed. Showalter, pp. 86–91. See also William O'Neill, *Last Romantic: A Life of Max Eastman* (New York, 1978).

169. **the crisis of ornamentation:** See Anderson, *Kafka's Clothes*, p. 182, on the antiflorid impulse in modernist Prague.

170. **"We wanted each object":** Eastman, *Enjoyment of Living*, p. 411. On ad-stripping, see Wilson, *Labor of Words*, p. 57.

 "entertainment, education and the livelier kinds of propaganda": "Editorial Notice," *Masses*, Dec. 1912, p. 31. The masthead declaration is reprinted in Eastman, *Enjoyment of Living*, p. 421.

171. **"We had a custom":** Eastman, *Enjoyment of Living*, p. 439.

 "Labor people came to it": Vorse, *Footnote to Folly*, p. 42.

 "A good part of New York's intelligentsia": Eastman, *Enjoyment of Living*, p. 439.

 "A cozy room": Unidentified news clipping, quoted in Zurier, *Art for The Masses*, p. 49.

 "As Floyd read along": Vorse, *Footnote to Folly*, p. 42.

173. **"Bourgeois! Voting!":** Young, *On My Way*, p. 281.

the reputation of bohemian playboy: Eastman was a leading anti-Stalinist and drew fire from Communist intellectuals. His stress on the hard work he and Floyd Dell did at the *Masses*, as opposed to the fooling around of the editors, can be seen in *Enjoyment of Living*, p. 399. A bitter debate on the seriousness of his political involvements with the journal broke out between him and Joseph Freeman of the Communist *New Masses*. See Freeman, "Greenwich Village Types," *New Masses*, May 1933, pp. 18–20; Eastman, "Bunk about Bohemia," *Modern Monthly*, May 1934, pp. 200–08, and "New Masses for Old," *Modern Monthly*, June 1934, pp. 292–300; Bob Brown, "Them Asses," *American Mercury*, Dec. 1933, pp. 403–11. The burst of recriminations was a response to Eastman's anti-Stalinism as well as to the publication of Albert Parry's *Garrets and Pretenders*. It is unclear if Parry was a member of the Communist Party, but his portrait of Eastman as a frivolous good-timer who lacked political backbone was in line with Communist accusations and galled Eastman. For a summary of the charges and countercharges, see O'Neill, *Last Romantic*, pp. 164–66.

"There would arise": Vorse, *Footnote to Folly*, p. 42.

"Bolder and freer": Sherwood Anderson, quoted in Eastman, *Love and Revolution*, p. 17.

"frank and free": Joseph Freeman, *An American Testament: A Narrative of Rebels and Romantics* (New York, 1936), p. 61.

"Nasty, dirty, smutty": Letter to the editor, *Masses*, Apr. 1916, p. 25.

174. **"So loud, so bitter":** Ida M. Keigman to Rose Pastor Stokes, Nov. 15, 1913, Stokes Papers.

"Vulgar beyond anything": Villard, quoted in Eastman, *Enjoyment of Living*, p. 401.

"I think it is distinctly injurious": George Foster Peabody, quoted in Eastman, *Enjoyment of Living*, p. 401.

"unconditioned freedom of expression": Eastman, quoted in Luhan, *Movers and Shakers*, p. 154.

the same market segment: Dell, *Homecoming*, pp. 194–95, 218.

"We have perfect faith": John Reed, unpublished manuscript, quoted in Zurier, *Art for the Masses*, p. 37.

175. **"Most of alert young America":** Genevieve Taggard, quoted in Zurier, *Art for the Masses*, p. 66.

Georgia O'Keeffe: Zurier, *Art for the Masses*, p. 195, n. 112; Benita Eisler, *O'Keeffe and Stieglitz* (New York, 1991), p. 70. On Field's subscription, see Field to C. E. S. Wood, Oct. 29, 1913, Field/Wood Collection. On Cahan's support, see Cahan to Max Eastman, May 19, 1917, Eastman Papers. On Reedy's interest, see Reedy to Eastman, May 1, 1913. On Bryant, see Eastman, *Enjoyment of Living*, p. 566.

176. **intimate address:** Kristin Vassallo, "Imagined Friendship and the Nation at Stake: Authors, Readers, and the Nineteenth Century American Conduct Book," unpublished junior essay, Princeton University, 1996. Readers were no doubt socialized into a receptive relationship to the (usually unnamed) magazine voice through their acquaintance with magazine advertisements, which as early as the 1890s invoked personal relationships through a mode of direct address—friendly, advising, encouraging, not overbearing. Ohman, *Selling Culture*, p. 193.

"You know how Washington Square": John Reed, "The Capitalist," *Masses*, Apr. 1916, p. 1.

"From my garret window": Allan Ross Macdougall, "New York Letter," *Little Review*, Apr. 1916, p. 29.

"Never yet have I entered" . . . "There is no place for me": Melville and Gogol, quoted in Irving Howe, "The City in Literature," *The Critical Point: On Literature and Culture* (New York, 1973), pp. 39–58.

177. **"I have just had the January number":** *Little Review*, Mar. 1915, p. 56.

6/WRITER FRIENDS: LITERARY FRIENDSHIPS AND THE ROMANCE OF PARTISANSHIP

178. **"Every writer I came to know":** Brooks, *Days of the Phoenix*, pp. 19–20. See also Brooks, *Confident Years;* Daniel Aaron, *Writers on the Left: Episodes in American Literary Communism* (New York, 1992); Eric Homberger, *American Writers and Radical Politics, 1900–39: Equivocal Commitments* (London, 1986).

179. **imagined affinities:** For a philosopher's treatment of the role of literary empathy in modern politics, see Martha C. Nussbaum, *Poetic Justice: The Literary Imagination and Public Life* (Boston, 1995).

"Mary dear": Flynn, quoted in Dorothy Gallagher, *All the Right Enemies: The Life and Murder of Carlo Tresca* (New Brunswick, 1988), p. 57.

180. **literary enthusiasts for labor . . . were novel:** Compare Michael Denning, who agrees on the absence of writer friends before the 1910s but views the Greenwich Village left as "only a harbinger" of the literary solidarities of the Popular Front in the 1930s (*The Cultural Front: The Laboring of American Culture in the Twentieth Century* [New York, 1996], p. 3).

families subsisting on bread, molasses, and beans: Kornbluh, *Rebel Voices*, p. 6; Dubovsky, *We Shall Be All*, ch. 10; William Cahn, *Lawrence 1912: The Bread and Roses Strike* (New York, 1977); Ardis Cameron, "Bread and Roses Revisited: Women's Culture and Working-Class Activism in the Lawrence Strike of 1912," *Women's Work and Protest: A Century of U.S. Women's Labor History*, ed. Ruth Milkman (New York, 1985). Van Gosse makes extremely interesting observations about the impact of Lawrence in "Paterson 1913," *Radical History Review* 48 (1990): 174. On the Lawrence strike, see also Gerald Sider's "Cleansing History" and my "Response" in *Radical History Review* 65 (1996).

181. **"the brotherhood of man":** Richard Washburn Child, "The Industrial Revolt at Lawrence: Where the American Melting Pot Has Boiled Over," *Collier's*, Mar. 9, 1912, p. 13.

"The Lawrence strike touched": Walter Lippmann, *A Preface to Politics* (New York, 1913), p. 208. For coverage, see Vorse, "The Trouble at Lawrence," *Harper's Weekly*, Mar. 16, 1912, p. 10; Ray Stannard Baker, "The Revolutionary Strike," *American*, Sept. 1912, p. 3019; Child, "Industrial Revolt." An interesting contrast can be drawn to the Pullman strike, where the absence of any contingent of sympathetic writers left unchallenged the conservative Chicago papers' representation of the strikers as bloodthirsty anarchists (Sklar, *Florence Kelley*, pp. 272–73).

the first strike to attract sympathetic coverage: At the trial of Wobbly leaders in 1907 for the murder of Frank Steunenberg, the former governor of Idaho, the papers were more or less hostile. At McKee's Rock, Pennsylvania, three years earlier—the big IWW strike that preceded Lawrence—steelworkers were treated to the usual newspaper condemnations, moderated only by the mildly sympathetic investigations of social conditions published by one progressive magazine, *Survey* (Dubovsky, *We Shall Be All*, pp. 204–06). The late J. Anthony Lukas confirmed to me from his research that the IWW in its trials and strikes before Lawrence made little or no effort to reach out to sympathetic journalists (personal communication, July 28, 1995). See Lukas, *Big Trouble: A Murder in a Small Western Town Sets Off a Struggle for the Soul of America* (New York, 1997), on the Steunenberg trial, where the lack of sympathetic coverage is striking.

"Gentle, alert, brave men": Reed to Eddy Hunt, quoted in Rosenstone, *Romantic Revolutionary*, p. 121. I owe my understanding of the shifting valence of IWW manliness to David Kirkpatrick, "Knights and Wobblies: The Gender of Radical Labor at the Turn of the Century," seminar paper, Princeton University, 1991. Dubovsky discusses the image of the cutthroat saboteur in *We Shall Be All*, p. 146.

"The working class and the employing class": Quoted in Kornbluh, *Rebel Voices*, p. 12. The IWW position derived from European syndicalists' sharp distinction between workers and intellectuals, motivated by their dislike of the ideologues and lumbering bureaucracy of the German Social Democrats (Fink, *Progressive Intellectuals*, pp. 127–29).

182. **"It was a wonderful strike":** Haywood, *Bill Haywood's Book*, p. 255. For Haywood's changing views of intellectuals, see Golin, *Fragile Bridge*, pp. 119–20, 174.

"the greatest victory in American labor": *International Socialist Review*, April 1912, p. 613.

"The question of 'Will the I.W.W. Grow?'" Quoted in Dubovsky, *We Shall Be All*, p. 260. The burst of organizing is also described there and in David Kirkpatrick, "Gender in the Industrial Workers of the World: Jane Street and Denver's Rebel Housemaids," senior thesis, Princeton University, 1992.

183. **the arrival of the Lawrence children:** Dubovsky, *We Shall Be All*, pp. 250–52.

Writers and political intellectuals spoke at mass meetings: Upton Sinclair, Lincoln Steffens, William English Walling, Rose Pastor Stokes, and Inez Haynes Gillmore all churned out publicity material. A total of as many as ninety people from Manhattan were involved (Golin, *Fragile Bridge*, p. 164).

surely Mabel Dodge couldn't drive: Very few people knew how to drive in 1913 and even fewer women. Learning to drive a motorcar, in fact, became a daring feminist act, but to my knowledge Mabel Dodge hadn't done it yet.

"a new field of force": Golin, *Fragile Bridge*, p. 9.

the pageant in Madison Square Garden: Golin, *Fragile Bridge*; Linda Nochlin, "The Paterson Strike Pageant of 1913." Robert Edmond Jones went on to become a successful set designer. On Max Reinhardt's spectacles, see J. L. Styan, *Max Reinhardt* (Cambridge, Eng., 1982).

184. **"In the future"**: Luhan, *Movers and Shakers*, p. 206.
   the Mesabi Range: Dubofsky, *We Shall Be All*, p. 326.
   The McNamara brothers: There is much about the trial in the Field/Wood Collection at the Huntington Library, since Field covered the trial for an Oregon journal and Wood was present as a legal observer. On the Mooney trial, see Richard H. Frost, *The Mooney Case* (Stanford, 1968).
185. **"His understanding of the peon soldiers"**: Cook, "New York Letter," *Chicago Evening Post*, May 1, 1914.
186. **"I am a Personage in here"**: Reed to Eddy Hunt, quoted in Rosenstone, *Romantic Revolutionary*, p. 121.
   "I see the *American*'s circulation booming": Bobby Rogers, quoted in Rosenstone, *Romantic Revolutionary*, p. 122.
187. **Reed's writing was prosaic**: Christopher Wilson, "Broadway Nights," *Prospects* 13 (1988): 280–84.
   socialist-tinged *Metropolitan*: Sonya Levin, a socialist and feminist born on the Lower East Side and a habitué of the Village, was managing editor. There are letters from Levin in the Rose Pastor Stokes Papers. On Whitney's takeover of the *Metropolitan*, see Hicks, *John Reed*, p. 112.
   Steffens vouched for Reed: The Harvard English professor Charles Copeland would also have enhanced Steffens's admiration, since Steffens had looked to Copeland's classes as a source of promising young writers since the days of the *Commercial*. Moreover, Steffens must have been feeling especially kindly toward Reed, since Reed was one of his few defenders in Greenwich Village when he returned to New York in disgrace after his unsavory involvement in the McNamara trial in Los Angeles in 1912. The deal that Steffens had worked out for the McNamara brothers— confessions in return for short sentences—aborted, resulting in convictions with long prison terms and a political debacle in Los Angeles. The labor movement lost tremendously in public support, and the promising socialist candidate in the mayoral election went down in defeat (Rosenstone, *Romantic Revolutionary*, p. 88).
   Trailed by Mabel Dodge: For the Dodge-Reed affair at this stage, see Rudnick, *Mabel Dodge Luhan*, pp. 91–98. Reed's letter (to Eddy Hunt) about Mabel's hunting jacket is quoted in Rosenstone, *Romantic Revolutionary*, p. 151.
188. **"One could see the square, gray adobe houses"**: John Reed, *Insurgent Mexico* (New York, 1914), p. 60.
189. **"It's so much Reed"**: Carb, quoted in Rosenstone, *Romantic Revolutionary*, p. 167.
   "I read Jack Reed's Mexico": Leo Stein, quoted in Luhan, *Movers and Shakers*, p. 425.
   In reality, Villa's army: *Encyclopedia of Latin American History and Culture*, vol. 4, ed. Barbara A. Tenenbaum (New York, 1996); James D. Cockcroft, *Mexico: Class Formation, Capital Accumulation, and the State* (New York, 1983), esp. pp. 104, 125; Alan Knight, *The Mexican Revolution*, vol. 2 (New York, 1986), pp. 115–29; Jim Tuck, *Pancho Villa and John Reed: Two Faces of Romantic Revolution* (Tucson, 1984); Bobbie Ferguson and George Agogino, *Tracing John Reed's 1914 Desert Route: The Haciendas* (Portales, 1979); Friedrich Katz, *The Life and Times of Pancho Villa* (Stanford, 1998).

191. **"A dreadful, an eerie town"**: Isaac Babel, *1920 Diary*, ed. Carol J. Avins, trans. H. T. Willetts (New Haven, 1995), pp. 69–70 (entry for 18 Aug. 1920). See Avins's fine introduction. Babel, of course, made his own generic choices when he transposed the diary material into the stories of *Red Cavalry*, choices made far more acute by the politics of Bolshevik publishing.

     "A painful two hours": Ibid., pp. 36–37 (entry for 25 July 1920).

     "Your first two articles": Lippmann to Reed, March 25, 1914, Reed Papers (bMS Am 1091[568]).

192. **"pen pictures"**: Katherine Hoyt to Reed, March 21, [1914?], Reed Papers (bMS Am 1091[502]).

     The president of Reed's New York bank: A. S. Frissell, president of Fifth Avenue Bank, to Reed, Apr. 27, 1914, Reed Papers (bMS Am 1091[444]).

     "Legendary John Reed": *New Republic*, Dec. 26, 1914, pp. 15–16. Amid the political uproar in downtown Manhattan over the unemployed and the Ludlow massacre, professional and political logic also sent Reed to Colorado, where he wrote an unusually crisp piece of investigative reporting on the strike for the *Metropolitan* ("The Colorado War," *Metropolitan*, July 1914, reprinted in *The Education of John Reed: Selected Writings*, ed. John Stuart [1955; Berlin, 1972], pp. 106–45). The events at Ludlow pushed the writer friend, for the first time, to expand the role into a political activism beyond writing. He joined a national committee to win support for the strike and took advantage of his celebrity status to speak publicly.

     For Reed's encounter with the president, see Rosenstone, *Romantic Revolutionary*, p. 176.

193. **"It seems to us"**: Macmillan firm, publishers, to Reed, July 18, 1916, Reed Papers (bMS Am 1091[588]).

     Leached of its "color": Reed complained to Carl Hovey that the revolution was losing its "color" and proposed that he leave the Villatistas to find the forces of Emiliano Zapata in the south, a band of mostly Indian rebels whose remote situation and ethnic exoticism seemed more promising. No American journalists had yet reached Zapata, and his story, Reed promised his editor, was bound to be "as marvelous as an Arabian Night" (Reed to Hovey, quoted in Rosenstone, *Romantic Revolutionary*, p. 163).

194. **"ghastly"**: Reed, quoted in Rosenstone, *Romantic Revolutionary*, p. 193.

     no American did succeed . . . until Hemingway: Paul Fussell, *The Great War and Modern Memory* (New York, 1975); David M. Kennedy, *Over Here: The First World War and American Society* (New York, 1980), pp. 213–30.

     Sympathy for England: See Steel, *Walter Lippmann*, ch. 8 for an account of the demographics of support for Britain during the war.

195. **"I have come to hate Europe"**: Reed, quoted in Rosenstone, *Romantic Revolutionary*, p. 213.

     "great stuff ahead": Ibid., p. 217.

     Sales were minuscule: Ibid., p. 245.

196. **"How far I have fallen"**: Reed to Bryant, July 15, 1917, Reed Papers (bMS Am 1091[78]).

     "desperate grind": Ibid., June 28, 1917 (bMS Am 1091[68–69]).

     "I realize how disappointed": Ibid., July 10, 1917 (bMS Am 1091[75–76]).

He planned to go: "Harvard Alumni Association," Jan. 20, 1917, Reed Papers (bMS Am 1091[476a]).

197. **Max Eastman and a socialite friend:** Eastman, *Love and Revolution*, p. 63. Bryant could get credentials—although probably not her passage paid—from a syndicate, but Reed couldn't.

198. **"She was so unbelievably beautiful":** Eunice Tietjens, *The World at My Shoulder* (New York, 1938), p. 66.

199. **"life to her was a rapidly taunting mixture":** Bodenheim, *Blackguard*, pp. 137–38.

    the finest collection of modern writing: Even as William Carlos Williams blasted contemporary poetry magazines, he gave the *Little Review* a nod of respect: "Margaret Anderson is the only one of them all who gets up a magazine which is not a ragbag" ("Belly Music," *Others*, July 1919). See also Holly A. Baggett, "Aloof from Natural Laws: Margaret C. Anderson and the *Little Review*, 1914–29," Ph.D. dissertation, University of Delaware, 1992; Abby Ann Arthur Johnson, "The Personal Magazine: Margaret C. Anderson and the *Little Review*, 1914–29," *South Atlantic Quarterly* 73 (1976): 351–63; Susan Noyes Platt, "The *Little Review*: Early Years and Avant-Garde Ideas."

    her political allegiances dropped away: During World War II in France, she fled the German advance along with her dying lover, Georgette Leblanc. Although opposed to the Nazis and capable of small gestures of defiance, she had no ties to the Resistance. See the second volume of her memoirs, *The Fiery Fountains* (New York, 1951).

200. **"the higher joys":** Anderson, *My Thirty Years' War*, p. 9.

    "Life is a glorious performance": "Announcement," *Little Review*, Mar. 1914, p. 1.

201. **"Our point of view":** *Little Review*, Mar. 1914, p. 1.

202. **criticized a Chicago literary critic:** "Editorial," *Little Review*, May 1915, p. 36; Lucian Cary, "Literary Journalism in Chicago," *Little Review*, June–July 1915, p. 1.

    "Why didn't someone shoot": Margaret Anderson, "Toward Revolution," *Little Review*, Dec. 1915, p. 5.

    "We can not weather all this gold": H. D., "Late Spring," *Little Review*, Jan.–Feb. 1916, p. 1.

    If you'd ever felt: "Announcement," *Little Review*, Mar. 1914, p. 1.

203. **identification of femininity with bourgeois mediocrity:** Burke, *Becoming Modern*, p. 168; Lisa Tickner, "Men's Work? Masculinity and Modernism," *differences: A Journal of Feminist Cultural Studies* 4 (Winter 1992): 2–24.

204. **"Everyone who came to the studio":** Anderson, *My Thirty Years' War*, p. 74.

    "I have no place in the world": Ibid., p. 4.

    "higher journalism": Rubin, *Making of Middlebrow Culture*, p. 15.

    "A great many of the people": *Little Review*, July 1914, p. 67.

    "As for you, haughty young woman": Letter from the Rev. A.D.R., Chicago, *Little Review*, Nov. 1914, p. 69.

205. **"I like these IWW people a lot":** Anderson, "Mother Jones and Elizabeth Gurley Flynn," *Little Review*, Apr. 1915, p. 18.

206. **"We were considered heartless":** Anderson, *My Thirty Years' War*, p. 154.

Elsa von Freytag-Loringhoven: Watson, *Strange Bedfellows*, pp. 270–71; Anderson, *My Thirty Years' War*, pp. 179–82. Freytag-Loringhoven starred in a 1921 film made by Duchamp and Man Ray, *Elsa, Baroness von Freytag-Loringhoven, Shaves Her Pubic Hair*. Man Ray portrayed the barber (*Conspiratorial Laughter*, p. 25). Claude McKay encountered her in Berlin in the 1920s, poverty-stricken and selling newspapers on the streets (*Long Way from Home*, pp. 105, 241). Phillip Herring has pulled together most of the extant information in *Djuna*, pp. 112–17; see also the summary in Naumann, *Making Mischief*, p. 184. The expatriate Mary Butts's short story "The Master's Last Dancing," about an exhibitionistic woman in Paris who wears bizarre clothing, is clearly modeled on the baroness. The story appeared in the *New Yorker*, Mar. 30, 1998.

"will any of you who are overburdened with money": "Surprise!" *Little Review*, Apr. 1916, p. 25.

"It wasn't like a beginning": Anderson, *Thirty Years' War*, p. 145.

207. **"the most creative work":** "Surprise!" *Little Review*, Apr. 1916, p. 25.

"unbelievably pretentious": Lippmann, quoted in Steel, *Walter Lippmann*, p. 69. For the Pound/Quinn/Anderson relationship, see B. L. Reid, *The Man from New York: John Quinn and His Friends* (New York, 1968), and Stephen Watson's account, based on archival research in the Quinn Papers, in *Strange Bedfellows*, pp. 342–48.

Pound's relationship to the female avant-garde: Ronald Bush provides a complex interpretation in his introduction to the Pound section in *Gender of Modernism*, ed. Scott, pp. 353–57. A general discussion of the "fear of emasculation" in high-modernist circles is in Gilbert and Gubar, *No Man's Land*, p. 42.

"sugar teat optimism": Pound, quoted in Watson, *Strange Bedfellows*, p. 310. "Widows and spinsters" is Pound's description of the editor Harriet Monroe and her readers (quoted in Reid, *Man from New York*, p. 286). See also Jayne Marek, *Women Editing Modernism: Little Magazines and Literary History* (Lexington, 1995), p. 188. Marek provides a judicious treatment of Pound and his relations with women of letters in chapter 3 (on Anderson) and chapter 6 (on Pound).

one English journal edited by feminists: The *Freewoman*, edited by Dora Marsden and Rebecca West, which Pound converted to the *Egoist*.

208. **"The spirit of the old *Little Review*":** Letter to the Editor, *Little Review*, Sept. 1917, pp. 31–33.

"When I compare the first year": Letter to the Editor, *Little Review*, Dec. 1918, p. 64.

"his vituperations": Lola Ridge, Letter to the Editor, *Little Review*, ibid., p. 63.

"Vive the anarchists!": Anderson, *Thirty Years' War*, p. 174.

cheeky . . . Too damn fresh: Pound and Quinn, in Baggett, "Aloof from Natural Laws," p. 257.

209. **the doomed generation of golden young men:** Despite the elegiac veil that his friends cast over his memory in the 1920s, it was Reed, not Bourne, who made it into the American pantheon of tragic youth. Perhaps this is because Bourne was physically disabled; certainly his deformities have made historians and chroniclers reluctant to treat him as anything except

pure mind, so that he is almost unknown today, a man for the historians of ideas. Or perhaps it is because his work and politics did not lend themselves, after his death, to any institutional sponsor, as Reed's books and life lent themselves to the Communist Party.

On Bourne, see the authoritative biography by Clayton, *Forgotten Prophet;* the introduction to *The World of Randolph Bourne,* ed. Lillian Schlissel (New York, 1965); Louis Filler, *Randolph Bourne* (Washington, D.C., 1943); John Adam Moreau, *Randolph Bourne: Legend and Reality* (Washington, D.C., 1966); Christopher Lasch, "Randolph Bourne and the Experimental Life," *New Radicalism;* Casey Nelson Blake, *Beloved Community: The Cultural Criticism of Randolph Bourne, Van Wyck Brooks, Waldo Frank, and Lewis Mumford* (Chapel Hill, 1990); and Michael Walzer, "The War and Randolph Bourne," *Company of Critics.*

neither could he project himself into . . . reportage: Bourne to Alyse Gregory, Feb. 16, 1914, *Letters,* ed. Sandeen, p. 221.

210. **"a strategic elite":** Bender, *New York Intellect,* p. 227. Scholars have generally stated that Beard offered Bourne the job, but Dorothy Teall, a friend who planned to write a biography, uncovered more confusing evidence (Teall to Agnes de Lima, n.d., "148 East Forty-eighth Street, New York City," Bourne Papers). A letter from Charles Beard to Bourne (May 15, 1914, Bourne Papers) supports the first interpretation.

211. **"who talk with a bravado":** Bourne to Carl Zigrosser, Nov. 16, 1913, *Letters,* ed. Sandeen, pp. 174–75.

"sound and disinterested thinking": The *New Republic*'s credo was published in the first issue, Nov. 7, 1914.

"a more spacious order of living": Walter Lippmann, quoted in Steel, *Walter Lippmann,* p. 63. For the *New Republic,* see Steel, *Walter Lippmann,* ch. 7; Wertheim, *New York Little Renaissance,* pp. 167–72. On Hackett, see Dell, *Homecoming,* pp. 194–95. Bender discusses Croly's background in *New York Intellect,* p. 223.

"We have got to be thoroughly critical": Herbert Croly to Bourne, Sept. 15, 1914, Bourne Papers.

212. **The magazine seemed a charmed circle:** Bourne to Prudence Winterrowd, Jan. 19, 1915, *Letters,* ed. Sandeen, p. 287.

the choicest books went to more powerful editors: A close look at the pattern of Bourne's publications in the *New Republic* suggests that he tried to publish a longer essay along with two short reviews every month. Many of these essays went unpublished, he complained to friends. A list of publications is appended to *The Radical Will,* ed. Hansen, pp. 541–45.

The Gary schools: Clayton, *Forgotten Prophet,* pp. 144–46.

213. **"It would be so glorious":** Bourne to Alyse Gregory, Dec. 1, 1914, *Letters,* ed. Sandeen, p. 278.

two books: *The Gary Schools* (Boston, 1916) and *Education and Living* (New York, 1917).

"a fearful thing": Bourne to Elizabeth Shepley Sergeant, Sept. 23, 1915, *Letters,* ed. Sandeen, p. 333.

214. **the special 1915 supplement:** "Votes for Women," supplement, *New Republic,* Oct. 9, 1915. The supplement was written by Charles Beard,

Lippmann, Croly, Frances Hackett, Alvin Johnson, and Walter Weyl. See Bourne to Elizabeth Shepley Sergeant, Oct. 10, 1915, *Letters*, ed. Sandeen, p. 339.

"Its coming ... always gives": Bourne to Alyse Gregory, July 24, 1915, *Letters*, ed. Sandeen, p. 312.

"a book one would have given": Bourne to Dorothy Teall, June 14, 1915, *Letters*, ed. Sandeen, p. 303.

"nothing at all of permanence": Bourne to Elizabeth Shepley Sergeant, June 25, 1915, *Letters*, ed. Sandeen, p. 306.

"suave and discreet disapproval": Bourne to Elizabeth Shepley Sergeant, Nov. 15, 1915, *Letters*, ed. Sandeen, p. 344.

215. **"We stand at the threshold":** Walter Lippmann, quoted in Rodgers, *Atlantic Crossings*, p. 279.

"with the idea of themselves controlling the war-technique": Bourne, quoted in Desley Deacon, *Elsie Clews Parsons: Inventing Modern Life* (Chicago, 1997), p. 181.

antiwar essay: "A Glance at German Culture," *Lippincott's Monthly*, Feb. 7, 1915, pp. 22–27.

"I have become": Bourne to Elizabeth Shepley Sergeant, Oct. 10, 1915, *Letters*, ed. Sandeen, p. 339.

his salary diminished: Bourne to Elizabeth Shepley Sergeant, Sept. 20, 1916, *Letters*, ed. Sandeen, p. 375.

216. **"I really thirst for fame":** Ibid.

"beloved community": "Trans-National America," *Atlantic Monthly*, July 1916, reprinted in *The Radical Will*, ed. Hansen, p. 264. See Blake, *Beloved Community*; Sara Evans, *Personal Politics: The Roots of Women's Liberation in the Civil Rights Movement* (New York, 1979); Charles Marsh, *God's Long Summer: Stories of Faith and Civil Rights* (New York, 1997).

217. **"To make real this striving":** Ibid.

John Dewey's influence: In an early essay Dewey argued that "democracy means that *personality* is the first and final reality" (quoted in Blake, *Beloved Community*, p. 87; see also the introduction).

"radical pet": Bourne to Elsie Clews Parsons, quoted in Deacon, *Elsie Clews Parsons*, p. 169.

218. **"merely stagy":** "Traps for the Unwary," *Dial*, Mar. 28, 1918.

"Why in the world do you (and I) fiddle around": Bourne to Alyse Gregory [late Oct. 1916], *Letters*, ed. Sandeen, p. 381.

"I am coming to think": Bourne to Esther Cornell, Aug. 10, 1917, *Letters*, ed. Sandeen, p. 401.

"When I get away": Bourne to Alyse Gregory, Nov. 10, 1916, *Letters*, ed. Sandeen, p. 382.

219. **"This should have been the soil":** Bourne to Alyse Gregory [Jan. 1917], *Letters*, ed. Sandeen, p. 394.

a Village community: Bourne's circle included Elsie Clews Parsons, Elizabeth Sergeant, and Frances Anderson—all writers from the *New Republic*—Esther Cornell (his lover—a Bryn Mawr graduate and actress), Agnes de Lima (a Vassar graduate and educational reformer). See the moving account of Bourne's friendship and conversation with Parsons in Deacon, *Elsie Clews Parsons*, ch. 9.

Seven Arts: See Sandeen's notes on *Seven Arts* and Bourne's other new venue, the *Dial*, in *Letters*, pp. 351–58; see also Blake, *Beloved Community*.

"The brighter color of a new day": James Oppenheim to Waldo Frank (1916), quoted in Wertheim, *New York Little Renaissance*, p. 174. Although the editors and many of their writers (including Van Wyck Brooks, Paul Rosenfeld, and Louis Untermeyer) moved in Village circles, they pointedly set up shop at a remove from the downtown scene, in offices on Madison Avenue on the East Side.

"You wouldn't allow me": Oppenheim, "Story of the *Seven Arts*," p. 163.

220. **"by which middle-class radicalism":** Randolph Bourne, "The Price of Radicalism," *New Republic*, Mar. 1916, reprinted in *The Radical Will*, ed. Hansen, p. 299.

"a sort of angelic wrestle": Dorothy Teall to Agnes de Lima, n.d., Bourne Papers.

"that tireless research": Dorothy Teall, "Bourne into Myth," *Bookman*, Oct. 1932, p. 599.

"Though he was to so large an extent": Gregory, *Day Is Gone*, p. 135.

"having led the experimental life": Bourne to Alyse Gregory, Nov. 19, 1916, *Letters*, ed. Sandeen, p. 385.

221. **the "laboring" of American culture:** Denning, Introduction, *Cultural Front*.

222. **"A man like Randolph Bourne":** Lasch, *New Radicalism*, p. 102.

7/SEXUAL MODERNISM

225. **"When the world began":** Hapgood, *Victorian in the Modern World*, p. 152.

"The awakening and liberation of women": Max Eastman, Editorial, *Masses*, Jan. 1913, p. 5.

"the removal of the barriers": Langner, *Magic Curtain*, p. 68. Langner was the impresario of downtown theater and a Liberal Club member.

226. **"Feminism is going to make":** Floyd Dell, "Feminism for Men," *Masses*, July 1914, p. 19.

explicit antipathy to women: See Gilbert and Gubar's *War of the Words* and *Sexchanges;* also Scott, *Gender of Modernism*, and Tickner, "Men's Work." A reformulation of the questions that have dominated feminist analysis can be found in Maria DiBattista's introduction to *High and Low Moderns: Literature and Culture, 1889–1939*, ed. DiBattista and Lucy McDiarmid (New York, 1996).

227. **"Feminism Will Give—Men More Fun":** *Delineator*, July 1914, p. 17.

the French *féminisme*: Nancy F. Cott, *The Grounding of Modern Feminism* (New Haven, 1987), p. 14. On feminism in these years, I have relied on Cott; Ellen Carol Dubois, "Working Women, Class Relations, and Suffrage Militance: Harriot Stanton Blatch and the New York Woman Suffrage Movement, 1894–1909," *Unequal Sisters*, ed. Vicki L. Ruiz and Ellen Carol Dubois (New York, 1994), pp. 228–46; Dubois, *Harriot Stanton Blatch and the Winning of Woman Suffrage* (New Haven, 1997); Mari Jo Buhle, *Women and American Socialism*. Cf. Joan Wallach Scott on a similar individualist strain in French feminism (*Only Paradoxes to Offer: French Feminists and the Rights of Man* [Cambridge, Mass., 1996], ch. 5).

228. **"so new":** This quotation and the others are all in Cott, *Grounding*, pp. 13–15.

   "All feminists are suffragists": Ibid., p. 15.

   "To me it seemed the big fight": Eastman, *Enjoyment of Living*, p. 306.

   New York was a hotbed of suffragism: Dubois, "Working Women," p. 237; Dubois, *Harriot Stanton Blatch*, ch. 4.

229. **"Polite up-town rich ladies":** Vorse, quoted in Cott, *Grounding*, p. 33.

   Ettie Stettheimer: Margaret Barry, "The Brontës of Manhattan," *Barnard*, Fall 1995, pp. 24–25.

   Wage Earners' League for Woman Suffrage: Orleck, *Common Sense and a Little Fire*, pp. 96–97.

   Men's League for Woman Suffrage: Eastman, *Enjoyment of Living*, pp. 306–08.

   "The question of sex equality": Max Eastman, Editorial, *Masses*, Jan. 1913, p. 5.

   "a mob of women trooping": John Reed writes about the Harvard Men's League for Woman Suffrage in "Harvard Renaissance," pp. 57, 62, 71.

   participation in suffrage was pretty much de rigueur: See the bills for mass meetings at Cooper Union in 1914 reproduced in Cott, *Grounding*, p. 12; see also Lingeman, *Theodore Dreiser*, vol. 2, p. 153.

231. **"half-way through the door":** *New York Evening Sun*, Feb. 17, 1917.

   "They are all social workers": Randolph Bourne to Prudence Winterrowd, Apr. 28, 1913, *Letters*, ed. Sandeen, p. 82. The Bourne/Winterrowd correspondence is fascinating for what it reveals of literary relations between periphery and center as well as of Bourne's complex relationships with women. Winterrowd was no slouch, and her retrospective musings on their letters, available in the Bourne Papers, Columbia University, are affecting in what they show of a middle-class woman's efforts to remake herself in the early century far away from the resources of college or the East Coast.

232. **the brainy young women:** Gluck, *Georg Lukács*, pp. 37–42; Pawel, *Nightmare of Reason*, passim. For the fin-de-siècle women, see Suzanne Keegan, *The Bride of the Wind. The Life and Times of Alma Mahler-Werfel* (London, 1991). Examples can be added: the German Jewish poet Else Lasker-Schüler, whose career was inseparable from her deep associations with men, and Mina Loy, who began her life as an artist in the Munich circle in the 1890s and observed several of these legendary femmes fatales from a distance. See Hans W. Cohn, *Else Lasker-Schüler: the Broken World* (London, 1974); Burke, *Becoming Modern*, ch. 3; Robert Michels, "On the Sociology of Bohemia and Its Connections to the Intellectual Proletariat," *Catalyst* 15 (1983): 1–25.

   "dingy" England: Randolph Bourne to Alyse Gregory, Oct. 11, 1913, *Letters*, ed. Sandeen, p. 160.

   "The educated daughters": Ibid., Nov. 1, 1913, p. 166.

   But nowhere in Europe: The intellectual underpinnings of the distrust and fear of women were provided by Otto Weininger's *Sex and Character* (1903), tremendously influential in Europe but much less so in the United States. Weininger's images of woman influenced the circle around Wyndham Lewis in Britain and the Italian Futurists around Marinetti (Gilbert and Gubar, *No Man's Land*, p. 22).

233. **"In this age of feminist aspirations":** Louis Fraina, quoted in Daly, *Done into Dance*, p. 162.
 "it is the setting of mothers free": Floyd Dell, *Women as World Builders: Studies in Modern Feminism* (Chicago, 1913), pp. 9, 104.
234. **The preoccupation with the self:** Nancy Cott contrasts the feminist idealization of personality with the mainstream construction of personality as people-pleasing (*Grounding*, p. 296, n. 40).
 "Masculine brutalities and egotisms": Randolph Bourne to Prudence Winterrowd, Apr. 28, 1913, *Letters*, ed. Sandeen, p. 82.
 birth control: Linda Gordon, *Woman's Body, Woman's Right: A Social History of Birth Control in America* (New York, 1977), chs. 9–10; Chesler, *Woman of Valor*; Constance Chen, *"The Sex Side of Life": Mary Ware Dennett's Pioneering Battle for Birth Control and Sex Education* (New York, 1996).
235. **Michael Higgins:** Sanger, *Autobiography*, pp. 12ff.; Chesler, *Woman of Valor*, ch. 1.
236. **a neo-Malthusian conference:** Goldman, *Living My Life*, vol. 1, pp. 268–73.
 popular working-class interest: Gordon, *Woman's Body*, p. 229.
237. **the "Rebel Girl":** See Baxandall's introduction to *Words on Fire*. Flynn titled her autobiography *The Rebel Girl*.
 the dance halls and nickelodeons: Kathy Peiss, *Cheap Amusements: Working Women and Leisure in Turn-of-the-Century New York* (Philadelphia, 1986).
238. **"look the whole world in the face":** Quoted in Chesler, *Woman of Valor*, p. 98.
 "The right to be lazy": Ibid., p. 99.
239. **A luminous Carnegie Hall meeting:** Sanger later complained that she received no support from the Village radicals, but this was not the case (*Autobiography*, pp. 186–87). Dell mentions the response to the *Masses* advocacy in *Homecoming*, p. 252; see also Gordon, *Woman's Body*, p. 232.
 shlepping bags of food: Chesler, *Woman of Valor*, p. 156.
 In 1917, Sanger was on her way: Ibid., pp. 161–62. As one of her last acts in association with the intellectuals, Sanger starred as herself in a silent movie about birth control supported with money from Mary Ware Dennett's organization (Rose Pastor Stokes, too, tried to turn her involvement into scripts that she peddled in Hollywood). See letters to Stokes from various producers (Jan. 21, Aug. 1, Nov. 6, Nov. 24, 1916, Stokes Papers).
241. **"hellhole of free love":** William Sanger, quoted in Chesler, *Woman of Valor*, p. 91.
 Bill Shatoff: Ben Reitman spoke of the "Radical Jews" who owned copies and of the pamphlet's being translated into "Jewish" (Gordon, *Woman's Body*, p. 218).
 "As human beings we must have work": Dubois, "Working Women," pp. 233–34.
242. **27 percent of the workforce was female:** Yellowitz, *Labor and the Progressive Movement*, p. 43. For the garment strikes, see Orleck, *Common Sense*, pp. 57, 77–78.
 Elizabeth Gurley Flynn: Golin, *Fragile Bridge*, pp. 124–26; Kirkpatrick, "Knights and Wobblies"; Elizabeth Gurley Flynn, *The Rebel Girl: An Autobiography. My First Life, 1906–1926*, 2nd ed. (New York, 1973), p. 280.
243. **the Freewoman:** Dell, *Women as World Builders*, p. 104.

"women adrift": Joanne J. Meyerowitz, *Women Adrift: Independent Wage Earners in Chicago, 1880–1930* (Chicago, 1988), p. 115.

Middle-class feminists . . . idealized young workingwomen: Dye, *As Equals and as Sisters: Feminism, the Labor Movement, and the Women's Trade Union League of New York* (Columbia, 1980), pp. 55–56.

"a way of life and a soul": Quoted in Buhle, *Dreamer's Paradise*, p. 82. The recognition of shared struggles broke with traditional views of working-women on both the right and left, which stressed the debilitating effects of wage earning and work in the world on women's future roles as wives and mothers (Orleck, *Common Sense*, p. 78).

"Working girls have a chance": "Women Workers," *Weekly Bulletin of the Clothing Trades* (1906), quoted in Dye, *As Equals*, p. 56; see also Penelope A. Emily Harper, "Investigating the Working Woman: Middle-Class Americans and the Debate over Women's Wage Work, 1820–1920," Ph.D. dissertation, State University of New York at Binghamton, 1997, p. 153.

"a poor working-girl": Anderson, *My Thirty Years' War*, p. 33.

244. **"She had seen no romance":** Day, *Long Loneliness*, pp. 46–47.

   a woman from Australia: Eastman, *Enjoyment of Living*, p. 297.

   Jessie Ashley: Ashley died during the influenza epidemic of 1918–19 at her home on the Upper East Side. She ran as a socialist for a New York judge-ship in 1912. A practitioner of direct action, she was arrested for distribut-ing birth control information and, in 1917, for refusing to stand during the singing of the "Star-Spangled Banner." She headed the support committee at Paterson. Mary Heaton Vorse wrote of her, "She had a clear, fearless mind which permitted no middle course" (obituary in *New York Times*, Jan. 22, 1919; Sanger, *Autobiography*, p. 71; Golin, *Fragile Bridge*; Vorse, *Footnote*, p. 57).

   Crystal Eastman: Introduction to *Crystal Eastman: On Women and Revolution*, ed. Blanche Wiesen Cook (New York, 1978).

   Ida Rauh: Information comes from her obituary in the *New York Times*, Mar. 12, 1970, enrollment records at the NYU law school archives, and an interview with the then-elderly Rauh that June Sochen utilized for *The New Woman in Greenwich Village*, p. 17. A newspaper clipping about Rauh's British experiences is in the Ida Rauh Eastman Collection, University of Wyoming. Rauh told Sochen that she never practiced law because, after a spell working in surrogate court for the Legal Aid Society, she found it meant fraternizing with Tammany Hall hacks.

245. **female lawyers had great difficulty practicing their profession:** The diffi-culty persisted into the 1960s; see Linda K. Kerber, *No Constitutional Right to Be Ladies* (New York, 1999).

   women in the professions: Cott, *Grounding*, p. 217; for a case study of the creation of new fields around gender difference, see Elizabeth Lunbeck on psychiatric social work, *The Psychiatric Persuasion* (Princeton, 1994).

   "could force their way into the professions": Gregory, *Day Is Gone*, p. 147.

   "really for women a golden age": Vorse, quoted in Garrison, *Mary Heaton Vorse*, p. 44.

246. **"New York was largely run by women":** Luhan, *Movers and Shakers*, p. 143. Compare Carroll Smith-Rosenberg, who observes that feminist mod-ernists wished "to free themselves completely from considerations of gen-

der, to be autonomous and powerful individuals, to enter the world as if they were men" ("The New Woman as Androgyne," p. 295).

In Margaret Anderson's account: Anderson, *My Thirty Years' War*, pp. 28–31.

"I wanted to go on picket lines": Day, *Long Loneliness*, p. 60. Day, writing as a religious ascetic after many years leading the Catholic Workers Movement, condemned her youthful desire: "How much ambition and how much self-seeking there was in all this."

"out to hurt their mother": Vorse, quoted in Garrison, *Mary Heaton Vorse*, p. 21.

247. **"Am I the Christian gentlewoman":** Genevieve Taggard, "Poet out of Pioneer," *These Modern Women*, ed. Showalter, p. 66. For Ann Douglas, the matricidal impulse is a prime mover of cultural history in the 1920s (*Terrible Honesty*, passim). See Deacon, *Elsie Clews Parsons*, pp. 14–15, on Parsons's view of the rebellion of the daughters.

Dorothy Day had grown up: Day, *Long Loneliness*, p. 38.

248. **"The rooms were large and well furnished":** Ibid., p. 57.

"they lacked the real economic and institutional power": Smith-Rosenberg, "New Woman," p. 296.

249. **marriage without a sexual charge:** A moving case from England is that of Beatrice Webb, who at great personal cost forswore a marriage to Joseph Chamberlain, whom she loved madly, for a prosaic but functional marriage to Sidney Webb (Nord, *Apprenticeship of Beatrice Webb*, pp. 96–103).

the release of female expression in work: Cott, *Grounding*, p. 41.

250. **the artist Man Ray and his lover:** The poet was Adon Lacroix. See Baldwin, *Man Ray*, pp. 39–40; *Conspiratorial Laughter*, pp. 5, 21; Avrich, *Modern School Movement*, pp. 159–60.

"the invention of heterosexuality": Jonathan Ned Katz, *The Invention of Heterosexuality* (New York, 1996).

a mecca for gay people: George Chauncey, *Gay New York: Gender, Urban Culture, and the Making of the Gay Male World, 1890–1940* (New York, 1994), ch. 9.

mentions . . . were heavily coded: A Harvard friend joked, for instance, that theater director Lee Simonson used ten different kinds of hair perfume. Bobby Rodgers to John Reed, June 1913, Reed Papers (bMS Am 1091[754]).

"warm friendships for other men": Luhan, *Movers and Shakers*, p. 45. For Van Vechten's marriage to Fania Marinoff, see *Letters of Carl Van Vechten*, ed. Kellner. When Van Vechten was in the epistolary company of other gay people, he was pretty close to explicit about his sexual life. After reading *Tender Buttons*, he wrote to Gertrude Stein, "the last part refers, I am sure, to things you and I do very well indeed" (*Letters*, p. 11). Florine Stettheimer painted an enchanting portrait of a queenly Van Vechten in his apartment in 1922.

251. **"Sex was never much":** McKay, *Long Way from Home*, p. 245. McKay got to the United States because a patron, a wealthy white gentleman in Jamaica, paid for his education. It appears that the two were lovers, although there is no conclusive evidence. McKay's attempt to create an ingenuous, Pan-like eros in his autobiography is reminiscent of Langston Hughes. See

Wayne F. Cooper, *Claude McKay: Rebel Sojourner in the Harlem Renaissance* (Baton Rouge, 1987).

Sophisticated people aimed to share: Christina Simmons, "Companionate Marriage and the Lesbian Threat," *Frontiers* 4 (Fall 1979): 54–59; Ellen Kay Trimberger, "Feminism, Men, and Modern Love: Greenwich Village, 1900–1925," *Powers of Desire: The Politics of Sexuality*, ed. Ann Snitow, Christine Stansell, Sharon Thompson (New York, 1983), pp. 132–33.

"I could not imagine a love affair": Sara Bard Field to C. E. S. Wood, May 8, 1913, Field/Wood Collection.

252. **"He is quite inspired by us":** Louise Bryant to John Reed, June 12, [1916], Reed Papers (bMS Am 1091[242]).

"The girl was clever": Luhan, *Movers and Shakers*, p. 421.

253. **"She asks for life":** Sara Bard Field to C. E. S. Wood, Feb. 6, 1916, Field/Wood Collection.

"It is experience": Ibid., Jan. 9, 1916.

"Sarah, our relationship": Louise Bryant to Sara Bard Field, June 16, 1916, Field/Wood Collection.

"my people are in no way": Louise Bryant to John Reed, June 9, 1917, Reed Papers (bMS Am 1091[262]).

"I only want my honey": Ibid., Apr. 6, 1919 (bMS Am 1091[289–90]).

254. **"China is going to be":** Ibid., Dec. 9, 1916 (bMS Am 1091[259]).

255. **"Just wait until we get well":** Ibid., Dec. 9, 1916. Mabel Dodge created in her memoirs an image of a Bryant who continuously resented and undermined Reed for his superior gifts. "Oh, *you're* not so much," she has Bryant screeching at her husband (*Movers and Shakers*, pp. 419–22).

"to keep close to each other": Louise Bryant to John Reed, Dec. 2, 9, 1916, Reed Papers (bMS Am 1091[254–5, 259]).

"It will be so fine": Ibid., Dec. 9, 1916.

"*Be careful* what you *write now*": Ibid., July 2, 1917 (bMS Am 1091[269]).

256. **"soldiers, civilians":** Ibid.

Inez Haynes: Louise Bryant to John Reed, July 8, July 15, 1917. Mention of the Irwins' travels during the war, with Inez featured as an unnamed wife lacking any profession, are in Will Irwin's *The Making of a Reporter* (New York, 1942), p. 364. The British closed the front to all women journalists, and the French arranged only chaperoned tours of the rear (Irwin, *Making*, p. 341).

257. **"I am twenty-nine years old":** Reed, "Almost Thirty," pp. 124–44.

258. **"moved freely up and down the earth":** Vorse, quoted in Garrison, *Mary Heaton Vorse*, p. 78.

cooperative housekeeping: For the Village scheme, see Wertheim, *New York Little Renaissance*, p. 89; Sochen, *New Woman*, pp. 48–52.

259. **percentage of women in domestic service:** the proportion of servants in the female labor force declined from one-third in 1910 to one-fourth in 1930. Mary P. Ryan, *Womanhood in America*, 2nd ed. (New York, 1979), p. 187.

Grace Mott Johnson: Gardner, *"Friend and Lover,"* pp. 330, 337.

Floyd Dell: Dell, *Homecoming*, pp. 193, 198, 234.

Heterodoxy: Schwarz, *Radical Feminists*, p. 60. Divorces in the country as a whole in 1900–20 ran between four and eight per thousand marriages.

260. **"For the usual modern type"**: Crystal Eastman, "Marriage under Two Roofs," *Crystal Eastman*, ed. Cook, p. 81.

the Zorachs: Charlotte Streifer Rubinstein, *American Women Artists* (New York, 1982), pp. 172–76.

261. **"I begin to feel"**: Neith Boyce to Hutchins Hapgood, Apr. 13, 1899, Hapgood Family Papers.

"I wonder if putting as much energy": Ibid., c. 1901–05. Ellen Kay Trimberger has collected some of the correspondence in *Intimate Warriors*.

"She has no high shoes": Neith Boyce to Hutchins Hapgood, "Wed.—p.m." [1916?]; "Wednesday" [1915?]; "Sept. 6" [1907], "Champéry," Hapgood Family Papers. Mabel Dodge, a friend of both partners, had some tart observations on the inequities of the Hapgood household in Westchester. "Neith did nearly all the housework," she writes in *Movers*, p. 47.

263. **the Village apartment of Madeleine Doty**: Rauh, like Crystal Eastman, was rooted in the Village reform circles connected to the Lower East Side; her friends included the A Club resident Arthur Bullard; the artist Jo Davidson; Mary Field Parton, her best friend and fellow WTUL organizer, Helen Marot; and Marot's companion, Caroline Pratt, founder of a progressive private school (Eastman, *Love and Revolution*, p. 4; *Enjoyment of Living*, p. 342). Rauh is an occluded figure, recoverable through scattered—and almost unanimously glowing—recollections of her friends, an odd, mute archive of her poetry (the Ida Rauh Eastman Papers at the University of Wyoming), a few letters deposited in other collections, and Eastman's extended, unrelenting put-downs in his memoirs. Djuna Barnes knew her from the Provincetown Players and chose her as an enigmatic modernist character in one of her involuted sketches (Mary Lynn Broe, "Djuna Barnes," p. 22).

"Ida was a truant": Eastman, *Enjoyment of Living*, pp. 266–67.

264. **"dramatic and exciting"**: Ibid., pp. 354–56.

"NO 'MRS.' BADGE OF SLAVERY": Ibid., pp. 380–83; see also O'Neill, *Last Romantic*, p. 25.

265. **"noble-looking, like a lioness"**: Luhan, *Movers and Shakers*, p. 199.

But the ménage fell apart: On the disintegration of the marriage, see Eastman, *Enjoyment of Living*, pp. 360–64, 379, 388–94, 488, 519–21, 527 562, 572–73.

Isadora Duncan's young dancers: Irma Duncan, *Duncan Dancer: An Autobiography* (Middletown, 1965).

266. **failure to make good as a war reporter**: Eastman, *Enjoyment of Living*, p. 534.

"Why not refer to our marriage": Rauh, 1949, quoted in O'Neill, *Last Romantic*, p. 250.

left New York for New Mexico: For a time Rauh and Daniel Eastman lived with Andrew Dasburg, who also was a single parent, apparently having separated from Grace Mott Johnson. On Daniel Eastman and his father, see Eastman, *Enjoyment of Living*, pp. 576–77.

She "talks so tragically": Sara Bard Field to C. E. S. Wood, Jan. 2, 1916, Field/Wood Collection.

"Why is it that there seem": Ibid., July 15, 1915.

267. **"suppleness, inventiveness, erotic ambivalence"**: DiBattista, *High and Low Moderns*, p. 18.

"Please don't leave me": Randolph Bourne to Alyse Gregory, Jan. 1915 [?], *Letters*, ed. Sandeen, p. 283.

"You cannot think": Ibid., Dec. 1, 1914, p. 278; see also Bourne to Prudence Winterrowd, Nov. 3, 1913, p. 171.

268. **"As I read over your letter"**: Randolph Bourne to Alyse Gregory, Jan. 5, 1914, *Letters*, ed. Sandeen, p. 200.

"I don't like to hear": Ibid., July 24, 1915, p. 311.

269. **"uncomplicated and happy march"**: "Mon Amie," reprinted in *The Radical Will*, ed. Hansen, pp. 435–42.

"Karen": Ibid., pp. 443–47; see also "Suffrage and Josella" [1918?], *The Radical Will*, ed. Hansen, pp. 453–56. "Karen" was apparently Frances Lundquist, a writer and a member of the Patchin Place circle (Zigrosser, "Florence King," p. 100). "Josella" was almost certainly Alyse Gregory.

271. **"all of the girls"**: Dell, *Homecoming*, pp. 288.

the tramp: For Britain, see Nord, *Walking the Victorian Streets*, pp. 230–33; Tickner, "Men's Work?" pp. 9–17. For the United States, see Brevda, *Harry Kemp*, pp. 71–76, 114–20. Eastman describes his stint of tramping in *Enjoyment of Living*, ch. 24. Even in his later, politically conservative years, he relished being lumped by an editorialist in 1914 in a crowd of "professional hoboes" that included Pancho Villa and Frank Tannenbaum (*Enjoyment of Living*, p. 479). Wilson, *Labor of Words*, pp. 56–63, discusses the "popular naturalism" of tramping literature in the United States. For the IWW link, see *Rebel Voices*, ed. Kornbluh, p. 67. Kenneth S. Lynn, *Charlie Chaplin and His Times* (New York, 1997), discusses the newfound fascination (ch. 5). In 1914, Chaplin took his own poverty-stricken, dejected working-class childhood and refashioned it, dreamlike, into *The Tramp*, turning the hobo into an enchanting ideal, an object of fantasy and desire.

"homoerotic humanism": Fussell, *Great War*, p. 287. The homoerotic energies of left-wing writing are examined in Michael Moon, "Neglected Histories and Geographies of Oklahoma," paper presented at the Center for the Critical Analysis of Contemporary Culture, Rutgers University, Nov. 1994, p. 18.

272. **"I shall never forget the sensation"**: Dell, *Homecoming*, p. 233.

8/TALKING ABOUT SEX

273. **Truth telling and equality, not a church ceremony:** A version of this argument is in my "Talking about Sex: Early-Twentieth-Century Radicals and Moral Confessions," *Moral Problems in American Life: New Perspectives on Cultural History*, ed. Karen Halttunen and Lewis Perry (Ithaca, 1998), pp. 283–308.

274. **"nature of a crusade"**: Langner, *Magic Curtain*, p. 68.

"night by night": Dell, *Homecoming*, p. 289.

John Reed and Louise Bryant: Bryant to Reed, Dec. 9, 1916, Reed Papers (bMS Am 1091 [259]).

275. **you certainly could deplore women:** Quoted in Cott, *Grounding*, p. 43. For other objections to the "repeal of reticence," see Hale, *Freud and the Americans*, ch. 10.

to speak of female desire: The situation hampered Victoria Woodhull, the most outspoken American woman sex radical of the nineteenth century, who, even in her scandalous speeches, scarcely sounds different in her description of erotic pleasure from the coded language of novels.

276. **"They were free"**: D. H. Lawrence, *Lady Chatterley's Lover* (1928; Harmondsworth, 1961), pp. 6–7. Thanks to Nancy Cott for the reference.

a long political and intellectual tradition: Ellen Carol Dubois, "Feminism and Free Love," unpublished paper in my possession; Gordon, *Woman's Body*, ch. 5.

277. **"varietism"**: The most important nineteenth-century advocates were the residents of John Humphrey Noyes's Oneida colony, who practiced "complex marriage."

an anarchist/free-love commune: Charles Pierce Le Warne, *Utopias on Puget Sound, 1885–1915* (Seattle, 1975); Patricia Brandt, "Organized Free Thought in Oregon: The Oregon State Secular Union," *Oregon Historical Quarterly* 87 (Summer 1986): 176; Carlos A. Schwantes, "Free Love and Free Speech on the Pacific Northwest Frontier," *Oregon Historical Society Quarterly* 82 (Spring 1981): 271–93; Taylor Stoehr, "Introduction," *Free Love in America* (New York, 1979); Veysey, *Communal Experience*, pp. 39–43 and passim.

Elizabeth Gurley Flynn: Baxandall, *Words on Fire*, p. 6.

Djuna Barnes's father: Broe, "Djuna Barnes," p. 21. See Phillip Herring's account of Barnes's amazing free-love grandmother, a follower of Victoria Woodhull, in *Djuna*, chs. 1–3.

278. **Cook's sexual radicalism:** This is amply expressed throughout the Cook Papers; see also Humphrey, *Children of Fantasy*, pp. 95–102.

C. E. S. Wood: Wood served in the Nez Perce campaign of 1877. He was the officer who actually wrote down Chief Joseph's great speech of surrender. Biographical information is in Edwin R. Bingham, "Experiment in Launching a Biography: Three Vignettes of Charles Erskine Scott Wood," *Huntington Library Quarterly* 35 (May 1972): 221–39; Erskine Wood, *Life of C. E. S. Wood* (privately published, 1978; available at the Huntington Library).

"Sappho": Louise Bryant to John Reed, Dec. 29, 1915, Reed Papers (bMS Am 1091[237]).

279. **"great love" . . . "the pulsing thought"**: C. E. S. Wood to John Reed, Mar. 2, 1910, Reed Papers (bMS Am 1091[942]).

not very Victorian in their sexual lives: Christina Simmons, "Modern Sexuality and the Myth of Victorian Repression," *Passion and Power*, ed. Kathy Peiss and Simmons (Philadelphia, 1989), pp. 157–77.

280. **Naomi:** See Bercovici, *It's the Gypsy in Me.*

"we all talked free love": Edgar Lee Masters, *Across Spoon River* (New York, 1936), pp. 183–86. On Goldman and Berkman, see Wexler, *Emma Goldman*, p. 57.

In the Yiddish press: Buhle, *Women and American Socialism*, p. 261.

281. **Ethel Lebe:** Durant and Durant, *Dual Autobiography*, pp. 20–21.

"bully material": Hutchins Hapgood to Neith Boyce, Sept. 28, 1905, Hapgood Family Papers.

282. **"the hot-bed of the Middle West":** Hutchins Hapgood, *The Spirit of Labor* (New York, 1907), p. 12.

"sex novel": Hutchins Hapgood to Neith Boyce, Oct. 20, 1905, Hapgood Family Papers.

"the need to work and love": Hapgood, *Spirit of Labor*, p. 168.

283. **"Very anarchistic ideas":** Hutchins Hapgood to Neith Boyce, Oct. 9, 1905, Hapgood Family Papers.

puritanism: Gurstein, *Repeal of Reticence*, pp. 129–34.

tales of vulnerable women: Whatever the actualities of Marie's story, Hapgood's rendering of her coming-of-age partook of the highly sexualized understanding of single young workingwomen current in progressive social investigation, which saw promiscuity as a major social problem but attributed it to environmental rather than moral causes. Hardship, not innate depravity, produced in young girls an understandable "desire to taste pleasures, to escape into a world of congenial companionship," that usually ended disastrously, as Jane Addams succinctly stated the common view. Rescue required the intervention of sympathetic friends, be they settlement workers or decent, loving men, who provided hapless women with healthful pleasures and affinities: social clubs, respectable work, marriage, and family life (*Twenty Years at Hull House*, p. 245).

284. **He became something of a free lover himself:** The onset of the affair with Marie can be gleaned from Hapgood's letters to Boyce in the late months of 1905 (Hapgood Family Papers).

"These last two months": Hutchins Hapgood to Neith Boyce, Dec. 6, 1905, Hapgood Family Papers.

285. **he became his subject's lover:** "I am trying to get her to write her life," he confided to Boyce, who pressed him to disclose the exact nature of his "entanglements" in Chicago. "She began it, but the anarchist she lives with discouraged her, and now she has stopped." Ibid., Nov. 25, 1905 [?].

"Varietism": Neith Boyce to Hutchins Hapgood, Dec. [?] 1905, Hapgood Family Papers.

"What haven't I got to say to you!": Hutchins Hapgood to Neith Boyce, Dec. [?], 1905.

286. **prostitutes' union in New Orleans:** Kirkpatrick, "Knights and Wobblies," p. 16.

"the wife who married for money": Emma Goldman, "The Traffic in Women," reprinted in *Red Emma Speaks*, ed. Shulman, p. 151.

287. **the *Masses* editorial board:** Zurier, *Art for the Masses*, p. 43.

In a group of short stories: Reed's sketches—"Where the Heart Is," "A Taste of Justice," "Seeing Is Believing"—are collected in Reed, *Adventures of a Young Man*. For the placement of the stories in Reed's writing about the city, see Wilson, "Broadway Nights."

"I shut him up hard": Luhan, *Movers and Shakers*, p. 234.

288. **the verities of the modern city:** Wilson, "Broadway Nights," p. 285.

John Sloan's sketches and paintings: Patricia Hills, "John Sloan's Images of Working-Class Women," *Prospects* 5 (1980): 157–96; Suzanne L. Kinser, "Prostitutes in the Art of John Sloan," *Prospects* 9 (1985): 231–54.

289. **Dorothy Day remembered with shame:** Day, *Long Loneliness*, p. 100.

291. **the reigning romantic imagery:** A few years later, Mary Heaton Vorse rhapsodized to Joe O'Brien that "you come into an inner piece of my spirit that I have kept closed always." Despite the Greenwich Village provenance,

their letters hearken back to images exalted by Victorian virtues of domesticity and sentiment. "I pray to the god inside me," O'Brien replied, "to make me work very hard and always be kind, so that my Mary will put up her folding-up rose-leaf of a hand in mine and go with me to the edge of life and find contentment and singing things" (quoted in Garrison, *Mary Heaton Vorse*, p. 57).

"I am naughty tonight": Hutchins Hapgood to Neith Boyce, "Late, Saturday night," 1914 [?], Hapgood Family Papers.

292. **"I wish you could be with me now!":** Ibid., "Tuesday night," n.d.

So he sent her Marie's letters: Ibid., Nov. 25, 1905 [?].

"Tell me you love me": Ibid., "Late, Saturday night," 1914 [?].

Hapgood chatted with Emma Goldman: Ibid., "Wednesday," 1909 [?]; Ibid., 1912.

293. **He invited the confidences of Ruby Darrow:** Ibid., "Tuesday night," 1904.

"You say you are sensitive": Ibid.

"She is so pretty": Neith Boyce to Hutchins Hapgood, undated letter [1907], Hapgood Family Papers.

"she is the one person": Ibid., Sept. 10, 1907.

294. **an intensely revelatory and detailed account:** Falk, *Love, Anarchy*; Alice Wexler, "Emma Goldman in Love," *Raritan* 1 (Summer 1982): 116–45.

"[I] would devour you": Emma Goldman to Ben Reitman, quoted in Falk, *Love, Anarchy*, p. 79.

"The day seems unbearable": Ibid.

"pour your precious life essence": Emma Goldman to Ben Reitman, quoted in *Emma Goldman*, p. 148.

295. **acquainted with Freudian thought:** It is unclear from Goldman's memoirs whether she attended any of Freud's lectures in Vienna or just heard about Freud (*Living My Life*, vol. 1, p. 173). For the Clark lecture, see Mari Jo Buhle, *Feminism and Its Discontents: A Century of Struggle with Psychoanalysis* (Cambridge, Mass., 1998); Hale, *Freud and the Americans*, pp. 5, 22, 269–70.

a Dostoyevskian cast: Goldman, *Living My Life*, vol. 1, p. 420.

a subculture known to the cognoscenti for its homosexuality: George Chauncey, *Gay New York*, pp. 75–86, 88, 90–91. Kirkpatrick points out that the migrant laborers of the IWW were also implicated in homosexual practices ("Knights and Wobblies").

296. **"For a woman of your knowledge":** Sperry, quoted in Falk, *Love, Anarchy*, p. 173; Wexler, *Emma Goldman*, 182–83.

297. **sexual connections:** For the erotic ties between Hapgood, Sperry, Reitman, and Goldman, see Wexler, *Emma Goldman*, p. 309, n. 35.

Hurtful secrets, hypocrisy, the sexual double standard: "The private self was an anachronism, a survival of the hated Victorian past—to be modern was to tell all" (Lunbeck, *Psychiatric Persuasion*, p. 138).

"the relief of telling the story": Dell, *Homecoming*, p. 26.

298. **"should have taken place":** Day, quoted in Watson, *Strange Bedfellows*, p. 158.

"I immediately wrote her a note": Luhan, *Movers and Shakers*, p. 261.

299. **"two women who love *one* man":** Sara Bard Field to C. E. S. Wood, undated letter [1914], Field/Wood Collection.

"smutty": Ibid., Aug. 20, 1919.

"not lovely to me": Ibid., Jan. 7 [1917].

"a bit shop-worn, I fear": Ibid., Oct. 6, 1917.

"I cannot conceive of such a thing": Ibid., undated letter, Nov. [1913].

"female world of love and ritual": Smith-Rosenberg, "The Female World of Love and Ritual," *Disorderly Conduct.*

300. **"I never had anyone believe":** Sara Bard Field to C. E. S. Wood, "Saturday, Aug. 9, Hotel St. Francis, San Francisco" [1914?], Field/Wood Collection.

301. **the Provincetown Players and Eugene O'Neill:** Pfister, *Staging Depth*, pp. 107–08.

the Liberal Club Players: Some plays, all authored by Floyd Dell, have been published: *King Arthur's Socks and Other Village Plays* (New York, 1922); *The Angel Intrudes* (New York, 1918); *Sweet and Twenty* (Cincinnati, 1921).

the Little Theater: Mary C. Henderson, "Against Broadway: The Rise of the Art Theater in America (1900–1920)," *1915: The Cultural Moment*, ed. Adele Heller and Lois Rudnick (New Brunswick, 1991), pp. 217–21. Chicago's Little Theater was the crown jewel of the movement.

"everybody's private affairs": Dell, *King Arthur's Socks*, p. 144.

the Village Ibsen: Richwine, "Liberal Club," p. 133. Richwine has compiled a list of the plays and the extant descriptions (pp. 130–44).

302. **psychoanalysis arrived in force:** On psychoanalysis, hysteria, and Village physicians, see the references to Dr. Lorber in Eastman, *Love and Revolution*, pp. 40–41, and to Dr. Brill and Dr. Smith Ely Jelliffe in Eastman, *Enjoyment of Living*, p. 490; Liber, *Doctor's Apprenticeship*, p. 590; Rudnick, *Mable Dodge Luhan*, p. 137; and Dearborn, *Queen of Bohemia*, p. 60. On the uses of the hysteria diagnosis with Sara Bard Field, see Field to C. E. S. Wood, Aug. 20, 1919, Field/Wood Collection; with Emma Goldman, see *Living My Life*, vol. 1, p. 187. For the nineteenth-century model of the problems rendered by an unused uterus, see Luhan, *Movers and Shakers*, p. 44. Dell and Eastman both wrote about psychoanalysis for the magazines.

Eugene O'Neill: O'Neill had entered Princeton in the class of 1910, dropped out after one year, and knocked around the New York area. The previous winter he had studied playwriting at Harvard with George Pierce Baker, one of the new lights of the Harvard faculty and the mentor of John Reed's friends Robert Edmond Jones and Lee Simonson.

303. ***Enemies:*** Ellen Kay Trimberger argues for Boyce's authorship in *Intimate Warriors*, p. 180. The play is reprinted on pp. 186–95.

307. **he talked like a thug:** Lingeman, *Theodore Dreiser*, vol. 2, p. 154.

9/LOVING AMERICA WITH OPEN EYES

311. **the First World War:** Fussell, *Great War;* Lasch, *New Radicalism;* Steel, *Walter Lippmann;* David M. Kennedy, *Over Here.*

"It is tremendously exciting here": *Letters of Carl Van Vechten*, p. 11.

"excited, pleased, happy": Dodge, *Movers and Shakers*, p. 295.

"former people": Malcolm Cowley, *Exile's Return* (1934; New York, 1986), p. 67.

312. **No Euro-American person:** Fussell, *Great War*, p. 21.
313. **"Pictures and poetry poured in":** Dell, *Homecoming*, p. 293.
    "psychic complex": Randolph Bourne, "Below the Battle," *Seven Arts*, July 1917; reprinted in Schlissel, *World of Randolph Bourne*, p. 162.
    work stoppages: On the labor situation, see Buhle, *Dreamer's Paradise*, pp. 49–52; Robert K. Murray, *Red Scare: A Study in National Hysteria, 1919–1920* (Minneapolis, 1955); Dubofsky, *We Shall Be All*, chs. 12–13.
    Max Eastman was nearly lynched: Eastman, *Love and Revolution*, pp. 53–57.
314. **Prosecutions and convictions:** A federal judge in North Dakota described a bloodthirsty situation in the courts: "I tried war cases before jurymen who were candid, sober, intelligent businessmen . . . who under ordinary circumstances would have had the highest respect for my declarations of law, but during that period they looked back into my eyes with the savagery of wild animals, saying by their manner, 'Away with this tiddling, let us get at him' " (Charles Fremont Amidon, quoted in Zechariah Chafee Jr., *Freedom of Speech* [New York, 1920], p. 77).
    Early roundups of dissenters: Chafee, *Freedom of Speech*; David M. Rabban, *Free Speech in Its Forgotten Years* (New York, 1997); Murray, *Red Scare*; William Preston Jr., *Aliens and Dissenters: Federal Suppression of Radicals, 1903–1933* (Cambridge, Mass., 1963); Higham, *Strangers in the Land*, ch. 8; H. C. Peterson and Gilbert C. Fite, *Opponents of War, 1917–1918* (Madison, 1957).
    a tremendous wave of strikes: Labor militancy had been high during the war, too, as I have noted. In 1919, there were fewer strikes but more people involved (Murray, *Red Scare*, pp. 5–9). Most of the strikes were conducted by the AFL, but employers smarting from two decades of pro-labor progressive initiatives seized the chance to cast trade unionism as the work of Bolsheviks. Networks of spy-catching patriots, now calling themselves America Firsters, served as conduits to the public for propaganda equating the open shop with patriotism and inciting the extirpation of the foreign menace in schools, workplaces, and local government.
    haven for insurrectionaries: Gregory, *Day Is Gone*, p. 154; Buhle, *Dreamer's Paradise*, p. 68. Bukharin and Trotsky got into an acrimonious fight, but apparently none of the Village radicals noticed them and, their sights on Russia, they themselves did not notice any of the English-speaking radicals. See Stephen F. Cohen, *Bukharin and the Bolshevik Revolution* (New York, 1974), pp. 43–44; Frederick C. Giffin, "Leon Trotsky in New York City," *New York History* 49 (Oct. 1968): 391–404. Trotsky's presence and his speeches in Russian and German were later reported to the Red-hunting Lusk Committee (Joint Legislative Committee Investigating Seditious Activities, *Revolutionary Radicalism: Its History, Purpose, and Tactics* [Albany, 1920], vol. 1, p. 628).
    a strong showing by the Socialist Party: In the 1917 election, the SP mayoral candidate came in a strong third and there were numerous winners in municipal and state offices (Julian F. Jaffe, *Crusade against Radicalism: New York during the Red Scare, 1914–1925* [Port Washington, 1972], p. 71).
315. **"intolerable":** Butler, quoted in Bender, *New York Intellect*, p. 298. On the situation at Columbia, see pp. 296–300. The resistance to Butler culminated in Charles Beard's resignation.

For Emma Goldman and Alexander Berkman: Wexler, *Emma Goldman*, p. 231.

During a suffrage protest: See Floyd Dell's account of the fracas in which he and his feminist lover found themselves in *Homecoming*, pp. 341–42.

The playing of the "Star-Spangled Banner": Peterson and Fite, *Opponents of War*, p. 197; Eastman, *Love and Revolution*, p. 35; Jaffe, *Crusade against Radicalism*, p. 7.

The Justice Department: Chafee, *Freedom of Speech*, p. 79; John Sayer, "Art and Politics, Dissent and Repression: *The Masses* Magazine versus the Government, 1917–1918," *American Journal of Legal History* 32 (Jan. 1988): 64.

Red-hunting agents: New York became a hotbed of surveillance and harassment, to a degree that has gone unnoticed by historians. The Lusk Committee, set up in Albany after the Armistice, generated its proceedings not from oral testimony (in the manner of the Red hunters of the 1950s) but from printed materials supplied by spies: intercepted telegrams and letters, purloined organizational minutes and lists, transcripts of speeches taken down in shorthand. Nothing is known about how café life fared on the Lower East Side, but the frequency of charges brought against Russian Jews from the neighborhood and the volume of materials seized from Yiddish- and Russian-language organizations for perusal by the Lusk Committee indicates the presence of spies there as well. In the landmark *Abrams* case, the anarchist defendants, young people from Goldman's circle, were snagged because someone picked up the pro-Bolshevik pamphlets they had tossed out a factory window onto the street.

The Heterodoxy group: On their activities during the war, see Schwarz, *Radical Feminists*, pp. 32–34; Baker, *Fighting for Life*, p. 182.

Agents tapped phones: Madeleine Doty, a feminist writer who had been with Reed and Bryant in Petersburg, found her phone tapped after her lover, Roger Baldwin, refused conscription and went to jail as a conscientious objector (Doty, "Chapter on Roger Baldwin," p. 38, Baldwin Papers, Seeley Mudd Library, Princeton University). The Lusk Committee hearings depended heavily on intercepted telegrams.

"Neither a middle ground": Bender, *New York Intellect*, p. 297.

316. **Even John Dewey:** Dewey was not involved in downtown life to any extent, but Randolph Bourne and Max Eastman were both his students. In 1916, he had lent his stature to testifying in a successful *Masses* protest against the removal of the journal from the subway newsstands. During the war and the Red Scare, however, Dewey did not take a position against the arrests in New York and the reprisals on his own Columbia campus. He valued disagreement and skepticism but as provocations toward an unfolding of a succession of provisional consensuses rather than as values in their own right (Dewey, "Are We Indecent?" *Masses*, July 1916, pp. 21–24; Robert Westbrook, *John Dewey and American Democracy* [Ithaca, 1991], pp. 210–11; Alan Ryan, *John Dewey and the High Tide of American Liberalism* [New York, 1995], p. 198).

"a license for Bolshevik thuggery": John Wertheimer, "*Freedom of Speech*: Zechariah Chafee and Free-Speech History," *Reviews in American History* 22 (1994): 369.

The postmaster denied mailing privileges: Sayer, "Art and Politics," p. 53. The Lusk Committee material on publications is in Joint Legislative Committee, *Revolutionary Radicalism*, vol. 2. The *Little Review* escaped scrutiny, probably because it was off the stands at the moment the committee focused on "propaganda"; virtually every other liberal or left-leaning New York publication was called before the committee, with the exception of the *New Republic*.

317. **"I know exactly what I am after":** William H. Lamar, Solicitor to the Postmaster General, quoted in Sayer, "Art and Politics," p. 53. A fellow civil libertarian reported back to Roger Baldwin after a trip to Washington that the postmaster viewed "high-brow" publications as worse than pro-German material (Harry Laidler to Baldwin, Dec. 23, 1918, Baldwin Papers).

The *Masses* editors: Young, *On My Way*, pp. 290–98; Sayer, "Art and Politics"; Eastman, *Love and Revolution*, p. 119.

318. **"every man and woman in the U.S.":** John Dos Passos, *The Best Times* (New York, 1966), p. 76.

But the New York leaders: Charges were eventually dropped against Elizabeth Gurley Flynn, Carlo Tresca, Joseph Ettor, and Arturo Giovannitti (Camp, *Iron in Her Soul*, pp. 78–82). Flynn most likely drew on her Heterodoxy connections since bail was posted by a committee of New York women. See Dubofsky's damning interpretation of Flynn's actions in *We Shall Be All*, pp. 425–28.

319. **Only a handful of American reporters:** Bessie Beatty, a San Francisco reporter; Albert Rhys Williams, a Social Gospel minister; and Madeleine Doty (Whitman Bassow, *The Moscow Correspondents: Reporting on Russia from the Revolution to Glasnost* [New York, 1988]).

a reverse emigration: There is a list of emigrés in Rosenstone, *Romantic Revolutionary*, p. 287. Irving Howe found that, between 1917 and 1921, some 21,000 Russian Jews left the United States (*World of Our Fathers*, p. 336). Dell mentions the influential Lower East Sider Alex Gumberg in *Homecoming*, p. 335. See also Bassow, *Moscow Correspondents*, pp. 22, 25–26, 29.

"the greatest story of my life": Reed to Lincoln Steffens, June 1918, quoted in Rosenstone, *Romantic Revolutionary*, p. 320.

American soldiers' cheerful, peppy accounts: Kennedy, *Over Here*, pp. 214–15.

320. **"The old world crumbles down":** Trotsky, quoted in *Ten Days That Shook the World* (New York, 1977), p. 269.

***Ten Days* became a paradigmatic text:** Originally published by Boni and Liveright with an enthusiastic preface by Lenin, the book was translated into Russian and published in the Soviet Union in 1923 with an additional foreword by Lenin's wife, Nadezhda Krupskaya. There were twelve subsequent Soviet editions until 1930, when publication was suspended: although some two hundred people are named in the book, there is virtually no mention of Stalin. Later in the 1930s, as Stalinist terror proceeded, so many of the people Reed mentions were killed or exiled that the book became suspect. Publication was revived after de-Stalinization was initiated in 1956. See *John Reed and the Russian Revolution: Uncollected Articles,*

Letters, and Speeches on Russia, 1917–1920, ed. Eric Homberger and John Biggart (London, 1992), pp. xiv–xv.

"this is how it happened": Howe, *World of Our Fathers*, p. 336. As the literature of World War I came to shape soldiers' memories of it, so *Ten Days* dictated reminiscences of the October days, so that the book seemed to take on additional truth value through the memoirs that constituted the first wave of history making of the revolution.

a powerfully expansive term: Peter G. Filene, *Americans and the Soviet Experiment, 1917–1933* (Cambridge, Mass., 1967), p. 46; Cott, *Grounding*, p. 62.

he was persona non grata: Fifth Avenue Bank to John Reed, Dec. 12, 1918; Harvard Club to Reed, Feb. 15, 1919, Reed Papers (bMS Am 1091[478]).

They responded with an urgent sense of engagement: See letters in the Reed Papers from Theron Castner, May 20, 1919; Charles J. Finger, Apr. 17, 1919; Ben Fletcher (an imprisoned Wobbly), May 10, 1919; David Webster, June 24, June 27, 1920 (bMS Am 1091[334, 438, 440, 915, 916]). In Leavenworth, "the book was generally circulated among us," wrote Bill Haywood (*Bill Haywood's Book*, p. 308).

321. **"capable of extension through space":** Bender, *New York Intellect*, p. 245. Eastman points out that in 1918 none of the key Bolshevik texts had yet been translated. Louis Fraina's *The Proletarian Revolution in Russia*, which contained translations from Lenin and Trotsky, appeared sometime in 1918. Lenin's "Letter to the American Workingman" was smuggled into the United States at the end of 1919 and published with John Reed's aid (Eastman, *Love and Revolution*, p. 107; Buhle, *Dreamer's Paradise*, pp. 75–77; Rosenstone, *Romantic Revolutionary*, p. 342). On Americans' grasp of Russian politics, see Filene, *Americans and the Soviet Experiment*, ch. 1, although Filene deals with opinions among liberal elites. For the Lower East Side, see Howe, *World of Our Fathers*, pp. 335–39.

323. **"it will be our gain":** Goldman, quoted in Wexler, *Emma Goldman*, p. 232.

cagey equivocation, precise arguments, and rousing declarations of principle: On advocating violence, for example, Goldman insisted she only advocated the *understanding* of violence, while Berkman placidly allowed that "we all believe in violence and we all disbelieve in violence; it all depends upon the circumstances." On the conspiracy, Berkman pointed out that two people who had opposed militarism for thirty years could hardly be said to have joined together to "conspire" against the draft. See Drinnon, *Rebel in Paradise*, ch. 21; Wexler, *Emma Goldman*, pp. 230–36; Goldman, *Living My Life*, vol. 1, pp. 612–23; Anderson, *My Thirty Years' War*, pp. 195–96. Goldman in her memoirs holds that from the beginning she and Berkman had no hope of winning and saw the proceedings as a farce, but the tenor and earnestness of the defense and their skill in evading legal snares indicate otherwise. Anderson, who went to court every day, remembered them as so "naively optimistic" they could sway any judge (*My Thirty Years' War*, p. 195).

"the man who loves a woman": "Address to the Jury," *Red Emma Speaks*, ed. Shulman, pp. 323–24.

324. **"Nothing better could have happened":** Goldman, quoted in Wexler, *Emma Goldman*, p. 240.

"I felt myself transferred to Russia": Goldman, quoted in Rosenstone, *Romantic Revolutionary*, p. 350.

"Every once in awhile": E. M. Boyd to Roger Baldwin, Nov. 20, 1918, Box 12, Folder 1, Baldwin Papers.

"She had, despite all, been rich in love": Letters to Reitman and Fitzgerald, quoted in Wexler, *Emma Goldman*, p. 273; Falk, *Love and Anarchy*, pp. 292–95.

326. **thumbed her nose at the lot:** The story is retold in Drinnon, *Rebel in Paradise*, p. 276.

"there was almost never a week": Anderson, *My Thirty Years' War*, p. 146.

"It is a great thing": Jane Heap, "Push-Face," *Little Review*, June 1917, p. 4.

(Emma Goldman took a copy to jail): Drinnon, *Rebel in Paradise*, p. 233.

327. **Even John Quinn:** Pound was excited over the chance to sponsor the publication of a masterpiece but wary lest he offend Quinn; he tried to mediate by asking Joyce to take out some of the offending lines, a request that Joyce adamantly refused. Ben Huebsch, the downtown publisher who had taken on the first two books, would not even touch the manuscript unless Joyce agreed to excise scatological and sexual sections.

In the spring they went to press: On the publication of *Ulysses* and the ensuing trial, see my essay "Margaret Anderson" in *Forgotten Heroes of the American Past*, ed. Susan Ware (New York, 1998); Edward de Grazia, *Girls Lean Back Everywhere: The Law of Obscenity and the Assault on Genius* (New York, 1992); Anderson, *My Thirty Years' War*; Reid, *Man from New York*; Jackson R. Bryer, "Joyce, *Ulysses*, and the *Little Review*," *South Atlantic Quarterly* 66 (Spring 1967): 144–64; Baggett, "Aloof from Natural Laws."

the American Civil Liberties Union: In an interesting exchange with Theodore Schroeder, a leading light of the Free Speech League, Roger Baldwin, director of the ACLU, dismissed litigation about personal liberty and expression as incidental to the "wider political question which we are discussing" (Rabban, *Free Speech*, p. 310). Baldwin's lessons under duress in the storm of wartime and Red Scare prosecutions—he himself went to jail as a conscientious objector—caused him to narrow the focus of free speech so that the ACLU took on only explicitly political speech, and political speech of a certain cast, for that matter. It was Baldwin's genius to sense a political opening as pro-war progressives and well-placed politicians wearied of the Palmer raids. He took advantage of flagging support for the attorney general, steadily distancing the ACLU from labor and immigrant cases and resorting to a rhetoric of Anglo-Saxon liberties, putting his work in line with a "real" America of white middle-class Protestants. While too principled to cater to prejudice, he still moved free speech away from embarrassing associations with erotic novels and immigrant Jews and tidied it up. Anglo-Saxonism pervades many of the letters he wrote from jail, along with his courtroom speech (widely reprinted), available in the Baldwin Papers.

despised Anderson and Heap: Lesbians and litigation went hand in hand, in Quinn's view. If Anderson and Heap were in trouble, it was only what they deserved. "All pederasts want to go into court. Bringing libel suits is one of the stigmata of buggery. The bugger and the Lesbian constantly think in terms of suits and defenses" (quoted in Baggett, " 'Aloof from Natural

Laws,' " p. 257). The association probably came from the Oscar Wilde case, although Quinn conveniently ignored the fact that no one was being sued, they were being prosecuted.

328. **"Girls lean back everywhere":** Heap, quoted in de Grazia, *Girls Lean Back Everywhere*, p. 10.

In 1922, Anderson emigrated: Not too much later, the fortunes of *Ulysses* turned. With publication blocked in the United States, the American expatriate Sylvia Beach, owner of a bookstore in Paris, published Joyce's book under the shop's imprint. Backed now by leading French critics, the novel won acclaim as a masterpiece. In the States, critics and writers circulated underground copies from Paris and filled newspaper columns lamenting the puritanism of an American culture that forebade legitimate publication in this country. Perhaps out of embarrassment, perhaps from ignorance, the latter-day defenders did not mention Margaret Anderson, except to denigrate her efforts: when someone challenged a critic for the *New York Herald-Tribune* on his past evaluation, he replied that he had misjudged *Ulysses* because the *Little Review* installments contained so many spelling errors (Anderson, *My Thirty Years' War*, pp. 175–76).

329. **"cosmically efficacious and well-bred war":** Randolph Bourne, "Below the Battle," *Seven Arts*, July 1917, reprinted in Schlissel, *World of Randolph Bourne*, p. 162.

"A war made deliberately by the intellectuals!": Randolph Bourne, "The War and the Intellectuals," *Seven Arts*, June 1917, reprinted in Schlissel, *World of Randolph Bourne*, p. 147.

330. **"A man must glow":** Walzer, *Company of Critics*, p. 55.

Bourne lived in chronic fear: Oppenheim, "Story of the *Seven Arts*." Van Wyck Brooks was frightened for his friend and tried to nudge him back to writing about art and literature (Clayton, *Forgotten Prophet*, pp. 218–19). While *Seven Arts* escaped the censors, when *Mother Earth* reprinted Bourne's piece on the intellectuals, the censors confiscated the issue (Deacon, *Elsie Clews Parsons*, p. 182).

A Columbia English professor: The professor was John Erskine, whose genteel, cultivated approach Bourne despised. Bourne's defender was Harry Dana, of the distinguished Boston family (Harry Dana to Alyse Gregory, June 30, 1948, Bourne Papers; John Erskine, *The Memory of Certain Persons* [Philadelphia, 1947], pp. 194, 252–53). On the hike up the Connecticut shore, see Agnes de Lima to Alyse Gregory, n.d., Bourne Papers. On Bourne's suspicions of Dewey, see Dorothy Teall to Agnes de Lima, n.d.

the supreme peacefulness of being at war: Bourne, "War and the Intellectuals," reprinted in *World of Randolph Bourne*, ed. Schlissel, p. 156.

"The big game is over": Bill Haywood to John Reed, Sept. 1, 1918, Reed Papers (bMS Am 1091[482]). Serving time in prison for the first time became a part of left-wing politics; prison was seen as a charged place where one deepened commitments and acquired a transcendent spiritual strength and freedom by taking one's place beside the country's outcasts. "While there is a soul in prison, I am not free," Eugene Debs avowed in his moving summary in a sedition case in 1919, but it was not just Debs who came to view jail as a special place. A conscientious objector, for instance, testified to fellow c.o. Roger Baldwin that he was relieved at the prospect of sharing "the world's shame, and of having an actual personal part with the disinherited of the earth" (Robert Whitaker to Baldwin, Jan. 17, 1919, Baldwin Papers). The shift suggests a change in the psychology of political commitment, especially in emerging ideas of middle-class collective guilt. The Wobblies, in contrast, seem to have taken a bluffer, more practical view of jail as a predictable consequence of labor militancy, to be endured and joked about. See the wonderful IWW prisoner letters to Baldwin (box 12, folder 1, Baldwin Papers).

331. **"malcontents":** Bourne, "Twilight of Idols," *World of Randolph Bourne*, ed. Schlissel, pp. 202–03.

"What shall we do with our America?": Bourne, "Trans-National America," *Radical Will*, ed. Hansen, p. 262.

book reviews and short essays: See especially Bourne's review of Bertrand Russell's *Political Ideals*, "A Primer of Revolutionary Idealism," *Dial*, Jan. 17, 1918, p. 69.

332. **"It was the good fortune":** Lewis Mumford, "The Image of Randolph Bourne," *New Republic*, Sept. 24, 1930, p. 152. On Bourne's postmortem career, see Dorothy Teall, "Bourne into Myth," *Bookman*, Oct. 1932, pp. 590–99; Elsie Clews Parson, "A Pacifist Patriot," *Dial*, Mar. 1920, pp. 367–70.

"abounding vitality and moral freedom": Bourne, "The History of a Literary Radical," *Radical Will*, ed. Hansen, p. 434.

"took into account": Waldo Frank, *Our America* (New York, 1919), p. 200; see also James Oppenheim's tribute in his introduction to *Untimely Papers* (New York, 1919).

"a resonant instrument of certain strains": Dorothy Teall, quoted in letter to [Blanche?] Messitte, uncataloged ms., Bourne Papers.

333. **"this blundering, wistful, crass civilization":** Bourne, "Below the Battle" (1917), *World of Randolph Bourne*, ed. Schlissel, p. 164.

single-issue, single-sex movement: Cott, *Grounding*, ch. 2.

334. **some of the downtown men:** Greenwich Village bildungsromans include Max Eastman, *Venture* (New York, 1927); Floyd Dell, *Moon-Calf*; Harry Kemp, *Tramping on Life: An Autobiographical Narrative* (New York, 1922) and *More Miles*; Carl Van Vechten, *Peter Whiffle* (New York, 1922); Bodenheim, *Blackguard*. The new publishers—the Bonis, Liveright, Knopf—produced most of these books. See also the beginning of the Village memoirs with Will Durant, *Transition: A Sentimental Story of One Mind and One Era* (New York, 1927); Dell's short stories collected in *Looking at Life* (New York, 1924) and *Love in Greenwich Village*; and his "A Spiritual Autobiography of My Own Generation" in *Intellectual Vagabondage* (New York, 1926).

Sleazy Guido Bruno: Watson, *Strange Bedfellows*, p. 232. A popular tourist guide that embodied these changes was Egmont Arens, *The Little Book of Greenwich Village* (New York, 1918). Alfred Kreymborg describes his transformation into a performer in Guido Bruno's garret in *Troubadour*, pp. 214–15. In Chicago, the most famous outpost of bohemia suffered a similar fate. The Dill Pickle became a nightclub for slumming tourists and Chicago fraternities who wanted exotic Bohemian Nights for their members. BRAINS—BRILLIANCY—BOHEMIA, one advertisement proclaimed (flyer in Dill Pickle Club Papers, Newberry Library). See also Harry Kemp, who in *More Miles* describes "the Greenwich Village of fifteen years ago, the true one . . . the one that existed before the present invasion of slummers in search of the Bohemian life of sly naughtiness and semi-artistic tawdriness that, in turn, had its origins and sole being in the brains and fancies of a few sensational hacks, space-writers and reporters"; Anna Alice Chapin, *Greenwich Village* (New York, 1920); Ware, *Greenwich Village*, pp. 14–15.

335. **Way down South in Greenwich Village:** Bobby Edwards, "The Village Epic," *The Little Book of Greenwich Village: A Handbook of Information concerning New York's Bohemia* (New York, 1922).

"The American middle class": Dell, *Homecoming*, p. 360.

"It was a bitter thing": Ibid., p. 326.

336. **a conquered country:** Cowley, *Exile's Return*, p. 71.

"former anarchists": Ibid., p. 67.

They had negotiated a transition: This is Mary Daly's formulation of the inability of Isadora Duncan to relate to the culture of the 1920s (*Done into Dance*, p. 208).

new order: Compare Lawrence Levine, who argues in *Highbrow/Lowbrow: The Emergence of Cultured Hierarchy in America* that Americans moved toward an increasing hierarchy of culture in the twentieth century, drawing rigid divisions between high and low forms, tasteful and vulgar audiences. See also his "Jazz and American Culture," *The Unpredictable Past: Explorations in American Cultural History* (New York, 1993), p. 176. My view is that a paradigm of rigid cultural hierarchy does not explain the incredible cross-fertilizations and hybridizations of modern American arts and letters, both high and low.

Acknowledgments

I am grateful to the Institute for Advanced Study, to Joseph Taylor, Princeton's Dean of Faculty, and to the John Simon Guggenheim Memorial Foundation for giving me time free from the obligations of teaching. I thank my colleagues at Princeton who, both knowingly and unwittingly, have enriched my scholarship: Natalie Zemon Davis, Maria DiBattista, Hendrik Hartog, Daniel Rodgers, and especially Philip Nord. Laura Engelstein, Anson Rabinbach, Stephen Kotkin, James Richardson, Jeremy Adelman, James Wood, and David Montgomery took time and care to answer my questions.

Over a number of years, seminars on cities at the New York Institute for the Humanities helped me understand metropolitan culture in new ways, and I still benefit from what I learned there from Thomas Bender, Richard Sennett, and William R. Taylor. Paul Berman was unstinting of his time and his copious knowledge of the bohemians; he kindly read a draft of the entire book. Ann Hulbert also read the book at an early stage and brought to bear her fine literary and cultural imagination.

At Metropolitan Books, Sara Bershtel's fascination with the book, the insights she's offered, and her criticism and editing have been extraordinary; I thank her and Riva Hocherman, who likewise gave the book fastidious attention and care. I was fortunate to have the benefit of Marc Aronson's historical knowledge of the period. Lucy Albanese designed a beautiful book, lending it the spirit of the "new." Geri Thoma gave generously and thoroughly of support and interest. Nicole Sackley's intellectual company came to mean as much to me as her superb assistance in research; I thank her for her absorption in my own questions, large and small. Jay Turner, with patience and meticulousness, helped tie up loose ends. James Wilentz's interest in the bohemians has affirmed my sense of their continuing importance. Hannah Wilentz's pride and interest in my writing have been unanticipated, glorious gifts.

Without Judy Fiskin, friend across a continent, Katherine Fleming, friend across generations, and Deborah Epstein Nord, colleague and coconspirator, I can hardly imagine how I could have written this book. Their qualities of artfulness and mindfulness, their courage and intelligence, and the achievements of each in the experimental life have inspired and sustained me more than I can say. As for Sean Wilentz, I still think that meeting him by accident long ago was one of those huge, fabulous pieces of luck with which New York City abounds. I am deeply grateful for his conversation, his abiding interest in my work, and his wonderful historical acuity. Above all I thank him for his faithfulness to the enterprise of modern love.

Index

Page numbers in *italics* refer to illustrations

Praise for

continued . . .

family, and 'veddy British' tradi-
...orbing debut sparkles with glints of
...cy Mitford and Julian Fellowes."

—Stephanie Clifford, *New York Times* bestselling author of *Everybody Rise*

"Hornak's wry, masterful portrayal of a family in crisis is filled with flawed and funny characters who will capture—and break—your heart."   —Fiona Davis, author of *The Dollhouse* and *The Address*

"If you like your families dysfunctional and your novels whip-smart, then Hornak's delightful debut about a family discovering the unexpected benefits of forced quality time over the holidays will enchant your inner ironist and sentimentalist alike."

—Courtney Maum, author of *Touch* and *I Am Having
So Much Fun Here Without You*

"Hornak offers a tragicomic holiday tale that's perfect for fans of family sagas and multiperspective narratives like *Love Actually*."   —*BookPage*